CONSUMING HABITS

Drugs in History and Anthropology

Edited by
Jordan Goodman, Paul E. Lovejoy and Andrew Sherratt

London and New York

First published 1995
by Routledge
11 New Fetter Lane, London EC4P 4EE

Simultaneously published in the USA and Canada
by Routledge
29 West 35th Street, New York, NY 10001

Transferred to Digital Printing 2003

Routledge is an imprint of the Taylor & Francis Group

Typeset in Palatino by Florencetype, Stoodleigh, Devon
Printed and bound in Great Britain by
Intype London Ltd

British Library Cataloguing in Publication Data
Consuming Habits: Drugs in History and
Anthropology
I. Goodman, Jordan
394.1409

Library of Congress Cataloguing in Publication Data
A catalogue record for this book is available from the
Library of Congress

ISBN 0-415-09039-3

CONSUMING HABITS

CONTENTS

FIGURES AND TABLES

FIGURES

TABLES

NOTES ON CONTRIBUTORS

David T. Courtwright is Professor and Chair of History at the University of North Florida. He is the author of *Dark Paradise: Opiate Addiction in America before 1940* (Cambridge, Mass., Harvard University Press, 1982) and other works on drug use and addiction. He is currently writing a book about single men and social disorder in American History.

Alexander von Gernet teaches anthropology at the University of Toronto. His recent contributions include 'The construction of prehistoric ideation' (*Cambridge Archaeological Journal*, 1993, vol. 3, pp. 67–81). His current research relates to archaeological and ethnohistorical theory, and to the symbolic context of Amerindian tobacco use.

Jordan Goodman is Lecturer in International Economic History at the University of Manchester Institute of Science and Technology. He is the author of *Tobacco in History: The Cultures of Dependence* (London, Routledge, 1993) and is currently researching the history of pharmaceutical research in Europe and the United States since 1800.

Eric Hirsch is a lecturer in social anthropology in the Department of Human Sciences at Brunel University. He is the co-editor of *Between Place and Space: Landscape in Anthropological Perspective* (Oxford, Oxford University Press, 1995) and is currently completing a research monograph based on his fieldwork in Papua New Guinea.

Stephen Hugh-Jones teaches social anthropology at the University of Cambridge. He is the author of *The Palm and the Pleiades* (Cambridge, Cambridge University Press, 1979) and is currently researching a book on social and economic change in north-west Amazonia.

Paul E. Lovejoy is Professor of History at York University, Canada. He is the co-author of *Slow Death for Slavery: The Course of Abolition in Northern Nigeria, 1897–1936* (Cambridge, Cambridge University Press, 1993) and other works on slavery, the kola and the salt trade. He is currently working on a history of slavery and the slave trade in nineteenth-century West Africa.

Kathryn Meyer teaches East Asian history at Lafayette College. She has written several articles on drug control policy and is currently completing a co-authored book provisionally entitled *Dirty Money: A Study of the International Narcotics Traffic*.

Jacob M. Price is Professor Emeritus of History at the University of Michigan. In addition to many articles, his books touching on tobacco include *The Tobacco Adventure to Russia* (1961), *France and the Chesapeake* (Ann Arbor, Michigan, University of Michigan Press, 1973), *Capital and Credit in British Overseas Trade* (Cambridge, Mass., Harvard University Press, 1980) and *Perry of London* (Cambridge, Mass., Harvard University Press, 1992).

Andrew Sherratt teaches archaeology and anthropology at the University of Oxford where he is responsible for the prehistoric collections in the Ashmolean Museum. He is a Fellow of Linacre College and a lecturer at New College. A volume of his collected papers about prehistoric Europe is to appear shortly from Edinburgh University Press.

Woodruff D. Smith teaches European history and currently serves as an administrator at the University of Texas at San Antonio. His most recent book is *Politics and the Sciences of Culture in Germany, 1840–1920* (New York, Oxford University Press, 1991). He is currently writing a book on the demand for overseas commodities in Europe, 1600–1800.

PREFACE

The essays in this volume focus on the history or anthropology of a group of substances which are generally considered to be neither food nor medicine, but have in common the fact that they are psychoactive – in the sense that they alter, to a greater or lesser extent, the state of consciousness of the user. While it has become customary to equate psychoactive substances with 'drugs' as a category of illicit commodities, it should be remembered that some of the world's most widely consumed products, such as tobacco, coffee, tea and cocoa, have these mind-altering properties. Consumers of tobacco and coffee, for example, habitually self-administer psychoactive compounds – nicotine and caffeine – in the most efficient manner possible by smoking and drinking respectively. Although these are both legal substances (tobacco's status is currently contested), the categories of licit and illicit are neither static nor rigid. Some substances that are presently illegal in the West were legally consumed here not too long ago: opium, cannabis, cocaine and LSD, for example. And the opposite is true. In some times and places, both tobacco and coffee have been classed as illicit commodities with heavy penalties for use or (in this classification) abuse. Some substances, moreover, are classed as licit in one culture and illicit in another: alcohol, for instance, is forbidden in Islamic societies, but in most of the rest of the world it has usually been legally available, at least to adult males. The boundary between illicit and licit is a shifting and negotiable one, historically and cross-culturally. As Richard Rudgley reminds us in his recent study, restrictions on psychoactive substances embody the outcome of conflicts over who has access to the means to alter consciousness and behaviour, such as bodily control. Such proscriptions specify who is permitted to alter their state of consciousness and under what circumstances. Which states of consciousness have been encouraged, tolerated or forbidden have been culturally and politically specific.

It is now generally recognized that the consumption of these substances reaches back into prehistory and across most cultures. The issues that historians and anthropologists raise about the production, distribution and consumption of other goods and commodities are just as appropriate, therefore, for psychoactive ones. Yet psychoactive substances have not attracted the scholarly attention they deserve, except from those involved in or commenting upon contemporary issues which address, generally, the problem of addiction and 'abuse' rather than use and context. The agenda is mostly set by pharmacologists, psychologists, sociologists and policy makers. We hope that the publication of this book will encourage research into the historical and cultural contexts of these psychoactive substances, and particularly the significance which they have had for their users. For this purpose, the very word 'drug', is an obstacle, and it is a theme – spoken or unspoken – of many of these papers that other ways of thinking about this topic are more appropriate. While the title of this volume uses the conventional word 'drug', the intention of the book is to undermine it as a category. This is a necessary stage in realigning phenomena for the purposes of comparison, and bringing together matters which are illuminatingly considered in conjunction, but which would otherwise be kept artificially apart.

The title of the volume contains a deliberate ambiguity: it is both about habits of consumption and habits which may, in certain circumstances, come to consume their users. The net has thus been deliberately cast widely, including ancient and modern, eastern and western. The choice of psychoactive substances considered in this volume is not exhaustive and inevitably, therefore, it is to some extent arbitrary. It reflects the interests of the contributors as much as the state of current research; and many other examples could have been chosen. While, for example, there is an essay on the consumption of betelnut in Papua New Guinea, there is not one on *kava* in Polynesia. Similarly, we do not include essays on *qat* or cannabis, despite their importance – either locally (in the Horn of Africa) in the case of *qat*, or internationally in the case of cannabis. This selectivity is deliberate, since it allows the contributors to be deployed very widely in time and space, and to raise a whole spectrum of issues that could not otherwise be addressed within the compass of a single volume. Even so, much remains unsaid. There are many connections between individual contributions that it would have been profitable to pursue – such as the often invisible social and economic ties which now bind the indigenous users of coca in north-west Amazonia in Chapter 2, and urban North American consumers of cocaine in Chapter 10. Such an investigation would involve international politics as well as economics; and it would encompass military as well as legal aspects. Many of the issues raised here in a historical context, concerning the perception of new substances, their control or fiscal exploitation, and the consequent development of trading patterns, have a contemporary relevance to questions which are of growing importance at the present time, and to crucial political decisions for the future. Thus while the book is largely retrospective in its subject matter, it is contemporary in its topicality. Although our concern here is not to enter contemporary debates about the use and abuse of drugs, we hope that this book will stimulate both historians and anthropologists to join in this discussion and offer constructive perspectives and ideas. It would be especially valuable if it were to provoke further consideration of the processes by which current perceptions arose, in the nineteenth century, by changes in world trading patterns, in habits of consumption, and the growth of images of deviancy: themes that are raised, but not fully explored, in the chapters that follow.

These issues are set out at greater length in the following Introduction by one of the editors, and then exemplified in studies that range from prehistory to the twentieth century, and from Papua New Guinea to Europe, North and South America, West Africa and Japan. An Afterword by the other editors closes the discussion and points more specifically to further lines of enquiry, assisted by the consolidated Selected Bibliography which ends the volume. This book had its origins in a conference organized by the Past and Present Society in London in July 1991, under the title of 'Peculiar Substances: the history of stimulants and narcotics'. The editors would like to thank the organizers of the Past and Present conference for their insight in choosing the rewarding topic of psychoactive substances, and in perceiving its potential scope. Earlier versions of five of the ten studies which make up this volume were delivered at the conference; the other half were specially commissioned for this book. While the title is different, the intention is the same: to pursue a vital historical question with imagination and originality.

INTRODUCTION
Peculiar substances
Andrew Sherratt

DRUGS: ATTITUDES AND APPROACHES

It is one of the paradoxes of Western, twentieth-century life that, although we have access to more information than ever before, the nature of our industrial society makes it harder to perceive other cultures except through categories which are largely inappropriate. This, in turn, makes it harder to see our own culture in comparative perspective. The case of what we call 'drugs' is an outstanding example. The term is used for a category of substances taken into the human body for purposes other than nutrition: 'drug', in this sense, is opposed to 'food'. Its contemporary usage encompasses two broad areas of meaning: medicinal preparations and chemically similar compounds consumed primarily for hedonistic purposes – where changes in body chemistry are sought for their psychological rather than physiological effects. 'Drugs' of both kinds are typically controlled by law, either by a system of medical prescription or by legal proscription, with penalties for their unauthorized possession; and the use of psychoactive materials in a non-medical context tends therefore to be characterized as drug 'abuse'. In this case, they are often described (particularly in American usage) as 'narcotics' – a term which more properly refers to substances causing sleep or insensibility, but which now usually carries implications of illegality.[1] The fact that they are often associated with a range of social and medical problems, through their use by deprived or disturbed groups within society, colours the terms in which the substances themselves are described.

Such usages and definitions, however, are very recent ones, since they have arisen within the context of capitalism and the Industrial Revolution; and they are misleading as a framework for approaching the great variety of ways in which organic substances have been used by human beings to alter their mental states. They relate specifically to societies with the technical capacity to manufacture chemically refined products, and to economies within which these products circulate as commodities (whether legal or illegal). This combination of conditions has obtained for no more than a century or so: but the existence of these powerful, purified psychoactive substances has created new and potentially dangerous modes of use which are not constrained by traditional social practices and contexts of consumption. At the same time the professionalization of medicine and pharmacy, and the introduction of systems of medical discipline, has led to increased state control over the actions of individuals in their uses of such substances. These developments, unique to the recent experience of humankind, have not only created a rupture with earlier folk usages, but have separated what are now thought of as 'drugs' from other kinds of widely used substances which also affect the mind and its moods as well as the body. The simple categories of 'drugs' and 'food' leave no place for an important range of preparations with psychoactive properties that form part of everyday consumption: either as food or drink (in the case of coffee, tea and chocolate) or as other 'habits' (I can find no more suitable collective description) such as smoking, sniffing or chewing, typically of tobacco (or, more innocuously, of peppermint-flavoured sugar). Yet such products are of great economic and social importance, and this prominence is due in no small part to their mental effects and often habituative tendencies – whether these have a physiological or a social basis. Some once widely consumed substances, such as cannabis, have crossed the line and been classified as dangerous drugs along with industrial preparations like morphine; others, like tobacco, have not. From a historical and anthropological point of view, it seems more useful to address these 'peculiar substances' collectively, and to trace the changing social and cultural contexts in which such psychoactive materials have been, and are, consumed. It is this emphasis on the embeddedness of culture in social practice that unites the contributors to this volume, whether they are concerned with small-scale, 'traditional' societies or the larger scope of capitalist economies on a global basis. Only by understanding the subtle relationships between culture, consumption and society can we hope to come to terms with the nature of the problems confronting the world today.

This enterprise forms part of a current trend towards breaking down the compartments between different areas of scholarship and allowing their disciplines to cross-fertilize. It gives problems to booksellers and librarians, since the results do not conform to established categories, but it ultimately increases understanding. The present topic is no exception, for it has often been most illuminatingly explored by writers who have come to it from unusual angles. One is Wolfgang Schivelbusch, whose recently translated book, *Tastes of Paradise*, followed his equally stimulating histories of street-lighting and railways.[2] Schivelbusch considers substances consumed for pleasure rather than nutrition (*Genußmittel* as opposed to *Nahrungsmittel*), including spices, condiments, tobacco, tea and coffee, as well as alcohol, opium and cannabis. His book is replete with anthropological insights, not least his notion of 'performance in the process of enjoyment', which stresses consumption as a social activity and leads to observations on the etiquette of buying drinks or the gestures and mannerisms of drinking tea.

Another innovative writer is Piero Camporesi, who from a detailed knowledge of Italian literature has written in rapid succession a whole series of studies, from popular views of hell to the use of perfumes as aphrodisiacs, in which the eating and drinking of a variety of substances has played a prominent role. Three publications in particular address themes relevant to this book.[3] The most recent, *Exotic Brew*, parallels Schivelbusch's subject matter in examining how the rising classes of the eighteenth century used a new cuisine to express their social and cultural aspirations. Its predecessor, *The Magic Harvest*, gave a broad survey of food and popular culture, rich in ethnographic detail; but it was in the first of these volumes, *Bread of Dreams*, that the most radical hypothesis was raised. Here, Camporesi describes the mass of people in early modern Italy as constantly in fear of famine, and the consequent symbolic force of eating and abundance, especially of bread. But that bread was often adulterated, or even infected with ergot; and in any case, to stave off hunger, starving villagers ate a variety of mind-numbing herbs, while hunger itself produced hallucinations. Whether this dismal vision of a permanently narcotized society, periodically erupting in outbreaks of St Vitus' dance, has any validity must be judged by specialists; yet the ubiquity of mind-altering agents in traditional societies cannot be doubted – just as the moods of industrial societies are set by a balance of caffeine, nicotine and alcohol, among many others. Camporesi shows that some usages of psychoactive substances might be described, as today, as hedonistic; some, as with wine, were permeated with meaning and ritual; others were, as always, the remedies of the desperate. Such studies give some idea of the common territory which is being opened up between history and anthropology.

The aim of the studies in this volume is similarly to form a bridge between various bodies of specialist literature that have hitherto existed largely in isolation: the history of food (which has not often explored the psychoactive properties of its ingredients); the history of drugs, whether in traditional or modern societies (where pharmacological rather than social aspects have usually been the focus of attention); and that part of economic history concerned with the production and distribution of consumable commodities (in which psychoactive products have played a not inconsiderable role). By providing a set of case studies which demonstrate the inter-relationships between these often arbitrarily divided topics, we hope to show the relevance of these different discourses to each other.

The essays that follow fall broadly into two groups: those dealing with traditional societies largely outside Western Europe (Chapters 1 to 5), and those dealing with societies whose economies were – and are – locked together by international trade (Chapters 6 to 10). While the opportunities for creating profit (either by states or other groups: Chapters 8 and 9) from trade in these materials are enormously greater in the latter contexts, the distinction between the two groupings is not so fundamental as to preclude comparisons and similar approaches. Indeed, it is precisely by applying concepts developed in describing the former that we may illuminate important aspects of the latter, and come to see familiar phenomena in a new light. This requires a rather broader set of concepts than the 'drug'-centred discourse which prevails in much of the literature, and benefits from an approach via the *mentalités* prevailing at the time. Many systems of thought concerning the body and substances taken into it – whether Indian Ayurvedic medicine or the medieval doctrine of humours – have insisted on a balance between often highly specific elements of diet and their relation to general behaviour and health. These have their counterparts in contemporary attitudes, such as the new climate of thought (centred in the USA) which emphasizes physical fitness and has revolutionized attitudes to tobacco smoking and to some extent also to the use of alcohol; and similar considerations affected the reception of 'colonial' products in Europe from the sixteenth century onwards (compare Chapters 10, 6 and 7). Reference to such indigenous modes of classification is a recurring theme throughout the book. Equally relevant are the social contexts in which particular substances are consumed. Many psychoactive substances form the focus of specific social occasions, both in their cultures of origin and (in rather different forms) in societies to which they have been introduced (Chapters 1, 2, 3, 4, 5 and 7). Just how important these 'consumption rituals' (which often have their own particular items of equipment) still are in contemporary culture is shown by the effort currently devoted to elaborating the packaging and presentation of various kinds of mineral water, to substitute for the alcoholic drinks formerly considered indispensable for hospitable behaviour. The inappropriate biological effects (in terms of impaired concentration, ability to drive, etc.) of a traditional psychoactive substance for certain elements of the middle classes in an increasingly technical world conflicts with the established cultural role of alcoholic drinks in Western society; so the conspicuous consumption of excessively expensive soft drinks serves to continue, in non-intoxicating form, the everyday rituals and social practices to which alcohol was formerly essential. To understand the ways in which people make use of (or desist from) the various psychoactive substances at their disposal, it is necessary to situate these materials in belief and social practice, and to understand the meanings which they have for their users – whether in historical, ethnographic or contemporary cultures.

Historical circumstances are also relevant to the rejection and proscription of psychoactive substances. This is not just the contrast between simple preparations and chemically purified forms – 'soft' and 'hard' drugs. Even powerful alkaloids such as morphine (isolated in 1804 from opium) and cocaine were widely sold in advanced countries in the later nineteenth century, both in commercial preparations as patent medicines and in pure form for personal use as narcotics. While opiate preparations such as laudanum were displaced in everyday use by new analgesics such as aspirin, changes in recreational or hedonistic usage owed more to social conventions. It was the increasing social tensions and consequent imposition of discipline (aimed initially at munitions workers) at the time of the First World War and its aftermath, that produced first the UK licensing laws and then the Dangerous Drugs Act (1924) that put an end to the socially acceptable use of these drugs.[4] In addition to these general tendencies towards the increased socio-political control of consumption, a further important factor in the categorization of substances such as opium and cannabis was their association with specific ethnic groups when increased population mobility in the nineteenth and twentieth centuries led to direct cultural contact with the customs of immigrant populations. These circumstances led to their stereotyping and an ethnocentric reaction against 'alien drugs' and their predominantly working-class users; in Britain the association of opium with Chinese immigrants was an important factor in the development of attitudes to it in the nineteenth century,[5] while the association of cannabis with West Indians repeated the process in the early 1960s and led to the inclusion of cannabis and its products in the Dangerous Drugs Act. This was in marked contrast to the earlier positive reception and adoption, initially by the upper and middle classes, of exotic substances such as tea, coffee and cocoa, which had an elite background in the donor cultures and whose users posed no such perceived threat. The fact that introduced stimulants have generally been preferred to narcotics (sensu stricto) in recent Western societies – though with some interesting but temporary exceptions – is also of relevance in the construction of modern industrial culture and diet.[6]

While it requires a special effort, in discussing plant products whose derivatives are now classified as 'drugs' and subject to legal restrictions and prohibition, to overcome the inhibitions which our recent history has imposed, the discourse of 'drugs' is no model for the often subtle uses of psychoactive substances either in the past or in those areas of the world where the plants are indigenous and traditional practices continue. What is needed is a more inclusive conception of the subject, with a special sensitivity to context.

REDEFINING THE FIELD

The interest of modern readers is to some extent a retrospective one: to understand the indigenous origins and uses of substances which have been promoted to global importance and which in some cases present acute problems to contemporary society. This 'genealogical' approach must, however, be broadened if it is to achieve a comprehensive understanding of other cultures. The wide range of 'folk remedies' surviving in modern Europe,[7] and the inadequately documented but very extensive 'ethnobotany' of indigenous peoples throughout the world, demonstrate an extensive understanding and use of the medicinal characteristics of particular plants and their preparations, including mood-altering as well as physically restorative substances. There is now a growing literature on the indigenous usage of psychoactive substances,[8] which embraces a wide range of societies and social situations. At one end of the continuum, powerful hallucinogens may be employed to give particular individuals privileged access to the sacred on specific ritual occasions. Weston La Barre and Peter Furst, in particular,[9] have explored this 'shamanic' aspect of Siberian and New World ethnography, where the context of altered consciousness is a specifically 'religious' one. At the other end of the scale, milder stimulants or narcotics may have a variety of uses, ranging from the 'practical' employment of *qat* or coca to aid physical performance in Ethiopia and the Andean region respectively, or kola (cola) as a social relaxant in West Africa. Such more widespread uses should not, however, be regarded as unstructured and informal; as Chapters 2 and 5 make clear, the cultural importance of these substances is expressed in a variety of contextually appropriate usages in which the substances themselves are often taken as a metaphor for a variety of social relationships. These properties are not uniquely restricted to psychoactive substances and can also apply to a range of special foods which serve to carry meaning and metaphor.[10] Those with perceptible mood-altering properties, however, are particularly likely to cross cultural boundaries and become indigenous items of trade;[11] and indeed (as the origin of the trade name Coca-Cola indicates) to be promoted to patent formulae in the context of international industrial capitalism.

From a broader comparative perspective, therefore, the study of psychoactive substances is part of the anthropology of consumption. Such substances thus take their place alongside a variety of other meaningful consumables: not only spices, flavourings and medicines or other non-staple elements of food,[12] but also preparations which are not necessarily even ingested – body paints and cosmetics, soaps, ointments, incense and perfumes. This formulation is valuable because it is also a reminder of the variety of ways in which organic substances can enter the human body – by anointment[13] or inhalation of smoke, as well as consumption by mouth either of liquids or solids, or even by rectal insertion.[14] These differing modes of access may be indicative of wider cultural or even cosmological conceptions of the human body and its relationship to a physical and spiritual environment, and to the permeability of the boundaries which separate them. They thus relate to notions of bodily purity and hygiene which have themselves been illuminatingly explored in the writings of Norbert Elias and the historians whom he has inspired.[15] Georges Vigarello's *Concepts of Cleanliness*, for example, traces the changing moral properties attributed to the human body, reflected in attitudes to washing, clothing, perfume and the process of personal privatization. What is striking in such accounts is the way perceptions even of such everyday substances as water have changed radically since the Middle Ages. These attitudes to the substances of the natural world, and notions of cleansing and purification, are as fundamental to understanding how practices such as tobacco smoking were integrated into prevailing European conceptual schemes as they are to the significance of the Scythian 'smoke-bath' described by Herodotus (see Chapter 1).

Psychoactive substances can therefore be considered not so much a category in themselves but as one aspect of a potentially wide range of social activities. Such an approach situates the subject matter of this book alongside other consumable commodities which have been given special social and cultural significance, not all of which have distinctive psychological effects. The case of sugar is a well investigated example:[16] a substance which began as a rare, medicinal preparation with almost mystical recuperative properties, reserved for kings and aristocrats, became a symbolic cultural marker for a wider set of elite consumers, and finally a major mass-produced commodity of trade which was not only a major component of industrial diet, but fundamental to the set of economic dependencies between Europe, slave-supplying West Africa and the colonial Caribbean. This process of promotion, from restricted to mass consumption, parallels that of tea, coffee and tobacco and suggests that the psychoactive character of the latter substances has merely enhanced – through their tendency to mildly addictive use – the features of a more general process of intercultural transmission and amplification,[17] though the propensity of psychoactive substances to acquire social meaning has often given them a special role. Only a few of the substances which have been prominent in their cultures of origin, however, have undergone the process of selection in an increasingly unified world, to achieve either general acceptability or the ambiguous status of widely consumed but internationally proscribed drugs (or, in the case of tobacco, to be currently in an interesting transitional state between the two). Betelnut ('catechu', cf. *cachou*) was brought to Europe, but did not catch on as a habit.

Conversely, psychoactive preparations which were formerly widely used may tend to disappear. In Polynesia, for instance, *kava* has recently declined in importance (and was described in a recent monograph as 'the abandoned narcotic'[18]), to be replaced by the wider use of betelnut as the older formal and religious contexts of *kava* use have disappeared. This can be related to the largely secular employment and ease of preparation of betelnut, though it has itself acquired new meanings in a changed set of uses. In China, similarly, cannabis which had been known since ancient times was given up a thousand years ago in favour of opium. Psychoactive substances are constantly available as symbols for reinterpretation, and can move in and out of particular social roles as circumstances change (compare Chapters 4 and 10). Understanding these principles may help us to predict the future of currently widely used, though contested, substances such as alcohol.

This emphasis on the social and experiential aspects of psychoactive substances should not obscure their economic dimension: precisely because of their social importance, drugs are big business. Nor is this simply a consequence of capitalism, since such substances tend to be valuable and widely traded even in their indigenous contexts, from Australian aboriginal *pitcheri* to West African kola. Much of the traffic of prehistoric times must have involved organic substances (even though these are less prominent in the archaeological record than durable items like stone axes or bronze ornaments); and the wine trade was undoubtedly a mainstay of the ancient Mediterranean economy in Greek and Roman times. All of these movements provided opportunities for profit and attempts to control them, even before the emergence of the transcontinental maritime trade that marked the appearance of the modern world system. This growth in scale in the early modern period, however, provided an unparalleled occasion to enhance state revenues (see Chapter 8), and such trade became a major factor in the course of world history with the growth of intercontinental specialization in production. The imposition of taxes on these trades created a new growth industry, smuggling, with both political and cultural consequences; it was the attempt to avoid lost revenues by collecting tea taxes in Boston that 'turned Americans into rebels and coffee-drinkers at the same time'.[19]

On the other side of the world, another substance was being mobilized as a weapon of the trade war: to stem the outflow of bullion to China in return for tea, Europeans promoted the use of one of their oldest indigenous crops (see Chapter 1) – the opium poppy. The East India Company established a monopoly over the production and sale of opium in India, and large quantities were then shipped to Canton. This product, vainly resisted by the Chinese authorities, thus took its place among the commodities of the world economy. Ironically, then, it was the diaspora of Chinese labouring populations, along with their acquired consumption habit, that triggered the reaction to 'alien drugs' which in part led to its proscription as a legal commodity – first on a national basis and subsequently by international convention. At the same time, the rise of drug companies manufacturing refined opiates for medical purposes introduced a new element, and the newly illegal status of all forms of prepared opium thus opened the way for new kinds of underground activity and the kinds of ambiguous traffic (and their social and political consequences) which are considered in Chapter 9. Since the value of a crop of opium poppies may increase over a thousandfold between harvesting and sale, the economic consequences (both to dependent consumers reduced to crime to pay for their habit, and indeed to producers whose cash-crops may displace subsistence ones) have often been more malign than the use of the substance itself – at least in chemically unpurified form.

This intertwining of cultural and economic factors is emblematic of the many-sided relationships of the peculiar substances and their consuming habits considered in this volume. With a better grasp of what their social role has been in the past, we shall be better placed to understand issues of value, dependence and control, and the nexus of relationships between industry, private enterprise, state intervention and crime, that have created the scale of contemporary problems. As Eric Wolf has written in a related context: 'Only by understanding ... names as bundles of relationships, and placing them back in the field from which they have been extracted, can we hope to avoid misleading inferences and increase our share of understanding.'[20] Deconstructing 'drugs' is a first step towards understanding the complex history of the consumption of psychoactive substances.

NOTES

1 All terms in this field are notoriously slippery, and tend to incorporate moral judgements in what were originally more precise usages: 'intoxication' (with original implications of poisoning) is now widely used as an equivalent for 'inebriation' or other specific behavioural descriptions. This is why the neutral term 'psychoactive' has been generally used in this volume.

2 W. Schivelbusch, *Tastes of Paradise: A Social History of Spices, Stimulants and Intoxicants*, New York, Pantheon Books, 1992 (originally *Das Paradies, der Geschmack und die Vernunft: eine Geschichte der Genußmittel*, Munich/Vienna, Carl Hanser Verlag, 1980).

3 P. Camporesi, *Bread of Dreams: Food and Fantasy in Early Modern Europe*, Oxford, Polity Press, 1989; *The Magic Harvest: Food, Folklore and Society*, Oxford, Polity Press, 1993; *Exotic Brew: The Art of Living in the Age of Enlightenment*, Oxford, Polity Press, 1994.

4 M. Cohn, *Dope-Girls*, London, Lawrence & Wishart, 1992. Current attitudes to 'drugs' were hardened during the 1960s, in response to their employment in a sub-culture of protest.

5 V. Berridge and G. Edwards, *Opium and the People: Opiate Use in Nineteenth Century England*, London, Allen Lane, 1981.
6 E. Hobsbawm, *Industry and Empire* (Pelican Economic History of Europe, vol. 4), Harmondsworth, Penguin, 1968; S. Mintz, *Sweetness and Power: The Place of Sugar in Modern History*, Harmondsworth, Penguin, 1985.
7 See, for example, C. F. Leyel, *Elixirs of Life* (Culpeper House Herbals), London: Faber & Faber, 1948.
8 Botanists such as Richard Schultes and William Emboden have described the variety of the world's plants which are appreciated for their psychoactive properties: R. E. Schultes, 'The botanical and chemical distribution of the hallucinogens', *Annual Review of Plant Physiology*, 1970, vol. 21, pp. 571–94; W. Emboden, *Narcotic Plants: Hallucinogens, Stimulants, Inebriants and Hypnotics; Their Origins and Uses*, London, Studio Vista, 1979. A wide-ranging collection of studies, published in two volumes in 1981 to accompany a museum exhibition, affords an invaluable survey and bibliography: G. Völger (ed.) *Rausch und Realität: Drogen im Kulturvergleich*, (*Ethnologica* NF 9), Köln, Rautenstrauch-Joest-Museum (also published with K. von Welck by Rohwohlt, Hamburg). Richard Rudgley's recent account, inspired by the same interests as the present volume (and cross-fertilized in Oxford tutorials), offers an excellent introduction to the scope of the subject: R. Rudgley, *The Alchemy of Culture: Intoxicants in Society*, London, British Museum Press, 1993.
9 W. La Barre, *The Peyote Cult*, New Haven, Yale University Press, 1938; P.M. Furst (ed.), *Flesh of the Gods: The Ritual Use of Hallucinogens*, New York, Praeger, 1972; idem, *Hallucinogens and Culture*, San Francisco, Chandler & Sharp, 1976.
10 Mintz, op. cit., pp. 8–13.
11 P. Lovejoy, *Caravans of Kola: The Hausa Kola Trade 1700–1900*, Zaria, Ahmadu Bello University Press, 1980.
12 J. Goody, *Cooking, Cuisine and Class*, Cambridge, Cambridge University Press, 1982; C. M. Foust, *Rhubarb: The Wondrous Drug*, Princeton, Princeton University Press, 1992.
13 As with atropine in European witchcraft: 'Die Salbe gibt den Hexen Mut' – *Faust*.
14 Such 'local cultures' are still evident in variations in everyday European medical practice: for instance, the northern preference for the oral ingestion of pills as opposed to the southern use of suppositories. Rectal insertion can be an effective method of consuming drugs.
15 N. Elias, *The Civilising Process: The History of Manners*, Oxford, Basil Blackwell, 1978; G. Vigarello, *Concepts of Cleanliness: Changing Attitudes in France since the Middle Ages*, Cambridge, Cambridge University Press, 1988.
16 Mintz, op. cit.
17 Mintz, op. cit.; see also H. Hobhouse, *Seeds of Change: Five Plants that Transformed Mankind*, London, Sidgewick & Jackson, 1985.
18 R. Brunton, *The Abandoned Narcotic: Kava and Cultural Instability in Melanesia*, Cambridge, Cambridge University Press, 1989.
19 E. R. Wolf, *Europe and the People without History*, Berkeley, University of California Press, 1982, p. 255.
20 Wolf, op. cit., p. 3.

1

ALCOHOL AND ITS ALTERNATIVES

Symbol and substance in pre-industrial cultures[1]

Andrew Sherratt

CONSUMPTION RITUALS AND THE CONSTRUCTION OF SOCIAL IDENTITY

Food and drink are perhaps the most fundamental, if short-lived, media of material culture. The serving and sharing of these essential elements make up one of the central daily activities of the human domestic group. It is the everyday practices of who provides sustenance for whom, and in what circumstances, that give family relationships and social classifications their substance; and it is here, both through the provision of daily bread and the rarer occasions of sacrifice, that the major metaphors of religious thinking have their origin.

Human diet is notoriously broad; our dentition resembles that of the omnivorous pig rather than that of specialized carnivores or herbivores. Even the poisonous roots of bitter manioc, the pungent fruits of peppers and the bulbs of the onion family have their role in the spectrum of human uses of plants.[2] The selection of sources of nourishment from the environment is an infinitely variable set of decisions that is only partly explicable on grounds of calorific rationality; the choice of consumables and the transformation of edible resources into food is at the heart of the cultural process. The harvesting of plants and the killing of animals are not simply practical activities but occasions for rites of passage in the production of eatable substances.[3] The use of fire to break down resistant tissues and release nourishment is itself a uniquely human characteristic, practised for over a million years; and its consistent application to the preparation of food serves to reinforce a separation of the raw from the cooked, the natural substance from its cultural transform, and makes possible the infinite varieties of cuisine.[4]

Food is not simply a system of alimentation, then, but also a system of non-verbal communication; and its syntax can be illuminated by the kinds of structural analysis that have been applied to mythology and visual art.[5] Only certain products and combinations are contextually appropriate, either to a society as a whole or to certain groups, gatherings and individuals within it. At its most basic level, this involves cultural definitions not only of food itself but of what constitutes a 'meal' or other forms of consumption event. At the same time, however, it has a socio-economic dimension in that these choices are constrained both by natural availability and social access. Not everyone in a given society is in a position to obtain the materials and appurtenances necessary for the more elaborate modes of presentation.[6] Different practices are appropriate to different social positions; typically these involve classifications of age, gender and status, membership of particular groups and notions of exclusiveness or hospitality between them. They also involve different degrees of ostentation and formality, and the use of a whole range of items of material culture concerned with the preparation and serving of food and drink. To consume a certain substance in a certain way embodies a statement, but this assertion can be either accepted or controverted by others involved in the process of social reproduction. 'Acceptable practice' thus evolves through a constant network of negotiations and serves to define the identities of individuals and groups. It is the social, rather than the biological, interpretation that makes sense of Ludwig Feuerbach's old aphorism – *der Mensch ist was er ißt* ('man is what he eats').

This process operates at several levels, including both the formal and the informal definition of groups, allowing strategies for the inclusion or exclusion of individuals through the use of characteristic 'marking rituals'.[7] At the domestic level, this may be no more than the prevalent conception of how everyday acts are properly done – Pierre Bourdieu's *habitus*;[8] in larger communities or associations it takes on greater formality in rarer and more explicitly symbolic occasions. Participation in such activities is often a defining characteristic of membership of these larger social groups, and the form of public consumption itself is often emblematic of their identity, constitution and structure.[9] Ritualized forms of consumption may be explicitly religious acts, as in the Christian Eucharist or the complex wine-offerings to the ancestors in the elaborate bronze vessels of Shang and Zhou dynasty China. Such overtly symbolic uses help to fix the meanings of a wider range of social ceremonies and hospitable occasions, when eating and drinking may be combined with other forms of performance and recitation – as in the Polynesian *kava*-ceremony or the Greek *symposion*.[10] In these more fluid social circumstances, entertainment involving eating and drinking may become a competitive arena of social display (both in the provision of food and in the syntax of its use[11]) as appropriate groupings, boundaries and relative standings are actively negotiated. The choice and combination of particular items of food and drink thus embody notions of status and value, as well as conceptions of identity and belonging, whether actual or desired.

It is not surprising, therefore, that the word 'consumption' should denote not only the process of eating and digesting food but also the whole social arena of using material culture,[12] from its acquisition to the abandonment of its residues, over a whole range of societies from the ethnographic to the capitalist[13] – much as 'taste' is extended to other forms of social discrimination.[14] The consumption of food is a paradigm for understanding the 'consumption' of other materials, goods and services. Its constant physical necessity, and the variety of experiences which it encompasses, make it an especially useful medium for apprehending the ways in which societies and cultures are constituted and the manner in which they change.

A particularly relevant instance is offered by the way in which Western societies since the sixteenth century have accommodated the whole diversity of new plant products made available by the colonial experience (some of which are described in more detail by Goodman and Smith in Chapters 6 and 7 of this volume), which formed an important part of what has been described as the 'consumer revolution' of the eighteenth century.[15] These recent examples offer clues to the ways in which substance and symbol interact and provide opportunities for the acquisition of contextual meanings. Their absorption into Western culture and ultimately into global consumerism has involved a structural accommodation to earlier practices centred on the use of various forms of alcohol. Considering only the products consumed in liquid form, it is clear that they have given rise to a whole set of graded consumption rituals and contextually appropriate usages, based on perceived oppositions such as those between wine and beer, tea and coffee, as well as various forms of sugar and chocolate (among many others). These aligned with other category distinctions: inebriant versus stimulant, cold versus hot, silver versus ceramic. From an archaeological and art-historical point of view, it should be noted that each of these substances was associated with its own material culture, in the form of particular vessels and materials appropriate for their serving and consumption: the adoption (and adaptation) of 'China' porcelain for tea is a case in point. From a sociological perspective, what is interesting is the way in which they came to embody statements and aspirations. Since wine drinking was so closely associated with traditional aristocratic culture, the 'cups/That cheer[16] but not inebriate' (William Cowper, *A Winter Evening* 1785) came to be an obvious symbol of middle-class revolt against the values of the *ancien régime* (as, incidentally, was opposition to hunting and the warrior aristocracy's cult of the horse).[17] Economic changes were a fundamental part of this process, but its operation cannot simply be understood in economic terms: 'the use of commodities such as sugar, coffee and tea is not simply a sign of more "real" or "basic" socioeconomic changes but an active process of cultural construction in itself'.[18] Rather, the use of these consumables became 'one of a number of significant elements of a cultural pattern that had meaning because it both signified and constituted the respectability of the people who participated in it.... All of these things constituted a demand for respect.'[19] Food and drink embody not only statements, but also rhetorical statements.

In this perspective, the introduced novelties of the seventeenth and eighteenth centuries are only one chapter in the more general transformation of European societies which had been in process since the later Middle Ages.[20] The growth of courtly society and the formation of new foci of power were accompanied by the elaboration of eating practice and entertainment which replaced the quantitative contrasts of 'feast and fast' with a more subtle and differentiated cuisine.[21] These practices provided a model for a broadening class of bourgeois imitators, in which the contrary principles of social distancing and wider recruitment were played out: as spices became more accessible to the bourgeoisie, so aristocratic tables emphasized game and natural flavourings instead, and placed a greater stress on the *style* of eating.[22] These processes, too, had their material culture concomitants, in the form of a wider range of eating equipment, with a proliferation of tablewares such as *maiolica*, as well as forks, linen napkins and tablecloths.[23]

The choice of foods and drinks, therefore, and their manner of preparation and serving, is fundamental to the definition – and, indeed, the creation – of social groups and classes. While it is not unique in these attributes, which it shares with many other forms of material and oral culture, it has the double significance (like poetry) of being a form of satisfaction both in itself and in what it conveys. Being perishable and constantly consumed, foods and drinks must be constantly produced, so that they are continuing elements of the relations of production and distribution: a continuous flow around the networks of exchange. As a commodity, they can generate wealth; as a possession, they embody value; in their consumption, they express the values embodied in them. Moreover, if the consumption of food or drink also affords some additional experience (if it has behavioural as well as nutritive effects) then it carries a further importance both in the sensations that it gives and the cultural significance attributed to them.[24] It is these properties which explain the cultural prominence of substances such as alcohol[25] and its alternatives, and indeed of the whole variety of psychoactive substances which have been incorporated into human culture and diet. It follows from the analysis presented above, however, that the meanings associated with consumption of these substances are not static. Everyday practices and explicitly symbolic usages will vary according to the constitution of the social group, and may be tactically employed as a dynamic element in its formation and maintenance. There can be no simple equation between particular acts of consumption and a single ideology or set of meanings. The history of psychoactive substances is a continuing process of transformation, involving complex patterns of incorporation, interaction and opposition. The remainder of this chapter attempts to exemplify some of these principles in relation to Old World uses of alcoholic drinks, and to situate them in a wider comparative context.

THE SOCIAL USES OF PSYCHOACTIVE SUBSTANCES

The use of psychoactive products covers a spectrum of practices which from a modern, Western point of view might be described as religious, medical and secular. Where only one such substance is available to a society, it may indeed combine all three aspects – though 'secular' uses are likely to be subject to contextually appropriate use and prescription. Isolated and archaic societies may have just one such privileged plant, as with *pitcheri*[26] among certain Australian aboriginal tribes. More complex societies, in contact with a diversity of neighbouring groups, are likely to acquire several such substances, especially since their high value and low bulk make them highly appropriate as commodities for long-distance exchange and trade, well illustrated in the case of kola.[27] In these circumstances their uses are likely to separate into different spheres of consumption, with some occupying a ritually prominent and highly circumscribed context (perhaps echoed in lesser everyday rituals of hospitality), others, for instance, a medicinal or pleasure-giving role. Stephen Hugh-Jones' discussion of the complementary meanings assigned to coca, tobacco and *yagé* in a South American context in Chapter 2 in this volume is a good illustration of these subtleties. In urban societies, with their more widespread contacts, a great variety of such substances may be used, each in a different context and social setting.

It is important, therefore, that evidence for the employment of substances such as opium or cannabis at various times in the past should not immediately be interpreted as an indication either of profound ritual significance or of widespread employment for largely hedonistic purposes: they may simply belong to the *materia medica*. Nevertheless, even this latter category is not a neutral one, for the availability of psychoactive products is a constant temptation to 'misuse' – a term that implies less a medical judgement than a social one, in the sense of an unrestricted (and possibly habit-forming) hedonism. Few cultures allow this privilege to more than a fraction of their members, whether this fraction is defined by gender, status, wealth, or a combination of all three. One reason for this is the powerful potential of such substances to accrue symbolic meanings, and to provide focal experiences in the formation of dissident communities. Such factional usage is appropriately described as 'cult', in that it is the practice of a minority and exists in opposition to established forms of consumption. This is evident not only in current 'drug sub-cultures' in the Western world, but also ethnographically – the most literal example being the 'peyote cult', a messianic movement among American Indians based on a hallucinogenic cactus.[28] In milder form, the phenomenon could also be seen as exemplified in the 'coffee cult' of early modern Europe – remember Bach's *Coffee Cantata* ('*Hat man nicht mit seinen Kindern hunderttausend Huderlei?*').[29] For this reason, the employment of psychoactive substances which are not otherwise ritualized, outside a 'medical' context (itself often subject to rules laid down by religious authority), is likely to be subject to strong social condemnation. This appears to have been the case with opium in ancient Israel (see below, note 121). Conversely, such initially restricted minority or cult practice may become the hallmark of a group which ultimately attains power, and may in its turn become the badge of orthodoxy. In this case, the formerly dominant substance may itself become the token of minority cult, if not demoted further to the status of an element of folk medicine, treated as deviant, or even tabooed.[30]

The uses of 'drugs' are therefore constructed at three levels: at the level of practical choice (in the selection of the plant for the collection and preparation of a product); at the level of experience (in learning how to use the substance to produce an appropriate response);[31] and in the social assignment of contextual meaning to the act of consumption. All three aspects may vary through time. Their appropriateness also varies with the degree of social complexity: different kinds of drugs are appropriate to different sorts of society. Substances causing marked behavioural alteration, including some loss of physical control, may be powerful symbols of access to esoteric knowledge and communication with other worlds.[32] Such qualities may be attractive for individuals in small communities or in societies where political power is in the process of formation; but they are less appropriate for societies which emphasize self-control (*sensu* Elias),[33] for instance, for the holders of offices where responsible decision-making is required – except, perhaps, on occasions of 'ritual inversion' (funerals, year's end).[34] Powerful hallucinogens of 'magic mushroom' type may thus be prominent in the earlier stages of social evolution, less so thereafter; though they may continue to have contextually appropriate uses, for instance, employment in battle (e.g., by *berserkers*). Mild intoxicants, such as *kava* or alcoholic drinks (or tobacco) are more appropriate for ceremonies at which larger numbers participate, and which are occasions for male bonding, entertainment, speeches and negotiation. Since the psychological experience of these substances is itself culturally constructed to a large extent, they may come to be used in a more 'moderate' way, even if initially employed to induce trance-like states. Overt drunkenness and its associated boorish behaviour[35] may be enviable in an aristocracy with privileged access to alcohol, but needs to be tamed in more bourgeois circumstances, and becomes merely pathetic when alcohol is plentiful. Conversely, the moderation of orthodox usage allows the wilder, ecstatic employment of psychoactive substances in the context of cult – for example, in Dionysiac *orgia* (wine, perhaps even 'spiked' with something stronger),[36] or in the practices of European witchcraft.[37]

Also important is the relationship between 'drugs' and 'food'. There is an obvious contrast between, say, *pitcheri* specially procured by trade for the purpose of privileged consumption, and the production of beer by cereal-cultivating societies (who may devote up to half their crop to its preparation).[38] The former has economic (and political) as well as ritual rationing; the latter requires a more subtle gradation of consumption events to express the social appropriateness of its use. With poppies and hemp, the crops also have other economic uses – for oil and fibre as well as for the preparation of narcotic opium and cannabis; and these substances may be taken in a 'food-like' way, through ingestion, as well as a non-food way, by inhaling smoke. The latter mode relates to other practices, such as the burning of incense or other sweet-smelling substances, which may relate to ideas of cleansing and purification. This spectrum of usages offers a variety of symbolic roles for the consumption of particular drugs, and opportunities for a diversity of interactions and oppositions among them, which might be expected to relate to social, cultural and ethnic differentiation and competition in complex societies.

WINE IN MEDITERRANEAN ANTIQUITY

Wine in the Mediterranean region is practically synonymous with civilization. *Yn, wayana, wo-no, oinos, vinum, yayin,* wine:[39] the word is universal. Whether in Levantine, classical or Christian contexts, the imagery is ubiquitous, the topic fundamental both to cultural and economic history. The spread of urban life was everywhere associated with the consumption of wine, and usually the cultivation of the vine; the material-culture remains studied by archaeologists – whether the 'Greek vases' and Roman *terra sigillata* which were the *maiolica* of the ancient world, or the silver and gold drinking-sets of the seriously rich whose style they imitated – were in no small part the paraphernalia for its consumption.[40] Even the humble amphorae which have been recovered in their thousands from Mediterranean wrecks by looters and underwater archaeologists are eloquent of the scale on which wine was transported, and give valuable information on the changing patterns of its production and trade – even though it is a besetting sin of archaeologists to write the history of containers rather than that of their contents.[41]

Wine had a multitude of uses: it was an anaesthetic, a solvent and a coolant; as vinegar, an organic acid; and a disinfectant – the first aid offered by the Good Samaritan was to pour oil and wine on the wounds. As a drink, it kept better than beer and even improved with age; it was an important element of Mediterranean diet,[42] and as such provided an exportable commodity for those areas specially suited to its production. The variety of local conditions gave rise to differences of taste and quality, and the regional production of especially desirable vintages was as much a feature of ancient as of modern times.[43] Then as now it was a social lubricant, and an essential element of hospitality: 'wine that maketh glad the heart of man'. The consumption of wine therefore provided a stock of metaphors which permeated Mediterranean religious and secular traditions.

The place of wine within the Judaeo-Christian tradition provides a point of entry to these meanings. The equation of red wine with sacrificial blood is a metaphor which underlies the central rite of Christianity, the Eucharist: *Hic est calix novum testamentum in sanguine meo* (Luke 22.20), the blood of the new covenant, shed for the remission of sins;[44] and in Orthodox practice it is offered to the communicant warm, with the consecrated bread (the 'Lamb'), on a spoon. In ancient Jewish tradition, wine formed an element in sacrificial ritual, offered as a libation (*nesekh*) after the animal and the corn-offering, as well as accompanying the services of the Sabbath and the celebration of the Passover meal, and ceremonies of passage such as marriage. The spring festival of Purim is celebrated with copious cups, to the point of mellowness, so that enmities are forgotten. The inebriating qualities of wine are recognized in Psalm 23, in the line which Protestant reformers translated as 'my cup runneth over', but which in the Vulgate preserves an alternative reading of its original ambiguity: *Et calix meus inebrians quam praeclarus est* ('my chalice inebriateth me').[45]

Ancient Israel was at the centre of early wine production: Levantine wines were exported to Egypt in the Bronze Age (where, for climatic reasons, grapes could only be cultivated in the Delta),[46] and Syrian wines (and also ice) were sent to northern Mesopotamia.[47] Wine as an elite drink, however, only came to replace beer in Mesopotamia in the early first millennium (the Neo-Assyrian period), when extensive vineyards were laid out, capable of producing the 10, 000 skins of wine drunk at the inauguration of the new capital built at Nimrud by Assurbanipal II.[48] The motif of the royal banquet, accompanied by wine and the symbolic fecundity of the grape, came to be an important icon of power and fertility; and Assyrian reliefs frequently depict the king holding a wine-bowl.[49] It is at this time that the elaborate set of metal vessels appropriate to the ancient 'wine ceremony' began to be formalized – the mixing-vessel, ladle, pouring-vessel, filter-funnel and a variety of cups[50] – which were to spread around the Mediterranean as equipment for the *banquet couché* that was the hallmark, in a variety of local interpretations, of the Orientalizing period, and most famous as the Greek *symposion*.[51]

As in the Levant, vines had been cultivated in the Aegean since the third millennium BC, but the growth of wine (and olive oil)[52] production was closely associated with the capital concentration and organization provided by the Minoan and Mycenaean palace-centres in the second millennium, under whose influence wine drinking probably first reached Italy. Precious metal vessels for wine drinking, and their pottery substitutes, formed part of the elite style of living and already show the elaboration of mixing, pouring and drinking customs. With the disorganization of the Dark Age which accompanied the transition from bronze to iron, the intensity of cultivation and the opportunities for high living diminished, so that access to wine and the ability to provide ostentatious feasts were important levers of political power: the Homeric hero 'feasts at equal feasts', forming alliances and securing the following of his own warrior band. Wine was not then the everyday commodity that it was to become by the second century BC, when Cato allowed seven amphorae of wine a year for his slaves – a bottle a day.[53] The dynamics of such chiefly or aristocratic societies have parallels both in ethnographic descriptions and in the world of the Norse sagas.[54]

The tradition of aristocratic feasting continued into the Archaic period when trade with the east Mediterranean grew to a larger scale, and the Greek city-state developed; and the style and significance of wine consumption was heavily influenced by Near Eastern practice.[55] In these circumstances, when the military role of the armed aristocrat had given way to the hoplite phalanx, the *symposion* became an all-male institution devoted to *euphrosyne* (delight) and *hesychia* (tranquillity) – the political harmony and convivial sociability associated with civic life, and associated with music and poetry.[56] The symposion itself had a ritual character, and took place under the sign of Dionysos, who had tamed the madness-inducing drug by teaching humankind to mix it with water. Later in Greek history these drinking clubs became famous both for political conspiracy and for philosophical discourse like Plato's *Symposion*, and for the literary form of learned disquisitions, such as Athenaeus of Naucratis' *Deipnosophistae*, which is itself a compilation of information about sympotic behaviour, drinking customs, and equipment.

The elaboration of serving and drinking equipment is best shown by the proliferation of 'black-glaze' vessels decorated with black and red figured scenes that epitomize classical Greece in museum displays: the *krater, hydria, oinochoe, kylix, rhyton*, etc. (the last showing Achaemenid

Persian influence). These pottery containers, often found in tombs, are now recognized as substitutes and surrogates – either for a less wealthy stratum of sympotic society, or deliberately bought for burial – for long-remelted originals in silver.[57] The association between wine drinking and silver vessels is a constant theme of ancient material culture,[58] and was propagated eastwards as far as China: when grapes and grape-wine production reached Tang China from Persia along the Silk Route in Sasanian times, silver cups made of sheet-metal travelled with them and revolutionized traditional Chinese metalworking practices, which had hitherto been based on casting, principally of bronze. This produced the range of elegant 'lotus-petal' forms, which thereafter became also characteristic of Chinese ceramics; and the attempt to produce fabrics in imitation of fine sheet-metal forms led to the development of white-wares,[59] and ultimately porcelain.[60] It is a permissible speculation that the value accorded to silver in Mediterranean and successor civilizations was due in part to this nexus of elite associations, formed during the Bronze Age and continued in classical and medieval times.[61]

Wine, therefore, in both secular and religious use, was the metaphorical lifeblood of Mediterranean civilization. It is thus ironic that while it continued to be the elite and sacramental drink of Byzantium and Christian temperate Europe, it was shortly to be banned in the area of its birth.

WINE, WHEELS AND SILVER: THE OPPOSITION OF ISLAM

The symbolic importance of wine and alcohol is thrown into stark relief by developments in the Mediterranean area in the later first millennium AD. Perhaps the best-known example of contrasting 'drug cultures'[62] is the opposition between the practices of Judaeo-Christian and Islamic societies in the western Old World. While the patterns of the present day or of recent historical times cannot be unproblematically projected into the past, the structure of this opposition is instructive as a model for the social and symbolic uses of psychoactive substances in general. Wine was the traditional inebriant of Near Eastern cultures for three and a half thousand years before the rise of Islam, and had its origins there (see below, p. 24). In many orthodox Islamic states at the present time, however, it is banned by law,[63] and its consumption is forbidden by religious authorities and frowned upon in traditional practice. In contrast, the consumption (usually by smoking) of cannabis and its products has been traditionally practised, while viewed with suspicion in the West, and internationally[64] proscribed as a dangerous narcotic. In situations of everyday hospitality in the present-day Islamic world, coffee and tea are served as accompaniments to many forms of entertainment and negotiation. Other stimulants, such as *qat*,[65] are locally employed both in private use and in social situations. The various social uses of alcoholic drinks are thus divided between other narcotics and stimulants.

Tea is a relatively recent introduction to these regions (probably seventeenth century); coffee (originally chewed, not infused)[66] has become widespread as a drink only since the sixteenth century, having been known in the Red Sea area in the fifteenth, and initially forbidden at Mecca in the early sixteenth, though soon widely consumed in the countries around the east Mediterranean.[67] It rapidly acquired its characteristic repertoire of brass coffee-pot and tray, iron roasting-pan and wooden mill – the equipment of hospitality. *Qat* is likely to have been used for longer, and seems at times to have been monopolized for religious use, for instance, in maintaining concentration during recitations of the Koran, but has now escaped to be a widely used (if only quasi-legal) commodity – often accompanied both by coffee and tobacco.[68] Kola was probably used, in the parts of West Africa to which it is native, in the pre-Islamic period: as one of the few local stimulants it played a similar role under Islam to *qat* further east, and its cultivation sustained an increasing trade especially during the eighteenth and nineteenth centuries. Cannabis (*hashish*, literally 'herb' or 'weed') was widely used in the medieval Islamic world, mostly in solid form, though its use was disparaged; smoking, in water-pipes, was apparently known before the introduction of tobacco: archaeological evidence from Ethiopia demonstrates its use in the fourteenth century, where it was employed to smoke cannabis products.[69] Smoking had a particular significance among societies whose prosperity had depended since the later second millennium BC on the incense trade with southern Arabia.[70] Although cannabis is often cited as a plant introduced from India and Persia in the twelfth century,[71] it appears (at least in its mild form) to have had a continuous history of use in the east Mediterranean since the later second millennium BC, and traces of tetrahydrocannabinol have recently been found (apparently as a medicament in the case of a difficult childbirth) associated with a fourth-century AD burial near Jerusalem.[72] It is possible, therefore, that it was promoted from medical to hedonistic or hospitable use under Islam – either by Arabs (who had for over a millennium been concerned with the incense trade) or under Turkish influence (since cannabis had been ritually employed on the Eurasian steppes for millennia). By the sixteenth century it was consumed in a variety of forms, either smoked on a hookah, chewed or drunk as an infusion[73] in secular situations, and also used in a religious context by dervishes as a means of inducing trance.[74]

While no single drug achieved universal and privileged use under Islam, a variety of 'peculiar substances' went through cycles of religious and secular usage, producing a suite of narcotics and stimulants with appropriate contexts of employment. All of these must be seen as alternatives to alcohol, brought to prominence in opposition to the drinking of wine. It is the symbolic significance of wine drinking that made its proscription so significant as a cultural marker. This attitude had its origins in the fundamental shift in the balance of power in the Near and Middle East during the first millennium AD, and most rapidly in the century around AD 700, from the older-established urban civilizations with their nuclei in the alluvial river valleys and Mediterranean coastlands to the occupants of the much wider spaces of steppe and semi-desert which separated them. It is this change in perspective which formed the background to the spread of Islam. The civilizations of antiquity had been centred in small areas of intensive agrarian production, linked by maritime or riverine trade (especially in products such as wine and olive oil) and supplied with specialist products such as incense from a desert hinterland. The new configuration was based on control of the intervening spaces and desert routes, pioneered in the course of the incense trade and given a new importance by use of the camel. Whereas earlier civilizations had been dominated by the urban wine-drinking aristocracies of the coasts and cultivated plains, the groups which came to power with Islam as their ideology were 'the top stratum of a tribal desert society based on camel breeding and caravan trading'.[75]

This shift in geo-political dominance had important effects on the cultural patterns of the Near and Middle East. It is symptomatic, for instance, that wheeled vehicles (always a relatively restricted and elite means of conveyance in these regions) effectively disappeared from large parts of the Middle East during the first millennium, to the extent that medieval Persian artists produced representations of wheeled vehicles with fundamental misunderstandings of their construction and harnessing.[76] In a remarkable book, *The Camel and the Wheel*, R. W. Bulliet has described the stages of this process, which was connected with the decay of the road network, and the growing scale of inter-regional connections in which wheeled vehicles were less efficient as a means of long-distance transport.[77] It would be a mistake, however, to attribute use of the camel and the rejection of the wheel simply to ecological rationality: equally important was its cultural symbolism of appropriate behaviour by the dominant group.[78] The new dominance of desert culture was also expressed in other aspects of living: in constructions such as the early Islamic (mid-eighth century) 'desert palaces' such as Qasr al-Hayr in Syria, and at a more fundamental level in everyday furniture, like the replacement of chairs and tables by cushions and brass trays on folding wooden frames.[79]

It is in this context that changing attitudes to alcohol must be situated; for it was in the sphere of diet, and especially drinking practices, that the symbolic opposition was most forcibly expressed. Wine is not generally a drink of the desert: it was avoided in the early centres on the incense route, even where viticulture was possible;[80] and it formed the most obvious token of resistance to, and superiority over, the older elites. Wine, especially of high quality, was imported to Mecca (mainly by Jews and Christians) at the time of Muhammed, and in the Koran the Prophet initially warned merely against its misuse – noting that its tendency to lead to sin was greater than its usefulness (Sura II, 216); but it came to be condemned explicitly (along with stone pillars and divination by arrows) as an abomination of Satan: 'Avoid them, that ye may prosper' (Sura V, 92).[81] The *Hadith* condemns the drinking, buying and selling of wine as incompatible with faith; it is a sign of the last days; it was inadvisable as medicine and condemned even as a means for preparing vinegar.[82] Jurists discussed whether the proscription covered date-wine as well as grape-wine, and extended the ban to drinks with intoxicating effects made from grapes, dates, honey or cereals – even to grape-must. Wine was equated with blood and urine: anyone who drinks a draught of wine shall on Doomsday have to drink a bowl of pus. The effects of the spread of Islam are perceptible archaeologically in the widespread abandonment of vineyards and grape-pressing installations in Palestine in the seventh and eighth centuries.[83]

The condemnation of wine drinking as a practice can be seen as an explicit attempt to enforce a new set of cultural codes in direct opposition to the established values of the older civilizations in the areas conquered by Islam (though gaining force only long after the conquest itself). Like the preference for riding over driving, it was an expression of the lifestyle of a newly dominant minority; but unlike the passive neglect and disdain for the easy modes of transport of the town-dwellers it had a religious force because of the ritual canonization of wine drinking in the Judaeo-Christian and Persian traditions. Along with the condemnation of eating pig (which had been the object of similar attitudes before, in a comparable situation: see note 30) it was a symbolic inversion of the most distinctive practices of conquered populations, and especially the established elites and their religious setting, which it was desired to supplant. What had formerly been an ecologically rational aspect of local practice had become a cultural symbol and marker. This aspect of the Islamic cultural transformation was so effectively aimed because it spanned both the prevailing habitus of everyday entertainment and social hospitality, and the ritual use of wine as a symbol in religious liturgy: a whole spectrum of cultural usages and practices. But it should not be imagined as a simple change of cultures (as archaeologists, above all, are perhaps wont to conceive events in the past); as a symbolic marker in a shift of power – not unlike the other non-alcoholic consumption rituals of seventeenth- and eighteenth-century Europe – it was the focus of continuing tension and negotiation. Earlier practices continued, especially in Persia (otherwise Omar Khayyám's famous line 'a loaf of bread, a jug of wine . . .' would not have been possible), in the *Bazm* ceremony, an elaborate feast with music, poetry and wine, recorded in the twelfth and thirteenth centuries.[84] Religious ordinances constantly sought to counter such indulgence, and to assert the ascetic values of the early conquerors against the resurgence of older urban practices. The *Hadith* literature combines such injunctions with others against related aspects of luxury, such as precious metal vessels[85] which were particularly associated with the consumption of wine: 'He who drinks from a silver vessel will have hellfire burning in his belly.'

The present attitudes of Islamic states, therefore, are a codified selection of a variety of attitudes to alcohol which grew up in rhetorical opposition to the wine-drinking practices of Mediterranean antiquity, rooted in the absence of the vine in the dry zone surrounding the early centres of urban civilization. The receptiveness to alternatives, such as cannabis, *qat*, and later coffee and tea, is consistent with traditional uses of the plants of the dry areas south and east of the Mediterranean, where wine had its origins. This survey affords the basis for a more speculative enterprise: what did the world look like *before* wine, and how was it changed by its appearance? When, in fact, did alcohol production begin?

THE ORIGINS OF ALCOHOL IN THE OLD WORLD

When the Flemish monk William of Rubruck visited the court of Mangu Khan at Karakorum in the middle of the thirteenth century, the Mongol ruler offered him a choice of grape-wine, rice-wine, mead or kumish.[86] These four sources of sugars – grapes (fructose), grain (maltose), honey (glucose) and milk (lactose) – were the principal materials for preparing alcohol in antiquity. Which was the first?

A symposium in the pages of *American Anthropologist* in 1953, under the title 'Did man once live by beer alone?', discussed the hypothesis that cereal crops were first cultivated for brewing purposes rather than bread-making. Although the idea is periodically reventilated,[87] the consensus was that this seemed most unlikely, and that early hulled cereals were probably 'popped' (like popcorn) and naked ones made into gruel or porridge. Only a small part of the world's cereal growers make their crops into beer, and the discovery of fermentation is not an inevitable consequence of cereal growing, since it requires a knowledge of malting and yeast. Beer was, however, brewed by the Bronze Age civilizations of Egypt and Mesopotamia, already familiar with date- and grape-wine, and a great deal of information is available from literary and pictorial evidence.[88] Beer drinking is identifiable both iconically and archaeologically, since it was usually drunk through a straw because of the quantities of mash still floating in it.[89] Although at certain periods it seems to have been an elite beverage (as the pictorial record indicates), it was also quite widely consumed, at least by urban populations. Beer was not characteristic of the wine-growing heartlands of the Greek Mediterranean world, and a separate tradition of beer-making seems to have been characteristic of temperate Europe. Archaeological evidence suggests that European alcoholic drinks in the Bronze Age used a mixture of honey, wild fruits and sometimes cereals, and that pure beers did not appear until the Iron Age.[90] Classical writers such as Pliny associated beer with either Egyptians or Celts; Dionysius of Halicarnassus noted that 'the Gauls have no knowledge of wine . . . but used a foul-smelling liquor made of barley rotted in water'.[91]

Beer, then, seems to have existed on the edges of the wine-making world; and mead fits a similar pattern. Although valuable as a sugar supplement, honey is unlikely to have been sufficiently plentiful to sustain an alcoholic tradition on its own. It was an important item of trade in ancient times, and beekeeping (in horizontal hives) was practised from the third millennium onwards in the Mediterranean region – although later in northern Europe, where forest beekeeping was the norm until the early centuries AD.[92] Mead was an expensive, elite drink, and its importance in Indo-European mythology[93] is likely to be a later development from the generalized honey/cereal/wild fruit brewing technology which grew up on the periphery of Mediterranean wine production. The same could be true of the production of kumish from lactose-rich mare's milk:[94] it is quite likely to have begun as a local substitute for the quantities of wine disbursed to the Scythians from the Greek Black Sea colonies, and to their successors by traders from Byzantium and Christian Europe.

The most plausible scenario for the beginnings of alcohol production lies in the domestication of the sugar-rich tree-crops of the Mediterranean and adjacent areas. The primary Neolithic cultigens were cereals and legumes, but by the later fourth millennium there is evidence in the Levant for the cultivation of fruit-crops: date, grape, olive, fig and pomegranate.[95] The timing is significant, for it coincides with the beginnings of urban life in the alluvial lowlands of Mesopotamia, with ramifications throughout the Near East. The date palm is one of the most concentrated sources of sugar, both in its fruits and its sap, and is subject to natural fermentation; and moreover the palms grow well in lowland areas, unlike vines.[96] (Palm-wine, from many different genera of palms, is made in many parts of Africa and southern Asia, though it keeps less well than grape-wine.) The experience of using fermentable fruits may well have offered the incentive to take other fruit-crops into cultivation, and vines would have been particularly suitable in extending cultivation in the Mediterranean hill country of the Levant and coastal Asia Minor, where viticulture on any scale probably began.[97] The experience with fermentation processes, and the transfer of the various natural yeasts which exist on wild fruits would have been instrumental in extending alcohol production to honey and cereals.[98]

By the third millennium BC, wine production was established in the Aegean, and the assemblage of silver and gold drinking vessels recovered by Heinrich Schliemann from the destroyed remains of the second city of Troy indicates that the equipment for serving it with due ostentation was already in existence. Moreover, the imitation of these shapes in pottery, over a wide area of south-east and central Europe, testifies to the impact which drinking and its associated rituals had on the native cultures of surrounding regions. Since vines themselves were not to be cultivated in these areas before Iron Age and Roman times, some two to three millennia later, this would seem to be precisely the set of circumstances in which alternative alcoholic traditions would have their genesis, and in which substitute fermentation processes involving honey and cereals might be pioneered. This argument is strengthened by the subsequent appearance over large areas of northern and western Europe of pottery drinking vessels – usually, though not exclusively, found associated with weaponry in the graves of adult males – which are so distinctive as to give their names to whole archaeological culture-complexes: the Corded-ware and Bell-beaker 'cultures'. Rather than representing a mass migration of 'Beaker Folk', as nineteenth-century prehistorians envisaged, it seems more plausible to see this widespread apparition as testimony to an equally fundamental episode in European prehistory – the spread of alcoholic drinks.[99] This phenomenon would form the first chapter in a continuing story of the acculturation of the temperate zone by elements of culture and diet with their origins in the Mediterranean: the spread of metal drinking vessels in the Bronze Age (first in gold, then in bronze), the arrival of wine (and silver vessels) in Celtic times, and the cultivation of the vine itself under the Romans; and not least the arrival of Christianity and its sacramental celebration of the fruit of the vine.[100]

BEFORE ALCOHOL?

If alcohol can be traced back to the domestication of tree-crops in the Mediterranean, and spread from there over temperate Europe and adjacent Eurasia, then what preceded it in the forest and steppe country north of the zone where vines and dates had their home? It has been fundamental to the arguments of this paper that human societies are more likely than not to have discovered the psychoactive properties of the plants in their environment, and to have canonized their usage in culturally characteristic forms of consumption and ritual. In this section

I want to explore the suggestion that the pattern of usage in temperate Eurasia rather resembled that of native North America (as described by Alexander von Gernet in Chapter 3 of this volume), it being essentially a zone of smoking cultures rather than drinking cultures.[101]

The first ethnographic evidence is that of Herodotus (*c.* 446 BC) and concerns cannabis. In his account of the Scythians, derived from an informant in Olbia on the northern coast of the Black Sea, he describes a Scythian purification ritual on the Pontic steppes after a funeral:

> On a framework of three sticks, meeting at the top, they stretch pieces of woollen cloth, taking care to get the joins as perfect as they can, and inside this little tent they put a dish with red-hot stones on it. Then they take some hemp seed, creep into the tent, and throw the seed on the hot stones. At once it begins to smoke, giving off a vapour unsurpassed by any vapour-bath one could find in Greece. The Scythians enjoy it so much that they howl with pleasure.[102]

The accuracy of this account was strikingly confirmed by the excavation in 1947 of a group of burial mounds at Pazyryk in the Altai mountains of Siberia dating to the fifth century BC, where each burial had been accompanied by a 1.2 m-high wooden frame tent, enclosing a bronze vessel with stones and hemp seeds, apparently left smoking in the grave. A leather pouch with hemp seeds provided supplies, and scattered hemp, coriander and melilot seeds were also recovered.[103]

How old was this practice? Hemp (*Cannabis sativa*) was a traditional fibreplant of the steppes, and had been cultivated in China since the Neolithic. Its pharmacological properties are described in early Chinese medical texts. The use of cord-impressions to decorate pottery is characteristic both of China and of the steppe region from the fourth millennium BC onwards; and on the Pontic steppes this ornament was first applied to small-footed pottery vessels interpreted as braziers (*kurilnitsy*), which are commonly found in graves of the so-called Pit-grave and Catacomb-grave cultures of the third millennium. Similar vessels occur in later cultures, indicating a continuity of practice down to Scythian times. In two cases, one in Romania and one in the Caucasus, braziers from third millennium graves have been found in association with hemp seeds. It seems, therefore, that the practice of burning cannabis as a narcotic is a tradition which goes back in this area some five or six thousand years and was the focus of the social and religious rituals of the pastoral peoples of central Eurasia in prehistoric and early historic times.[104]

This pattern, surviving on the steppes, may be a model for temperate Europe before the introduction of alcoholic drinks. The archaeological record from western Europe contains other examples of artefacts which find their most logical explanation as burners for narcotics, usually concealed under descriptions such as 'incense-cups' or *'brûle-parfums'*. A series of small vessels which appear as accessories in rich burials in the early Bronze Age of southern England (mid-second millennium BC), including examples with fenestrated walls, are a prime candidate.[105] These would be contemporary with the use of alcoholic drinks in the chronology which I have proposed. An earlier and more widespread set of examples of small braziers, dating to the earlier fourth millennium, pre-dates the appearance of highly decorated drinking vessels. These are the so-called 'vase-supports', typical of the megalith-building cultures of southern and western France, and often found in association with megalithic tombs. Their widespread occurrence and distinctively decorated appearance, as well as evidence of burning, makes them comparable with the cannabis-braziers described above; and it is likely that they were used for the ritual inhalation of some other narcotic, perhaps in the context of mortuary ritual and communication with the ancestors. It is significant that they are culturally associated with engravings inside megalithic tombs, such as those of Gavrinis in Brittany, which have recently been discussed as possible examples of entoptic images produced under the influence of hallucinogens.[106] While an unambiguous demonstration is not yet possible, the realization is gradually dawning on archaeologists that such practices, widespread in the ethnographic record, are inherently likely to have existed in prehistoric times. Small pottery burners, typically decorated with animal protomes, are known from the earliest farming societies in the Balkans and suggest a long-standing interest in the symbolism of flame, smoke and perhaps the burning of sweet-smelling or pharmacologically active substances. Early Mesopot-amians burned resinous wood such as pine or juniper before they obtained aromatic incense from further south; Siberian shamans used these, or the ericaceous shrub *Ledum palustre*, to accompany their trances. It seems entirely probable that in their practices and associated mythologies the societies of aboriginal Europe were 'smoking cultures', and in this respect resembled those of temperate North America as they were encountered in the sixteenth and seventeenth centuries AD.

Of the psychoactive substances likely to have been used by indigenous Eurasian peoples, only a few have achieved wider currency. Many, therefore, have been forgotten, and it would be a mistake to attribute all possible indications to the famous ones. Nevertheless, there is one which seems, like cannabis in central Eurasia, to have been a European donation to the rest of the world. The opium poppy (*Papaver somniferum*)[107] is a native member of the Mediterranean flora and was cultivated by the first Neolithic groups in central Europe (perhaps as a result of early contacts with the west Mediterranean). Finds of whole capsules from later Neolithic lakeside villages in Switzerland show that the plant was fully domesticated, in that (like cereals) it had lost its self-seeding mechanism. Opium-poppy capsules are known to have been buried with the dead in esparto-grass bags in Neolithic Spain, preserved under especially arid conditions in a burial-cave in Almería; and some sort of opiate would seem to be the prime candidate as the substance burned in the pottery braziers of Neolithic western Europe – perhaps even the privileged psychoactive substance of ritual observance.[108]

OLD WORLD INTERACTIONS: THE DOMINANCE OF DRINKING

By the second millennium BC, in the Bronze Age, these regional traditions had begun to interact, and complex patterns had begun to emerge. These conjunctions were less confrontational than the subsequent ideological clashes of the Islamic period, and often resulted in syncretic usages: substances formerly burned or chewed were accommodated to the drinking mode of alcohol. This model can be exemplified in three areas on the margins of alcohol-using regions. One important area of innovation was the contact zone between the central Asian steppes and the east Mediterranean: the desert plateau of Iran and its borderlands, from Turkmenistan to northern India. This region has received special attention because of the long debate over the sacred hallucinogenic drink known in Sanskrit as *soma* and in Avestan by the cognate word *haoma*, which is described in passages of the *Rig Veda* – written down in the first millennium BC, but composed earlier. The question has been confused by the enthusiastic advocacy of R. Gordon Wasson for the implausible view that *soma* was prepared from mushrooms;[109] but now archaeology has offered better answers.

In the oases of the upper Oxus and adjacent northward-flowing rivers in Turkmenistan and Tadjikistan, at the western end of the later Silk Route, a series of fortified citadel-like sites, built of mud-brick and dating to the second millennium, has been excavated by Russian and local archaeologists.[110] Many (e.g. Gonur south, Togalok 1 and 21) enclose temple complexes that include both ash repositories from sacred fires, and preparation rooms where vats and strainers for liquid were found. Pollen analysis of their contents has identified traces of *Ephedra*, *Cannabis* and *Papaver* – the first a shrub-like species of joint-pine producing the euphoriant norpseudoephedrine and the stimulant ephedrine (also found in *qat*, and now used illicitly by athletes), the others also well known as euphoriants. Some of these were prepared by grating with stone graters and pounding with distinctive fine imported stone pestles, and the products were consumed as liquids (perhaps through decorated bone pipes, showing wide-eyed faces). Cylinder seals show animal-masked figures, playing a drum or leaping over a pole. The association of fire shrines and the consumption of psychoactive drinks suggested to the excavator that this is the origin of the tradition of Iranian fire rituals,[111] which was reformed by the prophet Zarathustra in the early first millennium BC. The genesis of the tradition which gave rise to Zoroastrianism would thus have taken place in the context of interaction between oasis communities – probably familiar with alcohol, since wine had been prepared in western Iran since the fourth millennium – and steppe and desert tribes which were part of the expanding pastoralist complex described in the previous section. The ritual plant products traditionally consumed on the steppes in braziers would now have been prepared as euphoriant or inebriating drinks – including the substance later known as *haoma*.[112]

It was from this area, at some time during the second millennium, that Aryan-speaking groups infiltrated into northern India, to assimilate the Dravidian-speaking populations of the collapsed Indus civilization, and introducing the religious ideas described in the *Rig Veda*. It seems likely, therefore, that the drink described as *soma* involved the infusion of various plant products known earlier on the steppes, and that there is no single answer to the *soma* question. One further plant may be mentioned, however, since it fits well into this complex: harmel or Syrian rue (*Peganum harmela*). It was this latter plant which was originally identified by Sir William Jones in 1794 as the source of *soma*, and this suggestion has recently been repeated.[113] Since its first archaeological occurrence goes back to the fifth millennium BC in the Caucasus,[114] it is likely to have been used in the same way as the others described here, and it is burned in central Asia as an intoxicant as well as being used medicinally for its oil, as mentioned by Dioscorides. It is also a source of the red dye used in Persian carpets. Its action is more powerfully hallucinogenic than the others, however, since it contains harmine (formerly called telepathine) which was used as a 'truth drug' by the Nazis and also occurs as one of the active constituents of *Banisteriopsis caapi*, the South American vine used to prepare *yagé* (see Hugh-Jones' discussion in Chapter 2 of this volume). Two intriguing speculations suggest themselves: are the entoptic images produced by harmine reflected (as in Tukano art) in the geometric designs of traditional Persian and central Asian carpets; and did the hallucinogenic properties of this drug, and the flying sensation it induces, give rise to the motif of the 'flying carpet'?

The religious use of *soma* in second- and first-millennium India did not preclude the use of wine or other fermented drinks; and Ayurvedic texts recommend it as an element of diet. Proscription of alcohol began to be advocated in the sixth century BC, as Hindu dietary codes became more strict,[115] and in more recent times it has been forbidden to brahmins, who use an infusion of cannabis – which itself is widely smoked and consumed in food.[116]

The history of cannabis consumption here is likely to go back to the second millennium and to the usage of plants derived ultimately from the steppes (though an indigenous use of *Cannabis indica* is also possible), with cannabis gradually becoming a cultural and religious marker at a time of increasing contacts with the wine-using West. This increasing emphasis on the steppe inheritance to differentiate Indian culture from neighbouring groups contrasts with the continuity of a wine-using tradition (initially using rice and millet, then grapes) in China, where steppe influences were constantly resisted as alien in Chinese culture.[117]

The possibility that the Chinese alcohol-making tradition may have exercised an influence comparable to that which wine drinking in western Eurasia had on surrounding modes of consumption is one which deserves explicit formulation. Of the indigenous psychoactive substances of south-east Asia, the most widespread and perhaps the oldest is betel-nut.[118] This nut (*Areca catechu*) is traditionally chewed mixed with lime (like coca) and also with a leaf of the vine *Piper betel*. Remains of *P. betel* have been found at Spirit Cave, Thailand, in a context dating to *c*. 6000 BC. This plant is botanically related both to black pepper (our condiment) and to *Piper methysticum*, which is used in Oceania to produce *kava*. A long-standing interest in this group of plants can thus be inferred in this area. What, then, is the origin of *kava*? On the model suggested above for *soma*, it seems possible that products initially smoked or chewed came to be made into liquid infusions through contact with the fermentation practices associated with the preparation of alcoholic drinks. This is likely to have occurred in the second millennium BC. It is striking, therefore, that a distinctively decorated pottery known as Lapita Ware is known to have extended into Melanesia (an area ethnographically associated with *kava* consumption) around 1500 BC. It seems a plausible hypothesis, therefore, that these elaborate ceramic containers were used for the ceremonial[119] serving of a new beverage, with its origins on mainland south-east Asia, as a result of interactions between an indigenous usage of a species of *Piper* and the Chinese rice/millet wine-making tradition. The practice of infusing tea leaves may have a similar origin.

If this model is accepted, then a further regional example may be adduced. I referred in an earlier section to the disappearance of ceramic braziers in northern and western Europe, and the appearance in their stead of prominent forms of pottery drinking vessels. Corded-ware beakers and early Bell-beakers are ornamented with impressions of twisted cord: if these are hemp fibres, then the decoration may indicate that their contents were connected with cannabis. Similarly, funnel-neck beakers are often accompanied by collared flasks, shaped like an inverted poppy: were they used to contain infused opium? This theory has been elaborated elsewhere.[120] If this is the case, then they would represent a parallel process of accommodating local substances, previously smoked, to liquid form.

These last examples from temperate Europe date to the third millennium BC. By the second millennium BC the opium poppy was widely known in the Near East, and cultivated commercially on Cyprus for the production of a liquid opium preparation in an olive-oil base. It was exported to the nearby Levant and Egypt in characteristic flasks (juglets) in the shape of an inverted poppy capsule.[121] A comparable trade is inferred for seventh-century BC Greece from the distribution of small, coarse-ware jugs, often found in the graves of children or in sanctuaries of Demeter or Hera – vegetation and chthonic deities associated with death and resurrection.[122] Homer describes Helen as putting a drug called *nepenthes* into Menelaus' cup of wine, to quieten pain and induce forgetfulness (*Odyssey*, IV, 221), and this is likely to have been a liquid of this kind. Occasionally employed as a component of mysteries and chthonic cults (as of later witchcraft), plants such as poppy, henbane, belladonna, aconite and mandrake continued to be used in the twilight area between folk remedies and underground religion, for their soporific and analgesic properties and ability to set aside worldly cares; as Iago was to say of Othello (in a scene set also in Cyprus):

> Not poppy, nor mandragora,
> Nor all the drowsy syrups of the world,
> Shall ever medicine thee to that sweet sleep
> Which thou ow'dst yesterday.

CONCLUSION: THE ALCOHOLIC TRADITION AND THE GEOGRAPHY OF INTOXICATION

Alcohol has been the primary intoxicant of Western civilization, promoted throughout the world by the colonial diaspora of European populations; yet it was a comparative latecomer to the repertoire of behaviour-altering substances used by the human species. It was dependent on agriculture, and in the Old World was pioneered primarily by Mesopotamian and Mediterranean city-dwellers, although its preparation and use spread more widely to surrounding farming populations. In the temperate zone it apparently displaced narcotics inhaled as smoke. It was to some extent resisted in steppe areas, where this earlier practice continued, and more strongly in desert ones; and avoidance of alcohol became a badge of orthodoxy when control of the ancient river-valley civilizations passed to the previously peripheral populations of the arid interfluves. It remained central, however, to the Christian cultures of temperate Europe; and it followed European expansion across the globe. Its association with aristocratic values in Western societies nevertheless laid it open to challenges from other, more stimulating drinks acquired through the colonial experience, and more generally to the iconoclastic critiques of Puritanism which reached a high point in the era of Prohibition in the USA between 1919 and 1933. Yet its usage was so deeply embedded in the fabric of Western culture that alcoholic consumerism reasserted itself; and alcohol remains today as large a contributor to the finances of Western states through taxation as its extralegal alternatives are to the profits of international narcotics traffickers and the criminal organizations which distribute their products.[123]

The study of psychoactive substances, therefore, is an essential aspect of both anthropology and history, ancient and modern. This essay has merely scratched the surface of a rich historical and ethnographic literature in which dozens, perhaps hundreds, of the psychoactive substances used by human communities have been catalogued. It can no longer be doubted that these sorts of practices are fundamental to human social behaviour, and that the conventional categories of recent urban experience distort and simplify our perception of the past. Working backwards from the known, historical transfers of cultivated plants and their preparations, the outline of a prehistory becomes visible. The regularities encountered across the world suggest that the properties of each phytogeographical zone have been systematically explored by their human inhabitants. These explorations have taken place independently, though their discoveries have been shared and traditions of their use have interacted. In the central zone of the world's landmasses, where agriculture and urban life originated in both hemispheres, alcoholic drinks made from fruits and cereals are found and in the Old World have come to be the predominant culturally privileged intoxicants. North of this zone, narcotic leaves and seeds of annual herbs – poppy, hemp, tobacco, jimsonweed, each in its own area – have been consumed, commonly by smoking, and may belong to an older stratum of usage. South of this zone, stimulant leaves and fruits of perennial shrubs – kola, *qat*, coffee, tea, betel, coca, *pitcheri* – have been chewed, inhaled and sometimes infused. Chewing, sniffing or smoking thus seem to have been the original modes of ingestion; the use of liquid media for consuming psychoactive substances in many parts of the world can be argued to reflect practices originally associated with the various traditions of preparing alcoholic drinks. Cutting across these zones, though still changing from north to south, are the hallucinogens – mushrooms, cacti, tropical vines – that seem to be particularly concentrated around the Pacific. This last distribution may have its roots deep in the Palaeolithic period, with the dispersal of human populations from eastern Asia into the New World. The deliberate seeking of psychoactive experience is likely to be at least as old as anatomically (and behaviourally) modern humans: one of the characteristics of *Homo sapiens sapiens*.

In this perspective, psychoactive substances can be seen as integral to the constitution of culture. They have been fundamental to the nature of sociality and an active element in the construction of religious experience, gender categories and the rituals of social life. No ethnographic or culture-historical account is complete without a consideration of these matters. They have been central to the formation of civilizations, the definition of cultural identities and the growth of the world economy. They are, indeed, peculiar.

NOTES

This chapter attempts to apply an anthropological and 'macro-historical' perspective to the consumption of psychoactive substances in prehistory and early history, from the point of view of an archaeologist working primarily in later prehistoric Europe. The individual sections are not in strict chronological order; they work from the known to the unknown and back again.

1 I owe a constant debt to my colleagues with similar interests in the Ashmolean, especially Roger Moorey, Michael Vickers and Susan Sherratt. In preparing the Past and Present conference from which this volume began, my co-members of the organizing committee, Eric Hobsbawm, Virginia Berridge, Paul Slack and Charles Philpin, provided essential encouragement and help.

2 For a general survey of natural products and their preparation from a pharmacological point of view, see T. E. Wallis, *Textbook of Pharmacognosy*, London, Churchill, 1967.

3 The importance of cooking and food preparation is stressed in Marcel Detienne's introductory essay 'Culinary practices and the spirit of sacrifice', in M. Detienne and J.-P. Vernant (eds), *The Cuisine of Sacrifice among the Greeks*, Chicago, University of Chicago Press, 1989, pp. 1–20.

4 The theme runs through C. Lévi-Strauss, *Mythologiques* (3 vols), Paris, PUF, 1964–8. The nature of food preparation before the emergence of *Homo sapiens sapiens* is an unexplored area of speculation, but raises fascinating questions of how 'the artificial' was conceptualized before the emergence of fully human speech. The use of drugs does not necessarily depend on speech and conscious categorization, however, since a recent report in *Animal Behaviour* (139, p. 797) records the behaviour of chimpanzees in Tanzania which involves the selection and slow chewing in the early morning of *Aspilia* and *Lippia* leaves – plants with pharmacological benefits and stimulant properties, which are used in the same way by local people.

5 The pioneering examples are R. Barthes, 'Towards a psychosociology of contemporary food consumption', in R. Forster and O. Ranum, *Food and Drink in History: Selections from the Annales ESC*, Baltimore, Johns Hopkins University Press, 1979, 5, pp. 166–76; M. Douglas, 'Deciphering a meal', in idem (ed.), *Implicit Meanings*, London, Routledge, 1975, pp. 249–75; M. Douglas, 'Food as a system of communication', in idem (ed.), *In the Active Voice*, London, Routledge, 1982, pp. 82–104.

6 J. Goody, *Cooking, Cuisine and Class*, Cambridge, Cambridge University Press, 1982; in an older tradition, G. Simmel, 'Soziologie der Mahlzeit' in idem, *Brücke und Tür*, Stuttgart, K.F. Koehler, 1957.

7 M. Douglas and B. Isherwood, *The World of Goods: Towards an Anthropology of Consumption*, Harmondsworth, Penguin, 1978, pp. 74–84.

8 P. Bourdieu, *Outline of a Theory of Practice*, Cambridge, Cambridge University Press, 1977.

9 For a sensitive ethnographic account of the ways in which everyday material practices are used to construct hierarchy and induct children into accepted notions of role and social space, see C. Toren, *The Social Construction of Hierarchy in Fiji*, London, Athlone Press, 1990, e.g. p. 228; discussed in S. J. Shennan, 'After social evolution: a new archaeological agenda?', in N. Yoffee and A. G. Sherratt (eds), *Archaeological Theory: Who Sets the Agenda?*, Cambridge, Cambridge University Press, 1993, p. 57. Situations such as meal arrangements and precedence in drinking rituals both constitute and display hierarchy, so that children *experience* cognitive categories before they *conceptualize* them (if at all) in more abstract terms. The formalized communal behaviour of large groups may be reflected on specific occasions in smaller gatherings, so as to set up metaphoric relationships between the two: the head of the household is to the family as the chief is to the clan, etc.; 'domestic ritual' makes these analogies explicit. Conversely, public offices may be experienced as scaled-up versions of familial authority. Historians and anthropologists are converging on this form of analysis: see D. I. Kertzer, *Ritual, Politics, and Power*, New Haven, Yale University Press, 1988.

10 For *kava* see conveniently G. Koch, 'Kava in Polynesien' in G. Völger (ed.), *Rausch und Realität: Drogen in Kulturvergleich*, (*Ethnologica* NF 9), Köln, Rautenstrauch-Joest-Museum, 1981, pp. 194–9; M. Merlin, V. Lebot and L. Lindstrom, *Kava, the Pacific Drug*, New Haven, Yale University Press, 1992; R. Brunton, *The Abandoned Narcotic: Kava and Cultural Instability in Melanesia*, Cambridge, Cambridge University Press, 1989; for wine in the Greek *symposion*, O. Murray, 'Sympotic history', in idem (ed.),*Sympotica: A Symposium on the Symposion*, Oxford, Clarendon Press, 1990.

11 Cf. M. W. Young, *Fighting with Food: Leadership, Values and Social Control in a Massim Society*, Cambridge, Cambridge University Press, 1971; A. Appadurai, 'Gastro-politics in Hindu South Asia', *American Ethnologist*, 1981, vol. 8(3), pp. 494–511; R. Jameson, 'Purity and power at the Victorian dinner party', in I. Hodder (ed.), *The Archaeology of Contextual Meanings*, Cambridge, Cambridge University Press, 1987, pp. 55–65.

12 Or, on occasion, even more fundamental processes: see J. Parry, 'Death and digestion: the symbolism of food and eating in north Indian mortuary rites', *Man*, 1985, NS vol. 20, pp. 612–30.

13 Douglas and Isherwood, op. cit.; M. Thompson, *Rubbish Theory: The Creation and Destruction of Value*, Oxford, Oxford University Press, 1979.

14 P. Bourdieu, *Distinction: A Social Critique of the Judgement of Taste*, London, Routledge, 1984.

15 N. McKendrick, 'The consumer revolution of eighteenth-century England' in N. McKendrick, J. Brewer and J. H. Plumb (eds), *The Birth of a Consumer Society: the Commercialization of Eighteenth-Century England*, London, Europa, 1982.

16 Note that these new drinks like tea (in this case) and coffee were stimulants, appropriate to the alertness and good timekeeping of an increasingly commercial and industrial society. The prominence of Quaker families in chocolate manufacture is well known. The temperance movement was later to lead some Nonconformist Protestant groups to replace wine even in the Eucharist, and to substitute (as I remember, in central England some thirty years ago), the proprietary blackcurrant drink, Ribena. Coffee in itself, as the

occasion for informal socializing, has now established its own kind of orthodoxy and standard practice in religious observance: witness the widespread current reconstruction of Anglican churches, often in the form of the addition of an exonarthex (as at St Andrew's, north Oxford), to accommodate the 'Rite of Coffee', which in Evangelical usage seems now to be almost as important as the Eucharist itself.

17 K. Thomas, *Man and the Natural World: Changing Attitudes in England 1500–1800*, Harmondsworth, Penguin, 1983, p. 183. The taboo on eating horsemeat derives in part from the prominent role of the horse in elite culture; was the relaxation of this taboo in France an echo of revolutionary fervour?

18 R. A. Austen and W. D. Smith, 'Private tooth decay as economic virtue: the slave-sugar triangle, consumerism and European industrialization', in J. E. Inikori and S. L. Engerman (eds), *The Atlantic Slave Trade: Effects on Economies, Societies, and Peoples in Africa, the Americas and Europe*, Durham, NC Duke University Press, 1992, p. 193.

19 Austen and Smith, op. cit., p. 194. This was, of course, only one of many meanings attached to drinking coffee: for an alternative in a different context, see note 29.

20 N. Elias, *The Civilizing Process*, vol. 1, *The History of Manners* (1978), and vol. 2, *State Formation and Civilization* (1982), Oxford, Blackwell, 1978–82.

21 'Nowadays it is not the prodigious overflowing of dishes, the abundance of ragoûts and gallimaufries, the extraordinary piles of meat which constitute a good table; it is not the confused mixtures of diverse spices, the mountains of roasts, the successive services of *assiettes volantes*, in which it seems that nature and artifice have been entirely exhausted in the satisfaction of the senses, which is the most palatable object of our delicacy of taste. It is rather the exquisite choice of meats, the finesse with which they are seasoned, the courtesy and neatness with which they are served, their proportionate relation to the number of people, and finally the general order of things which essentially contribute to the goodness and elegance of a meal.' L. S. R., *L'art de bien traiter*, 1674, quoted in S. Mennell, *All Manners of Food*, Oxford, Blackwell, 1985, pp. 54–61.

22 S. Mennell, op. cit., pp. 73–4.

23 For *maiolica*, see R. Goldthwaite, 'The economic and social world of Italian Renaissance maiolica', *Renaissance Quarterly*, 1989, vol. 42, pp. 1–32, in which he relates the great expansion of this industry and the diversification of its wares to 'radically new market behaviour' in response to new patterns of consumption: containers for drugs and spices, and decorative tableware of intermediate value for a rising bourgeoisie; for the contemporary elaboration of napery and other forms of table implements, see F. Braudel, *The Structures of Everyday Life* (Civilization and Capitalism 15th–18th Century, vol. 1), London, Collins, 1981, pp. 203–7. For a comparable phenomenon in an Islamic context, see R. W. Bulliet, 'Pottery styles and social status in medieval Khurasan', in A. B. Knapp (ed.), *Archaeology, Annales and Ethnohistory*, Cambridge, Cambridge University Press, 1992, pp. 75–82.

24 E. Bourguignon (ed.), *Religion, Altered States of Consciousness, and Social Change*, Columbus, Ohio State University Press, 1973; B. M. du Toit (ed.), *Drugs, Rituals and Altered States of Consciousness*, Rotterdam, Balkema, 1977.

25 The term is used as a shorthand for alcoholic drinks: distillation of wine was not employed before 1100 (as a medicine), and brandy did not become popular in Europe before the sixteenth century; Braudel, op. cit., pp. 240–4. (The Arabic term *al-kohl* was not originally applied to describe what we now

call alcohol.) The literature on the anthropology of alcoholic drink is large, but three representative collections may be selected: M. Douglas (ed.), *Constructive Drinking: Perspectives on Drink from Anthropology*, Cambridge, Cambridge University Press, 1987; M. Marshall (ed.), *Beliefs, Behaviors and Alcoholic Beverages*, Ann Arbor, University of Michigan Press, 1979; M. Everett, J. Waddell and D. Heath (eds), *Cross-cultural Approaches to the Study of Alcohol*, The Hague, Mouton, 1976.

26 Otherwise *pituri* – a chewed narcotic made from leaves of the *Duboisia* shrub.

27 The nuts of the west African palm tree, *Cola nitida* or *C. acuminata*: see P. Lovejoy, *Caravans of Kola: The Hausa Kola Trade 1700–1900*, Zaria, Ahmadu Bello University Press, 1980; also his chapter in this volume. The potential economic importance of such substances is even better illustrated by the beans of *Theobroma cacao*, used to make the elite chocolate drink of the Aztec, which were employed as a medium of exchange in pre-Conquest Mesoamerica: R. Millon, *When Money Grew on Trees*, unpublished doctoral dissertation, Columbia University, New York, 1955.

28 The classic account is W. La Barre, *The Peyote Cult*, New Haven, Yale University Press, 1938, updated in idem, 'Twenty years of peyote studies', *Current Anthropology*, 1960, vol. 1, pp. 45–60. The most developed forms of the peyote cult explicitly echoed the form of the Eucharist, though emphasizing individual experience and spiritual participation without sacerdotal intermediacy. It is one of a series of 'rituals of rebellion', though stressing accommodation and resignation to the world of the Whites, rather than the active resistance of revivalist movements like the Ghost Dance. The use of cannabis played a similar role amongst Jamaicans.

29 'Doesn't one have a hundred thousand vexations with one's children?': the secular *Coffee Cantata* (*Schweigt stille, plaudert nicht*, No. 211), written *c.* 1732 with a text by Picander, is the complaint of an old man, Schlendrian, about his daughter Lieschen's coffee-drinking habits, and how his attempts to dissuade her are ignored. She is devoted to it, comparing it to kisses and wine:

> Ei wie schmeckt der Coffee süsse
> lieblicher als tausend Küsse,
> milder als Muscatenwein . . .
> Coffee muss ich haben;
> und wenn jemand will mich laben
> ach, so schenkt mir Coffee ein.

Finally it is revealed that the coffee habit is in part a 'hidden discourse' on the part of the women (excluded from the public rituals of the coffeehouse) of the family including both mother and grandmother –

> Die Jungfern bleiben Coffeeschwestern
> die Mutter liebt den Coffee-Brauch
> die Großmama trank solchen auch,
> wer will nun auf die Töchter lästern?

– so who can blame the daughters? This form of female protest (not unlike smoking by women in the inter-war years of this century) was nested within another protest: the radical role of the coffeehouse in contemporary (male-dominated) political life. The coffeehouse was only 'domesticated' into the café in the nineteenth century, when it ceased to be an exclusively male preserve.

30 These properties are not restricted to psychoactive substances, but may apply to any item of food – or, indeed, other aspects of culture. A relevant example is the pig, and the continuing taboo on eating pork in Jewish and Islamic culture. This is most plausibly interpreted as a symbolic reference to the pastoral origins of these cultures – where pigs are ecologically inappropriate, and yield no secondary products such as wool – maintained as a cultural marker in circumstances where abstinence from an otherwise practical source of meat emphasizes ritual purity. The whole taxonomy of eatable and uneatable animals was constructed around this distinction: see M. Douglas, *Purity and Danger*, London, Routledge, 1966, Ch. 3.

31 Cf. the now classic article (written in 1953) of H. S. Becker, 'Becoming a marijuana user', in *Outsiders*, New York, Free Press, 1963, pp. 41–58.

32 Cf. M. Eliade, *Shamanism: Archaic Techniques of Ecstasy*, London, Routledge, 1972 (where psychoactive substances are treated as a minor technological aspect of shamanism); M. Harner (ed.), *Hallucinogens and Shamanism*, New York, Oxford University Press, 1973 (where they are seen as more fundamental). *Amanita muscaria*, the fly agaric mushroom, is classically employed in Siberian shamanism; hallucinogenic mushrooms are also notable in the ethnography of New Guinea and many parts of central and south America, with similar usages.

33 Elias, op. cit., vol. 1 (1978), pp. 35–40, vol. 2 (1982), pp. 229–50. In the interpretative tradition of Elias, and concerned specifically with alcohol and its socio-cultural contexts in European history, see H. Spode, *Alkohol und Zivilisation: Berauschung, Ernüchterung und Tischsitten in Deutschland bis zum Beginn des 20. Jahrhunderts*, Berlin, Tara-Verlag, 1991; idem, *Die Macht der Trunkenheit: Kultur-und Sozialgeschichte des Alkohols in Deutschland*, Opladen, Esker & Budrich, 1993.

34 E. R. Leach, *Rethinking Anthropology*, London, Athlone Press, 1961, pp. 132–6.

35 Like the Greek *komos* (revel), whence 'comedy'.

36 Although also interpretable as a representation of wild, uncontrollable 'otherness' in opposition to conventional behaviour, especially on the part of women – the inverse of the *symposion*.

37 C. Ginzburg, *Ecstasies: Deciphering the Witches' Sabbath*, London, Hutchinson Radius, 1990.

38 Comparable figures may be derived for medieval Europe and for recent African millet- and maize-cultivators.

39 Ugaritic, Hittite, Mycenaean (Linear B) and classical Greek, Latin and Hebrew respectively; see also note 97. For a survey of the uses of wine in the ancient world, see essays in P. E. McGovern, S. J. Fleming and S. H. Katz (eds), *The Origins and History of Wine*, New York, Gordon and Breach, in press 1995.

40 M. Vickers and D. Gill, *Artful Crafts: Ancient Greek Silverware and Pottery*, Oxford, Oxford University Press, 1994.

41 See in general D. P. S. Peacock, *Pottery in the Roman World: An Archaeological Approach*, London, Longman, 1982; for a typical case study, A. Tchernia, 'Italian wine in Gaul at the end of the Republic', in P. Garnsey, K. Hopkins and C. R. Whittaker (eds), *Trade in the Ancient Economy*, London, Chatto & Windus, 1983, pp. 87–104; and more fully in A. Tchernia, *Le vin en Italie romaine: essai d'histoire économique d'après les amphores*, Paris, Bocard, 1986.

42 A common estimate for the Roman period (based on a variety of military and civilian sources) is that adult males consumed on average a litre of wine per day – a quarter of the daily caloric intake: see M. Broshi, 'Wine in ancient Palestine – introductory notes', *Israel Museum Journal*, vol. 3, pp. 21–40.

43 The varieties included red, white and clear wines, and also sweet varieties made from raisins and smoked or resinated forms. The wine was drunk diluted with water, with different degrees of dilution suitable for particular occasions and social categories. Various additives were used: balsam, wormwood, pepper, myrrh, syrup, seawater and various scents and spices – some to cover inferior or spoiled vintages, others to add extra elements of ostentatious luxury.

44 The imagery was already an old one, since it seems to underlie the use of animal-heads as *rhyta* (pouring-vessels) employed in the Bronze Age, which would appear to spout blood – though the animals represented (stag, bull) are usually wild, powerful and thus hunted ones, as opposed to the domestic animals of sacrifice.

45 Translations of this line neatly encapsulate the ambiguities and tensions between wine 'the mocker', that causes drunkenness, wrath and fornication, and wine as the symbol of the abundant banquet (see any concordance to the Scriptures for this range of associations); the Hebrew (and Syriac) versions use a word meaning 'saturated', with a secondary sense of being inebriated (cf. 'sozzled'); the Septuagint and Vulgate (Ps. 22, 5) make this latter sense explicit. Luther ('*Du . . . schenkest mir voll ein*'), and subsequent Protestant translators, returned to the alternative, more sober, meaning of the Hebrew original. I owe this fascinating information to Helen Hughes-Brock and Sebastian Brock.

46 L. H. Lasko, *King Tut's Wine Cellar*, Berkeley, Scribe Publications, 1977.

47 S. Dalley, *Mari and Karana: Two Old Babylonian Cities*, London, Longman, 1984, pp. 90–1.

48 D. Stronach, 'The imagery of the wine bowl: wine in Assyria in the early first millennium BC', in McGovern, Fleming and Katz, op. cit.

49 Stronach, op. cit., with examples.

50 P. R. S. Moorey, 'Metal wine-sets in the ancient Near East', *Irania Antiqua*, 1980, vol. 15, pp. 181–97.

51 J.-M. Denzer, *Le motif du banquet couché dans le Proche-Orient et dans le monde grec du VIIè au IVè siècle avant J.-C.*, Paris, Bocard, 1982; for the economic background to the Orientalising movement, see E. S. Sherratt and A. G. Sherratt, 'The growth of the Mediterranean economy in the early first millennium BC', *World Archaeology*, 1993, vol. 24(3), pp. 361–78. For the Greek *symposion*, see O. Murray, 'Sympotic history', in Murray, op. cit., pp. 3–13. Similar forms of aristocratic banquet emerged from the Orientalizing episode in different parts of the Mediterranean: in Etruscan Italy (where, unlike later Greek practice, it continued to be associated with food and the presence of women); and in Celtic Europe, where imported southern equipment was often used to serve local brews – as in the sixth-century burial at Hochdorf near Stuttgart, where an imported Greek *dinos* contained traces of mead.

52 These two tree-crops require similar intensity of cultivation, and both are useful as 'cash-crops' with the added value of special attention and manufactured products: see A. G. Sherratt and E. S. Sherratt, 'From luxuries to commodities: the nature of Mediterranean Bronze Age trading systems', in N. Gale (ed.), *Bronze Age Trade in the Mediterranean*, (Studies in Mediterranean Archaeology 90), Jonsered, Paul Åströms Förlag, 1991. Their desirability was neatly summed up by Pliny: 'There are two liquids most pleasing to human bodies, wine inside and oil outside', *Natural History*, 14, 150.

53 N. Purcell, 'Wine and wealth in ancient Italy', *Journal of Roman Studies*, 1985, vol. 75, p. 13.

54 As exemplified, for instance, in the work of Schuyler Jones, *Men of Influence in Nuristan*, London, Seminar Press, 1974, or the descriptions of Bjørn Qviller, 'The king in Dark Age Greece and medieval Norway; the evolutionary significance of sympotic kingship', MS, 1985; cf. Appadurai on 'tournaments of value' – A. Appadurai, 'Commodities and the politics of value' in idem (ed.), *The Social Life of Things: Commodities in Cultural Perspective*, Cambridge, Cambridge University Press, 1986, p. 21.

55 As were many other aspects of life: W. Burkert, *The Orientalising Revolution: Near Eastern Influence on Greek Culture in the Early Archaic Age*, Cambridge, Mass., Harvard University Press, 1992.

56 O. Murray, 'The Greek symposium in history', in E. Gabba (ed.), *Tria Cordia: scritti in onore di Arnaldo Momigliano*, Como, Edizione New Press, 1983, pp. 257–72; idem, 'The symposium as social organisation', in R. Hägg (ed.), *The Greek Renaissance of the Eighth Century BC* (Skrifta utgivna av Svenska Institutet i Athen, 30), Stockholm 1983.

57 Rather as *maiolica* and glassware were to be in Renaissance Europe: Vickers and Gill, op. cit.

58 The association is a continuing one, from the silver *tastevin* of the Burgundian cellarman to Robert Burns' cry 'Go fetch to me a pint of wine, and fill it in a silver tassie'. The choice of silver has a double rationale: it displays the colour and density of the wine, and it does not have the deleterious chemical reactions caused by copper, which interacts with the tannins in wine (which is why green tea is converted to black tea on copper trays).

59 The translation of silver as black in classical Athens and white in Song China relates to how the silver was cleaned: European practice was to encourage a dusky patina; Persian and oriental silver was cleaned (perhaps with lemon juice).

60 See J. Rawson, 'Tombs or hoards: the survival of Chinese silver of the Tang and Song periods, seventh to thirteenth centuries AD', in M. Vickers (ed.), *Pots and Pans: A Colloquium on Precious Metals and Ceramics in the Muslim, Chinese and Graeco-Roman Worlds, Oxford 1985*, Oxford, Oxford University Press, 1986, pp. 31–56. These Chinese wares themselves transformed Near Eastern and European ceramics, first by the transmission of techniques to Persia and the Mediterranean, and second through the direct export of porcelain by sea to Western Europe, accompanying tea. The interaction between elite consumables and material culture is part of the fascination of this topic.

61 The values accorded to different metals are cultural constructs, not universals; indigenous African societies rated copper more highly than gold, since its reddish hue was symbolic of power, while the light colour of gold was associated with death (as opposed to the dark colour of life): see E. Herbert, *Red Gold of Africa*, Madison, University of Wisconsin Press, 1984.

62 A shorthand for 'cultural complexes involving the symbolic use of psychoactive substances'.

63 It is ironic that in 1990 American troops at the outset of the Gulf War celebrated an alcohol-free Christmas in tents in the deserts of Saudi Arabia – and drank, instead, Coca-Cola!

64 Proscribed, that is, by Western-dominated international bodies.

65 Otherwise *khat*, the leaves of the shrub *Catha edulis*.

66 Although the name is often derived from Kaffa, a south-west Ethiopian ethnonym, it has plausibly been related to Arabic *qahwa*, 'intoxicating', originally applied to wine and transferred to the other drink: E. Haberland, 'Kaffee in Äthiopien', in Völger, op. cit., p. 492, quoting Arendonk.

67 Braudel, op. cit., p. 256.

68 On *qat*, see: A. Schopen, 'Qat in Jemen', in Völger, op. cit., pp. 496–501; S. Weir, *Qat in Yemen: Consumption and Social Change*, London, British Museum Publications, 1985; L. V. Casanelli, 'Qat: changes in the production and consumption of a quasilegal commodity in northeast Africa' in Appadurai, *The Social Life of Things*, op. cit., pp. 236–60. *Qat* is now used by Somali immigrants in Great Britain; and the question of its legal proscription there has already been raised (BBC news item, January 1993).

69 F. Rosenthal, *The Herb: Hashish versus Medieval Muslim Society*, Leiden, Brill, 1971; B. M. Du Toit, 'Cannabis in Afrika', in Völger, op. cit., pp. 508–21; N. J. van der Merwe, 'Cannabis smoking in 13th–14th century Ethiopia', in V. Rubin (ed.), *Cannabis and Culture*, The Hague, Mouton, 1975: the term 'narghile' is derived from the Sanskrit word for a coconut, from which waterpipes were originally made – see E. J. Keall, 'One man's coconut is another man's grenade', *Muqarnas*, 1993, vol. 10, pp. 275–85.

70 M. Artzy, 'Camels, incense and collared rim jars: desert trade routes and maritime outlets in the second millennium BC', *Oxford Journal of Archaeology*, 1994, vol. 13(2), pp. 121–47. For the mythological significance of aromatics in Greek society, see M. Detienne, *Les Jardins d'Adonis*, Paris, Gallimard, 1972.

71 This may be true of stronger varieties of cannabis, for example, *Cannabis indica* as opposed to *Cannabis sativa*.

72 J. Zias, H. Stark, J. Seligman, R. Levy, E. Walker, A. Breuer and R. Mechoulam, 'Early medical use of cannabis', *Nature*, 1993, vol. 363 (no. 6426) p. 215.

73 A. Saleh, 'Alkohol und Haschisch im heutigen Orient', in Völger, op. cit., pp. 488–91.

74 S. Anwari-Alhosseyni, 'Haschisch und Opium in Iran' in Völger, op. cit., pp. 482–7. Its association with the Nizari Isma'ili sect in Persia, described disparagingly as *Hashishiya*, led to the myth of the Assassins as accounts filtered to the West from Crusaders and travellers like Marco Polo.

75 Ibid., p. 109; cf. P. Crone, *Slaves on Horses: The Evolution of the Islamic Polity*, Cambridge, Cambridge University Press, 1980, Ch. 2.

76 When Alexander Kinglake set out from Belgrade on a tour of the Ottoman Empire in 1835, he recorded in a famous sentence his reactions on leaving Belgrade: 'I had come, as it were, to the end of wheel-going Europe, and now my eyes would see the Splendour and Havoc of the East.' It is significant that the criterion he chose to distinguish Christian Europe from the Islamic world was the use of wheeled vehicles, especially horse-drawn ones; and he exemplified this further in a passage when an injured companion had to be conveyed from Edirne to Istanbul:

> Methey was too ill to be kept in his saddle, and wheeled carriages, as means of travelling, were unknown. There is, however, such a thing as an 'Araba', a vehicle drawn by oxen, in which the wives of a rich man are sometimes dragged four or five miles over the grass by way of recreation . . . [but] . . . no one had ever heard of horses being used for drawing a carriage in this part of the world.
>
> A. Kinglake, *Eothen*, London, Century, 1982 [1842], 18.

77 R. W. Bulliet, *The Camel and the Wheel*, Cambridge, Mass., Harvard University Press, 1975.

78 This change was paralleled in the West by a growing dominance of horseriding rather than driving (which had in antiquity, in the form of the chariot,

been the symbol of the elite) until the development of the medieval carriage, though even then it remained a potent symbol of aristocratic power: S. Piggott, *The Earliest Wheeled Transport: from the Atlantic Coast to the Caspian Sea*, London, Thames & Hudson, 1983; idem, *Wagon, Chariot and Carriage: Symbol and Status in the History of Transport*, London, Thames & Hudson, 1992.

79 O. Grabar, *City in the Desert: Qasr al-Hayr East*, Cambridge, Mass., Harvard University Press, 1978; for furniture, F. Braudel, op. cit., pp. 283–9.

80 Hieronymos of Cardia (fourth century BC) is quoted by Diodorus Siculus (19, 94) as noting of the Nabataeans 'it is a law unto them not to sow corn nor to plant fruit trees, nor to drink wine': cited in Broshi, op. cit., p. 32. The Nabataeans eventually adopted all the habits of Mediterranean civilization; but groups further south on the incense route retained their ambivalence: G. W. van Beek, 'The Land of Sheba', in J. B. Pritchard (ed.), *Solomon and Sheba*, London, Phaidon, 1974, pp. 40–63.

81 A. J. Wensinck, article 'Khamr (Juridical Aspects)', in *Encyclopedia of Islam*, New Edn, 1978, vol. 4, pp. 994–7.

82 Ibid., p. 995.

83 Broshi, op. cit, p. 36; though a later (ninth- or tenth-century) date is arguable. This is supported by the continuing prominence of the very high quality wine of Beit Ras (ancient Capitolias), which was celebrated even in Arabia from the sixth century continuously down to the time of the Abbasids; see C. J. Lenzen and E. A. Knauf, 'Beit Ras/Capitolias: a preliminary evaluation of the archaeological and textual evidence', *Syria: Revue d'art oriental et d'archéologie*, 1987, vol. 64, pp. 34–42; I am grateful to Alison McQuitty for these observations. See also J. Sadan, 'Khamr (as a product)' in *Encyclopedia of Islam*, op. cit., pp. 997–8.

84 A. S. Melikian-Chirvani, 'Silver in Islamic Iran: the evidence from literature and epigraphy', in M. Vickers, op. cit., pp. 95–100.

85 For the *Hadith* literature, see G. H. A. Juynbol, 'The attitude towards gold and silver in early Islam', in Vickers, op. cit., pp. 108–13. The opposition towards precious metals was partly to ostentation, partly to hoarding when silver needed to be mobilized for charitable and economic purposes: a phenomenon noted by Schneider (J. Schneider, 'Was there a pre-capitalist world-system?', *Peasant Studies*, 1977, vol. 6(1), pp. 24–7) and paralleled in the substitution of pottery for silver as grave goods in cultures as diverse as Etruscan Italy and Tang China – see other articles in Vickers, op. cit.

86 William of Rubruck, translated in C. Dawson (ed.) *The Mongol Mission*, New York, Sheed & Ward, 1955. These beverages were drunk explicitly for their intoxicating qualities: 'To our misfortune our interpreter was standing near the cup-bearers, and got drunk immediately . . .'; William gave his speech of introduction, and 'the Khan began to reply "Just as the sun spreads its rays in all directions, so my power is spread everywhere". Up to this point I understood my interpreter, but beyond this I could not grasp a single complete sentence, which showed me he was drunk. And Mangu Khan himself seemed to be intoxicated': ibid., pp. 154–5. The drinks were served from a device made by a Parisian craftsman in the form of a silver tree with a figure bearing a trumpet on the top, with silver lions' heads pouring the drinks into bowls. When the drinks got low, the trumpet was sounded and the cup-bearers replenished their supplies. Alcohol is often served with ostentation.

87 'Symposium: did man once live by beer alone?' (query by R. J. Braidwood; responses by J. D. Sauer, H. Helbaek, P. C. Mangelsdorf, H. C. Cutler, C. S. Coon, R. Linton, J. Steward and A. L. Oppenheim), *American Anthropologist*,

1953, vol. 55, pp. 515–26; S. H. Katz and M. M. Voigt, 'Bread and beer: the early use of cereals in human diet', *Expedition*, 1985, vol. 28(2), pp. 23–34.

88 H. F. Lutz, *Viticulture and Brewing in the Ancient Orient*, Leipzig, Hinrichs'sche Buchhandlung, 1922; L. F. Hartman and A. L. Oppenheim, *On Beer and Brewing Techniques in Ancient Mesopotamia*, Supplement to the *Journal of the American Oriental Society*, 10, 1950.

89 Scenes of drinkers with straws are a common motif, from late fourth-millennium seals in Mesopotamia down to Cypriot-painted pottery of the early first millennium BC; the strainers from the ends of such straws can be identified archaeologically: see A. M. Meier and Y. Garfinkel, 'Bone and metal beer-strainers from the ancient Near East', *Levant*, 1992, vol. 24, pp. 218–23.

90 Summarized in A. G. Sherratt, 'Cups that cheered', in W. Waldren and R. Kennard, (eds), *Bell Beakers of the Western Mediterranean: The Oxford International Conference 1986*, Oxford, British Archaeological Reports, 1987, pp. 81–106, to be reprinted in Sherratt's *Economy and Society in Prehistoric Europe*, Edinburgh, Edinburgh University Press, forthcoming. The Norse word *bjórr* originally implied a fermented fruit and honey drink, as opposed to *öl* (ale). See also H. Kroll, 'Bier oder Wein' (Preliminary botanical report on the excavations at Feudvar, Serbia, 1986–90), *Bericht der Römisch-Germanischen Kommission*, 1991, vol. 72, pp. 165–77. Commenting on the occurrence there of wild vine, *Vitis vinifera sylvestris*, he notes the impossibility of making wine from it without some additional source of sugar (which would itself alter the character of the drink): 'Aus diesen Früchten kann man ohne Zuckerzusatz keinen Wein bereiten. Verwendete man Honig als Zuckerquelle, so entstände daraus ein Produkt, das man besser als Honigwein mit Fruchtwürze bezeichnete als Fruchtwein mit Honigzusatz.'

91 Pliny, *Natural History*, XIV, 29; Dionysius of Halicarnassus, *Roman Antiquities*, XIII, 10.

92 One interesting piece of archaeological evidence for this is the pollen analysis of a Bronze Age beaker from Scotland, which contained the pollen of lime (*Tilia cordata*) and the flavouring agent meadowsweet (i.e. 'mead-sweet', *Filipendula ulmaria*); lime trees did not exist in abundance in Scotland at that time: J. H. Dickson, 'Bronze Age mead', *Antiquity*, 1978, vol. 52, pp. 108–13. Honey was an important item of trade in early medieval times: the *Egilssaga* records that the father of Egil Skallagrimson sent a ship to England to procure it – a reference I owe to Bjørn Qviller. See in general E. Crane, *The Archaeology of Beekeeping*, London, Duckworth, 1983.

93 See, for example, J. Goosta, *The War of the Gods*, London, Routledge, 1985.

94 Described by William of Rubruck but not by Herodotus, as is often claimed.

95 D. Zohary and P. Spiegel-Roy, 'Beginnings of fruit-growing in the Old World', *Science*, 1975, vol. 187, pp. 319–27; D. Zohary and M. Hopf, *The Domestication of Plants in the Old World*, Oxford, Clarendon Press, 1993; L. Stager, 'The first fruits of civilisation', in J. N. Tubb (ed.), *Palestine in the Bronze and Iron Ages*, London, Institute of Archaeology, 1985, pp. 172–88.

96 There may have been extensive natural groves of date palms in the marshes at the head of the Persian Gulf, although the earliest archaeologically attested remains of *Phoenix dactylifera* are from Chalcolithic Ghassul and Nahal Mishmar in Israel. On dates, see N. Postgate, 'Palm-trees, reeds and rushes in Iraq ancient and modern', in M. Barrelet (ed.), *L'archéologie de l'Iraq du début de l'époque Néolithique à 333 a.n.è.*, Paris, CNRS, 1980, pp. 99–103.

97 It has been hypothesized that the word 'wine' had its origins in a cognate

of the Hittite *wiyanas* – and Noah himself is said to have planted a vineyard on the slopes of Mount Ararat; see Stager, op. cit.. If the word is indeed of Indo-European origin (which is not universally agreed), then it is itself interesting in relation to the antiquity of these languages in Anatolia; see A. G. Sherratt and E. S. Sherratt, 'The archaeology of Indo-European: an alternative view', *Antiquity*, 1988, vol. 62, pp. 584–95.

98 The production of 'wine' from rice in south and east Asia may not have required this association with a fruit crop, since a fermenting fungus, *Aspergillus oryzae*, is used, which accomplishes both saccharification and fermentation (i.e. the functions both of malting and yeast).

99 The southwards extension of cereal cultivation (maize in South America, millet – *Sorghum* and *Pennisetum* – in sub-Saharan Africa) into areas of root crop cultivation is likely to have been intimately connected with their use in brewing alcoholic drinks with social and ritual significance.

100 A. G. Sherratt and T. Taylor, 'Metal vessels in Bronze Age Europe and the context of Vulchetrun', in J. Best and N. de Vries (eds), *Thracians and Mycenaeans*, Leiden, Brill, 1990, pp. 106–34; M. Dietler, 'Driven by drink: the role of drinking in the political economy and the case of Early Iron Age France', *Journal of Anthropological Archaeology*, 1990, vol. 9(4), pp. 352–406.

101 A. G. Sherratt, 'Sacred and profane substances: the ritual use of narcotics in later Neolithic Europe', in P. Garwood, D. Jennings, R. Skeates and J. Toms (eds), *Sacred and Profane: Proceedings of a Conference on Archaeology, Ritual and Religion*, Oxford University Committee for Archaeology Monographs 1991, vol. 32, pp. 50–64.

102 Herodotus, *Histories*, tr. A. de Sélincourt, Harmondsworth, Penguin, 1954, IV, 75. Herodotus also notes (I, 201) a similar practice among the Massagetae ('eastward beyond the Araxes'), using 'a tree whose fruit has a very odd property . . . as it burns it smokes like incense, and the smell of it makes them drunk just as wine does with us'.

103 S. I. Rudenko, *Frozen Tombs of Siberia*, London, Dent, 1970, pp. 62, 284–5. It is interesting to note that in the ninth century AD Viking royal burials at Osebjerg, Norway, a purse in the 'Queen's Grave' also contained cannabis seeds: A. E. Christensen, A. S. Ingstad, B. Myhre, *Osebjergdronningens Grav*, Oslo, 1993, p. 233. I again thank Bjørn Qviller for this fact.

104 A. G. Sherratt, 'Sacred and profane substances', op. cit., p. 53. The Bronze Age *kurgan* (Pit- and Catacomb-grave) cultures, have been plausibly associated with the first speakers of Indo-Iranian languages. The succeeding Timber-grave and Andronovo cultures extended widely across the Eurasian steppes and affected a wide arc of cultures from Siberia to northern India.

105 For 'incense-cups' and other accessory vessels, see S. Gerloff, *The Early Bronze Age Daggers in Great Britain and a Reconsideration of the Wessex Culture*, Munich, Beck, 1975, pp. 225–32. In contrast to contemporary cultures of this period in central Europe, pottery drinking-cups are absent in the Wessex culture, suggesting that older practices had been reasserted in Britain after the emphasis placed on drinking in Bell-Beaker times.

106 In the same way as Tukano images produced under the influence of *yagé*: see M. Reichel-Dolmatoff, 'The cultural context of an aboriginal hallucinogen: *Banisteriopsis caapi*', in Furst, op. cit., pp. 84–113; idem, *Beyond the Milky Way: Hallucinatory Imagery of the Tukano Indians*, Los Angeles, UCLA Latin American Center, 1978.

107 A comprehensive account of its ancient uses is given in M. D. Merlin, *On the Trail of the Ancient Opium Poppy*, London and Toronto, Associated University Presses, 1984.

108 A. G. Sherratt, 'Sacred and profane substances', op. cit., pp. 52–7.

109 R. G. Wasson, *Soma: Divine Mushroom of Immortality*, New York, Harcourt Brace Jovanovich, 1971.

110 Summarized in V. Sarianidi, 'Temples of Bronze Age Margiana: traditions of ritual architecture', *Antiquity*, 1994, vol. 68, pp. 388–97, and reporting pollen analyses by N. R. Mayer-Melikiyan.

111 Was the interest in fire derived from the older, steppe custom of burning psychoactive substances, at a time when these substances were coming to be prepared as beverages?

112 Later sources, including inscriptions of the Persian kings Darius and Xerxes, refer to a group in this area (known to Herodotus as the *Amyrgioi*) as the *saka haumavarga*, the haoma-making Scythians. It is not clear whether the substance in question was inhaled or drunk: if the latter, this practice may have distinguished them from other Scythian tribes.

113 D. S. Flattery and M. Schwartz, *Haoma and Harmaline: The Botanical Identity of the Indo-Iranian Sacred Hallucinogen 'Soma' and its Legacy in Religion, Language and Middle-Eastern Folklore*, Berkeley, University of California Press, 1989; see also discussion in R. Rudgley, *The Alchemy of Culture: Intoxicants in Society*, London, British Museum Press, 1993, Ch. 3.

114 G. N. Lisitsyna and L. V. Prishchepenko, *Paleoethnobotanicheskie Nakhodki Kavkaza i Blizhnego Vostoka*, Moscow, Nauka, 1977, pp. 64, 71, 85.

115 For these changing attitudes, see L. E. Grivetti, 'Wine: the food with two faces', in McGovern, Fleming and Katz, op. cit.

116 E. Moser-Schmitt, 'Sozio-rituelle Gebrauch von Cannabis in Indien', in Völger, op. cit., pp. 542–5. The Sanskrit term widely used (in India and by extension in Africa) to denote cannabis, *bhangā (bhang, ganja)* passed into Persian as *banj*, meaning henbane, *Hyoscyamus niger*, (M. Meyerhof, 'Bandj', *Encyclopedia of Islam*, 1960, vol. 1, p. 1014). This is another plant with a long history of use in the Western Old World, occurring, for instance, at Bronze Age Feudvar in Serbia (Kroll, op. cit., p. 167). Its tranquillizing and sedative properties are due to the substance hyoscyamine, and it was used historically as an intoxicant and medicament. It has recently been identified in a late-neolithic grooved ware vessel from a ceremonial site in Scotland, added to a honeyed porridge. Along with belladonna (which also contains hyoscyamine), mandrake and opium-poppy, it was used psychoactively in classical and medieval times, though also capable of use as a poison.

117 While wine was recognized as dangerous in excess, it was never supplanted as the privileged intoxicant; and substances such as cannabis, opium and datura, although known and used, remained parts of the *materia medica*. That is not to say that hedonistic drugs were unknown: an aristocratic drug from the Han period was known as 'han-shi powder'. However, the influence of wine continued to be so dominant that when tobacco was introduced, the Chinese termed it 'dry wine': information from Mark Elvin.

118 W. Stöhr, 'Betel in Südost- und Südasien', in Völger, op. cit., pp. 552–9; S. Seyfarth, 'Betelkauen in Melanesien', in ibid., pp. 560–7; Brunton, op. cit.

119 The ritual context of *kava* consumption is emphasized by the way in which betel-chewing, as a largely individual and secular activity, has tended to replace it, as traditional authority and ceremonial has waned in recent times: Brunton, op. cit.

120 A. G. Sherratt, 'Sacred and profane substances', op. cit., pp. 56–7.

121 Robert Merrillees first promoted the idea that these flasks were used for opium, an idea since confirmed by chromatographic analysis of their residues: R. S. Merrillees, 'Opium trade in the Bronze Age Levant', *Antiquity*,

1962, vol. 36, pp. 287–92; idem., 'Opium again in antiquity', *Levant*, 1979, vol. 11, pp. 167–71; idem., 'Highs and lows in the Holy Land: opium in Biblical times', *Eretz-Israel* (Yadin Memorial Volume) 1989, vol. 20, pp. 148–53; J. Evans, 'Report' appended to the foregoing, pp. 153–4. The Hebrew word *rosh* ('head'), translated in the Bible as 'gall' (eg 'gall and wormwood'), is likely to refer to the opium poppy; a reference in the fourth century Jerusalem Talmud uses the Greek word *opion*. The association of *rosh* with wickedness and suffering would indicate both its bitter taste and the moral problems of misuse; Merrillees, 'Highs and lows in the Holy Land', op. cit., p. 150. The use of opiates seems to have spread eastwards from Europe and western Asia, to appear in south-east Asia in the first millennium AD.

122 N. Kourou, 'Handmade pottery and trade: the case of Argive monochrome ware', *Proceedings of the 3rd Symposium on Ancient Greek and Related Pottery*, Copenhagen, National Museum, 1988, pp. 314–24.

123 Conversely, the USA today spends almost as much on the suppression of 'drugs' as it does on defence.

2

COCA, BEER, CIGARS AND *YAGÉ*

Meals and anti-meals in an Amerindian community

Stephen Hugh-Jones

The primary concern of this essay is to document and analyse the use of coca, tobacco, beer and *yagé* (a hallucinogenic drink prepared from the bark of *Banisteriopsis caapi* vines) among the Barasana, a group of Tukanoan-speaking Amerindians living in north-west Amazonia on the frontier between Colombia and Brazil.[1] However, it is also intended to stimulate reflection on how anthropologists, historians and other scholars might contribute more widely to debates concerning 'drugs'. It is here that I shall begin.[2]

In their attempts to control the use of illicit drugs, government agencies have typically paid more attention to supply than to demand. To discuss why this should be so would take me far away from the intentions of this essay. Here I would merely make two observations. The first is that an emphasis on supply has, as one of its effects, the export of militaristic solutions to the perceived problem and the displacement of the violence and social upheaval that goes with them away from the wealthy consuming countries to the poorer producing countries and, in these, away from the cities towards centres of production located in rural areas.

My second observation would be that this focus on production and supply often seems to reflect a theory of demand phrased in terms of individual desires and needs. Debates about the 'drugs problem' are often characterized by an explicit or implicit assumption that demand for drugs is psychological or physiological in origin. This view of demand is especially prevalent in those many discussions of drugs which focus on the issue of addiction and which see the 'drugs problem' more in medico-legal than in socio-political terms. This reified emphasis on substances rather than on people results in a shift in attention away from the social forces that lie behind the consumption or prohibition of stimulants and psychoactive substances – what people do with drugs and why they do it – on to the apparent power of the substances themselves – what drugs do to people. The various campaigns against the indigenous use of coca in Latin America would be but one example of this common tendency to see drugs largely in medico-legal terms, to fetishize and exaggerate the inherent, dangerous potency of particular substances, to create 'problems' where none exist and fail to deal with real problems elsewhere.

Historians, sociologists, anthropologists and experts on cultural studies have all emphasized that consumption is a social activity, that demand is socially constituted and that the categorization and differential use of goods and services serve to create and maintain social distinctions and values. As Appadurai puts it, 'consumption is eminently social, relational, and active rather than private, atomic, or passive'.[3] Although a number of ethnographic case studies describe and analyse the use of stimulants in non-Western societies,[4] it is striking how little anthropological attention has been paid to 'drugs' closer to home and this despite their contemporary political, economic and social significance.[5] Most striking of all is that, despite their potential relevance to many of the arguments raised, 'drugs' are almost entirely absent from the recent literature on consumption.[6] Given the copious references to food and drink in these works and given also their emphasis on what Appadurai calls the 'politics of value', this neglect is surprising. If discussions of the 'drugs problem' might profit from recent studies of consumption, such studies might also profit by paying more attention to 'drugs'.

One reason for the scholarly neglect of drugs is that their illegal status tends to make them invisible. They are typically left out of statistics and other information on the economy – gathering reliable data about the production, distribution and consumption of drugs can be both difficult and dangerous. But this invisibility sometimes has other, more theoretical, sources as well. When, for example, Douglas and Isherwood define consumption as 'a use of material possessions that is beyond commerce and *free within the law*',[7] the illegal consumption of drugs is left in a theoretical vacuum. This explicit and rather arbitrary circumscription of the notion of consumption also finds echoes in a more widespread tendency to treat the category of 'drug' as unproblematic and self-evident and to extend it inappropriately to non-Western contexts.

Although anthropologists quite often employ it loosely as a general, cross-cultural category, the sense and meaning of the concept 'drug' are intimately linked to a particular institutional matrix – a state, established judiciary, police force and customs together with specialized and monopolistic medical and pharmacological professions and perhaps to an established clergy or priesthood as well. The concept also depends on a historically and culturally specific classification of substances and on a specific set of rules, norms and conventions concerning the appropriate ways in which these substances are to be distributed and consumed.

In common usage, the value of the term 'drug' frequently depends on a double contrast. On the one hand, 'drugs' are opposed to 'medicines' supplied legally by doctors and chemists to specified individuals and used for supposedly beneficial and non-recreational purposes; on the other hand, they are opposed to 'foods' which have to do with 'nutrition' or 'feeding' rather than with 'curing'. 'Foods' and 'medicines' are used, 'drugs' are 'ab-used'. However, this three-way contrast between 'drugs', 'foods' and 'medicines' appears to be both historically quite recent and confined to industrial societies;[8] it does not always map easily on to the way that substances are categorized elsewhere. Anthropologists have often documented the intimate relation between food and medicine in non-Western societies and it is clear that, above and beyond any nutritional value or physiological effects, food, drink, drugs and medicines all serve as vehicles for social interaction, as systems of communication and as expressions of social values in Western societies.

The implicit acceptance of the category 'drug' in anthropological analysis often goes together with a rather arbitrary allocation of different consumable substances – 'food', 'drink' and 'drugs' – into discrete analytical fields which might more profitably be discussed together. Two recent works on Andean societies provide examples. Johnsson analyses the social and cultural significance of food and drink among the Bolivian Aymara but ignores coca altogether, apparently on the grounds that it is not a 'food' but a 'drug'.[9] Inversely, Allen's otherwise excellent analysis of the use and significance of coca and alcohol in a Peruvian Quechua community is marred by her tendency to isolate these substances from a sustained consideration of more ordinary food and drink.[10] In a similar vein, Douglas' edited volume, *Constructive Drinking*, delivers a curious cocktail of alcohol, tea and *kava* but studiously avoids any mention of 'drugs'.[11] Despite this, many of the issues raised in the volume apply as much to 'drugs' in general as they do to drink in particular, a point which can be inferred from the remark that 'current interest in the alternative or black economy must turn more and more towards the anthropology of drink'.[12]

Partly aimed at stimulating reflection, these observations are also intended to make a specific point. What I am suggesting is not so much that more attention be paid to 'drugs' but rather that because 'drug' is a non-scientific category inseparable from its political and moral overtones, care should be taken to avoid the rather arbitrary divisions of relevant fields of discussion and analysis to which it so often leads. I want to use a specific case to suggest that while the category 'drug' often seems to divert attention away from 'food' and 'drink', an anthropology of 'peculiar substances' might usefully begin by thinking more about the consumption of stimulants or psychoactive substances in relation to the consumption of more ordinary fare. This would involve combining an ethnographic focus on behaviour, paying attention to the use of stimulant and psychoactive substances in the context of social interaction, and a more cultural approach focusing on categorization: of different consumable substances in relation to each other, of the relevant social occasions, and of the people involved.

With reference to the Barasana Indians of north-western Amazonia, I shall show how the consumption of powdered coca leaves accompanies verbal exchanges and serves as a vehicle for social interaction and how patterns of coca consumption are related to social divisions based on gender, age and kinship. I shall also show how coca use is related to the use of tobacco (in the form of cigars and snuff), alcohol (in the form of beer), and of *yagé*. Although some or all of these might be referred to as 'drugs', I shall try to avoid imposing an alien category; I want instead to show that an examination of the overall pattern of consumption of these substances in relation to that of other foods and drinks reveals an implicit categorization of substances into two contrasting sets each with an analogous internal structure.

Although the indigenous use of coca is usually associated with the Andean zone it is in fact also quite widespread in the western part of Amazonia. Coca itself is a semi-tropical plant and the coca consumed by the highland Quechua and Aymara is actually grown in the warmer montaña region on the eastern, Amazonian slopes of the Andes. In the lowlands further to the north and east, a different, Amazonian variety of coca is found. This variety, grown from cuttings rather than seeds and with a much lower alkaloid content, is used mainly by the Tukanoan and Witotoan-speaking groups in south-east Colombia and north-east Peru. Unlike in the Andes, where dried coca leaves are chewed whole mixed with lime, here they are first dried by stirring them rapidly in a pot heated on a fire and then pounded to a fine green powder to which ash from burned Cecropia or Pourouma leaves is added.[13] The wetted powder, stored as a lump in the cheek, is slowly swallowed; the widely used phrase 'coca chewing' is thus not really appropriate in this context.

The Barasana are one of some twenty Tukanoan-speaking Indian groups living in the southern part of the Colombian Comisaría del Vaupés. These intermarrying groups are exogamous, patrilineal units and (ideally) each speaks a different language. Relations between these groups are characterized by reciprocal exchanges of food and material goods, of feasts and of spouses in marriage. The external equality of status between groups stands in marked contrast to the ranked hierarchy within. Each group is sub-divided into a series of clans related as 'brothers' and ranked according to the birth-order of their founding ancestors. Ideally the clan is a single, co-residential unit. In practice clan segments made up of a group of brothers with their in-married wives and children live together in a communal, multi-family longhouse or *maloca*. Relative age and birth-order not only are the model for status differences between whole clans but also determine status differences between brothers within the clan or longhouse. As we shall see, this age-based hierarchy is reflected in the details of how coca is prepared and consumed. In addition to this linear ranking of clans, there is some evidence to suggest that all the different groups were once also divided into three ranked strata of 'chiefs', 'commoners' and 'servants', a class-like system that applied to Tukanoan society as a whole. Present-day Barasana state that, as in the pre-conquest Andes, coca consumption was once the prerogative of the higher-ranking groups.

The Barasana treat coca with a respect that gives the plant and all the products and activities associated with it a sacred-like status. The planting of coca bushes, the picking and processing of coca leaves and the consumption of coca powder are all ritualized and surrounded by elaborate etiquette. Coca is eaten by all adult men and by a few of the older women. It thus takes on the role of a sign, both of adult (principally male) status and of certain powers and attributes that go with this status. In particular, it signals the capacity to engage in communication with other human and spirit beings in the outside world. Though it is sometimes eaten when alone, coca consumption is essentially a social activity, accompanied by conventionalized speech and formalized behaviour which focuses less on the ingestion of the powder or its effects than on the act of exchanging or sharing the powder with others.

Coca is used in three different but overlapping contexts: at work during the day; in the men's conversation circle at night; and during periodic ritual dances involving visiting groups from other longhouses. At work, coca is often accompanied by a shared cigar and occasionally by snuff; at night, cigars and snuff are almost always taken, and boiled manioc juice (*manicuera*) is usually served soon after dark. At dances, *yagé* is added to the list of coca, cigars and snuff and boiled manioc juice is replaced by beer. In addition to differences in the kinds of substances consumed, each different context involves a different degree of formalization of behaviour and is associated with differences in both the style and the content of speech.

Although people rarely comment directly upon the physiological or psychological effects of coca, when they do, the effects they perceive or choose to emphasize also depend on context. In relation to work, they emphasize that coca gives them energy, stamina and concentration and that it staves off hunger; in relation to the men's circle, they say it elevates their mood, makes them more convivial and able to talk, helps them to think and to meditate, and keeps sleep at bay; in relation to ritual dances, they say that both coca and *yagé* help them to learn and concentrate on the complex verbal and bodily routines involved in dancing and chanting and that coca helps them to stay awake and do without food for twenty-four hours or more. Resistance to sleep and hunger are two of the virtues of adult men. They also emphasize the role of coca in facilitating communication with their fellow men and with their ancestors.

When they are engaged in solitary work, men sometimes eat coca on their own. Consumed in this way, coca comes close to having a purely instrumental use on a par with the 'snacks' eaten by hungry people. When work is done in company, eating coca takes on a more social aspect. Such work is usually done on behalf of a particular man who is expected to supply his fellow workers with coca and who orders the breaks when they are consumed. The coca is now referred to as a 'treat' or 'reward' (*bose*) and, like those for tea, coffee or cigarettes elsewhere, coca breaks allow people to rest and give rhythm and structure to the work in hand. After the break, the men return to their tasks with a wad of coca in their cheeks; when the wad is finished it is time for another break.

In my own experience, coca-picking is often a tedious and lengthy task, frequently carried out in hot sun and a cloud of biting flies. Privately, many Barasana men would agree with this view. For this reason, despite its official status as a quintessentially male occupation, they are not above sending their wives out to pick the leaves for them. Publicly, however, neither the picking nor processing of coca is classed as 'work' and, on the surface, every effort is made to present coca-picking as a pleasant period of quiet socializing between co-operating equals. Underneath, however, certain elements of hierarchy can be detected. The bushes being picked are owned by the (usually elder) man who planted them. It is he who invites the others to pick with him, who weeds the coca rows as the others start to pick, who determines the amount to be picked, who passes round coca and cigars during periodic rests, and who does most of the talking. He is as generous with his words as he is with the coca he supplies.

This disguised hierarchy emerges more clearly as the coca is processed. Coca-toasting is quite skilled – burned leaves have an unpleasant bitter taste – and is done either by the owner of the leaves or by another elder man, often a respected visitor who is invited to do the job. It thus has higher-status connotations. Once toasted, the leaves are pounded in a mortar by the most junior men present and it is also they who are usually sent to collect Pourouma or Cecropia leaves for the ash. A more senior man burns these leaves and he is in charge of sieving the powdered coca leaves. The pounded coca is mixed with the ash and placed in a bark-cloth sleeve fixed to the end of a long pole which is inserted into a long, hollow balsa-wood cylinder. By flexing the pole back and forth, the bag is made to bash against the inner sides of the tube causing the fine, green powder to fly out and collect in the bottom of the tube.

At the end of the sieving, the man tips the coca powder out of the tube into a hemispherical gourd which he presents to the owner. The owner then stores the coca away in a container: a round gourd, a pot, a bark-cloth bag with a bone-tube 'straw' or an empty tin. If a lot of coca has been made, he will give a share of the product to the other senior men present. The whole process is quite formalized and it is noticeable that the allocation of tasks and distribution of product depend on relative status. This is determined by a combination of ownership, age and whether people are hosts or guests. In the past, the hierarchy was apparently even more explicit. In those days, higher-ranking clans were the masters of servant clans made up of semi-nomadic hunters, the Makú. These servants were called 'the people who light cigars' (*bũdo yori bãsa*). Men would send their servants out to pick and process coca leaves for them. Occasionally this still happens today and under these conditions, coca-picking and processing has the status of plain hard work.

If coca breaks give structure and rhythm to work, the production and consumption of coca have a more general relation to time. Like the women's harvesting and processing of bitter manioc, the men's picking and processing of coca is a regular, daily and very time-consuming process. Men usually hunt, fish or do other work in the morning and then begin to pick and process coca in the afternoon, the task being timed to end around dusk. People say that, without coca, their day would have no structure; a myth about the origin of night describes the tedium of unstructured time when, with neither night nor coca to structure their lives, men sat around aimlessly, not knowing what to do or when.

Coca is never consumed with food nor food with coca. The only relatively fixed meal of the day happens soon after waking; thereafter, the day is punctuated by periodic but rather unpredictable meals and snacks whose timing depends largely on what is available and when. For men at least, the time between food or meals is largely given over to coca and, if enough is around, it is chewed throughout the day. Eating little is another male virtue. Women and children often continue eating after dusk but men eat little in the afternoon and, as soon as it gets dark, eat no food at all. Food and cooking are as strongly identified with women as coca and coca preparation are associated with men. Jokingly men refer to coca as *bõbi*, a word they also use to refer to boiled sweets brought in from outside; they also consider it to be their equivalent to the fruits and other sweet foods that women are said to prefer. The routine of coca preparation also bears a formal relation to the production of manioc bread and the two are talked of as analogous processes.[14]

For the men, both the minor alternation between eating food and eating coca during the day and the major alternation between day as a time for food and night as a time for coca also mark an alternation in their relations and contact with women. They eat food with women and children but eat coca almost exclusively with each other. The separation brought about by coca is most dramatic at night. The women, often nibbling little snacks, sit together in a group towards the rear of the house, with their men folk grouped in an open circle in the middle of the house, eating their coca, smoking cigars and taking occasional doses of snuff. The men eat no food but will sometimes drink *farinha* (toasted manioc granules) mixed with water or, more usually, drink *manicuera,* a warm, sweet drink made from boiled manioc juice which the women prepare at dusk. Night is the time of spirits and ancestors who, like the men after dark, consume only coca and tobacco. Here coca takes on another temporal aspect for, acting as a mediator and stimulating thought, it allows men in the present to enter into communion with these ancestors in the past.

The mood and tone of the nightly men's circle are of restrained formality, of calm conviviality, of serious talk and quiet meditation, a time for communion with other people and communication with the spirit world. The men sit on wooden stools, the shamans often blowing spells into gourds of food to ward off illness while the others talk quietly or sit in silence, weaving baskets, making string and rope from hanks of raffia, or doing nothing in particular.

The places where they sit say much about who they are. The headman of the longhouse usually sits close to a cluster of hourglass-shaped stands near the post where coca is sieved. These stands support gourds containing much of the paraphernalia of male ritual life: coca, snuff, cigars, lumps of tobacco and aromatic beeswax. Shamans prefer to sit leaning against a house post for these posts are vehicles of contact with the upper and lower worlds. The other men sit near the headman; when there are many people present there may be two vaguely defined arcs extending towards the front or men's door, with the most senior nearest the centre and the most junior furthest to the sides and front. If visitors are present they will sit on either side of the front door or close to one or other of the first two interior posts. A similar hierarchization of space and sitting arrangements appears to be a common feature of stimulant use in more formalized contexts elsewhere in the world.[15] The passing of coca obeys a strict etiquette. The headman, host and owner of the coca lights up a cigar, takes a few puffs, takes a mouthful of coca powder from its container (ideally a gourd with a tapir bone scoop), then passes both cigar and coca to the man next to him. Before smoking and eating, the recipient greets the donor saying 'Give it to me!' (*kwãya*!). As the donor acknowledges his greeting, the man puffs on the cigar, eats some coca and passes them on again. The cigar and coca pass from hand to hand with each man greeting those who have already been served, starting with the person who handed the coca to him and working in turn up the line to the host.

When cigar and coca have reached the end of the line they are passed back again exactly as they came. As they are passed back from person to person, each man says 'You've had some!' (*yikwahɨ!*) to all those to whom he passed the cigar and coca, beginning with the man who hands the gourd to him and ending with the man at the end of the line. When his greeting has been acknowledged, he takes another rapid puff of cigar, another brief scoop of coca, then passes both on back up the line towards the host. When the cigar and coca return to the host, he greets back down the line confirming that each man has had his fill. Tobacco snuff, blown into the nose through a v-shaped bone tube that bridges between mouth and nostrils, is passed round in a snail-shell container according to exactly the same routine.

This ritualized passing of coca continues periodically throughout the evening and it serves to underline the spatial hierarchy mentioned above. Like his position in the centre of the house, the headman's largely one-sided supply of coca and tobacco emphasizes his senior position. Senior visitors by the door and the other senior residents in the middle of the house who consider themselves the headman's rough equals usually make sure that they have their own coca and cigar to offer in return.

The hierarchization of space and of coca distribution is also reflected in patterns of speech. When talking about coca, men repeatedly stress its intimate relation to sociability, speech and conversation, a relation which is also obvious in their behaviour. Ideally, and also in practice on more formal occasions, their day is punctuated by a series of formal greetings in which the headman of the maloca puts the other men at their ease and tells them the order of proceedings: 'Soon we will go out to pick coca'; 'We have worked hard, now it's time to relax'; 'Now it is evening, it's time to sit down and talk'; 'We've had a good evening together, now it is time to sleep.' These greetings, too long to give in full, come like gifts from the head of the maloca and, like any serious talk, must be accompanied by the offering of cigars and coca. As formality increases, so also does the length of the speeches. Much of their content is taken up by detailed reference to picking, processing and eating coca so that coca and greeting become mutually-redundant vehicles, both medium and message.

The pattern of talk in the men's circle also mirrors that of coca distribution. The talk usually begins with relatively unstructured chatter and joking, but as the evening wears on, the conversation takes on a more quiet, serious and respectful tone with the headman or his deputy doing most of the talking. He talks in a near monologue, telling news and stories or outlining plans of action. His one chosen interlocutor supplies brief repetitions and comments to indicate his attention and assent while the others sit in silence. When visitors from other malocas are present, at some stage in the evening, the headman will make a point of going up and offering them coca before inviting them to tell him their news. Squatting in front of them he listens at length to what they have to say, then offers more coca before returning to his usual place.

In sum then, the headman's role as giver of coca parallels his role as giver of speech. The men's circle, focused around the consumption of coca, is an opportunity to exchange information, a forum for social interaction and a ritualized statement of the social order – a statement of hierarchy between men and women, seniors and juniors, of kin relations within the community, and of reciprocal equality between hosts and guests. It is also a playing out of the values that coca encapsulates, an expression of the importance attached to gregariousness, to good speaking, to the ability to tell stories, to peace and quiet, to wise, calm reflection and to the ability to do without sleep.

Coca is strongly associated with its owner, the man who plants it, who organizes its picking and processing, and who gives it out to others. This association between plant and person carries over to the level of the group as a whole. Each group owns one or more specific varieties of coca, planted from cuttings and coming from a common clone. The coca plants of each group are part of their ancestral inheritance, passed across the generations between father and son and maintained by an unbroken line of vegetative reproduction which is used as one of the principal images when speaking of the group's continuity through time. Like the group itself, their coca plants come from a common source, a continuous line of growth from an ancestral stock obtained by the ancestor of the group at the beginning of time. Just as the rows of coca in the gardens are compared to the individual men who own them, so the original plant is identified with the body of the ancestor. Coca serves as an intermediary between people and to give coca is to give out part of oneself, to offer and make manifest an aspect of one's identity. Each group also speaks and owns a distinctive language as another aspect of its patrimony and identity. This too is displayed and given out in the speech that goes with coca.

In the men's circle the main supply of coca is distributed asymmetrically from a single source, the headman or his deputy. This asymmetrical sharing at once emphasizes an in-group of co-resident men with common attributes and underlines the hierarchy, the ranking of clans and of individuals by age and seniority, which characterizes intra-group relations. By contrast, during rituals, when one longhouse community invites its neighbours to dance and drink beer, coca is exchanged on a reciprocal basis between all the senior men of the groups involved and it is here that its role as a gift emerges most clearly. These reciprocal exchanges of coca mirror other exchanges – of invitations, visits, beer, food, goods and of women – which take place between the members of affinally related communities of equal rank and status.

During ritual dances, sessions of dancing alternate with sessions of chanting. Each session of chanting, with hosts and guests sitting facing each other on two lines of stools, begins and ends with the passing of coca and cigars. The verbal etiquette remains the same as that of the men's circle but now, though it is the leader of the chant who begins the procedure, each senior man is expected to exchange with all the others present; by the end of the session, each will have eaten a sample of coca from everyone else.

This different, more egalitarian mode of exchange is paralleled by a different mode of speaking. The chanting is led by a single individual, a specialist chanter, but the words of each verse of his chant are repeated by the others, each in their own language, before the chanter begins the next. The chant is the analogue of the talk between host and guest at the men's circle but both the mode and content of the speech are different. Unlike the stories told at the men's circle, the chants or 'stories of the ancestors' (*bɨkɨra keti*) involve not the doings of the living but rather the doings of the first ancestors with whom the men are now identified. Much of the content of these chants concerns coca, tobacco, *yagé* and beer, the substances which give the chants their pretext. Chants about coca rework myths which tell how coca was created and how each group first obtained their own coca plants, and they make explicit the esoteric significance of the items of equipment used in processing coca leaves.

As they chant together, the men's coca now serves as an intermediary between them and their ancestors and as a communion meal at which the living, now identified with the ancestors, speak about them in their own archaic language and eat a substance identified with the ancestors' bodies. In daily life, coca eating is part of an unquestioned way of life that is not endowed with any explicit symbolic associations. But at dances these chants, and the spells which shamans blow over the gourds of coca before the dance begins, make explicit the mythological and symbolic associations of coca. Before discussing these associations, I must first say more about the relation between coca and food.

As I have explained, coca is never taken together with food. Not only is it physically quite unpleasant to mix the two together in the mouth; coca is also so effective in suppressing appetite that it can sometimes be positively nauseating to try to consume coca and food together. But beyond these purely practical considerations there are further social and cultural factors to take into account.

To begin with, it is not considered acceptable behaviour to eat coca and food together and any attempt to combine them would meet with strong disapproval. They are kept apart by a set of practices which puts them in opposition in terms of time, space and gender. Men eat coca preferentially at night and they eat it continuously throughout both day and night during rituals. By contrast, they will normally eat food only during the day. At the end of each ritual dance, a large meal, preceded by shamanic spells to render the food safe, marks the men's return to normal life. Men prepare coca towards the front of the house and eat it on their own in the middle while women prepare food at the rear of the house, eat together with their men folk at the sides of the house by day, and sometimes continue eating after dark, sitting by themselves towards the rear of the house.

Drinks – plain water, *farinha* (toasted manioc granules) or palm-fruit pulp mixed with water, boiled manioc juice (*manicuera*), manioc flour boiled in water (*mingau*) – are never consumed directly with food or meals. They are either taken just after eating or else consumed at other times when no food is served. When manioc beer, the most marked form of drink, is served no one eats at all until the beer is finished. Drinks and coca, though both peripheral to meals, are none the less quite often taken together. This combination is most marked at dances, when large amounts of beer and coca are served in a seemingly endless supply, but it also happens each evening when boiled manioc juice is served after the men have begun to eat coca and also in the day when men drink manioc starch boiled with water or *farinha* mixed with water as a refreshment after bouts of work. Finally, coca is usually accompanied by some form of tobacco, either cigars or snuff or both, and there is a strong expectation that the two should always go together.

From these and other observations, we can isolate two opposed complexes: 'food' and 'non-food'.[16] The division between these two complexes corresponds very roughly to that between the mundane and the spiritual, the everyday and the ritual. 'Food' comprises various fruits, tubers and gathered frogs, ants and insect larvae, different kinds of manioc bread and *farinha*, dips made from reduced manioc juice, chillies, fish, manioc leaves or palm-fruits together with fish and meat. 'Non-food' is made up principally of coca, tobacco (as cigars and snuff) and hallucinogenic *yagé*, the foods of the spirits and ancestors, but would also include the different manioc-based drinks mentioned above with which these substances may be consumed.

If we now look at how the different elements of each complex are combined together, we can see certain parallels between them. Snacks consist of fruit, boiled tubers, or pieces of dry, smoked fish or meat eaten with small lumps of manioc bread which hungry people of both sexes consume on their own and standing up. Proper meals are eaten communally with the participants squatting or sitting round one or more pots placed on the floor, with pieces of fish or meat dished out on a banana leaf. Sometimes men and women eat together, sometimes the men eat before the women and sometimes women eat on their own but, in all cases, meals are seen as something which binds the sexes and the community together.

That meals bind together the sexes is also suggested by the nature of what is eaten: meat or fish produced by men and manioc bread produced by women.[17] Those who eat fish or game without manioc bread are severely reprimanded and told that they must combine meat and bread together. The verb employed in this context is not *wɨo-* 'to mix physically' but rather *ɨko-* which has the connotation of mixing to produce some effect. This 'catalytic' quality is shown also in the substantive, *ɨko*, which refers to the leaf-ash added to coca and tobacco snuff to give it potency; to leaves which are added to *yagé* to make it more potent;[18] to the bait on a fish hook; and to any Western or non-Western 'medicine'. From different perspectives, this conjunction of protein and carbohydrate might be understood as the elements of a balanced diet, as marking the complementary relations between men and women in production and reproduction, as underwriting the ties that bind the community, or as part of a more general, symbolic pattern in which opposites are ritually united or interchanged to produce dynamic results.

Though drinks are often consumed with coca, they are never taken together with food. However, the meal itself has a liquid component, either a broth, heavily spiced with chilli pepper, in which the fish or meat has been boiled, or an ancillary 'pepper pot' made either from scraps of fish cooked with chilli peppers or from manioc juice and chilli peppers reduced by boiling until they form a dark, thick sauce. Manioc bread is dipped into the liquid and then eaten with pieces of fish or meat. Like British gravy, such peppery liquids add zest and serve to bind the more solid components together. In addition, like the terms 'hot' and 'spicy', the pepper pot in particular and chilli peppers in general carry with them a charge of sexual innuendo; a woman's sexual parts may be referred to as her 'pepper pot' and sexual intercourse as 'stirring' this same pot. Chilli peppers thus add a further, latent, dimension of sexual complementarity to each meal.[19]

In sum, as opposed to a snack, a proper meal must be eaten in company by people who either sit or squat on the ground and must have three components: meat or fish produced by men, manioc bread produced by women and some kind of liquid spiced with chilli peppers. This can be represented as in Figure 1.

A similar structure is visible in the case of 'non-foods'. Although coca is sometimes eaten alone as the equivalent of a snack, even at the most informal level when it is consumed during work there is an expectation that it will be accompanied by a cigar. As the level of formality increases, so also does the likelihood that snuff will be offered as well. Coca and

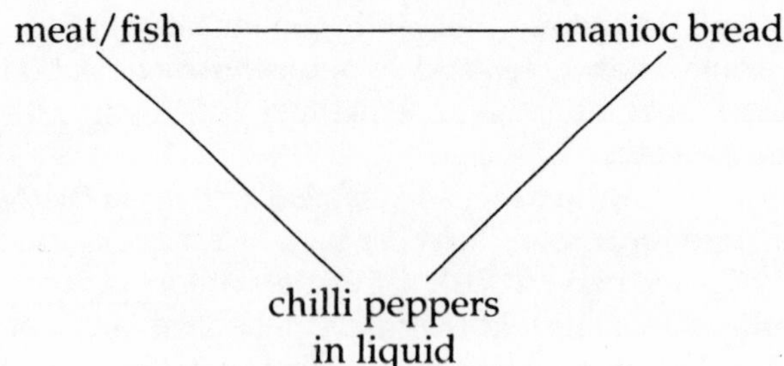

Figure 1 Food in Barasana society

tobacco are also linked together in other ways. Coca powder and tobacco snuff are prepared in exactly the same way, that is by mixing the dried and powdered coca or tobacco together with ash from burned leaves. The aromatic flavour which these burned leaves impart is highly esteemed and may sometimes be specially enhanced by blowing extra smoke into the ash through loose 'cigars' of rolled leaves; chips of Protium-resin incense may also be added to these leaf 'cigars' to impart yet more taste. Thus coca, like tobacco, is prepared with fire and ash and valued partly for its aromatic qualities. Finally, in addition to the obligatory accompaniment of coca by tobacco, some kind of manioc-based drink is usually drunk either just before coca is eaten or together with it. In short, whenever coca is eaten in company, it is consumed together with tobacco and a manioc-based drink in a pattern which recalls that of a meal. The general pattern can be summarized as in Figure 2.

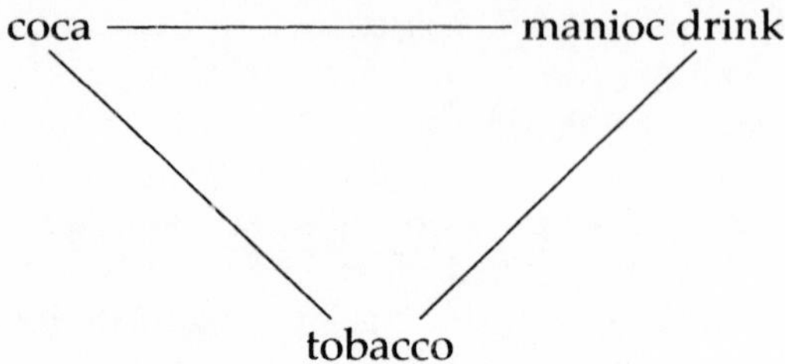

Figure 2 Non-food in Barasana society

However, in addition to that between 'food' and 'non-food' we need to add a further distinction between formality and informality and to bear in mind that, for most of the time, the consumption of both 'food' and 'non-foods' is a matter of habit. It is only on more formal occasions that people become self-conscious about what they do, consciously 'stick to the rules', and begin to make explicit some of the more esoteric associations of 'food' and 'non-food' which normally lie latent behind the taken-for-granted character of everyday objects and activities.

Ritual dances, sometimes attended by guests who may be quite distant strangers with whom relations are tense and ill-defined, are the most formal of all social occasions. They involve a shift to more marked and formal modes of speech and behaviour which accompany an increase in the quantity of 'non-foods' available. At a big dance, prodigious quantities of beer and coca may be produced and consumed. The hosts demonstrate their wealth, fertility and command over labour time by plying their guests with more than they can consume; the guests, under moral obligation to consume all they are offered, show their valour by finishing it all up even if they have to vomit out the excess to do so.[20]

This increase in quantity also goes together with a shift from less to more marked forms of the substances concerned. Let us begin with *yagé*, a hallucinogenic drink prepared from the macerated bark of *Banisteriopsis caapi* vines. Both coca and *yagé* are called *kahi* and distinguished, where necessary, by *bare* ('for eating') and *idire* ('for drinking'); *bare kahi* is coca while *idire kahi* is *yagé*. Coca and *yagé* are thus paired together in word and thought, the more marked form of *kahi*, *yagé*, being consumed only at dances.

This same relation between more and less marked forms is also apparent in the relation between beer and other manioc-based drinks. Generically, and when distinguished from 'food' (*bare* – 'stuff to eat'), all drinks are called *idire* ('stuff to drink'). But, unless otherwise qualified, *idire* on its own means 'beer'. Beer is thus quintessential 'drink' and the phrase 'to drink beer' (*idire idi-*) is the normal way to refer to a ritual dance. Beer is brewed from a base of boiled manioc juice fermented with various other ingredients such as toasted manioc bread, sugar-cane juice or pulped fruits or tubers. As a more marked form, served only at dances or formal gatherings, beer replaces the boiled manioc juice served each evening as the men's circle begins to form. Beer is also paired with *yagé*. The latter is intensely bitter and drinking it usually induces retching and vomiting. To help swallow it and to keep it down, a large gourd of beer is served as a chaser each time *yagé* is drunk. Finally, tobacco too has its more and less marked forms. As already mentioned, on formal occasions tobacco snuff is offered in addition to cigars. At dances, large doses of snuff are ingested up the noses of the participants as a necessary part of the ritual procedures which protect them from harm.

In sum then, the distinction between formality and informality goes together with that between the marked and non-marked forms of 'non-foods', but in each case the combination of these 'non-foods' is similar to that of the foods that make up a meal. Coca and *yagé*, produced by men, are served with drinks made from unfermented or fermented manioc juice, produced by women and accompanied by tobacco in the form of cigars or snuff as represented in Figure 3.

In addition, there is a further parallel this time between chilli pepper

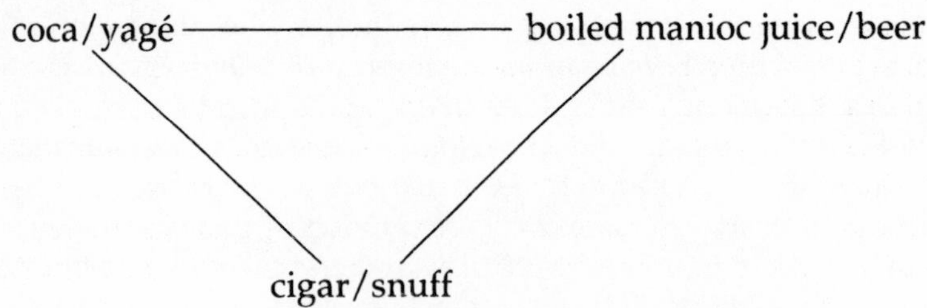

Figure 3 Marked and unmarked non-foods

and tobacco. Both are used more as essence than substance, more for their spicy, aromatic taste and stimulant effects than for providing bulk or sustenance, and both appear to play a similar 'catalytic' role, binding together male and female components. They also have a similar status with respect to smoke, fire and inhalation. Tobacco burned with fire produces a pungent smoke which is inhaled, while tobacco snuff, inhaled directly, produces a burning sensation which is compared to fire. Mythic precedent makes the snuff that shamans administer at dances equivalent to the heat and fire of the male Sun; it also makes the 'heat' of chilli peppers the equivalent of fire, but now fire of female ancestral origin.

Like snuff, the juice of chilli peppers may also be inhaled, but this time to cure hangovers and to produce the copious layer of facial grease which is both a sign of health and necessary for the aesthetics of facial painting. A condiment (*bia-bõa*, 'chilli-salt') made from smoked, dried and pulverized chillies mixed with salt smells quite similar to snuff but has more drastic effects. When burned on fire, dried chillies produce an asphyxiating smoke which is sometimes used as a punishment or fumigant and, in myth, used to smoke forest spirits from their lairs.

Finally, both tobacco and chilli have marked sexual connotations. If chilli peppers and pepper-pots are associated with female sexual organs, tobacco has similar associations with male organs. In myth, the first cigar was the penis of an ancestor and in ritual, a cigar placed in an inverted ritual cigar holder represents an ancestor with an erect penis, while pubic and auxiliary hair is sometimes referred to as 'tobacco hair'.[21]

What all this suggests, then, is that although 'foods' and 'non-foods' are kept apart in practice and opposed in thought, the different elements that make up these two complexes are regularly combined together in a similar fashion. In each case, the resulting 'meals' are made up of two substantial elements, one produced by men, the other by women, combined together in the presence of a third, more aromatic, substance which has more dynamic or 'catalytic' resonances of fire and sexual intercourse.

Although I have briefly mentioned myth in connection with the more esoteric connotations of chilli pepper and tobacco, thus far I have tried to confine myself largely to an analysis of the way 'foods' and 'non-foods' are used in practice and have emphasized that their consumption is not normally the subject of speculation. But if we now turn our attention to the mythology that the Barasana themselves see as providing the foundations of their everyday and ritual practices, we see that manioc and coca, the principal crops cultivated by women and men, are themselves identified with male and female ancestors and that the relation between them is also couched in sexual terms.

A long myth describes the marriage between the jaguar-like Yeba (Earth) and Yawira, the daughter of Fish Anaconda. This marriage establishes a primordial alliance between the Barasana as 'earth people' and their affines, the Bará, as 'water people'. Yeba is portrayed as an ignorant and wild man of the woods, civilized by his wife and father-in-law, who provide him with cultivated crops. Manioc itself comes in the form of Yawira and her sisters whose names are borne by some of the present-day varieties of this crop. Tobacco comes in the form of a fish which Yawira claims is her father's penis. As for coca, this has a double origin: first it comes from the finger of Yawira's baby brother and second from an amorous escapade between Yawira and Nyake, Yeba's younger brother. Yawira asks Nyake to help her carry manioc sticks to her garden for planting. When they get there, she seduces him and makes love with such vigour that he expires at the point of ejaculation, lying on the ground with arms and legs outstretched. His body becomes a variety of coca specific to the Barasana, which is planted alongside the coca originally obtained from their affines.

For the Barasana, this myth establishes a number of different points: why the expression 'planting coca cuttings' refers metaphorically to sex; why coca is planted in neat grid-like rows on to a blanket of manioc plants; why the eating of coca and manioc has a sacramental quality; and why these plants, as an essential component of the patrimonies of the groups concerned, are celebrated in word and deed during their ritual dances. Reproduced vegetatively from cuttings, manioc is passed on from mother to daughter while coca goes from father to son. They are treated as integral parts of the group identities which endure through time and which are transferred and recombined on marriage. These, then, are some of the resonances that lie behind the combination of gendered substances in the respective meals of 'foods' and 'non-foods'.

In this chapter, I have discussed Barasana consumption of coca from several different perspectives. In describing how coca is actually used, I have been concerned to document its role as a vehicle for different forms of social interaction, to show how its use plays a role in the expression and maintenance of a particular social order, and to draw attention to the close relation between exchanges of coca and verbal intercourse. As is usual with stimulant use throughout the world, the exchange of coca is used as a frame and pretext for heightened social interaction. In this instance, as formalization and ritualization increase, coca, tobacco, beer and *yagé* become so much the dominant focus of what is said and done that these substances become constitutive of the interactions themselves. This, I suggest, has to do with the fact that, in the culture of the Barasana and other Tukanoan Indians, language and a set of ritual possessions which include coca, tobacco, *yagé* and manioc plants, are crucial aspects of the identities of individuals and groups. These identities are being displayed and affirmed in interactions of this kind.

In discussing the conceptualization of coca and other 'drug-like' substances, I have examined the way in which different substances are combined together into meals in order to demonstrate the cultural construction of a particular pattern of consumption based around two opposed complexes, 'foods' and 'non-foods', each structured in a similar way. The evidence of myth clearly suggests that one aspect of this structuring has to do with a cultural emphasis on the potency of conjoining opposites conceived of in terms of gender.

In my discussion of 'food' and 'drugs', I have tried to demonstrate the importance of working through native cultural categories rather than imposing alien ones derived from a quite different cultural context. In particular, I have tried to avoid a physiological view of consumption, stressing instead that it is always a social activity informed by a cultural classification of substances. It is only at a level below that of the meal, in brief snacks of food or hurried scoops of coca, that the physiological effects of these substances – stopping hunger, giving energy – stand out. In all other contexts, these more pragmatic concerns are overlain by concerns of a quite different order: the creation and modification of social relations through feeding and giving, the expression and furtherance of a social and cosmological order through the combination of opposites and the reinforcement of the values that underlie them all.

NOTES

1 Fieldwork among the Barasana was carried out in 1968–71, 1979, 1984, 1990 and 1991 and was variously supported by grants from the Social Science Research Council, the Economic and Social Research Council, the British Museum and King's College, Cambridge. This support is gratefully acknowledged. For ethnographic details on the Barasana and neighbouring groups see C. Hugh-Jones, *From the Milk River*, Cambridge, Cambridge University Press, 1979 and S. Hugh-Jones, *The Palm and the Pleiades*, Cambridge, Cambridge University Press, 1979.

2 S. Weir, *Qat in Yemen: Consumption and Social Change*, London, British Museum Publications, 1985, p. 57 calls for an anthropology of all drug consumption practices.

3 A. Appadurai (ed.), *The Social Life of Things: Commodities in Cultural Perspective*, Cambridge, Cambridge University Press, 1986, p. 31.

4 C. Allen's study of coca and alcohol use in the Andes, *The Hold Life Has*, Washington, Smithsonian Institution, 1988, and S. Weir's *Qat in Yemen*, op. cit., are two shining examples of this genre.

5 Clearly such a claim depends partly on one's perspectives regarding both 'home' and the boundaries between academic sub-disciplines. There is a smattering of anthropological studies of cocaine and heroin use in the United States (see for example, P. Adler, *Wheeling and Dealing*, New York, Columbia University Press, 1993; P. Agar, *Ripping and Running*, New York, Academic Press, 1973; P. Bourgeois, 'Crack in Spanish Harlem', *Anthropology Today*, 1989, vol. 5, pp. 6–11); in this country there is also policy-oriented research of the kind undertaken, for example, by the Centre for Research on Drugs and Health Behaviour which sometimes involves anthropologically trained investigators who combine ethnographic techniques with more quantitative and questionnaire-based sociological methods. None the less, it remains true that anthropologists have typically paid more attention to the study of drug-production abroad than to consumption at home.

6 See, for example, M. Douglas and B. Isherwood, *The World of Goods: Towards an Anthropology of Consumption*, Harmondsworth, Penguin, 1978; P. Bourdieu, *Distinction: A Social Critique of the Judgement of Taste*, London, Routledge, 1984; Appadurai, op. cit.; and D. Miller, *Material Culture and Mass Consumption*, London, Blackwell, 1987.

7 Douglas and Isherwood, op. cit., p. 57 (my emphasis).

8 An exception to this generalization would be the Islamic world in which a distinction of this kind has a long history.

9 M. Johnsson, *Food and Culture among the Bolivian Aymara*, Stockholm, Almqvist & Wiksell, 1986.

10 Allen, op. cit.

11 M. Douglas (ed.), *Constructive Drinking: Perspectives on Drink from Anthropology*, Cambridge, Cambridge University Press, 1987.

12 Ibid., p. 14.

13 On the ethnobotany of Amazonian coca see R. Schultes and R. Raffauf, *The Healing Forest*, Portland, Dioscorides Press, 1990, pp. 166–76.

14 On this see S. Hugh-Jones, op. cit.

15 See, for example, Weir, op. cit., pp. 130–4 on *qat* and E. Bott, 'Psychoanalysis and ceremony', in J. La Fontaine (ed.), *The Interpretation of Ritual*, London, Tavistock, 1972, pp. 207–15 on *kava*.

16 I use inverted commas here to indicate covert categories not verbally labelled in local languages and of local application.

17 When men gather large quantities of insects, frogs or fruit, these may take the place of fish or meat but such foods are not to be considered as making up a paradigmatic 'proper meal'.

18 The leaves are those of *Banisteriopsis rusbyana*.

19 On the crucial integrative, binding function of gravy in British cuisine see A. Murcott, 'On the sociological significance of the "cooked dinner" in South Wales', *Social Science Information*, 1982, vol. 21, pp. 677–96. Advertisements for 'browning' and other products used in gravy-making frequently play upon the metaphorical role of gravy in binding the family together and more psychologically inclined advertisers see links between gravy and sexual fluids (Sue Byrne – personal communication).

20 This vomiting out of beer is not simply a matter of practical expedient; it has been widely reported in different parts of Amazonia, typically as a ritualized activity associated with ideas concerning fertility. For an excellent example of this, see E. Viveiros de Castro, *From the Enemy's Point of View*, Chicago,

Chicago University Press, 1992. That beer also loosens the bowels and that *yagé* causes both vomiting and diarrhoea both form parts of a whole Barasana philosophy of life-processes based on images of the digestive tube and its functions. (See S. Hugh-Jones, op. cit.). Similar ideas relating fertility to the force-feeding of food and coca are found in Andean communities (see Allen, op. cit., Ch. 6).

21 Tobacco forms one of a set of ritually marked male-owned crops, mostly 'non-foods' but also including maize and fruit trees, the usable parts of which are all borne above the ground. Apart from chilli peppers, all women's crops come from below the ground. This is a further aspect of the ritually marked status of chillies.

3

NICOTIAN DREAMS

The prehistory and early history of tobacco in eastern North America

Alexander von Gernet

ORIGINS OF TOBACCO SMOKING

The botanical origin of the genus *Nicotiana* has been traced to South America.[1] Ancient tobacco remains, smoking pipes and snuffing implements dating to various time periods have been recovered,[2] although the reconstruction of the human use of tobacco on that continent is preliminary.[3] Researchers have, however, been able to elucidate the South American tobacco complex as it existed in the interval between first European contact in the early sixteenth century and modern times. This complex included the ritualized consumption of nicotian substances, not only by smoking, but also by snuffing, drinking and even rectal injection.[4]

The use of *Nicotiana* during the Historic period was associated with slash-and-burn farming. Indeed, Wilbert has hypothesized that South American natives did not use the plant prior to the origins of horticulture, and that earlier forager societies were 'drug-free'.[5] But it seems far more likely that 'tobacco shamanism', as Wilbert calls it, was a vestigial trait of a hunter-gatherer lifestyle that was merely elaborated after the domestication of plants.[6] Wild species of tobacco were probably known to the earliest pre-horticultural societies in the Americas,[7] and it is reasonable to assume that the artificial selection of such species by foragers may even have contributed to the development of horticulture.[8]

Little is known of the origins of tobacco use in Central America, the West Indies and Mexico. Archaeological evidence suggests that an elaborate tobacco complex was present in both the Prehistoric and Historic periods.[9] While the relationship of this complex to the South American equivalent has not been studied, similarities in the smoking technology of prehistoric Mexico and the rest of North America have been demonstrated.[10]

The mechanism and timing of the spread of *Nicotiana* species into North America remains poorly understood.[11] While tubular smoking devices have been found on 3,000-year-old archaeological sites,[12] the recovery of pipes does not necessarily illuminate the origins of tobacco use, since dozens of non-nicotian plants were smoked by North American Indians.[13] Furthermore, the failure to recover pipes in earlier contexts does not suggest the absence of tobacco, since smoking devices were also manufactured from perishable materials and tobacco was consumed in other ways than by smoking. Chemical analyses of prehistoric pipe dottle and other residues have occasionally been successful in identifying alkaloids such as nicotine,[14] but the results have not always been conclusive.[15]

Despite these uncertainties, it is generally acknowledged that domesticated species of *Nicotiana* reached the northern continent through human agency and were introduced into eastern North America more than 2,000 years ago. Microscopic examinations of charred seed remains recovered by floating soil samples in water has resulted in the identification of over 4,000 tobacco seeds from a hundred archaeological sites in eastern North America. So far, the earliest specimens have been dated to the first century BC.[16]

The tobacco plant was probably incorporated into North American cultures because it could be readily adapted to an existing ideational context or set of beliefs. Cross-cultural analysis has enabled anthropologists to identify the underlying ideational stratum that gives native peoples in the New World a cultural unity. The ethnographic record suggests that the core elements of this belief system were linked to ecstatic shamanism and included an emphasis on altered states of consciousness. Dissociative states or out-of-body experiences were believed to facilitate communication with spirit beings and to permit transformation into such beings. The empirical support for this belief was found primarily in visual hallucinations as well as nocturnal dreams.[17]

Altered states of consciousness were induced by a variety of means, including prolonged isolation, rhythmic dancing, fasting and the adjustment of body chemistry through the ingestion of psychoactive substances. There is both cultural and botanical evidence that the latter practice is of considerable antiquity in the Americas. Indeed, anthropologists and ethnobotanists now argue that the earliest human foragers who migrated from Siberia to America at least 15,000 years ago carried with them a cultural predisposition for the use of psychoactive plants. As humans moved into new ecosystems they sought not only subsistence-related foods such as berries and nuts, but also flora which would help sustain and develop the basic tenets of a shamanistic ideology.[18]

Recent research has shown that *N. rustica*, the tobacco species propagated throughout prehistoric eastern North America, produces altered states of consciousness and even hallucinations if ingested in significant doses.[19] It appears that many native peoples favoured this species of tobacco because of the alkaloids it contained; hence, the original domestication process may have involved a gradual artificial selection of those plant populations which, when consumed, manifested the greatest potency or spiritual power.

While many psychoactive plants, including tobacco, were ingested through the gastrointestinal system, burning such substances and consuming the remains via the respiratory route has both physiological advantages and symbolic import. Not only do the lungs provide some alkaloids, particularly nicotine, extremely rapid access to the bloodstream, but the blowing and sucking of smoke are perceived to be shamanistic metaphors for the transfer of spiritual power. Hence it may not be coincidental that the earliest smoking-pipes resemble the sucking tubes used by shamans in healing rituals.[20] Over the course of millennia, the smoking complex appears to have evolved into a kind of democratized shamanism in which the use of pipes was, in many cases, no longer restricted to medico-religious specialists.[21] As a result, pipes are among the most salient features of the North American archaeological record.[22]

Despite the pivotal role of pipes in North American life and the 'sacred' nature of some of these smoking devices, these objects were not the basis of a specific Amerindian belief system. Contrary to assertions made in one recent work on the subject,[23] native peoples of North America did not practice a 'pipe-centered religion'. Rather, it is more helpful to consider permutations of the pipe complex as attenuated symbolic transformations of basic shamanistic principles.[24] While pipe symbolism has remarkable consistency throughout the continent, some similarities such as the presence of bird effigies and other ornithomorphic accoutrements, may be linked less to diffusion, and more to the constraining influence of shamanism and its animistic *Weltanschauung*.[25]

AMERINDIAN TOBACCO USE AT THE TIME OF EUROPEAN CONTACT

As European exploration of the eastern seaboard of North America intensified during the sixteenth and early seventeenth centuries, numerous observations on the indigenous inhabitants of the region were recorded. These ethnohistoric accounts document the use of tobacco and pipes in virtually every eastern North American culture from Québec to Florida. The following summary is gleaned from a detailed analysis of primary sources relating to the period 1500–1650.[26]

Since propagation of *N. rustica* required very little human intervention, it is unlikely that intensive horticultural preparation was necessary for a successful harvest.[27] Indeed, even foragers like the Micmac, who did not grow crops for subsistence, grew tobacco.[28] Some observers noted the presence of tobacco in clearings together with food crops, while others indicated that the plant was grown independently in small plots or among wild herbs and fruits.[29] Although agriculture was predominantly a female-related activity, there is evidence that tobacco was planted and collected by men.[30]

In much of eastern North America, tobacco was not only smoked but cast (as a dried powder or compressed leaf mass) into fires, water, and rock crevices. The reason for this was linked to the widespread belief that even inanimate objects had souls, and that spirits inhabited virtually every realm. Humans and spirit beings were thought to live in a social world where there was a perpetual obligation to fulfil an ancient contract. Spirit beings were particularly fond of tobacco and, hence, were offered the precious substance at every opportunity. The gifts were sent either directly to their terrestrial and underwater dwellings, or indirectly to the sky-world in the form of smoke. In return for these gratuities, which were invariably accompanied by invocatory prayers, the spirit beings were expected to provide certain favours. In some communities tobacco was offered daily to the rising and setting sun. It was also sprinkled on fires during occasional rites such as funerals, or at cyclical events such as corn harvesting. The rite was especially prominent in the sweatlodge, where it helped to divine the cause of illness, pacify various disease agents, or encourage a pestilence to leave a village. It was customary to carry extra tobacco during travel since humans were particularly dependent on the good will of spirits when away from home. Invocations were habitually performed at any change in the weather, or to pay homage to those responsible for violent storms on lakes. Moreover, it was deemed necessary to conciliate spirits when negotiating a canoe through difficult rapids and at portages where travellers felt exposed to ambush. Journeys were interrupted at any unusual or awe-inspiring natural features such as canyons and waterfalls, since these were believed to be the abodes of powerful beings who demanded tobacco. To ensure success in hunting, fishing and war expeditions, invocations were also performed before or during such ventures.[31] The universality of these rites is likely a consequence of the remarkable cultural continuity that characterizes the region.[32]

The infatuation with tobacco that was attributed to the spirits was arguably a reflection and extension of the high regard that humans had for the plant. Time and time again observers expressed astonishment at the tobacco addiction of many of the peoples they met in America. Both Iroquoian- and Algonquian-speaking peoples were seen with pipes in their mouths at all hours of the day and night, and tobacco figured prominently in the dreams they recalled. Not only was the leaf greatly prized, but many individuals seemed more ready to dispense with eating than with smoking. These impressions were corroborated by conversations with natives who sometimes admitted that there was nothing in the world they loved more than tobacco. Pipes were included as essential grave goods, for even the souls who travelled to the land of the dead were believed to be dedicated smokers.[33] As the Jesuit missionary Paul le Jeune recorded in 1634, the Montagnais, in what is now the Canadian province of Québec, had a

> fondness . . . for this herb [that] is beyond all belief. They go to sleep with their reed pipes in their mouths, they sometimes get up in the night to smoke; they often stop in their journeys for the same purpose, and it is the first thing they do when they reenter their cabins. I have lighted tinder, so as to allow them to smoke while paddling a canoe; I have often seen them gnaw the stems of their pipes when they had no more tobacco, I have seen them scrape and pulverize a wooden pipe to smoke it. Let us say with compassion that they pass their lives in smoke, and at death fall into the fire.[34]

Five years later Jérôme Lalemant found that the Huron of Ontario were anxious to know whether tobacco was available in heaven, claiming that they could not dispense with it in the Christian afterlife. Indeed, the Jesuits soon regarded abstention from smoking not only as a positive sign of conversion but as the most heroic act to be expected of any neophyte.[35]

With the exception of one apocryphal source on the Delaware, there is no evidence that women smoked in the pre-1650 period, and ample testimony that virtually every male had a pipe. Although Micmac children were eager to inhale the second-hand smoke emitted from their fathers' noses, the Pokanoket considered it odious for young boys to smoke.[36]

Prehistoric smoking devices recovered archaeologically in eastern North America are made from stone, or more often from clay.[37] Early French and English writers noted that Amerindian pipes were also manufactured from reed, wood, bone, antler and even lobster claws. By the early seventeenth century, copper and tin acquired from European traders supplemented these materials. Roger Williams observed that the Narragansett even learned the European craft of casting pewter and brass pipes. By the 1620s, these southern New England Algonquians also adopted steel drills. The Micmac and Delaware, by contrast, continued, after 1630, to employ drills made of traditional materials in the laborious task of piercing the stems and bowls of stone pipes.[38]

Early descriptions and illustrations suggest that the majority of smoking devices were either short, one-piece elbow pipes, or longer, two-piece versions having a stone or clay bowl with a detachable reed or wooden stem. Since the perishable stem is almost never recovered archaeologically, it has been difficult to assess the overall length of most two-piece specimens. The ethnohistoric sources indicate that these ranged from 30 cm to over 180 cm and were, occasionally, employed as leaning sticks. As John Smith noted in 1608, even the 75-cm pipes wielded by the Susquehannock were 'sufficient to beat out the brains of a man'.[39] Some authorities suggest that the separate-stemmed pipes may have served a different ritual purpose than one-piece devices,[40] but there is little documentary support for this assertion.

Both archaeological and ethnohistorical evidence suggests that pipes were highly valued. The Huron went to great lengths to prolong the use-life of ceramic smoking devices by carefully grinding and polishing chipped bowls and stems, and by using human blood as a bonding agent to repair fractures.[41] Among the Montagnais the breakage of pipes was common enough to have become a theme in their mythology. During his exploration of the St Lawrence River in 1603, Samuel de Champlain recorded a tale related to him by a chief named Anadabijou:

> He told me . . . that once upon a time there was a man who had a good supply of tobacco (which is a herb, of which they take the smoke), and that God came to this man, and asked him where was his tobacco-pipe. The man took his tobacco-pipe and gave it to God, who smoked tobacco a great while: after He had smoked enough, God broke the said pipe into many pieces: and the man asked Him, 'Why hast Thou broken my pipe? Surely Thou seest that I have no other?' And God took one of His own, and gave it to him, saying to him: 'Here is one that I give thee, carry it to thy grand Sagamore; charge him to keep it, and if he keep it well, he shall never want for anything whatever, nor any of his companions.' The man took the pipe, and gave it to his grand Sagamore, and as long as he kept it the savages wanted for nothing in the world; but afterwards the said Sagamore lost this pipe, and this is the reason of the great famine which sometimes comes among them. I asked him whether he believed all this; and he said yes, and that it was true.[42]

Smoking technology was not confined to pipes alone, but included a number of other accessories. At home, pipes were lit at a hearth using a live coal or a fire brand, while on journeys fire was produced by rubbing sticks or striking stones. By the early seventeenth century, these rudimentary methods of lighting pipes were supplemented with burning mirrors, steels and tinder boxes acquired from French and English traders.[43] The most oft-mentioned accessory was the tobacco pouch, which was observed hanging from the waist or neck of virtually every man. It was usually made of leather, although the specially prepared, severed hands of enemies were also used for this purpose. The Attikamek, Huron and other groups decorated their pouches, often using dyed porcupine quills. In addition to tobacco and pipes, pouches contained charms, mirrors and poisonous plants used in suicides. Tobacco pouches were valuable commodities which were occasionally requested by shamans in return for curing services or offered as stakes during gambling.[44]

Amid the frequent allusions to individual smoking, one also finds references to formal pipe ceremonialism at councils and other assemblies. As Pierre Biard wrote of the Micmac in 1611, 'all their talks, treaties, welcomes, and endearments are made under the fumes of this tobacco'.[45] Among many groups it was a common practice to smoke in silence for at least one half-hour before deliberations, speeches, or welcoming visitors. Participants either brought their own smoking devices or puffed on a communal pipe.[46] References to the 'peace-pipe' or *calumet* ceremonialism are rare in the pre-1650 literature,[47] although some 'passing-the-pipe' rituals almost certainly associated friendship with the sharing of tobacco before then.[48] Even the term 'smoking', when used as a figure of speech in Iroquois political rhetoric, symbolized peaceful, friendly discourse.[49] Pipes did not always have peaceful connotations, however, for they were occasionally employed in the torture of prisoners. In the 1640s the Mohawk seared their captives with red-hot pipes, burned their finger-tips in pipe bowls, and forced them to handle the live coals used to light their smoking implements.[50]

Smoking was a prominent feature of community festivals and dances. In fact, the Huron, Algonquin and Montagnais frequently had feasts at which nothing was consumed except tobacco. Pipes were also brought to sweatlodges and missionary sermons as well as taken on raiding expeditions. Storytelling sessions were often accompanied by pipe smoking, where even the myths alluded to tobacco. In short, there are few contexts in which references to smoking, pipes and tobacco pouches are not found.[51]

Amerindians did not, therefore, confine smoking to formal social, political, ceremonial and ritual occasions. In eastern North America tobacco use had, by the time of European contact, already become popularized but to describe it as secular would be to misconstrue the fundamentals of native belief systems and the role of tobacco in them. In native ideology virtually everything was permeated with a sacrosanctity. From a shamanistic viewpoint, pipe smoking was a means of facilitating communication with spirit beings and a vehicle for individual empowerment. The ubiquity of smoking as documented in the sixteenth and early seventeenth centuries should not be regarded merely as a profanation generated by the addictive properties of nicotine. Indeed, each inhalation and exhalation, while not always intended to produce altered states of consciousness or other manifestations of the sacred, afforded the lay person at least some access to the spiritual aspects of the cosmos, thereby curtailing the religious hegemony of the shaman in what were essentially egalitarian societies.

The use of tobacco was also linked to the practical exigencies of everyday living. There are reports that individuals smoked to suppress hunger and quench thirst.[52] The leaf was apparently regarded as a nutrient since it was not only smoked but occasionally eaten, either alone or as an ingredient in corn-bread.[53] Yet this form of consumption too may have been perceived as the ingestion of a metaphysical rather than physical substance. Like many other plants, tobacco was believed to be an animate leaf having a soul.[54]

EUROPEAN APPROPRIATION OF TOBACCO

Given the extraordinary Amerindian preoccupation with tobacco, it is not surprising that early European explorers expressed an interest in the herb. Exploration and colonization efforts in South America, Central America, the West Indies and Mexico brought Spain and Portugal in contact with tobacco-using natives during the late fifteenth and early sixteenth centuries.[55] By 1535, the French had encountered pipe-smoking Iroquoians along the St Lawrence River.[56] Twenty years later, a French writer described the cigar-smoking Tupinamba of Brazil.[57] It is almost certain that *N. rustica* had been imported and was growing in herbal gardens in the Low Countries by the 1550s, although there is no indication that tobacco was widely used anywhere in Europe before 1560.[58]

English explorers recorded the use of tobacco during a trip to Florida in 1565,[59] and the plant was apparently smoked by at least some Englishmen in the early 1570s – long before Raleigh is alleged to have introduced the custom. Nevertheless, the pipe was still a novelty during the penultimate decade of the century.[60]

The interval between the time the first descriptions of Amerindian pipe smoking appeared and the period of widespread appropriation of the habit by Europeans was remarkably short, especially in England. When Thomas Hariot, the English scientist who accompanied Ralph Lane's expedition to North America, encountered the North Carolina Algonquians smoking tobacco in 1585–6, he described the behaviour in terms which suggest that he was introducing his readers to something new:

> There is an herbe which is sowed a part by it selfe & is called by the inhabitants *uppówoc*: In the West Indies it hath divers names, according to the severall places & countries where it groweth and is used: The Spaniards generally call it *Tobacco*. The leaves thereof being dried and brought into powder: they use to take the fume or smoke thereof, by sucking it through pipes made of claie, into their

> stomacke and heade; from whence it purgeth superfluous fleame & other grosse humors, openeth all the pores & passages of the body: by which meanes the use thereof, not only preserveth the body from obstructions; but also if any be, so that they have not beene of too long continuance, in short time breaketh them: wherby their bodies are notably preserved in health, & know not many greevous diseases wherewithall wee in England are oftentimes afflicted.[61]

Shortly before 1590 the English began manufacturing pipes of white ball-clay as cheap and convenient alternatives to makeshift smoking devices. These early pipes resembled Amerindian versions recovered on archaeological sites along the eastern seaboard of North America, which suggests that the manufacturers used models brought back by Hariot or other survivors of the Roanoke expeditions.[62] By 1598, descriptions of smoking appeared in the European travel literature much as the Amerindian tobacco complex had been featured in earlier reports from the New World. Scarcely twelve years after Hariot had marvelled at the curious custom in America, a Silesian named Paul Hentzner described, with equal wonder and in similar terms, the identical habit during a visit to England:

> the English constantly use the Nicotian plant, which in the American language they call *Tabaca* (others call it *Petum*) and generally in this way. They have pipes made of clay for this purpose; in the lower end of these they put the plant, so dried that it can be easily reduced to powder, and light it. They draw smoke into their mouths from the upper end; this comes out again through the nose as if through funnels. It brings with it much phlegm and discharge from the head.[63]

Since smoking appears to have had no precedent in European history, it may seem amazing that it should have gained rapid and sweeping popularity in a society believing itself superior to 'savages' in matters of behaviour. As was the case with the selection of strong (and hence symbolically charged) *Nicotiana* species by prehistoric Amerindians, tobacco was appropriated by sixteenth-century Europeans because it could be easily adapted to existing contexts. The lower classes were undoubtedly introduced to smoking in European seaports by sailors returning from the New World. The potency of the imported varieties of Amerindian tobacco may have played a role during the early years of diffusion, since, as Pena and De l'Obel recalled in their celebrated herbal in 1571, sailors affirmed that 'their brains are lulled by a joyous intoxication' after smoking the leaf.[64] This observation confirmed one made a few years earlier by the Swiss scientist Konrad von Gesner who had experimented with the new plant. He named it *Vertiginosa* ('producing dizziness'), and noted that 'its power and speed in causing dizziness and a species of intoxication is indeed wonderful'.[65] It is no wonder, perhaps, that the social context of the consumption of tobacco was the tavern.[66] Unfortunately, little is known of the varieties and alkaloid content of the various *Nicotiana* species used in late sixteenth-century Europe, except that *N. rustica* was certainly among them; hence it is difficult to ascertain the degree to which the desire for recreational altered states of consciousness contributed to the early popularity of the habit.

Much more is known of the ideological context which set the stage for rapid diffusion beyond the seaports. This cultural predisposition had not, of course, anything to do with shamanism, but was, at least to some extent, linked to the humoral theory that prevailed as the central medical paradigm of the era. According to this theory, the healthy human body had a proper balance of 'humours', which had properties conceptualized in terms of dialectical oppositions such as hot/cold and dry/moist. Smoking fitted into this schema, since it seemed to dry out superfluous 'humours', thereby adjusting imbalances caused by inappropriate diet and climate.[67] In effect, tobacco entered the European theatre as a panacea which had long been sought by medieval alchemy. Here at last – as the title of an early treatise on tobacco suggests – was *Joyfull Newes Out of the Newe Founde Worlde*.[68]

The notion of a panacea was reinforced by a persistent rumour of uncertain origin that the Indians themselves favoured the herb because of its medicinal efficacy. This theme is frequently reiterated in the pre-1650 literature on North America. Tobacco was believed to heal wounds; assuage pain such as toothache; overcome extremes of weather; warm the body, brain and stomach; purge 'humidities' and superfluous moisture; counter rheumatic and respiratory problems; eliminate crudities, obstructions and indigestible matter; open pores, passages and bowels; induce sleep; calm passions; energize and restore strength; preserve general health and lengthen life. It was reasoned that, since harsh climates, diets and lifestyles made the inhabitants of the New World more prone to imbalances, native peoples needed to smoke frequently.[69] Even more imaginative was the view that tobacco acted as an anti-aphrodisiac, or, to borrow Marc Lescarbot's decorous language, 'hindered the functions of Venus'. This idea was invoked to help explain certain tendencies towards sexual modesty among both the Micmac and the Huron. It was hypothesized that smoke, directly entering the brain, depressed the senses and thereby inhibited promiscuity.[70] When combined with the salubrious effects of the plant, this additional characteristic made tobacco attractive especially to the clergy. Paradoxically, the regular ingestion that was intended to preserve a healthy and moral lifestyle soon led to widespread addiction and abuse. Indeed, several seventeenth-century popes were obliged to issue Bulls curtailing excessive tobacco use among ecclesiastical officials, and whether or not smoking broke the pre-communion fast was much debated in theological circles.[71]

By the first decade of the seventeenth century, two diametrically opposed positions about smoking had emerged. Some Europeans held that the devil had given tobacco to Amerindians to produce deceptive hallucinations in the shamans and their followers.[72] It was this link with the inherently diabolic characteristics of New World 'barbarism' that prompted King James I to issue his infamous *Counterblaste to Tobacco* in 1604, in which he encouraged his countrymen to consider 'what honour or policie can moove us to imitate the barbarous and beastly maners of the wilde, godlesse, and slavish *Indians*, especially in so vile and stinking a custome'.[73] This, and other vitriolic diatribes, fell on deaf ears since others, including influential physicians and herbalists, felt that tobacco was a gift from God sent to alleviate the suffering of humans. While it would have been preferable that the herb was discovered as a stray weed in the Vatican gardens, finding it in America did not preclude adapting it to a Christian life. As William Barclay noted in 1614, 'God honoured America and blessed it by this wonderful and sacred plant'. It was not long before tobacco was being hailed as 'the salvation of the world' and woodcuts of the plant appeared in illustrated renditions of the Psalms.[74] The endorsement of medical authorities, as well as the enthusiastic support of the aristocracy and the clergy, provided legitimacy for what was already becoming an unbridled social habit among the lower classes.

THE RETURN OF TOBACCO TO AMERICA

Histories of contact between Europeans and the native inhabitants of North America often emphasize how the imposition of technologies, behaviours and ideologies characteristic of state-organized nations brought about dramatic changes and 'acculturation' in tribal or band-level societies. It is clear, however, that culture contact involves a bilateral exchange that frequently results in 'transculturation'.[75] Hence researchers are beginning to recognize that the influence of the New World on the Old was as significant as the impact of Europe on the Americas.[76] Tobacco is, of course, only one of numerous examples; nevertheless, it is unique as the only important commodity that crossed the Atlantic in both directions and had sources and markets on both sides of the Ocean.

Once the English and French learned how to smoke, tobacco routinely accompanied sailors and explorers to the New World. The primary literature contains numerous allusions to the tobacco addiction of Europeans who lingered for extended periods in the nascent colonies. For example, Marc Lescarbot noted that the French, who had established a settlement at Port Royal (now in Nova Scotia) in 1606, were 'for the most part so bewitched with this drunkenness of tobacco, that they can no more be without it than without meat or drink'. Pierre Biard added that 'to inhale its fumes, they would sell their shirts'. Although the local Micmac were in a position to furnish the newcomers with the leaf, the French imported their own at a cost of 'a crown a pound'.[77]

Among Amerindians, the act of offering tobacco was part of a semiotic domain involving communication among humans, as well as between humans and spirit beings. This likely contributed to the prominence that smoking had in early contacts with French and English explorers. Once Europeans recognized the symbolic and transactional value of nicotian products, it was a logical step to transfer these substances from their own personal travel bags to the bale of trade goods destined for the natives. That Amerindians often had their own supply did not seem to matter, since protocol dictated that a pipe ceremony and gifts of tobacco preceded barter exchange.[78] Moreover, foreign tobacco *was* different, since it was imbued with the symbolic power often associated with the exotic.

The backwash of transculturation is documented as early as 1597, when Basque sailors offered tobacco to the Beothuk of Newfoundland in return for furs.[79] During the first decade of the seventeenth century, ships occasionally diverted to the West Indies to pick up tobacco before proceeding to the eastern seaboard of North America to trade with native peoples.[80] By 1604 Champlain had handed out quantities of the leaf to the eastern Abenaki whom he met along the coast of Maine.[81] A few months later, the chronicler of an English expedition noted that these same Abenaki 'gave us of their Tabacco in our pipes, which was excellent, and so generally commended of us all to be as good as any we ever tooke'.[82] During this early period the substance was passed back and forth between peoples who possessed roughly equal amounts.[83]

Meanwhile, efforts were under way to cultivate tobacco in England and reduce dependence on imports which, despite Anglo-Spanish hostility, often originated in Spanish colonial possessions.[84] By 1611, the struggling Virginia colony also turned its attention to nicotian production. For reasons which may for ever remain unclear, the Jamestown settlers found that, despite rave reviews from earlier explorers, the local *N. rustica* was simply unpalatable, and they were forced to import a West Indies seed known as *N. tabacum*. The crop was an instant success and the Governor soon complained that the colonists were feverishly 'rooting in the ground about tobacco like swine' instead of growing corn and wheat. King James I wanted to convert the colony to a silkworks, but the Amerindian plant, known in England for less than fifty years, rapidly became the economic lifeline of the first permanent English settlement in North America. The success of the Virginia experience soon prompted the French, the Dutch and the Swedes to establish 'tobacco colonies' in North America.[85]

By 1613–15 tobacco originating in the Spanish colonies in America was regularly purchased in Iberian ports and brought to France.[86] Some of these products were transferred to ships bound for the St Lawrence River and traded to the Montagnais and other Algonquian-speaking peoples.[87] As early as 1615, natives living as far inland as Ontario were canoeing hundreds of kilometres through the interior of Quebec to obtain European tobacco from French traders anchored at Tadoussac.[88] For two centuries thereafter, tobacco was one of the most important goods in the French and English fur trades. Ironically, Amerindians deemed the Virginia product to be unsuitable in all but the most desperate transactions. Despite the availability of cheap stocks in their own colonial backyards, European trading companies were forced to obtain imported Brazilian tobacco.[89]

While tobacco lubricated social relations and even facilitated colonial goals, seventeenth-century missionaries labouring in New France expressed ambivalence towards smoking. Although the Jesuits and Recollects affirmed the medical efficacy of the nicotian panacea and even experimented with the plant, they discouraged smoking among Amerindian neophytes, prohibited the practice in chapels and lauded converts who had abandoned the habit. At the same time they distributed tobacco bribes to encourage native peoples to attend sermons. They requisitioned tobacco from their superiors, claiming it was the only commodity acceptable to natives as payment for transportation, shelter and language tutoring. They destroyed sacred objects to which natives had traditionally offered the powdered leaf, and rewarded those converts who helped in this iconoclasm with presents of tobacco.[90]

Soon after the first Algonquian pipes reached Europe, English pipes were being made for export to America. Indeed, sailors exploring the coast of Maine were already distributing pipes to the natives in 1605.[91] Three years later, a 'Tobaco-pipe-maker' is listed among the tradesmen sent to the Virginia colony.[92] Archaeological evidence from native and colonial sites suggests that the typical pipe assemblage during this period included Amerindian pipes, European pipes, Amerindian pipes made in European styles, Amerindian pipes manufactured with the aid of European material and technology, as well as European pipes imitating Amerindian fashions.[93] Pipes manufactured by native peoples also ended up in Europe[94] where they were valued for their 'strength, handsomenesse, and coolnesse'.[95] Examples of smoking devices moving back and forth across the cultural divide abound in the literature of the colonial period.[96]

Some authorities have suggested that the influx of European tobacco and pipes made these commodities commonplace and threatened the 'dignity' of the Amerindian smoking complex,[97] but archaeological and ethnohistoric evidence suggests that European contact fortified and maintained what had already been a widespread habit in late prehistoric eastern North America.[98] The fur trade did, however, make tobacco and pipes available for the first time among some northern arctic and subarctic peoples. For example, the western Eskimo received tobacco and pipes from Asia, after the habit had circumnavigated the world on European ships. It was not long before they became the most important items in Russian–native trade.[99] Interestingly, early reports allude to giddiness, intoxication and prostration in Eskimo smokers,[100] suggesting that the leaf was easily adapted to the cataleptic trances of ecstatic shamanism.[101] Diffusion had come full circle and history had repeated itself.

As natives and newcomers sat across from one another, silently smoking and exchanging pipes and tobacco, they were lulled into thinking that the habit had always been part of their respective traditions. Ultimately, the popularity of tobacco on both sides of the Atlantic countered the European tendency to create an intellectual boundary between 'savagery' and 'civilization'. Hence when the pipe emerged as the symbol of British sophistication during the late nineteenth century, scholars tried to demonstrate that it had not originated among the Indians after all but, rather, had an honourable pedigree in an Old World civilization.[102] Smoking had become such an inextricable part of European life, the possibility that it had spread from the New World was simply inconceivable. Similarly, the aboriginal peoples of eastern North America were unaware that much of what they smoked after European contact came from Brazil. Nor, for that matter, did they recall that their own indigenous tobacco had originated in South America. Instead, they usually traced the plant to a single beneficent act by spirit beings that occurred at a specific time in their own history.[103] Ethnologists and folklorists have recorded comparable origin myths in almost every culture on earth where the habit is now prevalent. What makes tobacco an especially peculiar substance is that, while it was never necessary for human survival and while smoking it was a learned behaviour spread through diffusion, it nevertheless permeated cultures to such an extent that disparate peoples on several continents laid claim to having discovered it independently.

NOTES

1 T. H. Goodspeed, *The Genus Nicotiana: Origins, Relationships and Evolution of its Species in the Light of their Distribution, Morphology and Cytogenetics*, Waltham, Mass., Chronica Botanica, 1954.

2 E. F. von Nordenskiöld, 'Südamerikanische Rauchpfeifen', *Globus*, 1908, vol. 93(19), pp. 293–8. M. Uhle, 'A snuffing-tube from Tiahuanaco', *Bulletin of the*

Free Museum of Science and Art, 1898, vol. 4, pp. 159–77. J. Wilbert, *Tobacco and Shamanism in South America*, New Haven and London, Yale University Press, 1987, p. xvii.

3 J. C. Winter, 'Prehistoric and historic Native American tobacco use: an overview', paper presented at the Society for American Archaeology Annual Meeting, New Orleans, 1991.

4 D. Kamen-Kaye, 'Chimó: an unusual form of tobacco in Venezuela', *Botanical Museum Leaflets*, 1971, vol. 23(1), pp. 1–59. J. A. Mason, 'Use of tobacco in Mexico and South America', *Field Museum of Natural History Anthropology Leaflet* 16, Chicago, Field Museum Press, 1924. N. U. Mendoza, 'El tabaco entre las tribus indigenas de Colombia', *Revista Colombiana de Antropologia*, 1956, vol. 5, pp. 13–52. A. Serrano, 'El uso del tabaco y vegetales narcotizantes entre los indigenas de America', *Revista Geográfica Americana*, 1934, vol. 11, pp. 415–29. G. Stahl, 'Tabakrauchen in Südamerika', *Akten des 21. Internationalen Amerikanistenkongresses* [1924], Göteborg, Sweden, 1925, pp. 315–20. G. Stahl, 'Der Tabak im Leben südamerikanischer Völker', *Zeitschrift für Ethnologie*, 1926, vol. 57, pp. 81–152. J. Wilbert, 'Tobacco and shamanistic ecstasy among the Warao Indians of Venezuela', in P. T. Furst (ed.), *Flesh of the Gods: The Ritual Use of Hallucinogens*, New York, Praeger, 1972, pp. 55–83. J. Wilbert, 'Magico-religious use of Tobacco among South American Indians', in V. Rubin (ed.), *Cannabis and Culture*, The Hague, Mouton, 1975, pp. 439–61. J. Wilbert, *Tobacco and Shamanism*, op. cit.

5 Ibid., pp. 149–50.

6 A. von Gernet, [Review of] 'Tobacco and Shamanism in South America, Johannes Wilbert, Yale University Press, New Haven', *Man* 1989, vol. 24, p. 713.

7 Winter, op. cit.

8 P. T. Furst, *Hallucinogens and Culture*, Novato, California, Chandler & Sharp, 1976, p. 27.

9 A. E. Douglass, 'A portrait pipe from Central America', *American Antiquarian*, 1889, vol. 11, pp. 348–53. J. G. Elferink, 'The narcotic and hallucinogenic use of tobacco in Pre-Columbian Central America', *Journal of Ethnopharmacology*, 1983, vol. 7, pp. 111–22. Mason, op. cit. A. Oramas, 'Out of myths and legends emerges a real personage: the tobacco', *Cuba Tabaco International*, 1982, vol. 8, pp. 57–65. M. N. Porter, 'Pipas precortesianas', *Acta Anthropólogica*, 1948, vol. 3(2). F. Robicsek, *The Smoking Gods: Tobacco in Maya Art, History and Religion*, Norman, University of Oklahoma Press, 1978. M. H. Saville, 'Ancient smoking-pipes from Ecuador', *Indian Notes*, 1924, vol. 1, pp. 63–9. H. J. Spinden, *Tobacco is American: The Story of Tobacco before the Coming of the White Man*, New York, New York Public Library, 1950. J. E. S. Thompson, 'Some uses of tobacco among the Maya', *Notes on Middle American Archaeology and Ethnology*, 1946, vol. 3(61), pp. 1–5; idem, 'Tobacco among the Maya and their neighbors', in J. E. S. Thompson, *Maya History and Religion*, Norman, University of Oklahoma Press, 1970, pp. 103–23.

10 Porter, op. cit.

11 W. A. Setchell, 'Aboriginal tobaccos', *American Anthropologist*, 1921, vol. 23, pp. 397–414. Winter, op. cit.

12 D. F. Jordan, 'Adena and blocked-end tubes in the Northeast', *Bulletin of the Massachusetts Archaeological Society*, 1959, vol. 20(4), p. 49. W. A. Turnbaugh, 'Tobacco, pipes, smoking and rituals among the Indians of the Northeast', *Quarterly Bulletin of the Archaeological Society of Virginia*, 1975, vol. 30(2), p. 65.

13 V. J. Knight, Jr., 'Some observations concerning plant materials and aboriginal smoking in eastern North America', *Journal of Alabama Archaeology*,

1975, vol. 21(2), pp. 120–44. A. von Gernet, 'Hallucinogens and the origins of the Iroquoian pipe/tobacco/smoking complex', in C. F. Hayes III (ed.), *Proceedings of the 1989 Smoking Pipe Conference*, Research Records No. 22, New York, Rochester Museum and Science Center, 1992, pp. 171–85.

14 F. L. Gager, Jr., V. Johnson and J. C. Holmes, 'Ancient tobacco smokers', *Science*, 1960, vol. 132, p. 1021.

15 R. B. Dixon and J. B. Stetson, Jr., 'Analysis of pre-Columbian pipe dottels', *American Anthropologist*, 1922, vol. 24, pp. 245–6.

16 T. W. Haberman, 'Evidence for aboriginal tobaccos in eastern North America', *American Antiquity*, 1984, vol. 49, pp. 269–87. G. E. Wagner, 'Tobacco in prehistoric eastern North America', paper presented at the Society for American Archaeology Annual Meeting, New Orleans, 1991. Winter, op. cit. As recovery and identification methods are refined, the dating may become more precise.

17 M. Eliade, *Shamanism: Archaic Techniques of Ecstasy*, Princeton, Princeton University Press, 1964. W. G. Jilek, 'Altered states of consciousness in North American Indian ceremonials', *Ethos*, 1982, vol. 10, pp. 326–43. B. W. Lex, 'Altered states of consciousness in northern Iroquoian ritual', in A. Bharati (ed.), *The Realm of the Extra-Human: Agents and Audiences*, The Hague, Mouton, 1977, pp. 277–300. von Gernet, 'Pipe/tobacco/smoking complex', op. cit., pp. 172–3.

18 M. Dobkin de Rios, *Hallucinogens: Cross-Cultural Perspectives*, Albuquerque, University of New Mexico Press, 1984, pp. 6–7. P. T. Furst, *Flesh of the Gods*, op. cit., p. ix. Furst, *Hallucinogens and Culture*, op. cit., pp. 2–6. W. La Barre, 'Old and New World narcotics: a statistical question and an ethnological reply', *Economic Botany*, 1970, vol. 24, pp. 73–80. R. E. Schultes and A. Hofmann, *Plants of the Gods: Origins of Hallucinogenic Use*, New York, McGraw-Hill, 1979, pp. 27–30. von Gernet, 'Pipe/tobacco/smoking complex', op. cit., pp. 172–3.

19 The evidence is summarized in von Gernet, 'Pipe/tobacco/smoking complex', op. cit., pp. 176–7. Early historical records include: F. Du Creux, *The History of Canada or New France* [1664], P. J. Robinson and J. B. Conacher (eds), Toronto, Champlain Society, 1951–2, vol. 1, p. 108; M. Lescarbot, *The History of New France* [1618], W. L. Grant (ed.), Toronto, Champlain Society, 1907–14, vol. 3, pp. 177, 253. Ethnographic observations include: F. G. Speck, *Naskapi: The Savage Hunters of the Labrador Peninsula* [1935], Norman, University of Oklahoma Press, 1977, p. 226; D. Wilson, *Pipes and Tobacco: An Ethnographic Sketch*, Toronto, Lovell and Gibson, 1857, p. 22. Chemical analyses include: O. Janiger and M. Dobkin de Rios, 'Nicotiana an hallucinogen?', *Economic Botany*, 1976, vol. 30, pp. 149–51. Experimental studies include: R. K. Siegel, P. R. Collings, and J. L. Diaz, 'On the use of *Tagetes lucida* and *Nicotiana rustica* as a Huichol smoking mixture: the Aztec "Yahutli" with suggestive hallucinogenic effects', *Economic Botany*, 1977, vol. 31, pp. 16–23.

20 K. Birket-Smith, 'Drinking tube and tobacco pipe in North America', *Ethnologische Studien*, 1929, pp. 29–39.

21 von Gernet, 'Pipe/tobacco/smoking complex', op. cit., p. 178.

22 J. D. McGuire, 'Pipes and smoking customs of the American aborigines, based on material in the U.S. National Museum', in *Annual Report of the Board of Regents of the Smithsonian Institution; Report of the U.S. National Museum Part 1*, Washington, Smithsonian Institution, 1899, pp. 351–645. G. A West, 'Tobacco, pipes and smoking customs of the American Indians', *Bulletin of the Public Museum of the City of Milwaukee*, 1934, vol. 17, pp. 1–995. There

exists, in addition to these standard and oft-cited works, a staggering list of books and articles on the use of tobacco and pipes in North America. See A. von Gernet, 'The transculturation of the Amerindian pipe/tobacco/smoking complex and its impact on the intellectual boundaries between "savagery" and "civilization", 1535–1935', unpublished PhD thesis, McGill University, Montreal, 1988.

23 J. Paper, *Offering Smoke: The Sacred Pipe and Native American Religion*, Moscow, Idaho, University of Idaho Press, 1988, p. 113.

24 A. von Gernet, [Review of] 'Offering Smoke: The Sacred Pipe and Native American Religion, Jordan Paper, University of Idaho Press, Moscow, Idaho', *American Anthropologist*, 1990, vol. 92, pp. 1040–1.

25 A. von Gernet and P. Timmins, 'Pipes and parakeets: constructing meaning in an early Iroquoian context', in I. Hodder (ed.), *Archaeology as Long-Term History*, Cambridge, Cambridge University Press, 1987, pp. 31–42.

26 These works contain over 300 individual passages relating specifically to the Amerindian use of tobacco or pipes. Given the large number of citations germane to each topic, only partial lists of the most accessible references are furnished. A more thorough analysis may be found in von Gernet, 'Transculturation', op. cit.

27 J. Gerard, *The Herball or Generall Historie of Plantes*, London, 1597. Knight, op. cit., p. 126. R. Linton, 'Use of tobacco among North American Indians', *Field Museum of Natural History, Anthropology Leaflet*, 1924, no. 15, pp. 3–4. A. Skinner, 'Some Seneca tobacco customs', *Indian Notes*, 1925, vol. 2, p. 128.

28 Lescarbot, op. cit., pp. 252–4.

29 P. L. Barbour (ed.), *The Jamestown Voyages Under the First Charter 1606–1609*, Cambridge, Cambridge University Press, 1969, vol. 1, pp. 85, 140. H. P. Biggar (ed.), *The Works of Samuel de Champlain*, Toronto, Champlain Society, 1922–36, vol. 1, pp. 327–8. P. Boucher, *Canada in the Seventeenth Century*, E. L. Montizambert (ed.), Montréal, George E. Desbarats, 1883, pp. 47–8. H. S. Burrage (ed.), *Early English and French Voyages Chiefly from Hakluyt, 1534–1608*, New York, Charles Scribner's Sons, 1906, pp. 292, 349. T. De Bry, *A Brief and True Report of the New Found Land of Virginia* [*America*: Part 1 of *Grands Voyages*], Frankfurt-on-Main, 1590, plate 20. W. Strachey, *The Historie of Travell into Virginia Britania*, L. B. Wright and V. Freund (eds), Hakluyt Society, 2nd Series, no. 103, London, Hakluyt Society, 1953, p. 79. R. G. Thwaites (ed.), *The Jesuit Relations and Allied Documents*, Cleveland, Ohio, Burrows Brothers, 1896–1901, vol. 11, p. 7; vol. 23, p. 225.

30 Boucher, op. cit., p. 55. Thwaites, op. cit., vol. 15, p. 79. R. Williams, *A Key Into the Language of America: or, an Help to the Language of the Natives in that Part of America, Called New-England*, London, 1643, pp. 14–15.

31 References to tobacco rites are scattered throughout the early historical record. See, for example, the following sources: E. Arber (ed.), *Travels and Works of Captain John Smith*, Edinburgh, John Grant, 1910, vol. 1, pp. 21–2, 77, 372–3; Barbour, op. cit., vol. 1, pp. 104, 143, 145–6; Biggar, op. cit., vol. 1, pp. 443–5; vol. 2, pp. 301–2; De Bry, op. cit., p. 16; C. Le Clercq, *First Establishment of the Faith in New France* [1691], J. G. Shea (ed.), New York, J. G. Shea, 1881, vol. 1, p. 216; G. Sagard, *The Long Journey to the Country of the Hurons* [1632], G. M. Wrong (ed.), Toronto, Champlain Society, 1939, pp. 171, 189, 197–8; Thwaites, op. cit., vol. 10, pp. 159, 165–7; vol. 13, pp. 31–3, 203, 259–67; vol. 19, p. 87; vol. 20, p. 51; vol. 23, p. 55; vol. 26, pp. 309–11; vol. 39, p. 13.

32 J. W. Springer, 'An ethnohistoric study of the smoking complex in eastern North America', *Ethnohistory*, 1981, vol. 28, p. 229.

33 Arber, op. cit., vol. 1, pp. 78, 374. H. P. Biggar (ed.), *The Voyages of Jacques Cartier*, Publications of the Public Archives of Canada 11, Ottawa, F. A. Acland, 1924, pp. 183–5. Boucher, op. cit., pp. 47–8. Burrage, op. cit., pp. 375–6. De Bry, op. cit., p. 16. Le Clercq, op. cit., vol. 1, pp. 217–18. Lescarbot, op. cit., vol. 3, pp. 164, 176–7, 252–4. Sagard, op. cit., pp. 62, 88, 121. Strachey, op. cit., p. 94; Thwaites, op. cit., vol. 3, p. 117; vol. 5, pp. 111–13, 159–61; vol. 9, p. 273; vol. 10, p. 173; vol. 17, pp. 81–3, 127; vol. 18, p. 187; vol. 20, pp. 185–7; vol. 27, p. 157; vol. 29, p. 157; vol. 32, pp. 229–30; vol. 38, p. 253. Williams, op. cit., pp. 44–5.

34 Thwaites, op. cit., vol. 7, p. 137.

35 Thwaites, op. cit., vol. 17, pp. 81–3, 127; vol. 18, p. 187; vol. 20, pp. 185–7; vol. 27, p. 157; vol. 29, p. 157; vol. 32, pp. 229–30.

36 Biggar, *The Voyages of Jacques Cartier*, op. cit., pp. 183–5. T. C. Holm, *Description of the Province of New Sweden, Now Called, by the English, Pennsylvania, In America* [1702], P. S. Du Ponceau (ed.), Philadelphia, M'Carty and Davis, 1834, p. 122; Lescarbot, op. cit., vol. 3, pp. 252–4. Williams, op. cit., pp. 44–5. A. Young, *Chronicles of the Pilgrim Fathers of the Colony of Plymouth, from 1602 to 1625*, Boston, Charles C. Little and James Brown, 1844, p. 363.

37 D. G. Smith, 'Stylistic variation in Middleport smoking pipes', in Hayes III, op. cit., pp. 15–30. A. von Gernet, 'Analysis of intrasite artifact spatial distributions: the Draper Site smoking pipes', *Museum of Indian Archaeology Research Report* 16, London, Canada, University of Western Ontario, 1985, pp. 1–271.

38 Barbour, op. cit., vol. 1, pp. 135–6. Biggar, *The Voyages of Jacques Cartier*, op. cit., pp. 183–5. Burrage, op. cit., pp. 125–6, 333, 375–6. N. Denys, *The Description and Natural History of the Coasts of North America (Acadia)*, W. F. Ganong (ed.), Toronto, Champlain Society, 1908, pp. 424–5. Holm, op. cit., p. 130. J. F. Jameson (ed.), *Narratives of New Netherland 1609–1664*, New York, Charles Scribner's Sons, 1909, p. 57. C. H. Levermore (ed.), *Forerunners and Competitors of the Pilgrims and Puritans . . . 1601–1625*, Brooklyn, New England Society, 1912, vol. 1, p. 46; vol. 2, pp. 398, 411, 413–14. A. C. Myers (ed.), *Narratives of Early Pennsylvania, West New Jersey and Delaware 1630–1707*, New York, Charles Scribner's Sons, 1912, pp. 16–17. Thwaites, op. cit., vol. 7, pp. 137–9. Williams, op. cit., pp. 44–5. W. Wood, *New Englands Prospect* [1634], Boston, E. M. Boynton, 1898, p. 65.

39 Arber, op. cit., vol. 1, pp. 53–4, 350; vol. 2, p. 423. J. E. Brooks (ed.), *Tobacco: Its History Illustrated by the Books, Manuscripts and Engravings in the Library of George Arents. Jr.*, New York, Rosenbach, 1937–52, vol. 1, p. 320; vol. 2, p. 90. Denys, op. cit., pp. 424–5. Holm, op. cit., p. 130. Lescarbot, op. cit., vol. 3, pp. 252–4. von Gernet, 'Transculturation', op. cit., p. 116. Williams, op. cit., pp. 44–5.

40 J. Paper, 'The Iroquoian and pan-Indian sacred pipes: comparative ritual and symbolism,' in Hayes III, op. cit., pp. 163–9.

41 Sagard, op. cit., p. 197. von Gernet, 'Analysis of intrasite artifact spatial distributions', op. cit., pp. 146–53.

42 Biggar, *The Works of Samuel de Champlain*, op. cit., vol. 1, pp. 114–15.

43 Biggar, *The Voyages of Jacques Cartier*, op. cit., pp. 183–5. Lescarbot, op. cit., vol. 3, pp. 194, 252–4. Sagard, op. cit., pp. 98–9. Thwaites, op. cit., vol. 6, p. 173; vol. 7, pp. 137–9; vol. 12, p. 117; vol. 28, pp. 293–5. Williams, op. cit., p. 73.

44 Arber, op. cit., vol. 2, p. 429. Biggar, *The Voyages of Jacques Cartier*, op. cit., pp. 183–5. Burrage, op. cit., p. 348. De Bry, op. cit., plate 16. S. A. Dickson,

Panacea or Precious Bane: Tobacco in Sixteenth-Century Literature, New York, New York Public Library, 1954, p. 140. Lescarbot, op. cit., vol. 3, pp. 252–4. Sagard, op. cit., pp. 85, 102. Strachey, op. cit., pp. 174–204. Thwaites, op. cit., vol. 5, p. 131; vol. 10, p. 209; vol. 13, pp. 31–3; vol. 15, p. 155; vol. 19, p. 173; vol. 24, pp. 39–41, 89; vol. 25, pp. 123–5; vol. 38, p. 253. Williams, op. cit., pp. 44–5, 113. Young, op. cit., pp. 186–8. 194.

45 Thwaites, op. cit., vol. 3, p. 117.

46 Biggar, *The Works of Samuel de Champlain*, op. cit., vol. 1, pp. 98–101, 295; vol. 2, pp. 69, 282–4. C. C. Hall (ed.), *Narratives of Early Maryland 1633–1684*, New York, Charles Scribner's Sons, 1910, p. 45. Jameson, op. cit., p. 109. Lescarbot, op. cit., vol. 3, p. 204. Sagard, op. cit., pp. 88, 150. Thwaites, op. cit., vol. 10, p. 219; vol. 15, p. 27; vol. 26, p. 161; vol. 28, pp. 293–5; vol. 38, p. 253. Williams, op. cit., p. 55. Young, op. cit., pp. 210, 307.

47 The literature on the history and ethnology of calumet ceremonialism is vast. For useful summaries see: D. J. Blakeslee, 'The origin and spread of the calumet ceremony', *American Antiquity*, 1981, vol. 46, pp. 759–68; I. W. Brown, 'The calumet ceremony in the Southeast and its archaeological manifestations', *American Antiquity*, 1989, vol. 54, pp. 311–31; W. N. Fenton, 'The Iroquois eagle dance, an offshoot of the calumet dance', *Bureau of American Ethnology Bulletin*, 156, Washington, DC, Smithsonian Institution, 1953; G. Hafner, 'Das Calumet und seine Beziehungen zum nordamerikanischen Südwesten', in *Akten des 34. Internationalen Amerikanistenkongresses* [1960], Vienna, Ferdinand Berger, Horn, 1962, pp. 564–8; R. L. Hall, 'The evolution of the calumet-pipe', in G. E. Gibbon (ed.), *Prairie Archaeology: Papers in Honor of David A. Baerris*, University of Minnesota Publications in Anthropology, 1983, vol. 3, pp. 37–52; Paper, *Offering Smoke*, op. cit.; W. Schroeter, *Calumet: Der heilige Rauch, Pfeifen und Pfeifenkulte bei den nordamerikanischen Indianern*, Wyk auf Foehr, Germany, Verlag für Amerikanistik, 1989; Springer, op. cit.; W. A. Turnbaugh, 'Calumet ceremonialism as a nativistic response', *American Antiquity*, 1979, vol. 44, pp. 685–91; von Gernet, 'Transculturation', op. cit., pp. 291–302.

48 Holm, op. cit., p. 130. Lescarbot, op. cit., vol. 3, pp. 176–7, 252–4. Sagard, op. cit., p. 88. Thwaites, op. cit., vol. 27, pp. 285, 301.

49 F. Jennings, W. Fenton, M. Druke and D. Miller (eds), *The History and Culture of Iroquois Diplomacy: An Interdisciplinary Guide to the Treaties of the Six Nations and Their League*, Syracuse, Syracuse University Press, 1985, p. 121.

50 Thwaites, op. cit., vol. 24, p. 281; vol. 26, p. 43; vol. 39, p. 65.

51 Barbour, op. cit., vol. 1, p. 84. Biggar, *The Works of Samuel de Champlain*, op. cit., vol. 1, pp. 98–101, 114–15; vol. 2, pp. 86, 282–4. Denys, op. cit., p. 419. Jameson, op. cit., p. 177. Lescarbot, op. cit., vol. 3, pp. 252–4. Sagard, op. cit., pp. 112–13. Thwaites, op. cit., vol. 7, pp. 137–9; vol. 32, p. 271. Williams, op. cit., p. 189.

52 Brooks, op. cit., vol. 1, p. 256. Burrage, op. cit., pp. 125–6. Dickson, op. cit., p. 44. S. A. Dickson and P. H. O'Neil (eds), *Tobacco: A Catalogue of the Books, Manuscripts, and Engravings Acquired Since 1942 in the Arents Tobacco Collection at the New York Public Library*, New York, New York Public Library, 1958–69, vol. 2, pp. 86–7. Holm, op. cit., p. 121. Lescarbot, op. cit., vol. 3, pp. 190, 194, 252–4, 266. Sagard, op. cit., pp. 62, 199. Thwaites, op. cit., vol. 7, pp. 137–9; vol. 10, p. 203; vol. 32, p. 271.

53 Holm, op. cit., p. 121. Sagard, op. cit., p. 199. Thwaites, op. cit., vol. 10, p. 203; vol. 13, p. 157.

54 Thwaites, op. cit., vol. 7, p. 23.

55 Dickson, op. cit. von Gernet, 'Transculturation', op. cit., pp. 32, 86, 499.

56 Biggar, *The Voyages of Jacques Cartier*, op. cit., pp. 183–5.
57 Brooks, op. cit., vol. 1, pp. 217–19.
58 von Gernet, 'Transculturation', op. cit., pp. 21–34.
59 Burrage, op. cit., pp. 125–6.
60 von Gernet, 'Transculturation', op. cit., pp. 34–7.
61 De Bry, op. cit., p. 16.
62 von Gernet, 'Transculturation', op. cit., pp. 258–63.
63 Dickson, op. cit., p. 195.
64 Dickson, op. cit., p. 54.
65 Brooks, op. cit., vol. 1, pp. 271–4. von Gernet, 'Pipe/tobacco/smoking complex', op. cit., p. 177.
66 A seventeenth-century example of the association between tobacco and drunkenness is afforded by the title of a well-known treatise on the subject: J. Balde, *Die Truckene Trunkenheit*, Nürnberg, 1658.
67 K. T. Kell, 'Tobacco in folk cures in Western society', *Journal of American Folklore*, 1965, vol. 78, pp. 102–4. D. B. Quinn, *Set Fair for Roanoke: Voyages and Colonies, 1584–1606*, Chapel Hill and London, University of North Carolina Press, 1985, pp. 434–5. von Gernet, 'Transculturation', op. cit., pp. 24, 59–60.
68 N. Monardes, *Joyfull Newes Out of the Newe Founde Worlde*, J. Frampton (ed.), London, 1577. The tobacco-as-panacea idea persisted despite circumstantial evidence that tobacco had serious deleterious effects. For example, Thomas Hariot, whose early descriptions helped popularize the habit and who had been taught to exhale through the nasal passages by the North Carolina Algonquians, had, by 1615, contracted cancer of the nose, from which he eventually died (von Gernet, 'Transculturation', op. cit., p. 37).
69 Biggar, *The Voyages of Jacques Cartier*, op. cit., pp. 183–5. Brooks, op. cit., vol. 1, p. 322; vol. 2, p. 156. Burrage, op. cit., pp. 125–6. De Bry, op. cit., p. 16. Dickson, op. cit., p. 44. Lescarbot, op. cit., vol. 3, pp. 176–7, 252–4. Sagard, op. cit., p. 88. Thwaites, op. cit., vol. 3, p. 117. Williams, op. cit., pp. 14–15.
70 Lescarbot, op. cit., vol. 3, p. 164. Sagard, op. cit., p. 121.
71 von Gernet, 'Transculturation', op. cit., pp. 326–34.
72 Brooks, vol. 1, p. 226.
73 James I, King of England, *A Counter-Blaste to Tobacco* [1604], Pennsylvania and London, Rodale, Emmaus, 1954, p. 12. For a recent interpretation of this famous statement on tobacco and its place within contemporary English politics and medicine see D. I. Harley, 'The beginnings of the tobacco controversy: Puritanism, James I, and the Royal Physicians', *Bulletin of the History of Medicine*, 1993, vol. 67, pp. 28–50.
74 von Gernet, 'Transculturation', op. cit., pp. 69–77, 320–35.
75 The term *transculturation* was introduced by the Cuban scholar Fernando Ortiz (see Bronislaw Malinowski's discussion of the neologism in F. Ortiz, *Cuban Counterpoint: Tobacco and Sugar*, New York, Alfred A. Knopf, 1947, pp. ix–xi). I have revived it from the neologistic graveyard to describe the bilateral and interdependent historical trajectories of tobacco in post-Columbian America and Europe. See von Gernet, 'Transculturation', op. cit.
76 G. Arciniegas, *America in Europe: a History of the New World in Reverse*, San Diego, Harcourt Brace Jovanovich, 1986. W. Brandon, *New Worlds for Old: Reports From the New World and Their Effect on the Development of Social Thought in Europe*, 1500–1800, Athens, Ohio, University of Ohio Press, 1986. F. Chiappelli (ed.), *First Images of America: the Impact of the New World on the Old*, Berkeley, University of California Press, 1976.
77 Lescarbot, op. cit., vol. 3, pp. 252–4. Thwaites, op. cit., vol. 3, p. 117.

78 An excellent example of the prominent role of tobacco, pipes and smoking may be found in the records of the Hudson's Bay Company Fur Trade. See A. Ray and D. Freeman, *Give us Good Measure: An Economic Analysis of Relations Between the Indians and the Hudson's Bay Company Before 1763*, Toronto, University of Toronto Press, 1978, pp. 53–62.
79 D. B. Quinn (ed.), *New American World: A Documentary History of North America to 1612*, New York, Arno and Hector Bye, 1979, vol. 4, p. 120.
80 Ibid., vol. 5, p. 123.
81 Biggar, *The Works of Samuel de Champlain*, op. cit, vol. 1, pp. 283–4.
82 Burrage, op. cit., pp. 372–3.
83 von Gernet, 'Transculturation', op. cit., pp. 132, 255.
84 C. T., *Advice How to Plant Tobacco in England . . . With the Danger of the Spanish Tobacco*, London, 1615. The identity of C. T. remains unknown.
85 von Gernet, 'Transculturation', op. cit., pp. 77–8, 133–86.
86 J. M. Price, *France and the Chesapeake: A History of the French Tobacco Monopoly, 1684–1791, and of Its Relationship to the British and American Tobacco Trades*, Ann Arbor, University of Michigan Press, 1973, pp. 3–4.
87 Thwaites, op. cit., vol. 4, p. 207.
88 Biggar, *The Works of Samuel de Champlain*, op. cit., vol. 3, pp. 38–9.
89 von Gernet, 'Transculturation', op. cit., pp. 187–257.
90 Ibid., pp. 340–69
91 Burrage, op. cit., pp. 367–8, 370.
92 Arber, op. cit., vol. 1, p. 108; vol. 2, p. 412.
93 von Gernet, 'Transculturation', op. cit., pp. 264–5.
94 J. Neander, *Tabacologia*, Leiden, 1622.
95 W. Wood, *New Englands Prospect* [1634], Boston, E. M. Boynton, 1898, p. 65.
96 von Gernet, 'Transculturation', op. cit., pp. 312–14.
97 Turnbaugh, 'Tobacco, pipes, smoking and rituals', op. cit. W. A. Turnbaugh, 'Elements of a nativistic pipe ceremonialism in the post-contact Northeast', *Pennsylvania Archaeologist*, 1977, vol. 47(4), pp. 1–7.
98 von Gernet, 'Transculturation', op. cit., pp. 303–9.
99 E. S. Burch, Jr., 'War and trade', in W. W. Fitzhugh and A. Crowell (eds), *Crossroads of Continents: Cultures of Siberia and Alaska*, Smithsonian Institution, Washington, 1988, p. 235.
100 G. Sherman, 'Tobacco pipes of the Western Eskimos,' *The Beaver*, 1972, vol. 303, pp. 49–51.
101 Eliade, op. cit., pp. 288–97.
102 von Gernet, 'Transculturation', op. cit., pp. 380–485.
103 J. T. McCullen, Jr., 'Indian tobacco myths concerning the origin of tobacco', *New York Folklore Quarterly*, 1967, vol. 23, pp. 264–73.

4

EFFICACY AND CONCENTRATION

Analogies in betel use among the Fuyuge (Papua New Guinea)[1]

Eric Hirsch

INTRODUCTION

The people who form the focus of this chapter, the Fuyuge of Papua New Guinea, did not chew betelnut at the time of first European contact (*c.* 1900). This fact is brought out in accounts of the colonial administration patrols that first visited the area. The attention of the patrol officers appears to have been very quickly drawn to the teeth of Fuyuge men and women, and comparisons made between their white, unstained teeth and the heavily stained teeth of the betelnut-chewing coastal populations (with whom they had more familiarity). Eighty years later, as we shall see, this situation had altered radically.

There are three essential ingredients to the betelnut chew: the Areca palm nut; the leaf, stem or catkin of the *Piper betle* plant; and slaked lime. When using the term betelnut in this chapter reference is made to all three ingredients. Betelnut can be chewed either in quid form or in mixture.[2] Fuyuge men and women chew betelnut in the second of these two ways. A scene often observed among the Fuyuge today can be described as follows:

> A man or woman has an areca nut to share with others present and they all sit down together to enjoy the chew. The green palm nut, often the size of a golf ball, is cut open. Inside its tough, fibrous skin is the fruit, about one-half the size of the nut. This is divided into the requisite number of portions and one piece distributed to each of those present.[3] This is placed in the mouth and chewed with an aromatic leaf. Finally, portions of lime are added to the chew. Fuyuge men and women carry lime in small tin containers with tightly fitting lids (these are often used baking-powder tins from the mission station). Inside the tin is kept a short thin stick. The stick is wetted in the mouth, dipped in the lime and the lime cling-

> ing to the stick sucked into the mouth. This is done several times until the chewer has obtained enough lime to create the red saliva that is linked to the potency of the chew. Usually one lime container is passed around to each person present.[4]

Nine alkaloids form the active ingedients of the areca nut, with arecoline the most abundant and arecaidine also actively important.

> The former is hydrolized to the latter by calcium hydroxide, that is, by the lime that is chewed with the nut. The chewing of the three ingredients produces bright red saliva by a chemical process . . . the alkaloids from the nut and an essential oil from the betel pepper are responsible for the euphoric properties of the chew. . . . The suffused appearance, feeling of well-being, good humour and *the undoubtedly increased capacity for activity provide a typical picture.*[5]

Unlike more familar psychoactive substances such as coffee or tobacco, betelnut is not well known among European and North American populations. Its use, however, covers an extensive area – from the coast of East Africa to Polynesia and as far north as the China coast. As noted by Mac Marshall, between one-tenth and one-quarter of the world population regularly chew betelnut, 'making this humanity's fourth most widely used drug after nicotine, ethanol and caffeine'.[6]

In the Pacific context, betelnut is one of two prominent psychoactive substances, the other being *kava*. At the same time, *kava* use is similar to that of betelnut in that it is often consumed with little formal ceremony or as part of elaborate ritual systems. Earlier this century W. H. R. Rivers noted that the distribution of these two substances was almost mutually exclusive.[7] He attempted to account for this distribution with a theory of cultural migrations and diffusions of two separate peoples: the '*kava*-people' who came first, and the 'betel-people' who later displaced them. Although Rivers' theory is not taken seriously today, as Brunton has recently noted, Rivers identified an important problem: namely, the uneven and scattered distribution of *kava*, a problem that has preoccupied a number of recent scholars.[8] Similar attention has yet to be given to the distribution of betelnut use in the South Pacific. This may be due to its more widespread use beyond the societies of the South Pacific and its commonly accepted origins in the Malay Peninsula.[9] Given this widespread distribution, though, betelnut use has recently expanded into large population areas, such as highland Papua New Guinea, where previously its use was far more restricted.

Betelnut is chewed in mundane, everyday contexts, and quantities are 'concentrated' for specific uses in ritual, a point returned to below. When I came to live among the Fuyuge during the mid-1980s the situation had changed significantly from that reported earlier this century by

Williamson[10] and in colonial government-sponsored patrol reports.[11] Fuyuge men and women were now avid chewers of betelnut and were keen to obtain the chew at any opportunity. However, unlike their coastal neighbours, access to supplies of betelnut among the Fuyuge was very limited.[12] Betelnut's range of psychoactive properties can help account for its desirability and Fuyuge avidness for it as a chew. The effects associated with these properties were often mentioned to me as the reason Fuyuge men and women enjoyed chewing. The nature of these properties is an undoubtedly important factor in the adoption and widespread use of betelnut among the Fuyuge. But it is only part of the picture.

As significant are the changes in relations among the societies of Papua New Guinea that have been brought about since the arrival of Europeans. This is a complex history which involved, among other developments, the establishment of colonial states (British and German in the late nineteenth century) and more recently (1975) an independent nation-state. One of the important factors involved in this process is the marked change in inter-regional trade and exchange associated with the growth of towns, urban centres, and a monetary economy. Prior to colonial intervention, trade and exchange among societies throughout the region were symbiotic: the objective was not profit but sustenance. Valued cultural resources from one group (e.g., mountain-bird plumes) were traded for valued resources found among another group (e.g., coastal shells). Betelnut was one among numerous resources traded and exchanged in this manner. Since colonial intervention, and particularly after the Second World War, many of the systems of regional trade and exchange have discontinued, as valued resources are now channelled to commercial markets in towns and urban centres.

What has emerged are cultural groups which, because of their geographical proximity and local ecology, have been able to gain control of the urban market trade. This is particularly evident in the case of betelnut. Its consumption has now come to be associated with a distinctly Papua New Guinean metropolitan lifestyle. At the same time, the ecological sources of this substance are limited and as a result several cultural groups have been able to amass substantial monetary wealth to the exclusion of groups like the Fuyuge. In post-colonial Papua New Guinea betelnut has now emerged as an index of the ability to participate in a metropolitan-centred culture whose ascendancy has resonances in regions throughout Papua New Guinea. The prominence of betelnut in contemporary Papua New Guinea is linked to a rebalancing of power relations that has been brought about through the changes which have occurred to inter-regional trade and exchange systems.

In short, the psychoactive properties of betelnut have taken on a particular salience because the properties themselves are indicative of a set of experiences that extend beyond the betelnut chew itself. Betelnut has come to be perceived differently because the socio-historical context of a people like the Fuyuge has changed in relation to European incursion and the development of metropolitan centres, such as Port Moresby. The interest in betelnut among the Fuyuge is closely related to its prominence in this more distant context, but in a manner that relates to distinctly Fuyuge concerns and practices.[13]

Everyday and ritual uses of betelnut evoke particular analogies linked to the factors outlined above. Central among these are analogies between betelnut use and notions of efficacy and concentration. The avidness for chewing that Fuyuge men and women show towards betelnut in everyday contexts takes on a transformed appearance in the use they make of it in their ritual performances. In these performances large quantities of betelnut are brought together and displayed for varying periods as part of specific ritual sequences. There is thus a dynamic interaction between the accumulations attempted in ritual and the personal desire to chew and seek out betelnut for individual use. One context (everyday limited access) continually creates the conditions for the other context (ritual concentration).[14] It is through each that Fuyuge men and women make evident their efficacy in the transformed contexts created by European incursion.

EFFICACY AND CONCENTRATION

It is perhaps appropriate at this point to clarify briefly what is meant by the related notions of efficacy and concentration. An example from close to home may be used to set the scene. Consider the image of a smoke-filled room where important decisions and/or deals are made. In such rooms men and women meet to 'concentrate' their minds around some issue ('brainstorming' or 'deal-making'). The ability to solve a problem or strike a complicated deal can be defined as 'efficacy' and this quality is made apparent through particular forms of concentration (the room filled with cigarette/cigar smoke, focused minds around a space, e.g., a large table, where this is achieved). A person is efficacious if he or she obtains a desired outcome through concentration. In such contexts the consumption of food in an everyday manner is perceived as distracting and is consigned to a peripheral position (hence the emphasis on fast foods): to engage in everyday forms of eating would be seen as evidence of taking one's mind off the task at hand. The predominance of non-food substances (tobacco, coffee, etc.) allows the mind to be released from hunger and thinking of food, while at the same time sharpening it to the desired outcome.

In the Papua New Guinea context, as has often been observed, men and women perceive the outcome of any action or event as surrounded by uncertainty.[15] The ability to achieve an action or event as anticipated, is an indication of a person's capacities. A person is seen as having efficacy when he or she is perceived by others as having the ability to achieve actions and events in an anticipated manner. For example, there is a Fuyuge notion, *aked*, which I translate as efficacious men. Often during fieldwork I would ask someone when an anticipated event was going to take place. Invariably I would be told that he or she (the person I was asking) did not know, but that the *aked* knew (i.e. it was the *aked* who had the capacities to make things happen; it was 'they' – unspecified efficacious others – who 'knew').

In addition to the *aked* there is another category of persons that stands out in this regard: the person of the *amede*, which I translate as chief. Fuyuge men and women say that an *amede* allows them to sustain themselves as efficacious. He is seen as having specific 'holding together' capacities which become explicit in ritual contexts. In such contexts, persons and objects need to be 'concentrated' into a single space for the performance of ritual events. The ability to achieve these concentrations is fraught with uncertainty depending on the will and desires of others. The chief is perceived as able to co-ordinate such concentrations. To achieve this, the minds of men and women need to be focused or 'concentrated' in a specific manner. The notion of concentration, then, has two related meanings: physical accumulation and the focusing of the mind in order to achieve this – one is an index of the other. As we shall see, betelnut among the Fuyuge is inextricably linked with these two forms of concentration and the sense of efficacy demonstrated by the ability to achieve these.

As the presence of the person of the chief makes evident, there is a 'resistance factor'[16] that needs to be overcome in these forms of concentration. The more resistance (e.g., scarcity, will/desire) that needs to be mastered in accomplishing the anticipated outcome, the more spectacular the event will appear to those who have come to witness it. An analogous factor of resistance operates at the level of mundane consumption. As Alfred Gell, following Simmel, has noted, the symbolic value of a good is related to the amount of resistance (monetary, spatial, etc.) that needs to be overcome before any act of consumption can take place.[17] The 'symbolic load' that betelnut carries among the contemporary Fuyuge is directly related to the resistance involved in its acquisition. The social processes which make necessary the presence of the chief ('holding together', overcoming resistance) have brought betelnut into perspective and endowed it with a specific resistance-engendering symbolic value.[18] But this has only become possible under particular socio-historical conditions: on the one hand, where betelnut has become a widely sold market commodity in Port Moresby, and on the other hand, where its presence is extremely limited in contexts like that of the Fuyuge.

URBAN SCENARIO: VILLAGE ANALOGY

The casual vistor to Port Moresby will immediately notice men and women selling betelnut throughout the city on street-corners, on pavements next to the sides of buildings, or in large markets. In each context one finds the seller seated on the ground, usually in a cross-legged position with individual piles of betelnut neatly arranged on a cloth or opened-up sack laid out in front of her or him. Each pile has the same number of nuts (of roughly the same quality) with a set price for each pile. If one wants to buy betelnut from these sellers, individual piles of betel are purchased; one betel at a time, for example, cannot be bought (unless, of course, the 'piles' themselves consist of one item each). What is exchanged are one 'unit' of betelnut for one 'unit' of money.

This form of selling and buying, however, is not restricted to betelnut. All other foods for sale in the market (such as sweet potatoes, greens, yams, etc.) are sold in this same unit for unit way:

> Here vendors expect to sell their product in certain sized bundles. They do not lower prices or increase bundle sizes to meet flagging demand. On the contrary, women [for example] may prefer to take the produce home or return the following day to clear their stock. Yet their operating on a basis of one bundle of food for one denomination of money does not mean that the market rate is standardised. The size of the bundles may well fluctuate from day to day.[19]

As Modjeska has observed: 'Urban Melanesians do not ordinarily evaluate transactions on the basis of a quantity for quantity ratio (for example weight for price) but rather by comparing qualities per unit offered at unit prices.'[20]

More generally, then, as is evidenced by these transactions, there is a substitution of one unit for one unit. Men and women do not base their transactions on some underlying system of value to which the items are compared. Rather, value is an emergent property (made visible through transactions) and it is only units reckoned to be analogous to one another that can be exchanged (i.e. are substitutable).

The same holds true for persons in the village setting of the Fuyuge (and more generally in Melanesia). It is only by transforming themselves into 'units' (e.g., 'hosts', 'dancers', etc.) that relations between persons can be made. Betelnut is an element in the sets of analogies (substitutable units) that are made visible in Fuyuge ritual. Only persons transformed into units which are seen to evoke notions of efficacy (i.e. have been appropriately 'concentrated') can be brought into relationship. Betelnut has emerged historically in the Fuyuge context as an index of the capacity to mobilize or bring together and thus demonstrate efficacy in the ritual context.

ERIC HIRSCH

BETELNUT IN PAPUA NEW GUINEA

Many casual observers have likened betelnut-chewing to the Western custom of coffee drinking. It appears to occur at relatively frequent intervals and with little formal ritual surrounding its use. Its users even include young children. However, until the last few decades betelnut use in Papua New Guinea was confined mostly to coastal and riverain areas, many of the islands around the mainland and some highland fringe areas. Since then it has spread (via the highlands highway) and been adopted into New Guinea highland societies where the majority of the country's population resides.

The rapid expansion of betelnut use in the period after 1945 has been accompanied by commercialization: 'As urban centres have developed in the Pacific, a market for betelnut has grown up among those wage employees and others who have migrated to the city and have little or no access to land on which to grow betelnut ingredients'.[21] A large proportion of this demand in Port Moresby has been filled by the Mekeo people who live 100 km west of the city.[22] Since the 1970s they have been able to drive trucks on a daily basis to the city (along the Hiritano Highway) in order to sell betelnut at the numerous markets. Before the construction of this highway, the Mekeo brought their betelnut to Port Moresby by boat or by plane. As a result of this lucrative trade, the Mekeo have accumulated money which is used to purchase lorries and consumer durables. Other cultural groups are excluded from these sources of money, consumer goods and the practices that go with this lifestyle. The Fuyuge, as neighbours of the Mekeo, are one such people. On the other side of the country other groups who travel up the highlands highway from Lae to sell betelnut in the vast New Guinea highlands region accumulate equally large revenue.[23] The most desired types of betelnut derive from a limited number of ecologically suitable sites, none of which naturally occurs in highland areas.

The commercialization of betelnut is linked to its psychoactive properties. Betelnut allows the body to perform for extended periods of time without food, stimulates the mind to different forms of concentration, and, as noted above, sustains a general feeling of well-being. As Wari Iamo has noted among the Keakalo who live along the coast in the Central Province, east of Port Moresby, 'people chew betelnut to enhance work and other social activities in which they take part'.[24] This was a property stressed to me numerous times during my fieldwork among the Fuyuge. On those occasions when I ventured to Port Moresby my hosts would instantly ask for betelnut upon my return. The intense excitement and joy that were expressed when I produced betelnut for general consumption were an indication of how greatly it was valued, but also how limited were the local sources of this substance.

THE PERSPECTIVE FROM THE FUYUGE

The Fuyuge live in the Wharton Ranges about 100 km north-west of Port Moresby. The Fuyuge number around 14,000 and their population is concentrated in five river valleys. Each of these populations has a distinct origin and migration history. Within each river valley the population is divided into a number of named units based on a shared territory and dialect. These are referred to as places (*bu*) or more commonly 'homes' (*em*).[25] I lived in the 'home' of Visi which has a population of roughly 450.

The Fuyuge were incorporated into the colonial state over a period of several decades between 1900 and 1950.[26] Unlike their coastal neighbours or the demographically more dense highland populations on the New Guinea side of the country, the Fuyuge have not been integrated into the state and metropolitan markets via a major road. With the exception of a number of small mission or government airstrips, the Fuyuge remain relatively isolated from Port Moresby and its open-market economy where betelnut is sold.

When betelnut[27] is available men and women will chew it among themselves in small groups, dividing the nut into as many portions as there are persons present. As noted, it is chewed because of the psychoactive effects it produces as well as for its capacity to allow the person to sustain arduous activities while avoiding the effects of hunger. While other foods such as sugarcane are more frequently eaten for this latter purpose, the appeal of betelnut is due to its psychoactive effect, and the analogies this effect has with images and modes of conduct that may be construed as 'metropolitan'.[28]

Because (as with any food) it is not possible to exclude a person present when chewing betelnut, since to do so is to be labelled 'greedy', men and women take care only to disclose that they have betelnut when they want to share it. At the same time, to have it known that one has betelnut stored away which is not being shared with others is to fall into the same category of greediness. There is thus a precariousness present in the everyday use of betelnut because supplies and access are so limited. If it is known that one has betelnut, then this should always be disclosed and it shared out; if one does not have betelnut, one is always keen to find a source. This situation is, however, momentarily 'eclipsed' in the context of ritual performances.

Betelnut has a prominent place in contemporary Fuyuge ritual. The ritual is known as *gab* and is enacted by a 'home' or section of a 'home'. A specially built village is constructed for the purpose. It consists of an oval-shaped plaza with houses around its perimeter. All of the events of the ritual are staged and performed in this plaza. What is stressed by Fuyuge men and women is the ordering or staging of the ritual: the manner in which particular sequences are organized and accomplished in the plaza. Men and women are concerned with what they can see in this space. If a sequence is perceived to be performed incorrectly, men and women will not hesitate to indicate their disapproval. In this context the hosts can demonstrate their efficacy in performing the sequences in an expected way (or with permitted innovations) and spectators of various sorts can watch and scrutinize their efforts. These are not two separate activities (host and spectator) but rather two dimensions of a single process of image creation. Each sequence staged in the *gab* anticipates the following one.[29] At various points in this sequence large quantities of betelnut are gathered together from within Fuyuge lands, neighbouring lands and the coast and Port Moresby.

Men and women say that they come together to organize and perform a *gab* around an *amede* (chief).[30] As indicated above, a chief only manifests his capacities in the collective context of the *gab*. The Fuyuge say that without a chief they cannot perform the *gab* and without the performance of a *gab* they cannot sustain themselves as unshameful men and women.[31] To appear shameful is to appear as unefficacious and thus without purpose; that is, to appear peripheral. The chief is conceptualized as having 'holding together' (concentrating) capacities, in relation to persons, objects, words and minds.

Related to the image of the chief is the Fuyuge image of personhood. The Fuyuge person is conceptualized as someone brought into being through the social actions of others. The person is composed of a number of elements (body, mind, heart/will, spirit and skin). The significance of skin (*hode*) should be highlighted. The same word is used analogously to refer to bodily substance and the bark of trees. In addition, the land within any home is divided among a number of *hode*. Each person is composed of skin (*hode*) acquired from his or her father and mother. The significance of skin lies in its image of appearing to hold things together, bodies as well as social relations. Men and women imagine themselves as sharing a similar skin by drawing an analogy with a tree sharing a number of branches from a single trunk. The chief is like the base and persons (branches) are held together from this source. This image is given concrete form when betel bunches used in the *gab* are hung on branches of a tree placed in the centre of the ritual plaza.[32]

ANALOGIES IN A RITUAL CONTEXT

Fuyuge men and women say that they stage their *gab* ritual in a manner analogous to the way the bowerbird arranges his bower in the forests above their villages.[33] The bowerbird is said to construct his bower around the sapling of a young tree. Around this sapling the male bird creates the plaza in which he dances while female bowerbirds sit perched on nearby trees watching his performance. An analogous centre is formed as the focal point in the human *gab*, and it is here, on forest trees, that betelnut bunches are hung. The bird is said to decorate his bower with pieces of 'rubbish' from the forest floor – 'his yams'. Men and women say that like the bower they create a plaza around a centre of trees cut from the forest. Like the bowerbird they decorate the sides of their plaza – in this case, with cultivated yams. And again, like the bowerbird, men and women dance in the *gab* plaza to appear efficacious and powerful and in the course of which men and women become attracted to one another. Like the bowerbird, then, men and women say that they concentrate in a particular manner in order to appear efficacious.

The analogy made between the bowerbird *gab* and that of the human *gab* draws our attention to the way in which the Fuyuge, like other Melanesians,[34] reveal to themselves their conventions by having them concealed in different forms. What is important about the description above is the manner in which betelnut makes its appearance during different phases of the ritual: towards the beginning of the ritual when the ritual hosts make explicit their intention to engage in relations of exchange (substitution of units) with categories of invited 'guests' (dancers, exchange partners); and towards the end of the ritual when these intentions must be demonstrated as capacities to fulfil the anticipated outcome.

REVEALING THE INTENTION TO CONCENTRATE

Unlike the everyday use of betelnut, the large quantities of betelnut accumulated in the *gab* ritual are displayed so as *not* to be immediately chewed. Eventually they will be taken down from the branches of the tree in the plaza centre and distributed to those present. But the point of the display, both in terms of the quantities accumulated and the extent of their origins, is to make known to those present that the hosts are efficacious persons.

A *gab* is successful when the name of the *gab* and its hosts travel far and wide among the Fuyuge. This can only be accomplished, though, if persons from far and wide are invited to witness the capacities of the hosts and then return to their 'homes' with stories from the *gab*. The hosts, then, need to demonstrate that they have the capacity to concentrate and hold in one place (the *gab* village) persons and objects from near and far. In the contemporary context, the hosts must ensure that bunches of betelnut are brought from surounding 'homes', from cultural groups to the south, and from Port Moresby for this purpose. This acts as a visible sign of such intentions.

In the process of *gab* enactment, then, related 'units' are brought into existence (hosts and categories of invited persons). At the centre of this process (both spatially and conceptually) are placed numerous bunches of betelnut from mountain and coastal varieties. What is emphasized throughout by the hosts is that large amounts of betelnut will be seen displayed in the centre of the plaza. This image of plenty, concentrated in one place, resonates with other images of plenty that are anticipated in the plaza (dancers, pigs, money, etc.). Such concentrations are never certain until they are revealed. The gathering together of betelnut is indicative of the other anticipated concentrations.

The 'holding together' capacities that betelnut evokes are thus analogous to the chief who is conceptualized as the one who handles and speaks over betelnut in this setting. This relationship between person and object is made explicit at key moments of the ritual. When the chief is about to take the betelnut down from the tree and handle it, all the men and women present in and around the plaza remain motionless and do not utter a sound. All attention at this moment is focused on the chief. The entire ritual plaza is reduced to a silent, motionless state, to an image of singularity.[35] Minds and bodies are concentrated on the chief/betelnut.

CONNECTING IMAGES OF CONCENTRATION.

The hosts, then, are seen to have accumulated large quantities of betelnut and to have placed them in the centre of their village plaza on the branches of a tree. This is analogous to the large numbers of people who have been concentrated in the ritual village to witness the performances in the plaza (dances, pig-killing, distributions, etc.) Here the betelnut remains in anticipation of the dancers who have been invited to perform in the *gab*. Once the hosts have displayed the betelnut, the dancers begin the process of 'concentrating' themselves and making their way to the *gab*. In a manner that is analogous to the hosts, the dancers also attempt to amass a large group of performers by 'pulling' in men and women from neighbouring villages. As they approach the *gab* village their goal is to replicate in size that which the hosts have achieved: 'units' of substitutable magnitude.

In the process of forming themselves into such a unit, the dancers limit their food intake and consume large quantities of betelnut.[36] The goal is to make their skin and body appear glowing and trim – an image of strength. Avoiding food (except sweet potato) and sexual activity is the manner in which the mind and body can be concentrated towards this efficacious state. So, whereas the hosts have created an image centred around the display of betelnut, the dancers form themselves into an analogous image through consuming large quantities of this substance.

Two interlinked images are created. On the one hand, the hosts have gathered together large quantities of betelnut displayed in the village plaza. In other words, they are attempting to create an image of concentration which is external and visible. In an analogous manner, the dancers are consuming large amounts of betelnut in order to avoid ingesting food that might weaken them. Betelnut from this perspective is concentrated internally so as to focus the mind and body towards an effective performance. Thus while the hosts have concentrated large amounts of betel to be displayed in the plaza to appear efficacious, so the dancers consume large amounts of betel for an analogous reason.

The ability of the hosts to gather large quantities of betelnut in anticipation of the accumulation of pigs and yams is analogous to the dancers' ability to assemble large numbers of dancers, and that of the exchange partners to bring the desired valuables. It is the interrelations of these capacities which create the units (hosts and dancers) and thus allow them to be substitutable. Betelnut has entered this process in relation to the pulling (resistance) that is required to achieve the anticipated outcome. Betelnut has emerged as an index of the ability to concentrate – both physically and mentally – and thus to appear as efficacious: it is an index of the power to transform potential 'resistance' into an image of concentration.

CONCLUSION: MOMENTS OF REVELATION

The outcome of these anticipations, that is the efforts of the hosts and the performance of the dancers, however, is never certain until the actions of both are revealed. Men and women look for evidence that 'units' to be exchanged with one another are truly substitutable. Is, for example, the amount of betelnut accumulated in the plaza centre equal to, less than or more than the scale and magnitude of the dancers who have gathered? These are questions for which there are never clear answers, though, from the perspective of the various categories of persons present at the event, it is answers of 'certainty' that they all attempt to assert. This inherent uncertainty creates the conditions for the next event where these capacities can again be revealed.

Today, betelnut carries a heavy social, historical and symbolic load among the Fuyuge in relation to these ritual contexts. As we have seen, betelnut among the Fuyuge, as in Papua New Guinea more generally, is a highly desired psychoactive substance. At one level it is part of the experience of an emergent metropolitan culture to which the Fuyuge are only marginally connected. At another level, this highly desired substance is accumulated and takes centre stage in Fuyuge ritual process as an index of the collective's ability to transform itself into a concentrated and thus efficacious unit.

Betelnut has specific mind- and body-altering capacities. Pharmacologists and other medical scientists have been able to isolate the specific elements responsible for these effects. But these effects always exist within specific cultural contexts, shaped by history. At the turn of this century, before large-scale European incursion, the Fuyuge did not chew betelnut. Since the 1950s, however, the Fuyuge have become avid chewers and now display the same highly stained teeth of their coastal neighbours. Although the Fuyuge have remained increasingly marginalized from the metropolitan context of Port Moresby, the importance of betelnut both for individual consumption and for display in ritual has increased proportionally. Socio-historical developments which have included the incorporation of betelnut consumption into local practices cannot be 'read off' from the psychoactive properties of the chew. But as we have seen, without its specific properties, it is unlikely that betelnut would have the central place it does today both in Fuyuge ritual and in the emergent 'public culture' of contemporary Papua New Guinea. Indeed these psychoactive properties of concentrating the mind and body in specific ways have endowed the betelnuts with analogies of efficacy.

NOTES

1 This chapter has benefited from the helpful advice and comments of the editors, to whom I am most grateful. For any errors that remain I have only myself to thank. Field research was conducted in Papua New Guinea between 1983 and 1985 and was supported by the Wenner-Gren Foundation, Central Research Fund of the University of London and the London School of Economics. This support is gratefully acknowledged.

2 These two techniques have been described as follows: 'In the wrapped quid the lime and areca nut are wrapped in a betel pepper leaf before being chewed. In the non-wrapped quid or betelnut mixture the areca nut, the leaf or fruit, and the lime are placed in the mouth one at a time and worked into a quid with the tongue.' M. Marshall, 'An overview of drugs in Oceania', in Lamont Lindstrom (ed.), *Drugs in Western Pacific Societies: Relations of Substance*, Lanham, Md., University Press of America, 1987, p. 16.

3 The betelnut skin is often sucked by an adult or child but is not left to lie around, as the dried saliva may be used in sorcery against the person.

4 Some carry their lime in finished gourd containers which are more common on the coast. The lime is obtained via a long stick which is left in the mouth of the gourd. The stick is wetted in the mouth, placed in the gourd and the lime that attaches to the stick is taken into the mouth and licked off with the tongue and lips.

5 B. Burton-Bradley, 'Arecaidinism: betel chewing in transcultural perspective', *Canadian Journal of Psychiatry*, 1979, vol. 24, pp. 481–8 (my emphasis).

6 Marshall, op. cit., p. 15.

7 W. H. R. Rivers, *The History of Melanesian Society*, Cambridge, Cambridge University Press, 1914, 2 vols.

8 R. Brunton, *The Abandoned Narcotic: Kava and Cultural Instability in Melanesia*, Cambridge, Cambridge University Press, 1989; V. Lebot et al., *Kava: The Pacific Drug*, New Haven, Yale University Press, 1992.

9 Marshall, op. cit., p. 15.

10 R. Williamson, *The Mafulu Mountain People of British New Guinea*, London,

Macmillan, 1912, pp. 66, 288.

11 Now kept in the National Archives Office in Port Moresby.

12 That is, the large-fruited variety.

13 E. Hirsch, 'From bones to betelnuts: processes of ritual transformation and the development of "national culture" in Papua New Guinea', *Man*, 1990, vol. 25, pp. 18–34.

14 Individual (or particular) contexts and those of ritual should not be seen here as separate. Rather, it is perhaps more appropriate to view them as moments or phases in an ongoing 'totality' (see M. Mauss, *The Gift: Forms and Reasons of Exchange in Archaic Societies*, London, Routledge, 1990); or, where one is an anticipation of the other (see M. Strathern, *The Gender of the Gift: Problems with Women and Problems with Society in Melanesia*, Berkeley, University of California Press, 1988, Ch. 10).

15 Strathern, op. cit., p. 289.

16 See A. Gell, 'Anthropology, material culture and consumerism', *Journal of the Anthropological Society of Oxford*, 1988, vol. 19, pp. 43–8.

17 Ibid., p. 46.

18 The connection between betelnut and the chief is given further expression in Fuyuge myth. According to one narrative all forms of betelnut once existed within the lands of the Fuyuge but the most valued forms were 'lost' in the ancestral past – see Hirsch, op. cit. pp. 28–9.

19 M. Strathern, 'Qualified value: the perspective of gift exchange', in C. Humphrey and S. Hugh-Jones (eds), *Barter, Exchange and Value: An Anthropological Approach*, Cambridge, Cambridge University Press, 1992, p. 174.

20 Cited in ibid., p. 174.

21 Marshall, op. cit., p. 19.

22 See E. Hau'ofa, *Mekeo: Inequality and Ambivalence in a Village Society*, Canberra, Australian National University Press, 1981.

23 See P. Watson, 'Drugs in trade', in Lindstrom, op. cit., pp. 119–34.

24 W. Iamo, 'One of the things that brings good name is betel: a Keakalo conception of betel use', in Lindstrom, op. cit., p. 138.

25 In several previous publications these have been referred to as parishes. I now find the label of 'home' more appropriate. See E. Hirsch, 'Dialectics of the bowerbird: an interpretative account of ritual and symbolism in the Udabe Valley, Papua New Guinea', *Mankind*, 1987, vol. 17, pp. 1–14; Hirsch, 'From bones to betelnuts: processes of ritual transformation and the development of "national culture" in Papua New Guinea', *Man*, 1990, vol. 25, pp. 18–34.

26 During this time, French Catholic missionaries established themselves in the eastern area of the Fuyuge and gradually set up mission stations throughout all the river valleys to the west.

27 A small-fruited, wild mountain variety grows among the Fuyuge but is considered to be less potent and have an inferior taste.

28 See Hirsch, 'Bones to betelnuts', op. cit., p. 21.

29 All of which culminate in large-scale pig-killing and ceremonial exchanges.

30 Cf. C. R. Hallpike, *Bloodshed and Vengeance in the Papuan Mountains: The Generation of Conflict in Tauade Society*, Oxford, Clarendon Press, 1977; M. McArthur, *The Kunimaipa*, unpublished PhD thesis, Australian National University, Canberra, 1971; and for an analagous figure from island Melanesia see R. Wagner, *Asiwinarong: Image, Ethos and Social Power among the Usen Barok of New Ireland*, Princeton, Princeton University Press, 1986.

31 A man or woman will commit suicide out of shame (*fafi*) if their close

relations refuse to kill pigs in their name when they have reached the 'white hairs' life-crisis rite. During my stay among the Visi, a woman at the 'white hairs' stage of her life threw herself off a cliff when her husband refused to kill pigs for her.

32 The Fuyuge have given prominence to a number of rites associated with personal growth and maturity and also with personal decay and death. These life-crisis rites are associated with the experience of increasing social centredness and then with peripherality. This can also be correlated with increasing and then descreasing degrees of visibility and efficaciousness. The performance of these rites is never self-fulfilling and they are structured around the concentrating both of persons and valued objects (nowadays including large amounts of betelnut) into a *gab* space. The task of such concentration is always surrounded with uncertainty – depending on the will of others and/or the availability of valued objects. It is in relation to such uncertainty, and particularly in the context of the *gab*, that the person of the chief is conceptualized as pivotal: capable of achieving one talk (*av*), one work (*soso*), one mind (*sisibe*). The person, as similarly with the home, then, moves into and out of periods of uncertainly sustained efficaciousness (see E. Hirsch, 'Between mission and market: events and images in a Melanesian society', *Man*, 1994, vol. 29, pp. 687–711, where I use the notion of centredness as analogous to that of efficacy).

33 The bowerbird is any of various passerine birds native to Australia and New Guinea, the males of which build decorated 'bowers' during courtship (Oxford reference dictionary, 1986, p. 101.).

34 See M. Strathern, *The Gender of the Gift: Problems with Women and Problems with Society in Melanesia*, Berkeley, University of California Press, 1988, pp. 296–7.

35 See Hirsch, 'Between mission and market', op. cit.

36 Dancers invite men from coastal societies to visit the *gab* and trade coastal betelnut for mountain-bird plumes.

5

KOLA NUTS

The 'coffee' of the central Sudan

Paul E. Lovejoy

Kola nuts, which are eaten because they contain caffeine, theobromine and kolatin, are a popular stimulant in many parts of West Africa. Like other mild stimulants, including coffee, tea and cocoa, kola nuts are moderately addictive. Of the two most common varieties, *Cola nitida* contains from 1.0 to 4.0 per cent caffeine by weight and traces of theobromine, while *C. acuminata* has from 1.5 to 3.6 per cent caffeine and 0.02 to 0.09 per cent theobromine. Both caffeine and theobromine are alkaloids which stimulate the nervous system and the skeletal muscles. Both varieties also contain small amounts of kolatin, a glucoside heart stimulant, and tannin. In combination, these properties make kola as effective as other, mild stimulants, including coffee, tea and cocoa (Table 1). Although kola is not taken as a drink but is chewed, it has sometimes been compared with coffee, even being called the 'coffee of the Sudan'.[1]

Table 1 Caffeine and theobromine in mild stimulants [2]

Stimulant	*Caffeine(%)*	*Theobromine(%)*
kola	1.0–4.0	0.02–0.09
coffee	0.7–3.0	none
tea	1.0–4.7	traces
cocoa	0.07–0.36	0.8–4.0

There are at least forty-two varieties of kola,[3] but only *C. nitida* and *C. acuminata* have been particularly important historically. Of these, *C. nitida* was virtually the only kola exported from the producing areas in the forests of West Africa to markets in the Savanna to the north where they could not be grown; *C. acuminata* was eaten as well but almost entirely within the forest region where the nuts were cultivated. Hence *C. nitida* was the kola of long-distance trade and is the variety that is examined here. Many varieties of kola are found throughout the tropical African forests as far east as the Zaire River basin, but C. *nitida* was only grown west of the Volta River (modern Ghana) before the end of the nineteenth century, while C. *acuminata* grew only east of the Volta River, especially in the Yoruba and Igbo parts of modern Nigeria and areas further east still.[4] Hence the kola of long-distance trade was grown in a relatively restricted part of West Africa, more specifically in what is now southern Ghana, Ivory Coast, Liberia, Sierra Leone and Guinea-Bissau.

Other varieties of kola were cultivated in southern Cameroon and in areas further east, and in the second half of the nineteenth century some of these became the object of an export trade to the Savanna as well. C. *anomala* and C. *ballayi*, grown in southern Cameroon, were acceptable substitutes for C. *nitida* and hence were exported north along with small amounts of C. *acuminata*.[5] Further east, some other varieties of kola were sent north to Wadai and Darfur through Dar al-Kuti, and various 'false' kolas were exported in small quantities too.[6] None the less, C. *nitida* accounted for almost all kola that was traded beyond the areas of production.

The taste for kola is acquired because the nuts are bitter. Consumption of only a small piece of the nut affects the body, and hence consumers often break a nut into pieces; as a result there are a great number of terms for the size of a piece. Once a nut is broken open, moreover, it quickly oxidizes, turning dark red and then black as it dries. Consequently, nuts were (and are) frequently shared, which reinforced the social dimension of consumption. The taste of the nut lingers for some time after chewing and has the effect of making water taste sweet and refreshing, no matter how tainted the water might be from natron or other common minerals found in well water.[7] When consumed in sufficient quantity, kola stains the teeth and lips slightly red, which was often considered aesthetically pleasing and a sign of good health.

The fruit of the kola grows in pods that contain from three to twelve nuts. C. *nitida* nuts are divided into two cotyledons, which can be easily separated at the time of consumption, while C. *acuminata* has from two to five cotyledons. Each nut is about the size of a chestnut, approximately one to two inches in diameter. The nuts spoil very easily and must be kept damp and protected from the air. If cared for properly, C. *nitida* nuts can last for many months, even a year or more, subject to constant inspection to remove insect-infested nuts, mouldy nuts and others that have spoiled or withered. To protect the nuts in transit and during storage, they were wrapped in leaves, often in bundles containing one hundred, a common wholesale measure, or two thousand nuts, the amount of a head-load and one-half of a donkey load.

THE EVOLUTION OF THE KOLA TRADE

C. nitida (hereafter referred to as 'kola' unless otherwise specified) has been consumed in the western Sudan for at least a millennium and in the central Sudan (including modern northern Nigeria – the focus of this study) for at least 500 years. Because of their stimulating properties, consumers were willing to spend relatively large sums of money to acquire these nuts, and consequently, kola was an important commodity in the long-distance trade of West Africa, especially in Muslim areas, where alcohol was proscribed and other stimulants were not available.[8] The limits of this trade were determined by the perishability of the nuts, which had to be packaged carefully so that they would not dehydrate and thereby lose most of their properties. The nuts could be safely transported a thousand kilometres or so, which effectively became the radius within which they were consumed in substantial quantities. Although modern transportation has made it easier to move kola over greater distances, the area of consumption has not spread significantly beyond west Africa, although production within west Africa, especially in Nigeria, has expanded considerably in the twentieth century.

C. nitida originated as an export crop somewhere in the hinterland of Sierra Leone and Liberia, where people speaking one of the languages classified in the west Atlantic sub-family of Niger-Congo appear to have commercialized the nuts in the distant past, long before the Portuguese arrived in the fifteenth century.[9] The local word for kola, *gola* or *kola*, was subsequently adopted widely, eventually making its way into the languages of the western Savanna regions of Africa and into European languages as well.[10] People of the Mande sub-family who subsequently moved into the forest became major producers of kola by the fourteenth century. By then, Muslim merchants from the Mali Empire monopolized distribution. Known as Mande Juula (Dyula), these merchants were ultimately responsible for the spread of kola throughout the western Sudan. Small amounts of kola even reached North Africa in this period.[11]

By the fifteenth century, the cultivation of *C. nitida* had spread eastwards through the hinterland of Ivory Coast as far as the lower Volta basin of modern Ghana. The extension of cultivation made it feasible to distribute kola further east in the Savanna, so that by the end of the fifteenth century, at least, kola was transported from the lower Volta basin to the central Sudan, the area centred on modern northern Nigeria.[12] Thereafter the cultivation of *C. nitida* stabilized. Production was concentrated in the forests of Sierra Leone, Liberia and Guinea-Bissau; also in the forests of central Ivory Coast; and finally in the Akan forests of the lower Volta basin. Small amounts of *C. nitida* were also grown in the riverine districts of Nupe in the central Sudan, apparently being introduced in the eighteenth century at the latest. Local conditions along the Niger River made it possible for trees to bear some nuts, even though Nupe was in the Savanna.[13] Otherwise, there was no further movement of the crop eastwards until the last decade of the nineteenth century when *C. nitida* was introduced into the hinterland of Lagos in Nigeria. Why the crop did not spread further east before then is a matter of speculation. After 1700 the Volta kola groves were consolidated into the centralized state of Asante, which tightly controlled the export trade in kola, and the caravan routes from Asante to the central Sudan passed well to the north of the Nigerian forests.

The production of kola has increased dramatically in the twentieth century. Chevalier and Perrot estimated that 20, 000 metric tons of kola were produced in 1910; *C. nitida* accounted for 16, 000 tons of this amount, which probably represents the upper limit of total annual production in the past.[14] Cheaper transport within West Africa resulted in the rapid increase in demand and a corresponding expansion in production, which in Ghana alone reached 9, 743 tons in 1923–4.[15] By 1955 Ivory Coast was exporting 20, 000 tons of kola north to Mali.[16] The other traditional producers of *C. nitida* – Liberia, Guinea-Bissau and Sierra Leone – also increased the scale of exports as well.[17]

Southern Nigeria became the largest single producer by the middle of the present century, despite the fact that *C. nitida* was only introduced to this area after 1880. Previously, southern Nigeria had produced only *C. acuminata*, which was almost entirely consumed locally, except for small quantities that were exported north to the Savanna and overseas to Brazil.[18] The effective isolation of southern Nigeria from *C. nitida* seedlings ended when merchants began to import kola by sea from the Gold Coast and Sierra Leone in the late 1860s, and by the end of the century, this sea-borne trade began to rival the interior caravan routes. Yoruba farmers near Lagos began to plant *C. nitida* in groves, often adjacent to cocoa and coffee trees. While the coffee trees failed, cocoa and kola prospered.

The donkey caravans that had previously supplied the central Sudan dwindled in size after 1900, and eventually they stopped travelling altogether. For the first three decades of colonial rule, most kola came by sea from the Gold Coast and Sierra Leone, reaching a peak of 9, 679 tons in 1924, but this trade, too, was doomed in the rapidly changing conditions of the colonial era.[19] By the 1930s, imports from the Gold Coast and Sierra Leone declined as southern Nigeria began to satisfy the markets of northern Nigeria.[20] In 1957 southern Nigeria supplied 110, 000 tons to northern Nigeria, almost ten times the total production of *C. nitida* as estimated by Chevalier and Perrot in 1910.[21] Kola came to the attention of Islamic North Africa as early as the thirteenth century, at which time kola was being imported into Tlemcen in Morocco from Walata in the southern Sahara. Ibn Fadl Allah al-'Umari (*d.* 1349) referred to the nuts as 'âcres, désagréables au goût et les Noirs seuls les mangent'.[22] By the sixteenth century, kola was incorporated into the *matière médicale* of Islamic science. In 1586 al-Wazir al-Gassani, a doctor to Sultan Ahmad al-Mansur of Morocco, accurately described kola, and from at least that time small amounts of kola were imported into North Africa for medicinal purposes.

Portuguese mariners became aware of kola as early as the 1460s, when vessels first visited the rivers along the Sierra Leone coast where kola was grown. By the early sixteenth century, Portuguese merchants were heavily involved in the coastal trade along the upper Guinea coast, and kola almost certainly was a major item of transport from Sierra Leone as far north as the Gambia and Senegal Rivers. Because of royal restrictions on Portuguese activities, ship captains did not report this trade, which otherwise would have been taxed. None the less, an English privateer found kola on a Portuguese ship seized in 1564, and it seems likely that kola was a common cargo before that date. Kola was certainly well known to European merchants along the coast thereafter.[23]

Kola captured the imagination of European consumers in the last decades of the nineteenth century, first as a drug and then as a tonic. In Britain a medical preparation known as 'kola chocolate' that combined kola with sugar and vanilla was administered to invalids and convalescents as early as the 1870s; it was also recommended to travellers 'to allay hunger and relieve exhaustion'.[24] After considerable experimentation in Britain, France and the USA, kola became a basic ingredient in various potions that mixed kola with cocoa, coca, soda and other things, and it was used to improve poor quality chocolate. Kola extract was attributed with a variety of refreshing and restorative powers that ultimately resulted in the popular cola drinks. In 1886 the druggist John S. Pemberton of Atlanta, Georgia, invented Coca-Cola, which initially combined extracts from coca and kola, and was advertised as a 'brain tonic'.[25] Caleb B. Brabham, a North Carolina pharmacist, created Coke's principal rival, Pepsi-Cola, which was originally known as 'Brad's Drink' until 1893. It combined sugar, vanilla, oils, spices and kola. Like Coke, it was advertized as a medicinal tonic to relieve dyspepsia (upset stomachs) and peptic ulcers – hence the name.[26] By the 1890s, only Burroughs and Wellcome's Forced March Tabloid, still common in Britain, appears to have retained the original bitter taste of the nut.

Ultimately, none of the cola drinks relied on the nuts as an ingredient, despite the original inspiration. Alternative sources of caffeine and taste were cheaper to exploit. Modern advertising has sometimes recognized the connection with kola, but consumers have been generally unaware of the origin of cola pop. Today cola drinks are as fully 'uncola' as 7-Up. Incidentally, cola drinks are now popular in areas where kola nuts are chewed, not as a substitute but as another source of caffeine.

CONSUMPTION OF KOLA AND OTHER STIMULANTS IN THE CENTRAL SUDAN

The central Sudan was the eastern-most portion of the traditional market for kola and, as already noted, consumption of kola began there later than in areas further west – probably towards the end of the fifteenth century. None the less, this market became increasingly important because of the size of its population and the spread of Islam, which encouraged kola use and discouraged the consumption of most other stimulants and addictive substances. By the nineteenth century this region became one of the largest markets for kola, a position it retains to this day. Observations on kola use in this area, therefore, can be taken as representative of patterns throughout the region of kola consumption in West Africa.

The merchants who dominated the kola trade between Asante and the central Sudan came from the cities and towns of the Sokoto Caliphate, which was founded in a holy war (*jihad*) that began in 1804 and eventually consolidated most of the central Sudan into a single, Islamic state, divided into thirty emirates stretching from modern Burkina Faso in the west to northern Cameroon in the east. The kola merchants, particularly those from Kano Emirate, became very wealthy. By the end of the nineteenth century, they imported around 2,000 tons of kola per year, which, it should be noted, was modest by comparison with the volume of consumption only a few decades later and only a tiny fraction of current levels of consumption. It is instructive that the word for *C. nitida* in Hausa (*goro*) is derived from the common term that was in use further west.[27] By contrast, *C. acuminata* was referred to as *hannunruwa* in Hausa.

By the middle of the nineteenth century, kola nuts constituted 'one of the greatest luxuries of Negroland', according to Heinrich Barth who conducted research in the Sokoto Caliphate and Borno between 1849 and 1855. Barth reported that 'large sums are expended by the natives upon this luxury'.[28] Several decades later, the learned Muslim cleric, Imam Imoru, noted that kola was even accepted in lieu of the local cowrie currency: 'The Hausa people are so fond of kola . . . that it will buy anything; a man can give it as payment and it will be accepted.'[29] Both Heinrich Barth, the foreign scholar, and Imam Imoru, the local expert, establish how valuable kola was to consumers.

The principal reason for such demand had little to do with its symbolic meaning as a form of wealth or with its usefulness as a means of payment, however. As elsewhere, kola was wanted because of its stimulating properties, although Imam Imoru was surely exaggerating when he claimed that 'there are people in Hausaland who are addicted to kola; if they don't eat it, they feel like vomiting'.[30] None the less, there was clear recognition that kola could be consumed in excess: indeed an individual who chewed too much kola was called *sankara*, which was the Hausa name for the insects that damaged the nuts.[31] As this term suggests, such indulgence was the subject of scorn. Since the price of kola was very high before the twentieth century, it was seldom possible for individuals to consume enough kola to warrant such scorn. As with other mild stimulants, the determination of 'excess' is a culturally relative judgement anyway.

Consumers distinguished kola according to type, size and colour, among other factors. First, they identified kola according to botanical variety, *C. nitida*, *C. acuminata*, *C. ballayi*, *C. anamola* and 'false kola'. Second, *C. nitida* was distinguished according to colour (red or white), its province of origin, the season of harvesting and its size; if damaged, according to the degree of infestation with insects, the size of the piece that had been 'repaired', the extent of dehydration, or the nature of other maladies.[32] There were at least ten terms to indicate the size of a piece of nut broken off for consumption, for example.

Such detail reflects the extent to which consumption of this stimulant was taken seriously. It is no wonder that 'the arrival of a new consignment of kola nuts is as great an event for the Hausa as is the first appearance of a seasonal dish for a gourmet in Europe'.[33] Small quantities of kola, including clear distinctions among types, were even listed as separate items in the estate of one prominent Kano official who died in the late nineteenth century.[34]

Tobacco, alcohol and other addictive substances were available to consumers of the central Sudan in the nineteenth century, and probably earlier still, but kola was by far the most important item of consumption and tobacco was its only serious competitor; otherwise Muslims used virtually no other stimulant, intoxicant or narcotic.[35] Coffee and tea were rare because they had to be imported across the Sahara or from the West African coast, which made these stimulants prohibitively expensive. Cocoa was not introduced into West Africa until the end of the century, and then was not available in the Islamic Savanna until well into the twentieth century. Religious prohibitions made alcohol, whether imported or made locally, unacceptable for Muslims, although local pagan communities brewed millet beer and, in the more southerly regions, palm-wine was common. Wine and liquor were imported from Europe and the Americas, but little of these made their way into the Islamic Savanna.

For Muslims, the only alternative to kola was tobacco, usually chewed, occasionally taken as snuff, but almost never smoked.[36] Gustav Nachtigal, who provided the most thorough comparison of the different substances that were consumed, explained that people in Borno, the other major state in the central Sudan beside the Sokoto Caliphate, used tobacco to some extent in the 1870s, but not as much as might be thought. The people of Borno were:

> moderate in the consumption of tobacco, being distinguished from nearly all the tribes who live around them, and who either chew or smoke it, take snuff, or indulge in more than one of these methods of using tobacco. There are, to be sure, enough individuals [in Borno] who chew the small-leafed tobacco which is grown almost everywhere in the Sudan, but by far the greater number do not cultivate this habit, few are accustomed to taking snuff, and among the natives scarcely anyone has any experience in smoking.[37]

Tobacco was clearly of secondary importance to kola, although it was perceived as a substitute for kola when supplies were low.[38] Tobacco consumption appears to have varied in the central Sudan. More tobacco seems to have been consumed in the Sokoto Caliphate than in Borno, but the Islamic prohibition against smoking was widely respected. Smoking was rare, except in pagan areas.[39] Instead, most tobacco was chewed together with one or another type of salt or natron, and occasionally it was taken as snuff, again mixed with salt or natron.[40] Women also rubbed tobacco flowers on their teeth as a cosmetic, and inevitably ingested some nicotine as a result.

Coffee and tea were imported by Arab residents, but beyond the small North African population in the cities, very little coffee or tea was consumed.[41] There was little, if any, effort to develop the market for coffee in either the Sokoto Caliphate or Borno.[42] In his comparison of stimulants, intoxicants and narcotics, Nachtigal observed that even the mildly alcoholic beverages that were found in other Muslim countries were unknown, and beer drinking, which was common among pagan populations, was condemned.[43] For Muslims, kola and tobacco were the only substances that were in use, and of these kola was by far the most important of the two. As Nachtigal noted, 'the guro [kola] nut has become a luxury even more indispensable than is coffee or tea for other people, and it is regarded as a general calamity if a harvest failure or military operations diminish the flow into the market'.[44] Indeed, this was why North Africans referred to kola as the 'coffee of the Sudan'.[45] As far as other substances were concerned, Nachtigal was emphatic:

> Of the other narcotics and stimulants, such as opium and hashish (Indian hemp), the enjoyment of which is characteristic of many Muslim countries, there can be no question; neither of them is known, scarcely even by name, to the natives.[46]

Marijuana became popular among some sections of the younger population only after the middle of the twentieth century, and it was a recent introduction. Cigarettes, coffee, tea and beer have spread as well, but even now kola has continued to be the most common substance in use, in northern Nigeria at least. Kola was even more important in the past, and the depletion of kola supplies was considered a crisis. For example, when Emir Kwassau of Zaria was visiting his southern domains in the late 1890s and his entourage ran out of kola, he commandeered a passing caravan in search of new supplies. To the chagrin of all, the caravan had no kola, not even enough 'for medicine'.[47]

PATTERNS OF KOLA CONSUMPTION IN THE CENTRAL SUDAN

Because kola was expensive relative to the cost of living, the aristocracies of the Sokoto Caliphate and Borno were the principal consumers of kola in the nineteenth century. One kola nut often cost more than the amount that an individual spent on food for a day. Only the wealthiest commoners, often merchants, were able to afford its consumption. Officials and merchants also redistributed kola to their clients and dependants as gifts, but otherwise, kola was bought only for special purposes. Although it was valued as an item of prestige, ordinary people, let alone the large slave population, simply could not afford to buy kola. These people – the bulk of the population – only tasted kola on rare occasions. In the nineteenth century, kola use was very limited indeed and only became an item of mass consumption in the twentieth century.

Above all, kola was consumed in social settings, much the way people in other societies and other times drink coffee and tea, smoke tobacco products and imbibe alcohol. According to Paul Staudinger, the young entomologist in charge of the German expedition to Sokoto in 1885–6,

> The kola nut, goro in Hausa, is offered like a cigar at home [in Germany] and one may be sure it is never refused; on the contrary, it is considered good manners to share it round, even if only in small fragments, before helping oneself.[48]

In 1870 Nachtigal consumed half a nut after dinner 'instead of coffee', which followed the practice of wealthy people generally. As he observed, 'custom requires that one should offer to one's visitors one, or at least a half, guro nut, just as in Arab countries a cup of coffee is immediately placed before guests'.[49]

Nineteenth-century European accounts, which are laced with references to the consumption of kola in social settings and on official occasions, attest to the restricted and prestigious use of kola.[50] While in Muri in 1854, W. B. Baikie received a 'basket of fine guro or kola nuts . . . esteemed as a mark of great favour and friendship'.[51] In Borno also 'a gift of guro nuts is always a mark of particular friendship'; indeed it was 'a token of special goodwill', which a host usually distributed 'to the more distinguished of his guests'.[52] Sometimes kola was presented as a gift, and other times kola was expected as a form of *gaisuwa*, or official greeting that involved mutual gift-giving. Whether European, North African or African, all visitors were expected to honour local custom in giving kola nuts to subordinate officials, friendly merchants and other people who offered assistance.

Kola was distributed on Fridays to those who called on emirs and other officials.[53] Revd John Milum, for example, observed the dignitaries of Bida, one of the southern emirates, gathering at the palace in 1881 to talk and eat kola after reciting their prayers at the mosque.[54] Kola was also given as alms to clerics, which satisfied one of the tenets of Islam,[55] and it was customary for the wealthy to give kola to their subordinates. In 1885 Staudinger found that

> Such nuts, if sent by the king [emir], are a kind of present of honour, and people who have no money to buy them beg them from their friends. Rich people try to make themselves popular and to be regarded as 'big men' (*babba*) by distributing kola nuts, and for the noblemen chewing them is the favourite occupation.[56]

Kola was also given out at the Eid-ul-Fitr festival that followed the end of Ramadan, the month of fasting.[57]

Sometimes kola nuts formed part of tax payments, and in this way high-ranking officials acquired considerable stores of kola. Some emirates included kola as part of their tribute to Sokoto, emirate officials in turn receiving kola from merchants and lesser officials. And the Caliphs of Sokoto sent kola in return upon the installation of subordinate emirs.[58] Merchants gave kola to officials as part of their annual *gaisuwa* payments, which were customarily made to their political patrons. If they were kola importers, they usually made these payments upon their return from Asante.[59] Often these patrons had granted land and tax concessions to these same merchants, and the annual presentation amounted to something between an income tax and rent, that is a payment for special favours. Kola was also collected in lieu of tax on caravans coming from Asante, particularly at river crossings, even when the tolls were actually calculated in cowries.[60]

The nuts were consumed at all the major occasions common in Muslim society, including the naming ceremonies of children, marriage and funerals, just as the nuts were shared on religious holidays, at the social events of the wealthy and powerful and at important political gatherings. Kola was essential during courtship; it was a method of presentation to relatives, Muslim clerics and guests. Of course, the extent that kola was distributed at these rites of passage depended upon the wealth of those hosting the ceremonies.

On the sixth day after birth, a father publicly announced that his child would be named on the following day.[61] The father himself or his messengers visited the houses of neighbours, relatives and friends to invite them to the ceremony. Although it was not essential, kola was often distributed along with the invitation. According to Imam Imoru, 'some people give two kola nuts to those they tell and others give four'.[62] More kola was distributed at the ceremony itself, often amounting to a half a nut or more per person, according to the wealth of the family. There must have been many naming ceremonies in which very little, if any, kola was provided.

Suitors were expected to give kola at virtually every stage of courtship. Gifts were essential in winning the affection of the intended bride and the acceptance of her family. The practice of *bautar jaki*, which was common in Kano, Katsina, Sokoto, Zaria and Gwandu, required the presentation of gifts to the parents of the girl and often to the girl's sisters and brothers as well. According to an account dating from around 1907, older women served as intermediaries in approaching the families of eligible girls; as many as twelve nuts might be presented to the parents to indicate the interest of suitors. Subsequently, hopeful men had to provide fresh meat, money and more kola.[63] Once fathers approved of marriage, suitors were expected to reimburse disappointed rivals who had presented similar gifts, although sometimes the families of the intended brides helped by returning unconsumed items. To seal marriage agreements, suitors visited the houses of their brides-to-be, bringing fifty or a hundred kola nuts as further presents, whereupon prayers were recited. The day before weddings, the bride price was set in the presence of the Muslim cleric who would preside at the marriage, and this formality was yet another occasion to share kola. Of course, kola was also distributed at weddings.[64]

Kola also figured in the consummation of marriages. According to one account from the first decade of the twentieth century, the groom and his best man visited the room of the bride late on the night of the wedding, 'but when the best man speaks to her, she refuses to answer, until he gives her the cola-nuts "to open her mouth" – then the bride will allow herself to smile'. After the best man left, the newly married couple engaged in intercourse.[65] The metaphorical parallel between mouth and vagina should be noted. Kola consumption symbolically expressed the sexual submission of the bride, just as her acceptance or rejection of kola indicated consent or displeasure with the proposed marriage and the sexual intentions of the suitor.[66]

If a woman refused the kola overture, the male could try a charm which consisted of a mixture of kola, seven pieces of the *ramma* stalk, a piece of horse or donkey dung and water. The mixture was stored in a pot for seven days; each day expectoration was added before the suitor communicated with anyone. On the seventh day, the kola was presented to the girl. According to Ahmed A. Nasr, 'if she eats of it, when you are in bed that night you will hear knocking at the door'.[67] This sexual fantasy, culturally based but none the less powerful, combines the pleasure of imbibing kola and the anticipation of sexual fulfilment in the context of marriage. The pain of rejection is countered by the hope that the doctored kola will be accepted.

Whether or not fantasy became reality in the quest for a bride, kola was also a means of payment for sexual services outside of marriage, and it was associated with virility. According to Nachtigal, a few kola nuts were 'sufficient to purchase the favour of a frivolous girl'.[68] It was commonly believed that kola induced women to want men very much, indeed to crave them a lot.[69] As an antidote for impotency, kola was among many cures and aids; men resorted to verses of the Koran wrapped in leather pouches, various mixtures of natron and other ingredients that 'strengthened the penis' or 'increased the blood', but kola was specifically thought to intensify male sexuality ('Yana sa karefum maza [karfin maza]'). The nuts also increased the flow of semen ('Yana ded'a maniyi') and otherwise made men more desirable to women ('Yana sa maganin som mutane').[70] Of course, its property of reducing fatigue was a factor in overcoming the sexual frailties of men. Kola consumption was well advertised as a remedy for male inadequacies and as a means of overcoming female inhibitions.

Women turned to kola to combat male sexuality, especially while nursing. Cultural norms held that mothers were not supposed to engage in sexual intercourse for two years after giving birth, since it was believed that pregnancy would affect the flow of milk and thereby weaken nursing children.[71] Men often had more than one wife and concubines, but in cases where men wanted sexual access, no matter whether there were children or other women, mothers with infants attempted to avoid insistent husbands and reduce the risks of pregnancy if intercourse did take place by wearing a leather charm containing a kola nut around her waist.[72]

Kola consumption figured prominently in *bori* ceremonies, the spirit-medium cult that was widely practised by women in particular, although some men also participated. One *bori* spirit, Cigoro (eater of kola), distributed kola as a mark of possession.[73] The water spirit, Sarkin Rafi or Kogi, provided protection or refuge through kola; it was held that bad influences would pass into the kola. The spirit Bagudu ('no-running', i.e. as in battle) recommended kola as a means of syphoning off the urge to flee. Finally, kola was used in the initiation of people, usually women, into *bori*, which required the 'opening of the mouth' to facilitate possession. A female initiate remained silent for three days after the induction began, whereupon the woman and the spirit had 'mouths cut for them' to allow them to communicate with each other. Ten items were required to 'cut the mouth', including kola nuts.[74] The suggestion here is compelling. The susceptibility to spirit possession was perceived in oral terms that were analogous to the consumption of the stimulant kola. The parallel between eating kola and sexual penetration should again be noted.

The symbolic and metaphorical importance of kola in regulating and temporizing human relationships stands out.[75] Kola consumption was thought to overcome heartache ('Yana maganin ciwon zuciya') and otherwise settle the heart ('Yana maganin zaman zuciya'). It could also make someone wiser ('Yana dad'a wayon mutum'), improve self-discipline ('Yana sa kaifin hankali'), and make a person's conversation enjoyable ('Yana sa dad'in zance'). Not only would kola combat a curse ('Yana maganin bakin mutane'), but it was an antidote for sorcery ('Yana maganin maye'). The pharmacists who invented Coca-Cola and Pepsi-Cola as elixirs might have marvelled at these attributes, which were not so different from the properties they claimed for their own tonics.

Kola was also distributed during communal work parties (*gayya*) of young men. Such work parties were common in agriculture and were often accompanied by drumming. The kola was both a method of compensating the youths and a way of combating fatigue during the hard work. Food was provided as well.[76] There was no alcohol, unlike the work parties of other societies and other times. Kola was also appropriate when a new log was brought into the beating room where indigo was pounded into cloth, a craft specialization connected with the manufacture of expensive textiles.[77] Like the work party, the ritual associated with the heavy work of moving the log called for a celebration, and kola was an acceptable means of displaying appreciation. Kola was distributed when corvée labour was required to repair city walls as well.[78] Along the Shari River, fishermen believed that a few kola, divided into little pieces and thrown into the water, would hold the fish and thereby increase the catch:[79] presumably the fishermen chewed the kola first, and then spat the residue into the river.

Military officials dispensed kola to their soldiers before battle. It was thought to make men brave, even eager for combat ('Yana sa mutum ya yi yaki da yawa'), and it combated cowardice and the urge to flee on the battlefield because it made men tough ('Yana maganin tauri').[80] In 1852 Barth thought that the Sokoto army was addicted to kola: 'these fighting men, with a few exceptions, care only about their bodily comfort, and for a few "goriye", or Kola nuts, would be willing to sell the whole of their military accoutrements'.[81] Kola, along with other provisions, was distributed to troops the evening before campaigns. In 1853 James Richardson reported how the emir of Zinder used kola to incite his soldiers: 'At night the Sultan calls round him his chosen troops, and distributes gour-nuts, and makes presents of provisions.'[82] Richardson's observation was made on the eve of a slave raid.

Because kola stains the teeth red, it was used as a cosmetic. According to a poem by Imam Imoru,

> kola colors the women's teeth and our own,
> strengthening them
> and making our conversation better.
> It is a treatment
> for the bad teeth of old folks.[83]

Women in particular valued kola as a cosmetic for their teeth. The otherwise less desirable *C. acuminata* supplied this market to a considerable extent. In Borno women rubbed their teeth with a powder made from *C. acuminata* and tobacco.[84]

Contemporary medical treatises written in Arabic identify at least forty medicinal and psychological uses for the nuts. Among its medicinal properties, kola provided relief from hunger, fatigue and thirst, but it was also a cure for various aches and pains, including toothaches and sore gums. It relieved sore throats, could ease headaches, overcome nausea and reduce fevers. It was thought to prevent the loss of hair, counteract greying, improve eye-sight and strengthen the knees.[85] Its prescription for sexual disorders has already been noted.

KOLA IN POPULAR CULTURE

The miracles, stories and popular culture of the nineteenth century highlight kola, and in that sense, people came to have a perception of kola that was determined as much by manipulated demand as by personal desire. The references to kola in the miracles attributed to Uthman dan Fodio, the Muslim cleric who led the *jihad* that founded the Caliphate, amounted to a form of advertising. The Shehu was credited with making a supernatural trip to the kola markets of the middle Volta basin, where he rested in the shade of the kola tree.[86] Because of his supernatural abilities, he was able to navigate the shoals of brigandage, extortion and time. He is also credited with rescuing a kola caravan that had difficulty crossing a river.[87]

Kola and the kola trade are mentioned frequently in the stories, lore and history of the Caliphate.[88] One proverb used the distinction between the unpopular and rarely consumed *C. acuminata* and the common *C. nitida* to make the point that the unacceptable cannot be passed off as the 'real thing': 'hannunruwa ba goro ba, ungulu ba nama ba' – '*C. acuminata* is not *C. nitida*, anymore than [the flesh of] a vulture is meat [that can be eaten]'.[89] The destruction of Madugu Mijinyawa Mai Akokari's caravan in Borgu in the last quarter of the nineteenth century was a common story,[90] while there are many accounts of caravan organization and the Hausa communities along the trade routes to the kola forests.[91]

Malam Sulaimanu Ilorin, who wrote a pamphlet in Hausa on kola in the 1950s, records a poem that praises kola as the fruit of the money tree.[92] As is common in such poetry, this poem is characterized by personification, kola being addressed as a person. Its rhythmic dimension arises from the use of repetition, playing on the words *jatau, gindi, d'aure* and *kwance* to convey various levels of meaning. The nuts are lauded because they possess magic, extend honour, provide blessing and have power; they are truly full of wonder. Its epithet, *jatau* (light-brown), signified that kola was a means to wealth, a feature that was elaborated upon through the expression *jatau jan bagare*. This phrase, which contained the epithet for kola, was associated with a penalty in a popular gambling game; by analogy, the risks of the kola trade were compared with the possibilities of wealth through gambling.[93] Ilorin juxtaposes the distance one had to travel to see the roots (*gindi*) of the kola tree with the fact that it was necessary to leave one's homeland (*gindin uwa tasa*) in order to do so. Ilorin ironically ascribes to kola the power to imprison (*d'aure*) the person who ties the nuts up into bundles, just as kola can release the person who unties (*kwance*) the bundles.

In *Kitabul Mas-alati Tanbul*, a poem written around the turn of the twentieth century, Imam Imoru lauds kola consumption because 'it strengthens our body and decreases our hunger'; it 'provides wisdom and understanding to him whoever takes it'.[94] Indeed Imoru described kola as 'the pleasure of our hearts when available in our hands'. Its consumption encouraged friendship because the nuts were often broken into pieces and shared, an attribute which he praised: the nuts 'improve our relationships [because] if we get it, we distribute it among our friends'.

We accept kola as a gift even if only a piece.
The two good [halves] are very special indeed
As for the pieces, they are more than sufficient,
For he who gives either is of high standing and will be rewarded.[95]

As Imoru recognized, sharing a piece of kola was generous, while the gift of a whole cotyledon was 'very special'. As far as this learned *imam* was concerned, 'the ordeal of the grave would decrease' for those who shared kola and gave these nuts as gifts. Kola was a religiously sanctioned stimulant and, accordingly, Imoru also employed the name of the Prophet in praising its attributes.

Imoru associated kola with wealth and social position. Only the aristocracy and prosperous commoners could afford it, and hence conspicuous consumption of kola and the presentation of gifts marked the wealthy man.

It increases money and prestige for youth.
It is brought to us as bundled by its owner,

Presented in the palaces of the emirs where it is distributed.
For the young, it increases influence; its fruit,
Even if little, is expensive, if we are regular [consumers].
Who among the great would not like to eat it?
Which among the rich do not like to taste it with his money?
. . . It is the food for our great honorable men.[96]

Imoru suggests that the display of wealth through the consumption of kola was a means of enhancing one's influence. Young men with ambition somehow had to acquire the financial resources for such display.

The anonymous poet of *Kitab fawa-idul*, the 'book of kola', also reflected popular attitudes towards kola.[97] The poet warned consumers against buying kola without knowledge of the different types. Kola consumption was associated with health, wealth and eternal salvation:

It is better for your life, so my people tell me.
It prolongs your life, for the chewer has said it.
After prolonging your life, you get the blessing of
Health for the body and then wealth.
Afterwards would you never enter hell
Rather you would have all the goodness that is in Paradise
forever.

Even parents and other members of the family of the consumer would be absolved of their sins.[98] The frequent references to the Prophet, Allah, heaven and the absolution of sins not only reveal the religious tolerance of kola consumption but actually demonstrate the extent to which kola was legitimized in terms of Islam. In this society the mildly addictive quality of this stimulant was socially acceptable; indeed kola consumption received religious sanction and was openly encouraged.

Another poet, interviewed by A. Prietze in Cairo in 1911, lamented the impact of kola on both consumers and the merchants who dealt in it.[99]

Kola, tree of Gonja
[Worth] great sums of money,
The product of Asante,
Anyone who becomes addicted to you
Will never stop paying money.
Anyone who trades in you
Will stumble and fall
Until he dies in destitution.

Again through the technique of personification Prietze's poet, who was on pilgrimage to Mecca, appears to be criticizing the materialism associated with kola consumption and kola trading.[100] Considering the cost of kola in North Africa, moreover, the poet may have been suffering withdrawal symptoms as well.

Because of its value, 'kola' came to be synonymous with a gift, even a bribe. *Goro* referred to the reward given for the return of lost property, whether or not kola was actually given as the reward. When a person promised news that was anticipated as good news, the recipient often promised 'goro' in advance of hearing it. Even more generally, *goro* was the term used to refer to gifts that were offered in lieu of favours.[101] It is for these reasons that kola had some of the properties of money, as noted by Imam Imoru.[102] Kola was so valuable that it was recognized as a method of payment and reward, and today *goro* sometimes even refers to a bribe.

Even though the production and consumption of kola were religiously sanctioned, it was a luxury that was subject to the vagaries of trade in non-essential commodities. Kola was similar to other addictive substances in that demand was highly inelastic; no matter how much could be imported, there was always a market. No one really needed kola, despite the glorification of kola consumption that merchants, aristocrats and Muslim clerics encouraged. Kola is not a bad thing to chew if a caffeine and theobromine fix is desired. Packaging is easy, if kola is bought on the street and consumption commences within a few days of purchase. The side-effects are minimal, perhaps a little diarrhoea if the nuts are not clean, but normally nothing more than a little hypernervousness results from too much caffeine. Kola is an aphrodisiac, if for no other reason than it keeps lovers awake. Headaches are undoubtedly overcome if the cause of the pain is withdrawal symptoms from this mild stimulant. The other powers assigned to kola appear to be psychological and personal, however real the effects of ingestion may seem.

NOTES

1 James Richardson, *Travels in North Africa*, London, Richard Bentley, 1846, vol. 1, p. 254.

2 Various authorities differ in reporting the amounts of caffeine and theobromine in mild stimulants. Egil Ramstad (*Modern Pharmacognosy*, New York, McGraw Hill, 1959, pp. 316–17) states that cocoa has 0.8 to 2.3 per cent theobromine, with a tenth as much caffeine; that tea has 1.0 to 4.7 per cent caffeine; and that coffee has 0.7 to 2.3 per cent caffeine. Henry Kraemer (*A Text-Book of Botany and Pharmacognosy*, Philadelphia, J. B. Lippincott, 1910, pp. 332, 334, 381, 435) records cocoa with 0.07 to 0.36 per cent caffeine and 1.0 to 4.0 per cent theobromine; tea with 1.5 to 3.5 per cent caffeine and traces of theobromine; coffee with 1.0 to 2.0 per cent caffeine and no theobromine; and *C. acuminata* with 1.5 to 3.6 per cent caffeine and 0.02 to 0.09 per cent theobromine. Robertson Pratt and Heber W. Youngken, Jr. (*Pharmacognosy: The Study of Natural Drug Substances and Certain Allied Products*, Philadelphia, J. B. Lippincott, 1956, 2nd edn, pp. 285–8) state that

cocoa has 1.0 to 4.0 per cent theobromine and no caffeine; that tea has 1.0 to 4.0 per cent caffeine and traces of theobromine; that coffee has 1.0 to 3.0 per cent caffeine; and that *C. nitida* has 1.0 to 4.0 per cent caffeine and small amounts of theobromine. Table 1 records the lower and upper limits of the various reports. The various studies reported in August Chevalier and Em. Perrot, *Les kolatiers et les noix de kola*, Paris, Augustin Challamel, 1911, pp. 219–30, fall within the range cited here.

3 J. Hutchinson and J. M. Dalziel, *Flora of West Tropical Africa* (revised edn, R. W. J. Keay), London, Crown Agents for Overseas Governments and Administrations, 1958, vol. 1, part 2, pp. 321–2; T. A. Russell, 'The kola of Nigeria and the Cameroons', *Tropical Agriculture*, 1955, vol. 32, pp. 211–12; Richard M. Straw, 'Cola nut', *Encyclopedia Americana*, New York, American Corporation, 1964, vol. 7, pp. 232b–233; John Mitchell Watt and Maria Gerdina Breyer-Brandwijk, *The Medicinal and Poisonous Plants of Southern and Eastern Africa*, London, E. Edinburgh and S. Livingstone, 1962, 2nd edn, p. 1013.

4 Chevalier and Perrot, op. cit.

5 Russell, op. cit., p. 222; A. Wirz, *Vom Sklavenhandel zum kolonialen Handel*, Zurich, Atlantis-Verlag, 1972, pp. 157–8; Douglas Edwin Ferguson, 'Nineteenth century Hausaland, being a description by Imam Imoru of the land, economy, and society of his people', unpublished PhD thesis, UCLA, 1973, p. 386; Chevalier and Perrot, op. cit., pp. 180, 186; and Bernard-Aloys Nkongmeneck, 'Contribution a l'étude du genre cola au Cameroun', Thèse de docteur en sciences biologiques, Université de Yaounde, 1982.

6 Dennis Cordell has recorded information on the kola trade of Dar al-Kuti. Some kola was brought east from the Sokoto Caliphate and Borno, and some was imported from the south; personal communication, 5 June 1982.

7 This property was noted by Imhammed in 1789; see Henry Beaufoy, 'Mr. Lucas's communications', in R. Hallet (ed.), *Proceedings of the Association for Promoting the Discovery of the Interior Parts of Africa*, London, Hakluyt Society, 1967, vol. 1, p. 183. Also see Paul E. Lovejoy, *Caravans of Kola. The Hausa Kola Trade, 1700–1900*, Zaria and Ibadan, Ahmadu Bello University Press and University Press (Nigeria), 1980, p. 4.

8 For an overview, see Paul E. Lovejoy, 'Kola in the history of West Africa', *Cahiers d'Etudes Africaines*, 1980, vol. 20 (1/2), pp. 97–134; and George E. Brooks, 'Kola trade and statebuilding: Upper Guinea Coast and Senegambia, 15th–17th centuries', Working Paper No. 38, African Studies Center, Boston University, 1980.

9 Lovejoy, 'Kola in the history of West Africa', op. cit., pp. 97–134; and Brooks, op. cit.

10 Lovejoy, 'Kola in the history of West Africa', op. cit., pp. 103–8. Also see L. Marchese, *Atlas linguistique Kru*, Abidjan, IFAN, 1978, p. 208; and H. -C. Grégoire, *Etude de la langue Gouro (Région de Zuénoula)*, Abidjan, IFAN, 1975, p. 30. I wish to thank Joseph Lauer for additional references that elaborate on my earlier article.

11 H. P. J. Renaud, 'La première mention de la noix de kola dans la matière médicale des Arabes', *Hespéris*, 1928, vol. 8, pp. 43–57.

12 See Lovejoy, 'Kola in the history of West Africa', op. cit., pp. 97–134.

13 W. R. Elliot, Report on Labojie District, 24 November 1903, CSO 1/27/4, Nigerian National Archives, Ibadan; Edwardes, Report on Laboghi District, November 1902, Mss. Afr. s. 769, Rhodes House; B. A. Agiri, 'The introduction of Nitida kola into Nigerian agriculture, 1880–1920', *African Economic History*, 1977, vol. 3, pp. 2–5.

14 Chevalier and Perrot, op. cit., p. 358.
15 A. C. Miles, Report of a Cola Survey of the Eastern Ashanti Areas and a General Review of the Gold Coast Cola Industry, 20 March 1931, C. O. 98/59, Public Record Office.
16 Jean-Loup Amselle, 'Les réseaux marchands Kooroko', *African Urban Notes*, 1970, vol. 1(2), p. 145.
17 See, for example, Martin Ford, 'Kola production and settlement mobility among the Dan of Nimba, Liberia', *African Economic History*, 1992, vol. 20, pp. 51–63.
18 B. A. Agiri, 'The Yoruba and the pre-colonial kola trade', *Odu. A Journal of West African Studies*, 1975, vol. 12, pp. 55–68; idem, 'Trade in gbanja kola in south western Nigeria, 1900–1950', *Odu. A Journal of West African Studies*, 1986, vol. 30, pp. 25–45; and Agiri 'The introduction of Nitida Kola', op. cit., pp. 1–14.
19 Paul E. Lovejoy, 'The wholesale kola trade of Kano', *African Urban Notes*, 1970, vol. 5, no. 2, p. 141; and idem, *Caravans of Kola*, op. cit., p. 151.
20 For the Nigerian kola industry, see B. A. Agiri, 'Kola in Western Nigeria, 1850–1950. A history of the cultivation of *Cola Nitida* in Egba-Owode, Ijebu-Remo, Iwo and Ota areas', unpublished PhD thesis, University of Wisconsin, 1972; and Akanmu G. Adebayo, 'The kola nut trade in West Africa: A note on the Nigerian end of the trade under British rule, 1900–45', *FAB*, Frankfurt.
21 Samuel Onanuga Onakomaiya, 'The spatial structure of internal trade in delicacy foodstuffs in Nigeria', unpublished PhD thesis, University of Wisconsin, 1970, p. 87; C. L. N. van Eijnatten, 'Statistics on the production of kola nuts and the trade in this commodity, with special reference to Nigeria', Memorandum No. 1, Cocoa Research Institute of Nigeria, Ibadan, 1964. In 1964 rail shipments within Nigeria totalled 53,000 tons; see Ade Akinbode, *Kolanut Production and Trade in Nigeria*, Ibadan, NISER, 1982, p. 56. By this time, however, most kola was being transported in trucks; see Lovejoy, 'The wholesale kola trade of Kano', op. cit., p. 136.
22 As quoted in Raymound Mauny, *Tableau géographique de l'Ouest africain au Moyen Age, d'après les sources écrites, la tradition et l'archéologie*, Dakar, IFAN, 1961, p. 249. Also see Renaud, op. cit., and Nehemia Levtzion, *Ancient Ghana and Mali*, London, Methuen, 1973, pp. 182–3.
23 As discussed in Brooks, op. cit.
24 R. Austin Freeman, 'A journey to Bontuku, in the interior of West Africa', *Royal Geographical Society, Supplementary Papers*, 1893, vol. 3, p. 144.
25 Jaspar Guy Woodroof and G. Frank Phillips, *Beverages: Carbonated and Noncarbonated*, Westport, Conn., AVI Publishing, revised edn, 1981, p. 18; J. C. Louis and Harvey Z. Yazijian, *The Cola Wars*, New York, Everest House, 1980, p. 13–16; and John J. Riley, *A History of the American Soft Drink Industry*, New York, Arno Press, 1972. I wish to thank Peter Knights for his assistance on the origins of the cola drinks.
26 Louis and Yazijian, op. cit., p. 49.
27 Since the word for kola in the trading network of the Juula was *woro*, the Hausa word had to have been borrowed before the sound shift from 'g' to 'w' had occurred in Mande Juula, which suggests considerable antiquity. The Hausa word could not have been borrowed from the producers of kola in the Akan forests, who used *bese* as the word for kola and not the common root *-gola, -kola*. Such linguistic analysis is further proof that the original area of *C. nitida* production was in the far west. The Akan forests had several varieties of kola before the introduction of *C. nitida*, which apparently explains the use of an indigenous term rather than the adoption of a new

word deriving from the common root. See Lovejoy, 'Kola in the history of West Africa', op. cit. It should be noted that the sound shift between 'l' and 'r' is common.

28 Heinrich Barth, *Travels and Discoveries in North and Central Africa: Being a Journal of an Expedition undertaken under the Auspices of H.R.M.'s Government in the Years 1849–1855*, New York, Harper & Brothers, 1859, vol. 1, p. 514, based on his observations in Kano in 1851.

29 Ferguson, op. cit., p. 384. Imam Imoru wrote extensively on late nineteenth-century society and economy, and some of his writings have been translated into English by Ferguson. Imoru was also a noted poet and legal scholar. He was born and raised in Kano, but spent much of his adult life in the kola markets of the middle Volta basin. He was the *imam* at Kete-Krachi, which became part of German Togo, where he worked closely with the German scholar, Adam Mischlich, who published some of Imoru's work.

30 Ferguson, op. cit., p. 387.

31 G. P. Bargery, *A Hausa–English Dictionary and English–Hausa Vocabulary*, London, 1934, p. 899.

32 Lovejoy, *Caravans of Kola*, op. cit., p. 4. The entry under *goro* in Bargery's dictionary (p. 398) is very detailed.

33 Paul Staudinger, *In the Heart of the Hausa States*, Athens, Ohio University Press, 1990, tr. J. Moody, vol. 2, p. 147. Staudinger's observations apply to 1885–6.

34 The official was the *madaki*; see M. Hiskett, 'Materials relating to the cowry currency of the Western Sudan: a late nineteenth-century schedule of inheritance from Kano', *Bulletin of the School of Oriental and African Studies*, 1966, vol. 29, no. 1, p. 139.

35 See especially Lovejoy, *Caravans of Kola*, op. cit.

36 Paul E. Lovejoy, *Salt of the Desert Sun. A History of Salt Production and Trade in the Central Sudan*, Cambridge, Cambridge University Press, 1986, pp. 25–7.

37 Gustav Nachtigal, *Sahara and Sudan. Kawar, Bornu, Kanem, Borku, Ennedi*, London, C. Hurst & Co., 1980, tr. and ed. Allan G. B. Fisher and Humphrey J. Fisher, vol. 2, p. 203.

38 Staudinger, op. cit., vol. 2, p. 148. Staudinger also mentions that gum arabic was sometimes chewed in the sahel.

39 But see the accounts collected by Frank Edgar, *Litafi na Tatsuniyoyi na Hausa*, 1911, Belfast: as translated by Neal Skinner, *Hausa Tales and Traditions*, Madison, University of Wisconsin Press, 1977, particularly the story of the emir of Katsina, vol. 3, p. 119, which appears to refer to smoking among the pre-*jihad* aristocracy of Katsina.

40 Lovejoy, *Salt of the Desert Sun*, op. cit., pp. 25–7.

41 For the import of coffee and tea into Kano in 1885, see Staudinger, op. cit., vol. 1, pp. 222–3, 224, 228.

42 In the 1850s, Barth, op. cit., vol. 3, p. 363, found it curious that 'the natives do not feel the want of coffee', which he believed 'they might so easily cultivate'. In fact coffee cultivation was introduced to south-western Nigeria, southern Ghana, southern Cameroon, and other forest areas in the last decades of the nineteenth century, but the crop has never done as well as in other parts of the tropical world. None the less, Barth's comment still has relevance because it reveals the limited extent to which varieties of stimulants had dispersed to western Africa by the middle of the nineteenth century.

43 Nachtigal, op. cit., vol. 2, p. 201.

44 Ibid., vol. 2, p. 202.

45 Ibid., vol. 2, p. 201.
46 Ibid., vol. 2, p. 203.
47 See the story about Kwasau, Emir of Zazzau and Abubakar, Emir of Nupe, as translated by Skinner, op. cit., vol. 3, p. 108.
48 Staudinger, op. cit., vol. 2, pp. 145–6.
49 Nachtigal, op. cit., vol. 2, p. 201.
50 Dixon Denham, Hugh Clapperton, and Walter Oudney, *Narrative of Travels and Discoveries in Northern and Central Africa in the Years 1822, 1823, and 1824*, London, John Murray, 1828, vol. 1, p. 56; Nachtigal, op. cit., vol. 1, p. 111, vol. 3, p. 213; Staudinger, op. cit., vol. 1, p. 212.
51 William Balfour Baikie, *Narrative of an Exploring Voyage up the Rivers Kwora and Binue in 1854*, London, John Murray, 1856, p. 164.
52 Nachtigal, op. cit., vol. 2, pp. 111, 141–2, 202.
53 Staudinger, op. cit., vol. 1, p. 67.
54 John Milum, 'Note of a journey from Lagos up the River Niger to Bida, the capital of Nupe and Illorin in the Yoruba country, 1879–80', *Proceedings of the Royal Geographical Society*, 1881, p. 29.
55 See the story as translated by Skinner, op. cit., vol. 3, p. 82.
56 Ibid., vol. 1, p. 146.
57 Nachtigal, op. cit., vol. 2, pp. 283, 319.
58 A. Mattei, *Bas-Niger, Beneoue, Dahomey*, Grenoble, Vallier et Baratier, 1890; Jean Vuillet and H. Vuillet, 'Les kolatiers et les kola', *L'Agriculture pratique des pays chauds*, 1906, vol. 6, p. 329.
59 Testimonies of Muhammadu Kasori, interviewed 24 December 1969, Kano; Audu Ba'are, interviewed 18 January 1970, Kano; Gote Musa, interviewed 26 February 1970, Jega; and Muhammadu Dan Amarya, interviewed 5 March 1970, Gummi.
60 Paul E. Lovejoy, *Caravans of Kola*, op. cit., p. 109.
61 See 'The character of all Hausas', as translated by Skinner, op. cit., vol. 3, p. 222; and 'The descriptions', in R. Sutherland Rattray, *Hausa Folk-lore, Customs, Proverbs, etc.*, London, Oxford University Press, 1913, vol. 2, p. 186. Rattray based his book on the stories and accounts written down by Malam Sha'ibu, who gathered material from the members of Hausa caravans at the Volta River crossing of Yeji between 1907 and 1911.
62 Ferguson, op. cit., p. 251.
63 Rattray, op. cit., vol. 2, p. 150.
64 Ferguson, op. cit., pp. 276–7, 279. Also see Nachtigal, op. cit., vol. 2, p. 276, vol. 3, p. 60; Staudinger, op. cit., vol. 2, pp. 62, 147; A. J. N. Tremearne, *Hausa Superstitions and Customs*, London, Frank Cass, 1970 [1913], p. 142; Rattray, op. cit., vol. 2, pp. 152–64, 174–6; and Skinner, op. cit., p. 223.
65 Ibid., p. 224. It is not clear when this account was collected, but certainly between 1903 and 1911, either by Frank Edgar, who published the original in Hausa, or by Alder Burdon, whose collection of stories and histories was given to Edgar in 1903. Also see Ahmed Al Nasr, *Maiwurno of the Blue Nile. A Study of an Oral Biography*, Khartoum, 1980, p. 35.
66 Tremearne, op. cit., p. 77.
67 Al Nasr, op. cit., p. 35.
68 Nachtigal, op. cit., vol. 2, p. 202.
69 'Yana sa su so maza da yawa', and 'Yana sa su kwadayin maza da yawa'; according to a Muslim pilgrim interviewed in Cairo in 1912 by Rudolf Prietze; see 'Arzneipflanzen der Haussa', *Zeitschrift für Koloniale Sprachen*, 1913–14, vol. 4, p. 87. I have corrected Prietze's orthography according to Bargery, op. cit.

70 Prietze, op. cit., p. 87.

71 The subject of male and female sexuality has not been studied in any detail, more because it is taboo among scholars than because of an absence of data. As the discussion of kola demonstrates, there is considerable information on sexuality in oral data collected in the late 1960s and mid-1970s and in the written documentation from the end of the nineteenth and the early twentieth centuries. See, for example, the accounts as translated by Skinner (op. cit.), especially the discussion of the three types of males, depending upon the frequency and intensity of sexual desire, and the three types of women, depending upon the extent to which the clitoris is 'excessively developed' or 'deeply set in' (vol. 3, pp. 325–6). It is likely that the sources for these accounts were all men. For a discussion of the question of sexuality in the nineteenth century with respect to concubinage, see my 'Concubinage in the Sokoto Caliphate (1804–1903)', *Slavery and Abolition*, 1990, vol. 11(2), pp. 159–89.

72 Tremearne, op. cit., p. 151. Prietze, op. cit., p. 40.

73 M. Hiskett, *A History of Hausa Islamic Verse*, London, SOAS, 1975, p. 68.

74 Ibrahim Madauci, Yahaya Isa and Bello Daura, *Hausa Customs*, Zaria, Gaskiya Corporation, 1968, p. 81. Also see Tremearne, op. cit., p. 83.

75 Preitze, op. cit., p. 88.

76 H. B. Foulkes, Assessment Report, Dan Buram District, Kano Emirate, 1911, SNP 7/13 5785/1912 (Nigerian National Archives, Kaduna).

77 Ferguson, op. cit., p. 309.

78 Testimony of Nagudu Abdullahi, interviewed 5 November 1969, Kano.

79 Nachtigal, op. cit., vol. 3, p. 282.

80 Prietze, op. cit., p. 88.

81 Barth, op. cit., vol. 3, p. 122.

82 James Richardson, *Narrative of a Mission to Central Africa*, London, Chapman & Hall, 1854, vol. 2, p. 238. The raid to be launched by the emir of Zinder, the western province of Borno, was directed against Daura, one of the emirates in the Caliphate.

83 Arabic ms. No. 65, Kabprof M/AR4, translated by Abdullahi Bello, Zaria, 10 March 1975. Also see Prietze, op. cit., pp. 87–8.

84 Nachtigal, op. cit., vol. 2, p. 158.

85 Prietze, op. cit., pp. 87–8.

86 Gidado Dan Laima, *Raud al-jinan*, c. 1840, as translated by H. B. Harris, 'The Burden of Burdens', unpublished. The same miracle is described by Isa Dan Shaihu in *Wakar karamomin Shaihu*, the Hausa poem based on *Raud al-jinan*; see Mervyn Hiskett, '"The Song of the Shaihu's miracles": a Hausa hagiography from Sokoto', *African Language Studies*, 1971, vol. 12, p. 77. Also see Russell, op. cit., p. 210.

87 Two variants of this miracle are included in Edgar's collection, as translated and edited in Skinner, op. cit., vol. 3, pp. 9–12. For variants, see Abubakar Imam, *Magana Jari Ce*, Zaria, Gaskiya Corporation, 1937, pp. 112–18. For another story involving the Shehu and kola, see Sule Ilorin, *Tarihin Goro*, Zaria, Gaskiya Corporation, 1958, p. 2.

88 See, for example, Skinner's translations of 'The maiden, the frog and king's son' and 'Abdullahi, Emir of Kano, and the malam', in op. cit., vol. 2, p. 313, vol. 3, p. 82.

89 Rattray, op. cit., vol. 2, p. 254. Rattray records two other proverbs that pertain to kola, see vol. 2, p. 266.

90 'The caravan-leader, Mijinyawa-Mai-Akokari and all the other caravan leaders', as translated in Skinner, op. cit., vol. 3, pp. 245–7.

91 See the accounts by Imam Imoru which were reproduced and translated into German in Heinz Solken, 'Afrikanische Dokumente zur Frage der Enststehung der Hausanischen Diaspora in Oberguinea', *Mitteilungen aus der Ausland Hochschule*, 1939, vol. 42(3), pp. 79–100. Also see M. Heepe, 'Gottlob Adolf Krauses Haussa-Handschriften in der Preussischen Staatsbibliothek, Berlin', *Mitteilungen des Seminars für Orientalische Sprachen*, 1928, vol. 31, pp. xxviii–lxxx; and Jack Goody and T. M. Mustapha, 'The caravan trade from Kano to Salaga', *Journal of the Historical Society of Nigeria*, 1967, vol. 3(4), pp. 613–15, which includes an English translation of one of Krause's manuscripts. Also see 'Losing-on-the-exchange and the caravan-leader' and 'The trader and the Magajiya', in Skinner, op. cit., vol. 2, pp. 474–9 and 489–91.

92 'Goro goriya, d'an itace mai kud'i, mai sihiri, mai daraja, mai albarka, mai iko, mai ban mamaki! Jatau garinka da nisa, kowa ya zo ganin gindinka ya baro gindin uwa tasa. Jatau jan bagare, d'aure mai d'aure ka in ka so, kwance mai kwance ka in ka so'; see Ilorin, op. cit., p. i. I wish to thank Ibrahim Jumare for assistance in translating the poem, although the interpretation is mine.

93 Bargery, op. cit., pp. 57, 494.

94 No. 65, Kabprof M/AR4, translated by Abdullahi Bello, Zaria, 10 March 1975.

95 Ibid.

96 Ibid.

97 The author of *Kitab fawa-idul Jaur* was a cleric of Kano, whose name is not given; its composition dates from the early twentieth century or earlier still, Arabic ms. No. 73, Kanoprof C/AR4.

98 *Kitab fawa-idul Jaur*.

99 See Prietze, op. cit., p. 87. I have rendered Prietze's transliteration as follows:

> Goro, itacen Gwanja,
> D'umbun kud'i
> D'an Asance;
> Kowa ya saba da kai
> Bai ya barin kud'i.
> Kowa ya yi fataucin ka
> Ya fad'i
> Sai ya mutu da tsiya.

Gonja was the province north of Asante where the kola traders went to buy kola. While kola did not grow there, the trade was often referred to as 'the trade of Gwanja [Gonja]'. I wish to thank Ibrahim Jumare for assistance in translating Prietze's material.

100 Hiskett, op. cit., p. 80.

101 Bargery, op. cit., p. 398.

102 Ferguson, op. cit., p. 384.

6

EXCITANTIA

Or, how Enlightenment Europe took to soft drugs[1]

Jordan Goodman

> The vegetable kingdom offered its green deliria to the people and to those particular experts on nature's secrets who were present in the great 'pharmaceutical theatre'.[2]

> This delicious nectar has all the good effects of wine without the ill; a Liquor that warms without Inflammation, and exhilarates without intoxicating.[3]

Precise figures for European consumption of tobacco, coffee, chocolate and tea during the eighteenth century are lacking but available estimates provide evidence of a remarkable phenomenon. The consumption of these commodities grew as follows: tobacco, from 50 million to 125 million pounds; coffee from 2 million to 120 million pounds; chocolate from 2 million to 13 million pounds; and tea from 1 million to 40 million pounds.[4] Europe's population grew by more than 50 per cent but there was much more to this consumer revolution in soft drugs than demographic change alone.[5] The Age of the Enlightenment embraced a new lifestyle in which tea, coffee, chocolate and tobacco together with sugar, the fruits of overseas expansion and commercial capitalism, played a critical cultural role.[6] It was not, as might first be supposed, embraced by only the ruling or even the middle classes: all of these commodities were being mass consumed by the 1720s or 1730s in large parts of Europe.[7]

The explanation developed in this chapter has several parts to it. The first section I call Europeanization, an ongoing process of appropriation, development and definition which, in the case of the commodities under review in this chapter, began in the sixteenth century and reached its apogee in the eighteenth century. It was a multidimensional process comprising the full range of activities involved in consumption, production and distribution, plus a wide range of ideological, including medical, and symbolic constructions.[8] Europeanization not only made these commodities available to European consumers on a regular and reasonably predictable basis, but it also created historically unique combinations and configurations of these commodities in European form. The second section of the explanation concerns how and why Europeans consumed these particular commodities in the first place and how and why that consumption was sustained and grew over time. Interestingly these obvious questions have been virtually ignored or dismissed as trivial by historians, though not by other investigators.[9] What will be argued in this essay is that tea, coffee and chocolate substituted for indigenous commodities and tobacco for other herbal panaceas. The substitution was not simply commodity for commodity but was rather part of a large-scale transformation of the role of plants and the relationship between the natural world and Europeans that occurred during the seventeenth and eighteenth centuries. The final section of the explanation concerns the rituals associated with their consumption: their incorporation within and effects upon alimentary structures, principally the use of meals.[10] Piero Camporesi has referred to an aspect of this change – 'la science de savoir faire' – but it was more widespread, both socially and spatially, than he suggests.[11]

I

The rituals and meanings associated with the consumption of tea, coffee, chocolate and tobacco are deeply embedded in our culture. The habitual consumption of tea, coffee, chocolate and tobacco is a public affirmation of the central place of the consumption of a few, key, legal drugs in Western culture.[12] Significantly, these drugs are not nakedly consumed; they are clothed in a commodified form wherein is hidden an economic, social, cultural and political reality. Drinking tea, coffee, or chocolate and smoking cigarettes is quite different from consuming caffeine, theine, theobromine and nicotine. (Contrast this with the consumption of illicit drugs: heroin, cocaine, crack, even marijuana). Yet caffeine, nicotine, etc. are powerful alkaloids of their respective plants, with rather similar pharmacological properties and have been recognized for a long time as producing physiological changes primarily but not exclusively in the mind and as addictive.[13]

These rituals had their origin in the eighteenth century when they were used to proclaim a powerful ideology of sobriety and respectability. How the new soft drugs came to be associated with this ideology can partly be explained by the way in which Europe absorbed and transformed their mode of production, distribution and consumption.

Europe was the direct beneficiary of a prolonged period during which tea, coffee, chocolate and tobacco were brought to the point of commercial viability and consumer acceptance. This involved the process of botanical experimentation and selection, developments in methods of cultivation and processing leading to distinctive commodities with their own particular modes of consumption. These commodities, therefore, appeared in Europe replete with their own historical experiences often rooted in antiquity, enacted in China, the Near East and the New World. Tea and tobacco were certainly consumed in China and the Americas, respectively, by about 2000 BC.[14] Central American Amerindians were cultivating the cocoa tree at least a thousand years before Columbus reached the New World.[15] Coffee was probably being consumed in Ethiopia and Yemen by about AD 800–1000.[16]

Tobacco was the first of the new exotica to enter Europe as a direct result of the expansion of European interests overseas. Still, it took almost a century – from Columbus in 1492, to the publication in 1571 by Nicolas Monardes of his natural history of medicinal plants of the New World (which launched tobacco as an extraordinary panacea) – for Europeans to take up the nicotian habit.[17] Coffee made its first appearance in Europe, in Venice, in the first few decades of the seventeenth century, as part of its diffusion through the Middle East, from Yemen to the eastern Mediterranean lands, to the main cities of Islam, especially Baghdad, Cairo and Aleppo.[18] By the middle of the century, coffeehouses had sprung up in many of Europe's major cities, especially in Paris, London, Marseille and Vienna.[19] Until this time, coffee supplies into Europe were erratic and relatively small scale, traded across the Mediterranean into the ports of southern Europe, particularly Marseille.[20]

Chocolate, too, spread slowly from its homeland, Central America, to Europe. Though Columbus came across chocolate on his fourth voyage, the Spanish only became interested in it after the Conquest and it remained confined, in terms of consumption, to the populations of the newly conquered territories, both the indigenous Amerindians and the Spanish newcomers, for a long time. Shipments of chocolate to Europe date from the first decade of the seventeenth century (and possibly earlier than that) but not until the middle of the century did Europeans become familiar with the chocolate beverage.[21]

Tea faced a similar experience in Europe. Reports of its use in China and Japan were circulating in late sixteenth-century Europe and though some shipments of tea from China were made by the Dutch East India Company as early as 1606, the Company did not begin regular imports until the second half of the century.[22] The English East India Company started regular shipments of tea from Canton to London in the 1660s, though English acquaintance with tea drinking antedated the Company's involvement: Holland supplied the English market for the first half of the seventeenth century.[23]

Driven by the twin pillars of early modern economic ideology, colonialism and mercantilism, Europeans as a whole were not prepared to be supplied with these new drugs by non-Europeans, nor were they willing to be dependent on each other. Achieving control over production and distribution was a key feature of the Europeanization of these exotic commodities. Tobacco was the first commodity to undergo this transformation and its progress was very rapid. Europeans began cultivating tobacco in the New World and Europe in the final decade of the sixteenth century: Spanish colonists initially bartered tobacco from Amerindian producers in Venezuela but by the later years of the sixteenth century they had learned how to grow the plant from their neighbours.[24] This critical appropriation of Amerindian plant-lore and practice was rapidly overshadowed, however, by the remarkable success by English colonists in Virginia who, by the 1620s, were already meeting most of European demand.[25] Tobacco was a powerful instrument of European colonialism and settlement in the New World because it appealed to yeoman farmers, Dutch, French, Portuguese, English, even Swedish.[26] By the beginning of the eighteenth century, European consumption of tobacco was supplied principally by Virginia (almost 80 per cent) and the rest mostly by Brazil.[27] Cocoa cultivation also came to be controlled by Europeans, though there were some important differences when compared to tobacco. Unlike tobacco which was wholly incorporated within the European system – capital and labour were both European until the end of the seventeenth century – chocolate supplies to Europe came by way of the tribute system that Spain imposed on the conquered Amerindians, as the Aztecs had done before the Conquest.[28] Until the end of the sixteenth century, cocoa cultivation concentrated in those regions of central America where cocoa was a pre-Conquest crop. Thereafter, however, partly because of Amerindian depopulation in traditional cocoa-growing areas, cultivation expanded into Ecuador and especially Venezuela.[29] By the turn of the eighteenth century, Venezuela had become the New World's most important source of chocolate, a position which it held throughout the century: increasingly, after the middle of the seventeenth century, Venezuelan chocolate exports found their way to Holland and Spain, and from there were transshipped to European consumers.[30] Other European powers in the New World turned to cocoa cultivation as a possible staple crop but with varying degrees of success: Portugal, the most successful, Holland and France, less so and England, the least successful.[31] During the eighteenth century, Venezuela and the Amazon were the largest producers of chocolate, accounting for as much as 90 per cent of European consumption.[32]

Both tobacco and chocolate were rapidly Europeanized through colonialism and settlement. Coffee, by contrast, was grown outside the European colonial system and distributed to European buyers by a large number of intermediaries. The East Indies Companies, English, Dutch and French, were largely in the power of the rulers of Yemen when they came to purchase coffee and they were not the biggest buyers in the market until the eighteenth century. The Dutch East India Company was the first to break free of the Yemeni. In 1707 the Company ordered the planting of coffee bushes in Java, using seeds from a plant first grown in Ceylon in 1658. The first supplies reached Amsterdam and were sold at auction in 1712.[33] Fifteen years later Dutch merchants, once the most prominent buyers, were no longer to be seen in the coffee market in Beit el-Fakih: almost all Dutch consumption was now supplied by Java which, in the meantime, also rose to account for between 50 per cent and 75 per cent of the world's coffee trade.[34] Surinam began coffee cultivation in 1712 but shipments to Holland did not begin until 1718: thereafter coffee became the colony's second crop, after sugar – in 1772 Surinam produced over 12 million lbs of coffee.[35] The French, who were also big buyers in Mocha and Beit el-Fakih, profited directly from the Dutch success with the coffee plant. The Jardin des Plantes in Paris was able to produce seeds from a coffee plant that it had received from the Amsterdam Botanical Gardens.[36] These seeds were planted in Martinique in 1723.[37] From Surinam, the French introduced coffee cultivation into Cayenne in 1722 and, earlier, in 1715, another plant, apparently from Mocha itself, was planted successfully on Réunion, in the Indian Ocean, while in the same year cultivation began in St Domingue.[38] By 1789 St Domingue was exporting 77 million lbs of coffee and, according to one writer, was supplying about 60 per cent of the Western world's consumption.[39] After 1730 coffee from Martinique penetrated the Near Eastern market itself and the French began to withdraw as buyers from the region.[40] All of this was in contrast to the English who were slow to encourage coffee cultivation in their colonies: Jamaica, the most successful, produced insignificant quantities before the 1770s, and even though output finally exceeded 10 million lbs by the turn of the nineteenth century, this was considerably less than French planters produced in St Domingue or Martinique.[41]

The examples of tobacco, cocoa and coffee demonstrate above all the historical context within which the Europeanization of these commodities occurred. It was a primary strategy of the colonial enterprise to appropriate to itself as much of the production and distribution of exotic goods as possible. The colonial enterprise was eminently successful in tobacco, cocoa and coffee but tea was another matter. Until well into the nineteenth century China kept the tea plant to itself. The Dutch, urged by the Dutch East India Company, attempted to grow tea plants in Java from seeds procured in Japan from as early as 1684 but nothing came of this early venture into the tea transfer.[42] Other attempts to transfer the tea plant, even to Europe, were also made in the eighteenth century but without success.[43] Real success did not come in Java until the 1830s when technical assistance on how to prepare tea leaves for the market as well as sufficient seed was obtained from China.[44] Britain was even slower in transferring tea growing to its colonies: it was not until 1850 that Robert Fortune, a plant collector commissioned by the East India Company, arrived in India with plants and seeds from China.[45]

Even though the control over the production of tea eluded Europeans until the nineteenth century, they were, nevertheless, able to gain control over distribution from the port of Canton but this, too, was a protracted affair. In the seventeenth century, for example, Europeans received their tea from the Dutch East India Company by way of Chinese junks that supplied Batavia.[46] Access to the Chinese market was particularly difficult: the English East India Company did not drop anchor in the harbour of Canton before 1713 and it was not until the 1730s that European companies traded directly with the Chinese at Canton.[47] Once control over distribution occurred, the export of tea from China soared: legal exports increased more than twenty-fold in the period from 1719/25 to 1799/1806, from an average annual of 1.7 million lbs to 38 million lbs.[48]

Thanks to the European domination over the production and distribution of tea, coffee, chocolate and tobacco, their availability in Europe became more regular and on an increasingly large scale. European consumers benefited directly from the rapid absorption of these commodities into a highly sophisticated and efficient trading system within Europe.[49] Not only did these commodities enlarge the foreign trade sector of many European countries and become relatively more important as the early modern period progressed but they increasingly entered into the highly lucrative re-export trade.[50] Tea, coffee, chocolate and tobacco entered Europe, both officially and unoffcially, at myriad seaports and inland ports, providing therefore countless gateways to the market and the European consumer.[51] Remarking on the situation in England, Carole Shammas has cogently argued that 'the rationalization of overseas mercantile activity had, by the late 18th century, so far outstripped that of the domestic provisions business that consumers could often rely on the availability of sugar, tea, or tobacco more certainly than on the supply of dairy products and some cereals'.[52] Undoubtedly, the fact that tea, coffee, chocolate and tobacco were relatively non-perishable and came to the consumer in a processed and fairly standardized form, contributed to its widespread availability.

Europeanization can also be seen at work at the point of consumption. Medical authorities and botanists were of crucial importance here. They were responsible for assigning to the new commodities European meanings within the prevailing discourse. Precisely where, for example, the new substance would be located in therapeutic theory and practice was a matter of intense debate and for each of tobacco, coffee, tea and chocolate, a considerable literature was generated. This was not just an intellectual exercise, however; it was also a question of vested interests. Cornelis Bontekoe, one of the most enthusiastic advocates of coffee and tea drinking (in his 1685 treatise on tea, he advised that drinking anywhere from fifty to two hundred cups of the infusion daily was reasonable) was said by his critics to have been in the employ of the Dutch East India Company.[53] Another enthusiast of tea drinking, the Amsterdam physician and burgomaster, Nicholas Tulp, was a director of the Company.[54] Nicolas Monardes, the champion of nicotian therapy, had considerable interests in Spanish–American colonial trade, and no doubt there were others, such as Hans Sloane and Benjamin Moseley, who mixed medical and colonial interests.[55] The medical/botanical debate penetrated the structure of colonial commerce and there is no doubt that this stimulated demand for the new exotic substances.[56]

Another aspect of the Europeanization of these new commodities was the way in which they were consumed. As far as tobacco is concerned, European tobacco artefacts – pipes, cigars and snuff – were essentially imitations of Amerindian ones, but they were quickly transformed materially as were the rituals of their consumption. European tobacco consumption became incorporated into the culture of the tavern and it was consumed alongside alcoholic drinks.[57] This combination of drugs, alcohol and tobacco is, in this case, important to note.

As for the newly introduced hot beverages, these, too, were absorbed within European rituals while, at the same time, their consumption imitated practices of the source culture. Just as coffeehouses in the Near East were the preserve of men, incorporating leisure as well as business, so in Europe, coffeehouses were club-like and exclusively male.[58] Yet not all activities of the Near Eastern coffeehouse found their way to Europe: musical entertainments, ubiquitous in the Near Eastern coffeehouse, were practically unknown in the European variant, where counting house and political matters prevailed.[59] Once coffee consumption became established in its social and physical setting, tea and chocolate became available there too. Because of their assimilation within the culture of the coffeehouse, all three beverages were initially associated with a bourgeois masculinity, serious, purposive and respectable.[60]

The mid-seventeenth-century European coffeehouse may be seen as an adaptation of the Near Eastern establishment, but in its social dimension and the commodities it offered for consumption it was distinctly European. So, too, was the practice of sweetening and adding milk to these drinks. As far as we know, neither coffee, nor tea, nor chocolate were served sweetened in their source cultures. How and why the practice of sweetening evolved is a moot point.[61] Whatever the actual chronology, the fusion of tea, coffee and chocolate with sugar was a powerful force and symbol of European power overseas: it happened very swiftly and was rapidly taken for granted.[62]

Apart from transforming the mode of consumption of tea, coffee, chocolate and tobacco, Europeanization also involved the appropriation of the exotic through symbolic manipulation. The frontispiece of Sylvestre Dufour's influential treatise on coffee, tea and chocolate (most of it compiled from other texts) showed three figures in distinctive dress (Arab, Chinese and Amerindian) displaying the beverage of their culture. Dufour was a spice merchant and undoubtedly portrayed this unique meeting of three cultures as symbolic of Europe's economic prowess.[63] The cultural origins of the new commodities were used by their promoters: the Amerindian on tobacco wrappings and trade cards and names such as the Turk's Head for coffeehouses were affirmations of the ownership of exotic commodities by Europeans.[64]

II

The political economy of Europeanization was critical in making tea, coffee, chocolate and tobacco readily available to European consumers. Certainly, rising real incomes in Europe as well as novelty value also contributed towards making these commodities objects of mass consumption.[65] None of these factors, however, is sufficient to explain the specific cultural sites that these new commodities occupied in the seventeenth and eighteenth centuries.

To understand the appeal of the new commodities and their growing popularity, especially during the eighteenth century, it is necessary to investigate the possibility that they substituted for indigenous European plant products and drugs. This is a difficult task especially since historians have shown very little interest in what Europeans ingested apart from food. So great is the void that one can easily be forgiven for assuming that, apart from ingesting certain plants for demonological purposes, Europeans held a very conservative and protective attitude to the plant world around them.[66]

Our knowledge of the early modern European plant world is largely derived from the great herbals that appeared in print in the late fifteenth and early sixteenth centuries across Europe and continued to be published and translated widely well into the seventeenth century.[67] The herbals provided a compendium of plants describing their botany, cultivation and, most importantly, their 'vertues' or medicinal uses and abuses.[68] Various classifications were followed, but most herbals provided an index to their medicinal uses. They were therefore not simply an intellectual exercise in the botanic theatre but provided a robust pharmacopoeia and manual for health. Those uncultured in plant-lore could at least turn to a published guide: no wonder they were so popular.[69] Besides herbals, there were many other publications, including medical recipes for the poor and almanacs, that offered an entry into the living world of medicinal plants.[70]

It is quite clear that Europeans were not lacking either in the availability or knowledge of plants that when ingested produced physiological changes. Before the introduction of tea, coffee, chocolate and tobacco into Europe, Europeans had a very clear inventory of plant narcotics. Opium and cannabis were certainly two very well-known ones but there were others such as henbane, datura, senna and darnel that received close attention. Gaspard Bauhin's celebrated herbal of 1623 specially devoted one section to the narcotic plants (including nicotiana, it should be mentioned), but no herbal worth its weight could ignore these important plants.[71] John Gerard, who published a very influential herbal in 1597, recommended ointments made with the juice of Thorn-apple leaves (datura), certain to provoke mild hallucinations.[72]

While herbals and the like can inform us as to what was available and how it could be used, they cannot, of course, tell us who used the plants and precisely how they were used in practice. That the poor, both rural and urban, were consumers is certainly supported by available literary evidence.[73] And that much plant-lore was the domain of women is also supported by evidence.[74] Many plants were recommended as alternatives to food, yet their use was not without danger as many were highly toxic.

Reading through the promotional medical literature on tea, coffee, chocolate and tobacco, one is struck by the repetitive theme that out-distancing their many virtues was their uncanny ability to assuage and satisfy hunger and thirst, the latter effected by drinking the new beverages hot rather than cold or lukewarm.[75] There can be little doubt that the appeal for a large number of Europeans of products that nourished or even staved hunger (and thirst) was great, especially since the indigenous alternatives had side-effects.

Aside from countering specific problems such as hunger and thirst, the new commodities had their use generally in maintaining humoural equilibrium. Here, too, and perhaps on an even greater scale, there is some evidence that tea, coffee, chocolate and tobacco substituted for common European plants. Louis Ferrant, for example, Professor of Medicine at the University of Bourges and the author of one of the first treatises devoted exclusively to snuff (published in 1655), argued a strong case for the use of tobacco as a sternutatory. Before tobacco, he observed, there were other herbs used 'to heat and dry by irritation, to move the humours in the brain and ventricles and expel them'.[76] The herbs listed by Ferrant for this purpose included sage, thyme, lavender and ginger plus pyrethrum (chrysanthemum) and roots of iris. Tobacco, according to Ferrant was preferred to these because it was 'less harmful . . . less acrid and less hot'.[77] Earlier, John Gerard, in his herbal, also remarked that rosemary, thyme, savoury and sweet marjoram could all be smoked and 'doth stupifie or dull the scences, and cause that kind of giddines that Tobaco doth'.[78] Gerard also recommended valerian root as a sedative particularly for poor people – it decreased the physical desire for food, he noted. Other narcotics in Gerard's herbal included passiflora, roots of certain orchids and delphinium, as well as wild lettuce leaves.[79] John Coakley Lettsom, who wrote an important treatise on tea in 1772, recommended tea as an alternative to 'vegetable infusions' on the grounds of its superiority in 'taste and effects', as he put it.[80] Tea, coffee and chocolate were also highly praised as a real alternative to wine and cordial liquors as nourishment, as a cure for hangover and as a stimulant. As John Ovington remarked in his treatise on tea published in 1699: 'it is the proper vice of wine; 'tis quick indeed, and active as that liquor, but happily destitute of all the intoxicating quality'.[81]

That tea and tobacco and less so coffee and chocolate were being recommended as alternatives to formulations prepared from indigenous plants is highly significant in the history of the consumption of these commodities. If Europeans were following this advice, as argued here, then other social, economic and cultural changes occurring from the middle of the seventeenth century onwards helped to sustain the substitution effect. In the first place, physical accessibility to the countryside and therefore to herbal remedies and preparations became more difficult. Urbanization certainly contributed to this phenomenon as did the fact that the number of cities, that is agglomerations exceeding 10, 000 inhabitants, was growing very quickly, from around 200 in 1650 to over 360 in 1800.[82] In the countryside itself and in response to the urban growth, more land was brought into cultivation and gardens themselves began to be coveted not for their herbs and medicinal plants but rather for their flowers and ornamental plants.[83] This was, of course, the age of the formal and ornamental garden as well as that of the 'official' botanic garden.[84]

Accessibility to plants was not just a matter of physical location. There was also the question of the survival of a plant folklore in the wake of the intellectual changes occurring at this time. Folk cures were denounced; the publication of almanacs, frequently buttressing the medicine of cunning women and men went into decline; and medical orthodoxy was made more widely available through vernacular texts.[85] Botany separated itself from the tradition of the herbal and therefore from a preoccupation with medicine, becoming over the course of the eighteenth century a specialized intellectual pursuit; at the same time the number of books published on horticulture (including botany) grew fantastically.[86] All of these developments had the effect of distancing European consumers from plant lore and drawing them towards commodity gratification.

III

The scale of consumption as revealed by the figures at the start of this chapter reflected a crucial change in the social context of consumption, from public to domestic.[87] The best evidence for this is the proliferation of special utensils for serving and consuming these hot beverages.[88] Research on England, France and Holland shows a clear increase in the possession of tea and coffee equipment during the eighteenth century across all income bands.[89] As Peter Earle has remarked on the material culture of the new beverages as enjoyed by the London middle class: 'what was rare or unknown in the 1680's becomes commonplace in the reign of Queen Anne'.[90] The domestication of tobacco consumption also appears to have occurred during this time. The eighteenth century witnessed a phenomenal growth in the consumption of tobacco in the form of snuff and, with it, the ownership of snuff boxes, from the very simple to the incredibly ornate.[91] In a recent study of the material culture of lower-class Parisians during the eighteenth century, it emerged that by the end of the century, about one-third of the inventories examined included snuff boxes compared to less than 7 per cent at the beginning of the century.[92] It might be that, given the considerable fire hazards involved in lighting a pipe, snuff made the consumption of tobacco less hazardous, certainly in one's own home, not to mention someone else's.[93] Whatever the reason for it, there is little doubt that snuff enabled tobacco consumption to be more portable. Pictorial representations of tobacco consumption in the seventeenth century invariably show pipe smoking in taverns and *tabagies* while those in the eighteenth century frequently portray a snuff-taker typically on his or her own, or simply in company at home.[94]

The increasing consumption of coffee, tea and chocolate had a second important meaning in European culture: it had a profound effect on diet in general and the nature of meals and mealtimes. The greatest impact was probably on breakfast which, during the eighteenth century, became transformed for most people from a meal based around a grain porridge washed down with beer or wine to one centred on a sugared hot drink plus bread.[95] John Coakley Lettsom, writing in 1772, alerted his readers to the change in breakfast habits which had occurred recently: 'before the use of tea', he wrote, 'breakfasts were more substantial; milk in various shapes, ale and beer, with roast cold meat, and other additions . . . sack and wines for higher orders of mankind'.[96] He also remarked that tea had its impact on the afternoon meal as well.[97] Recent studies on the British diet point clearly towards the increasing consumption of tea and sugar and there is little doubt that the focus of change occurred at breakfast.[98] Coffee for breakfast with milk became established in France around this same time and its restructuring of the German breakfast some time after 1720.[99] According to Père Labat, the familiar French breakfast of coffee with milk together with a small piece of bread 'especially made for this purpose' was in place by the turn of the eighteenth century, as was the drinking of coffee at the end of the meal: 'one takes it on completing dinner, one has it in the evening in order to more easily prepare for supper. If not accompanied by coffee, dinner appears incomplete.'[100] Benjamin Moseley, the English physician and authority on diseases of the Tropics, confirmed in his treatise on coffee, first published in 1775, that it was the habit of the French not to add milk to their evening coffee.[101]

That these substances were psychoactive was understood by contemporaries though, of course, in their predominantly humoural terms. Their therapeutic value lay in two main areas: in their ability to 'ease the brain' by increasing alertness and wakefulness, to counter the effects of alcohol and opiate consumption and to assuage hunger and thirst.[102] The combination of tobacco plus either tea, coffee or chocolate (each of which contains very similar active alkaloids) with sugar was a critical component of diet and ritual in the eighteenth century and, by its incorporation within alimentary structures, their consumption became legitimated. The combination embodied moderation, as opposed to excess; mildness, as opposed to harshness; sobriety and wakefulness, as opposed to drunkenness and wantonness. By ritualizing the consumption of these substances within a domestic context (for example, at breakfast and afternoon occasions), sobriety itself became a domestic strategy and quality: by contrast, the consumption of alcoholic drinks, especially spirits, came to be focused on public spaces such as taverns, cafés and the streets.[103] Tea's advantage over wine, as a sober substitute as well as a hangover cure, was frequently repeated in the literature of the period.[104]

Tea, coffee, chocolate and tobacco were commercial capitalistic substitutes for indigenous European drugs, or 'vegetable substances', as they were called, some of which were dangerous and belonged to a rich but threatened folk tradition. The new soft-drug culture of the eighteenth century substituted for a much more ramshackle home-grown culture.[105] In his treatise, Lettsom remarked that tea, 'if not too fine, if not drunk too hot, nor in too great quantities, is perhaps preferable to any other vegetable infusion we know . . . its superiority in taste and effects to most other vegetables'.[106] The incorporation of the production and distribution of these commodities within the international commercial structure of early modern Europe ensured that the substitution for indigenous substances would be swift and find favour with all classes of consumers, for those who found it fashionable and respectable, and those for whom it became a necessity.

NOTES

1 The word 'Excitantia' is taken from the title of a chapter from the book by L. Lewin, *Phantastica: Narcotic and Stimulating Drugs*, London, Kegan Paul, Trench, Trubner & Co., 1931 in which the author attempts to classify drugs

by their primal physiological effects. All of the soft drugs discussed in this essay are in Lewin's chapter. Previous versions of this essay have been given as papers at the Social History Society Conference in London, York University (Toronto), Mount Holyoke College, the London School of Economics, the John Carter Brown Library at Brown University and the Victoria and Albert Museum. I would like to thank participants at these meetings for their helpful comments. Special thanks go to Ludmilla Jordanova and Dallas Sealy for their invaluable help.

2 P. Camporesi, *Bread of Dreams: Food and Fantasy in Early Modern Europe*, Oxford, Polity Press, 1989, p. 124.

3 J. N. Pechlin, *A Treatise on the Inherent Qualities of the Tea-Herb*, London, 1750; frontispiece.

4 These figures are taken from J. Goodman, *Tobacco in History: The Cultures of Dependence*, London, Routledge, 1993, p. 145; F. Braudel, *The Structures of Everyday Life*, London, Collins, 1981, p. 259; M. R. Trouillot, 'Motion in the system: coffee, color, and slavery in eighteenth-century Saint-Domingue', *Review*, 1982, vol. 5, p. 337; D. Alden, 'The significance of cacao production in the Amazon region during the late colonial period: an essay in comparative economic history', *Proceedings of the American Philosophical Society*, 1976, vol. 120, pp. 107–12, 132.

5 J. De Vries, *European Urbanization 1500–1800*, London, Methuen, 1984, p. 29.

6 P. Camporesi, *Le goût du chocolat*, Paris, Gasset, 1992.

7 Goodman, op. cit., pp. 59–61; C. Shammas, *The Pre-Industrial Consumer in England and America*, Oxford, Oxford University Press, 1990, p. 78. For limitations of and exceptions to the 'trickle-down' theory of the social diffusion of new commodities, see P. Lysaght, ' "When I makes Tea, I makes Tea . . .": innovation in food – the case of tea in Ireland', *Ulster Folklife*, 1987, vol. 33, pp. 44–71; S. Mennell, A. Murcott and A. H. van Otterloo, 'The sociology of food: eating, diet and culture', *Current Sociology*, 1992, vol. 40(2); J. J. Voskuil, 'Die Verbreitung von Kaffee und Tee in den Niederlanden', in N.-A. Bringéus et al. (eds), *Wandel der Volkskultur in Europa: Festschrift für Günter Wiegelmann zum 60. Geburtstag*, Münster, F. Coppernath Verlag, 1988; S. Mintz, *Sweetness and Power*, New York, Viking, 1985; and G. McCracken, *Culture and Consumption*, Bloomington, Indiana, Indiana University Press, 1988, pp. 93–103. See also the perceptive criticisms in A. Vickery, 'Women and the world of goods: a Lancashire consumer and her possessions, 1751–81', in J. Brewer and R. Porter (eds), *Consumption and the World of Goods*, London, Routledge, 1993, pp. 274–8. There is some evidence that the consumption of the new hot drinks of the period, coffee, tea and chocolate, diffused earlier and deeper in western than in eastern and northern Europe. See the important collection of essays giving various insights into this process – D. U. Ball (ed.), *Kaffee im Spiegel europäischer Trinksitten/Coffee in the Context of European Drinking Habits*, Zurich, Johannes Jacobs Museum, 1991, especially the following essays: J. Burnett, 'Coffee in the British diet, 1650–1990'; R. Sandgruber, 'Kaffeesuppe und "kleiner Brauner". Sozialgeschichte des Kafeekonsums in Österreich'; E. Kisbán, 'Coffee in Hungary: its advent and integration into the hierarchy of meals'; and M. Essemyr, 'Prohibition and diffusion – coffee and coffee drinking in Sweden 1750–1970'. See also E. Kisbán, 'Coffee shouldn't hurt: the introduction of coffee to Hungary', in Bringéus et al., op. cit.

8 For recent perspectives on analysing consumer culture from a historical and theoretical approach see, for example, J.-C. Agnew, 'Coming up for air: consumer culture in historical perspective', in Brewer and Porter, op. cit.; and

B. Fine and E. Leopold, *The World of Consumption*, Routledge, London, 1993.

9 See, for example, M. Douglas and Baron Isherwood, *The World of Goods: Towards an Anthropology of Consumption*, New York, Basic Books, 1981, and G. McCracken, op. cit. For examples of historians who have attempted to understand how new commodities enter into and are transformed by European cultural contexts see S. Mintz, op. cit.; S. Mintz, 'The changing role of foods in the study of consumption' and J. E. Wills Jr., 'European consumption and Asian production in the seventeenth and eighteenth centuries', both in Brewer and Porter, op. cit.; and C. Mukerji, *From Graven Images: Patterns of Modern Materialism*, New York, Columbia University Press, 1983. See also the discussion about the introduction of tobacco into Europe in the sixteenth century and the contrast with the rejection of coca in Goodman, op. cit., pp. 37–51.

10 See the interesting comments from differing perspectives in J. A. Husch, 'Culture and US drug policy: toward a new conceptual framework', *Daedalus*, 1992, vol. 121, pp. 293–304, and J. Gray, 'Gender and plebeian culture in Ulster', *Journal of Interdisciplinary History*, 1993, vol. 24, pp. 251–70.

11 Camporesi, *Le goût du chocolat*, op. cit., pp. 7–24.

12 W. A. Emboden, *Narcotic Plants*, London, Studio Vista. 1979.

13 W. Cullen, *Treatise of the Materia Medica*, Edinburgh, Charles Elliot, 1789; Lewin, op. cit.; A. Weil and W. Rosen, *Chocolate to Morphine*, Boston, Massachusetts, Houghton Mifflin, 1983; V. Berridge, 'Morality and medical science: concepts of narcotic addiction in Britain', *Annals of Science*, 1979, vol. 36, pp. 67–85; V. Berridge, 'Morbid cravings: the emergence of addiction', *British Journal of Addiction*, 1985, vol. 80, pp. 233–43; and H. G. Levine, 'The discovery of addiction', *Journal of Studies on Alcohol*, 1978, vol. 39, pp. 143–74.

14 P. Butel, *Histoire du thé*, Paris, Editions Desjonquères, 1989, pp. 13–14 and J. Wilbert, 'Does pharmacology corroborate the nicotine therapy and practices of South American shamanism?', *Journal of Ethnopharmacology*, 1991, vol. 32, p. 179.

15 Alden, op. cit., p. 103.

16 C. Van Arendonk, 'Kahwa', in *Encyclopedia of Islam*, 1978, vol. 4, pp. 449–51 and R. S. Hattox, *Coffee and Coffeehouses: The Origins of a Social Beverage in the Medieval Near East*, Seattle, University of Washington Press, 1985, p. 26.

17 Goodman, op. cit., pp. 44–7.

18 J. Schneider, '. . . Produktion, Handel und Konsum von Kaffee von 15 bis zum 19. Jahrhundert', *Kultur & Technik*, 1988, vol. 4, pp. 230–7, and Hattox, op. cit., pp. 79–91.

19 H. E. Albrecht, 'Coffee-drinking as a symbol of social change in continental Europe in the seventeenth and eighteenth centuries', *Studies in Eighteenth-Century Culture*, 1988, vol. 18, pp. 93–4.

20 M. Courdurié, 'Du café du Yémen au café des Antilles ou renversements de courants commerciaux sur la place de Marseille (XVIIe–XVIIIe siècles)', in *Le café en Méditerranée: histoire, anthropologie, économie XVIIe–XXe siècles*, Aix-en-Provence, Institut de Recherches Méditerranéennes, 1980.

21 Alden, op. cit., pp. 107–110 and A. Butler, ' "The Indian Nectar": the introduction of chocolate to seventeenth-century Europe', unpublished paper presented at Social History Conference, London, 1993, p. 2. Chocolate was not consumed in solid form until the mid-nineteenth century.

22 Writers who commented on tea at this time included the traveller Jan van Linschoten, the Jesuit missionary Matteo Ricci and the Jesuit historian Gian Pietro Maffei – see Butel, op. cit., p. 47; K. Glamann, *Dutch-Asiatic Trade, 1620–1740*, The Hague, Martinus Nijhoff, 1958, pp. 215–16; S. Schama,

The Embarrassment of Riches, London, Collins, 1987, pp. 171–2.

23 K. N. Chaudhuri, *The Trading World of Asia and the English East India Company 1660–1760*, Cambridge, Cambridge University Press, 1978, p. 386.

24 Goodman, op. cit., pp. 135–7.

25 R. R. Menard, 'The tobacco industry in the Chesapeake colonies, 1617–1730: an interpretation', *Research in Economic History*, 1980, vol. 5, pp. 109–77.

26 Goodman, op. cit., pp. 138–43.

27 Ibid.; Menard, op. cit.; and C. Lugar, 'The Portuguese tobacco trade and tobacco growers in Bahia in the late colonial period', in D. Alden and W. Dean (eds), *Essays Concerning the Socio-Economic History of Brazil and Portuguese India*, Gainseville, Florida, The University Presses of Florida, 1977.

28 Alden, op. cit., p. 104 and M. J. MacLeod, *Spanish Central America: A Socio-economic History, 1520–1720*, Berkeley, California, University of California Press, 1973, pp. 68–95.

29 Alden, op. cit., pp. 106–7.

30 Ibid., pp. 107–8; E. Piñero, 'The cacao economy of the eighteenth-century Province of Caracas and the Spanish cacao market', *Hispanic American Historical Review*, 1988, vol. 68, pp. 75–100; and R. J. Ferry, 'Encomienda, African slavery and agriculture in seventeenth-century Caracas', *Hispanic American Historical Review*, 1981, vol. 61, pp. 609–35.

31 Alden, op. cit., pp. 110–12; R. S. Dunn, *Sugar and Slaves*, New York, Norton, 1972, pp. 168–9; and N. Zahadieh, 'Trade, plunder, and economic development in early English Jamaica, 1655–89', *Economic History Review*, 1986, vol. 39, p. 208.

32 Alden, op. cit., p. 132.

33 Glamann, op. cit., p. 207.

34 C. R. Boxer, *The Dutch Seaborne Empire 1600–1800*, London, Hutchinson, 1977, p. 199 and G. J. Knaap, 'Coffee for cash: the Dutch East India Company and the expansion of coffee cultivation in Java, Ambon and Ceylon 1700–1730', in J. van Goor (ed.), *Trading Companies in Asia 1600–1830*, Utrecht, HES Uitgevers, 1986, p. 34.

35 C. C. Goslinga, *The Dutch in the Caribbean and in the Guianas 1680–1791*, Assen/Maastricht, Van Gorcum, 1985, p. 335–6.

36 W. H. Ukers, *All About Coffee*, New York, The Tea and Coffee Trade Journal Company, 1922, p. 728.

37 L. H. Brockway, *Science and Colonial Expansion*, New York, Academic Press, 1979, p. 51. The role of botanic gardens in the eighteenth-century diffusion of tropical plants deserves more attention than it has attracted. The nineteenth century is better served by D. Headrick, *Tentacles of Progress*, New York, Oxford University Press, 1988.

38 Ukers, op. cit., p. 728.

39 Trouillot, op. cit., p. 337.

40 Courdourié, op. cit; Braudel, op. cit., p. 260; and A. Raymond, *Artisans et commerçants à Caire au XVIIIe siècle*, Damascus, Institut Français, 1973, pp. 178–9.

41 R. L. Williams, *The Coffee Industry of Jamaica*, Kingston, Jamaica, The University of the West Indies Press, 1975, pp. 24–6.

42 W. H. Ukers, *All About Tea*, New York, The Tea and Coffee Trade Journal Company, 1935, vol. 1, p. 109.

43 J. C. Lettsom, *The Natural History of the Tea-Tree*, London, 1722, pp. 33–6. Lettsom remarked that there had been several attempts to transfer the tea plant to Europe but these had failed because of the bad state of seeds and

the poor way in which they were preserved. He suggested that one possible solution might be to sow seeds on the island of St. Helena and then transfer the young plants. Even if the transfer were successful, he doubted the future prospects of tea cultivation in Europe because of high labour costs. North America was also a possibility, he commented.

44 Ukers, *All About Tea*, op. cit., pp. 110–17.

45 R. Fortune, *A Journey To The Tea Countries*, London, John Murray, 1852, p. 340. Fortune realized that a successful transfer depended not just upon getting seeds and plants but also on getting experts to assist in the new cultivation. Until Fortune's visit to the tea districts and gardens in China, hardly anything was known about the plant's botany. Europeans mistakenly believed that black and green teas were different botanic varieties: Fortune showed that the difference in colour was caused by different processing techniques – ibid., p. 273.

46 Glamann, op. cit., p. 215; H. Mui and L. H. Mui, *The Management of Monopoly*, Vancouver, University of British Columbia Press, 1984, pp. 4–12; and Wills, op. cit., pp. 144–6.

47 Chaudhuri, op. cit., pp. 385–406; Glamann, op. cit., pp. 242–3.

48 L. Dermigny, *La Chine et l'Occident: le commerce à Canton au XVIIIe siècle, 1789–1833*, Paris, SEVPEN, 1964, p. 539.

49 J. Goodman and K. Honeyman, *Gainful Pursuits: The Making of Industrial Europe, 1600–1914*, London, Edward Arnold, 1988, pp. 33–67.

50 This is a very large and important topic. For some indication of the size, direction and importance of the re-export trade see Goodman, op. cit., pp. 150–65; Price's essay in this volume; Shammas, op. cit., p. 77; E. Schumpeter, *English Overseas Trade Statistics, 1697–1808*, Oxford, Oxford University Press, 1960, pp. 60–2; T. M. Doerflinger, 'The Antilles trade of the Old Régime: a statistical overview', *Journal of Interdisciplinary History*, 1976, vol. 38, pp. 397–415; and H. -C. Johanesen, 'How to pay for Baltic goods', in W. Fischer, R. M. McInnis and J. Schneider (eds), *The Emergence of a World Economy*, vol. 1, Wiesbaden, Franz Steiner Verlag, 1986.

51 For tea and tobacco see respectively H. Mui and L. H. Mui, 'Smuggling and the British tea trade before 1784', *American Historical Review*, 1968, vol. 74, pp. 44–73, and R. C. Nash, 'The English and Scottish tobacco trade in the seventeenth and eighteenth centuries: legal and illegal trade', *Economic History Review*, 1982, vol. 35, pp. 354–72.

52 C. Shammas, 'The eighteenth-century English diet and economic change', *Explorations in Economic History*, 1984, vol. 21, p. 267.

53 Schama, op. cit., p. 172; Ukers, *All About Tea*, op. cit., p. 32; Butel, op. cit., p. 47; Boxer, op. cit., p. 177; and E. Heischkel-Artelt, 'Kaffee und Tee im Spiegel der medizinischen Literatur des 17. bis 19. Jahrhundert', *Medizinhistorisches Journal*, 1969, vol. 4, pp. 250–60.

54 W. D. Smith, 'Complications of the commonplace: tea, sugar and imperialism', *Journal of Interdisciplinary History*, 1992, vol. 33, p. 268, and Schama, op. cit., pp. 119, 171, 184–7.

55 F. Guerra, *Nicolas Bautista Monardes: su vida y su obra*, Mexico City, Compañia fundidora de fiero y acero de Monterrey S. A., 1961, pp. 24–6, 79–82, and Dunn, op. cit., passim.

56 S. Mintz, 'The changing role of foods', op. cit., p. 265 and A. G. Olson, 'The Virginia merchants of London: a study in eighteenth-century interest-group politics', *William and Mary Quarterly*, 1983, vol. 40, pp. 363–88.

57 See, for example, descriptions in Goodman, op. cit., pp. 19–36, 59–89; A. von Gernet, 'The transculturation of the Amerindian pipe/tobacco/smoking

complex and its impact on the intellectual boundaries between "savagery" and "civilization", 1535–1935', unpublished PhD thesis, Montreal, McGill University, 1988, pp. 113–19; M. Vigié and M. Vigié, *L'Herbe à Nicot*, Paris, Fayard, 1989, pp. 56–61; and Schama, op. cit., pp. 193–201.

58 Hattox, op. cit., pp. 92–130. See also the discussion about the rituals of the European coffeehouse by Smith in this volume.

59 The literature on European coffeehouses is not extensive and many discussions repeat others. The following is a selection. Albrecht, op. cit.; H. E. Bödecker, 'Le café allemand au XVIIIe siècle: une forme de sociabilité éclairée', *Revue d'histoire moderne et contemporaine*, 1990, vol. 37, pp. 571–88; A. G. Olson, 'Coffee house lobbying', *History Today*, 1991, vol. 41, pp. 35–41; J. Pelzer and L. Pelzer, 'The coffee houses of Augustan London', *History Today*, 1982, vol. 32, pp. 40–7.

60 See Smith's essay in this volume for a discussion of this feature of European coffeehouses.

61 W. D. Smith, 'Complications of the commonplace: tea, sugar, and imperialism', *Journal of Interdisciplinary History*, 1992, vol. 33, p. 263, argues forcefully that 'the evidence points to the period between 1685 and the first years of the eighteenth century as the time at which the tea-and-sugar custom established itself in Britain and the Netherlands'. He also makes the interesting point that one should think of the tea–sugar combination as a way of moderating sugar consumption as much as sweetening the tea (pp. 270, 277). Not all contemporary evidence supports Smith's dating. Thomas Garway, frequently credited with being the first merchant to sell tea in London, certainly recommended sweetening the drink though, interestingly, he advocated honey and not sugar with milk – T. Garway, *An exact description of the Growth, Quality and Virtues of the Leaf Tea*, London, 1660. Johan Pechlin, physician at the Swedish Court in the late seventeenth century, wrote on tea in the 1670s and 1680s, and recommended sweetening with sugar, though only for Bohea (black tea) – Pechlin, op. cit, p. 10. Chocolate was sweetened with sugar by the middle of the seventeenth century; coffee not long after that; and there were other drinks such as lemonade that were prepared in this way – see H. Stubbe, *The Indian Nectar or a Discourse concerning Chocolata*, London, 1662, pp. 102–21; N. de Blegny, *Le bon usage du thé, du caffé et du chocolat*, Paris, 1687, 38; and M. Visser, *Much Depends on Dinner*, London, Penguin, 1989, pp. 273–4. In Paris, the *limonadier* frequently doubled as a coffeehouse owner – see J. Leclant, 'Coffee and cafés in Paris, 1644–1693', in R. Forster and O. Ranum (eds), *Food and Drink in History*, Baltimore, Maryland, Johns Hopkins University Press, 1979: p. 90.

62 Contemporary literature is full of the beverage–sugar connection. One good case in point is the comment on coffee in P. Pomet, *Histoire générale des drogues*, Paris, 1694, p. 205. Pomet, a Parisian apothecary and merchant, produced this very interesting compendium of plants and drugs available to European consumers at the end of the seventeenth century. His description of coffee is short and to the point: 'it has no use other than, after being roasted, as a drink made with water and sugar'. Other comments linking chocolate, coffee and sugar can be found in P. Labat, *Nouveau voyage aux isles de l'Amérique*, vol. 4, Paris, Delespine, 1742, p. 243; op. cit., vol. 6, pp. 369, 459; and *Calendar of State Papers*, Colonial Series, America and West Indies, 1724–5, London, pp. 121, 172.

63 S. Dufour, *Traitez nouveaux et curieux du Café, du Thé et du Chocolat*, Lyon, Girin et Rivière, 1685; W. Mueller, *Bibliographie des Kaffee, des Kakao, der Schokolade, des Tee und deren Surrogate bis zum Jahre 1900*, Bad Bockelt, Walter

Krieg Verlag, 1960, p. 66.

64 On the complicated role of the 'exotic' in stimulating demand, see the interesting comments in Wills, op. cit.

65 For some recent attempts to explain consumption patterns, principally of foodstuffs, during the early modern period, see C. Shammas, 'Changes in English and Anglo-American consumption from 1550 to 1800', in Brewer and Porter, op. cit.; S. Mintz, 'The changing role of foods', op. cit., in ibid. The volume edited by Brewer and Porter contains many important essays that bear, to some degree, on the problems raised in this chapter. For an analysis of the consumption of clothes and household goods in general see the essays by Vickery, Weatherill and Fairchilds. Jacob Price has also argued for a much closer analysis of demand rather than supply factors in understanding the nature of the transatlantic economy during this same period: see J. M. Price, 'The transatlantic economy', in J. R. Pole and J. P. Greene (eds), *Early British America*, Baltimore, Maryland, Johns Hopkins University Press, 1984.

66 There is almost an obsession with witchcraft and generally demonological and occult behaviour among those who have ventured into the history of the consumption of psychoactive substances in Europe. That witches and the like used psychoactive preparations is not beyond doubt. It is simply that whenever historians (and anthropologists) venture into the field of European plant-lore they inevitably confine their discussion to these activities. See, for example, the classic contribution to the subject by M. J. Harner, 'The role of hallucinogenic plants in European witchcraft', in M. J. Harner (ed.), *Hallucinogens and Shamanism*, New York, Oxford University Press, 1973 and L. Rothman, 'De Laguna's commentaries on hallucinogenic drugs and witchcraft in Dioscorides' Materia Medica', *Bulletin of the History of Medicine*, 1972, vol. 46, pp. 562–7. Two recent general treatments of psychoactive substances in culture continue to focus narrowly upon witchcraft in their discussion of European consumption patterns. See T. Hauschild, 'Hexen und Drogen', in G. Völger and K. von Welck (eds), *Rausch und Realität*, Hamburg, Rowohlt, 1981 and R. Rudgley, *The Alchemy of Culture*, London, British Museum Press, 1993, pp. 90–9. On the other hand, not many historians writing about witchcraft discuss the use of psychoactive substances. A recent example of one who does is C. Ginzburg, *Ecstasies: Deciphering the Witches' Sabbath*, London, Hutchinson Radius, 1990.

67 There are surprisingly few good histories of the herbals or of *materia medica* in general. The classic account of the 'Great Herbals' is given in A. Arber, *Herbals: Their Origin and Evolution*, Cambridge, Cambridge University Press, 1953. A more recent treatment but lacking in substantive analysis is F. J. Anderson's *An Illustrated History of the Herbals*, New York, Columbia University Press, 1977. See also K. M. Reeds, 'Renaissance humanism and botany', *Annals of Science*, 1976, vol. 33, pp. 519–42. There is much scope for research into this whole area, especially on the period after 1650.

68 See J. Stannard, 'The herbal as a medical document', *Bulletin of the History of Medicine*, 1969, vol. 43, pp. 212–20.

69 See the interesting discussion of medical publishing in the sixteenth century and the particular importance of the herbal in P. Slack, 'Mirrors of health and treasures of poor men: the uses of the vernacular medical literature of Tudor England', in C. Webster (ed.), *Health Medicine and Mortality in the Sixteenth Century*, Cambridge, Cambridge University Press, 1979.

70 On this important issue see the following: R. Porter (ed.), *The Popularization of Medicine 1650–1850*, London, Routledge, 1992, and P. Camporesi, *Bread of Dreams*, op. cit.

71 Arber, op. cit., p. 179, and W. E. Safford, 'Narcotic daturas of the Old and New World: an account of their remarkable properties and their uses as intoxicants and in divination', *Annual Report of the Smithsonian Institution*, 1920, pp. 537–67.

72 J. Gerard, *Gerard's Herbal*, edn of 1636, London, Spring Books, 1964, p. 94.

73 See, for example, Camporesi, *Bread of Dreams*, op. cit., pp. 108–50; K. Thomas, *Religion and the Decline of Magic*, London, Weidenfeld and Nicolson, 1971, pp. 177–211; A. Wear, 'The popularization of medicine in early modern England', in Porter, op. cit., pp. 29–32; and M. Ramsey, 'The popularization of medicine in France, 1650–1900', in Porter, op. cit., pp. 102–5.

74 Issues of gender are not given the prominence they deserve in discussions of popular culture and conflicts between the medical (male) establishment and those wise in the ways of popular medicine. For some guidance on these matters see Thomas, op. cit., pp. 177–211; Wear, op. cit., p. 34; and Ginzburg, op. cit., p. 304. It is interesting to note that in the eighteenth century, women were attracted to botany as an intellectual pursuit. For this, see A. B. Shteir, 'Linnaeus's daughters: women and British botany' and 'Botany in the breakfast room: women and early nineteenth-century British plant study', in P. Abir-Am and D. Outram (eds), *Uneasy Careers and Uneasy Lives: Women in Science 1789–1979*, New Brunswick, New Jersey, Rutgers University Press, 1987, as well as 'Botanical dialogues: Maria Jacson and women's popular science writing in England', *Eighteenth-Century Studies*, 1990, vol. 10, pp. 301–17.

75 Whether the new beverages should be drunk hot, warm or cold was the subject of debate. For an example of a position on chocolate, see H. Stubbe, *The Indian Nectar*, op. cit., p. 122.

76 L. Ferrant, *Traicté du tabac en sternutatoire*, Bourges, 1655, p. 22.

77 Ibid.

78 Gerard, op. cit., p. 89.

79 Emboden, op. cit., pp. 17–18.

80 Lettsom, op. cit., p. 50.

81 J. Ovington, *An Essay upon the Nature and Qualities of Tea*, London, 1699, p. 28. See also the comments on the substitution by tea of other products, including alcoholic drinks, made early in the nineteenth century by the Scottish historian, David MacPherson, quoted in Mintz, 'The changing role of foods', op. cit., p. 264.

82 De Vries, op. cit., pp. 29, 32–4, 39.

83 See Goodman and Honeyman, op. cit., pp. 19–32; K. Thomas, *Man and the Natural World*, London, Penguin Books, 1984, pp. 192–241; and J. Goody, *The Culture of Flowers*, Cambridge, Cambridge University Press, 1993.

84 We are just beginning to understand how and to what extent the eighteenth-century landscape was being transformed and what was its importance as the context as well as the object of social and political conflict. For an insight into landscape as political process see the following: G. B. Masefield, 'Crops and livestock', in E. E. Rich and C. H. Wilson (eds), *The Cambridge Economic History of Europe. Volume IV: The Economy of Expanding Europe in the Sixteenth and Seventeenth Centuries*, Cambridge, Cambridge University Press, 1967; Thomas, *Man and the Natural World*, op. cit., p. 284; P. Camporesi, *Le goût du chocolat*, op. cit., pp. 143–64; H. Ritvo, 'At the edge of the garden: nature and domestication in eighteenth-and nineteenth-century Britain', *The Huntingdon Library Quarterly*, 1992, vol. 55, pp. 363–78; and C. Mukerji, 'Reading and writing with nature: a materialist approach to French formal gardens', in Brewer and Porter, op. cit. This is another area where the scope for further and exciting research is substantial.

85 See for example Porter, op. cit.; B. Capp, *Astrology and the Popular Press: English Almanacs 1500–1800*, London, Faber & Faber, 1979, pp. 204–14; and L. Barrow, *Independent Spirits: Spiritualism and English Plebeians 1850–1910*, London, Routledge & Kegan Paul, 1986, pp. 213–28.

86 For an account of publishing in horticulture and natural history see B. Henrey, *British Botanical and Horticultural Literature before 1800*, Oxford, Oxford University Press, 1975, vol. 2, pp. 5–36, and D. E. Allen, *The Naturalist in Britain*, London, Allen Lane, 1976. An excellent social history of botany is offered in ibid., Ch. 2. See also Thomas, *Man and the Natural World*, op. cit., p. 225; F. Delaporte, *Nature's Second Kingdom*, Cambridge, Mass., MIT Press, 1982; and J. Browne, 'Botany for gentlemen: Erasmus Darwin and the Loves of Plants', *Isis*, 1989, vol. 80, pp. 593–620. For women botanists, see the works by Shteir cited in note 74.

87 During the eighteenth century there was a decline in the number of coffeehouses relative to population in Europe's main cities. In London, for example, the number of coffeehouses at the end of the eighteenth century was virtually the same as a century earlier – see Pelzer and Pelzer, op. cit.; Olson, op. cit.; and B. Lillywhite, *London Coffee Houses*, London, Allen & Unwin, 1963. Many had been turned into private clubs during the intervening years. In Berlin, at the end of the eighteenth century, the number of coffeehouses stood at only twelve, but the population of the city increased exponentially to 170,000 inhabitants from a figure of only 30,000 at the turn of the century – Bödecker, op. cit., pp. 571–4; P. M. Hohenberg and L. M. Lees, *The Making of Urban Europe*, Cambridge, Mass., Harvard University Press, 1985, p. 215. The same phenomenon occurred in France – see Braudel, op. cit., p. 258.

88 This phenomenon was part of a more general process involving two very important changes: a general increase in the ownership of consumer durables and a growing complexity in the material culture of the family table. On the former, much has been written. A good introduction to the subject is the recent edited volume by Brewer and Porter, op. cit.; as is the classic contribution by N. McKendrick, 'The consumer revolution of eighteenth-century England', in N. McKendrick, J. Brewer and J. H. Plumb (eds), *The Birth of a Consumer Society: The Commercialization of Eighteenth-Century England*, London, Europa, 1982. As for the material culture of the family table, this too has received some attention, though much more can be done. For the diffusion of tableware, dishes and cutlery, see C. Fairchilds, 'The production and marketing of populuxe goods in eighteenth-century Paris', in Brewer and Porter, op. cit., p. 230; Weatherill, op. cit.; L. Weatherill, *Consumer Behaviour and Material Culture in Britain 1660–1760*, London, Routledge, 1988; C. Shammas, *The Pre-Industrial Consumer in England and America*, Oxford, Oxford University Press, 1990, pp. 181–93; J.-L. Flandrin, 'Distinction through taste', in R. Chartier (ed.), *A History of Private Life III. Passions of the Renaissance*, Cambridge, Mass., Harvard University Press, 1989, pp. 265–8; and J. De Vries, 'Peasant demand patterns and economic development: Friesland, 1550–1750', in W. N. Parker and E. L. Jones (eds), *European Peasants and Their Markets: Essays in Agrarian Economic History*, Princeton, New Jersey, Princeton University Press, 1975, p. 221. For the increasing use of porcelain services, both imported from China and produced in Europe, see T. Volker, *Porcelain and the Dutch East India Company 1602–1682*, Leiden, Brill, 1954; Chaudhuri, op. cit., pp. 407–10; L. Weatherill, 'The growth of the pottery industry in England, 1660–1815', unpublished PhD dissertation, University of London, 1981; S. Tardieu, *La Vie domestique*

dans le Mâconnais préindustriel, Paris, Institut d'Ethnologie, 1964; R. Goldthwaite, 'The economic and social world of Italian Renaissance maiolica', *Renaissance Quarterly*, 1989, vol. 42, pp. 1–32; and the following, all by H. Desmet-Grégoire: 'Une approche ethno-historique du café: évolution des utensiles servant à la fabrication et à la consommation du café', in *Le café en Méditerranée: histoire, anthroplogie, économie XVIIIe–XXe siècles*, Aix-en-Provence, Institut de Recherches Méditerranéennes, 1980; 'Origine et évolution des objets du café à Marseille aux XVIIe et XVIIIe siècles', *Provence Historique*, 1988, vol. 38, pp. 69–87; and *Les objets du café*, Paris, Presses du CNRS, 1989. For an interesting and thoughtful discussion of the rituals associated with the table see M. Visser, *The Rituals of Dinner*, London, Viking, 1992.

89 See, for example, the following studies: C. Shammas, op. cit. pp. 169–93; C. Shammas, 'The domestic environment in early modern England and America', *Journal of Social History*, 1980, vol. 14, pp. 3–24; De Vries, 'Peasant demand patterns', op. cit.; Voskuil, op. cit.; and Fairchilds, op. cit.

90 P. Earle, *The Making of the English Middle Class*, London, Methuen, 1989, p. 295.

91 Goodman, op. cit., pp. 73–5.

92 Fairchilds, op. cit., p. 230.

93 G. A. Brongers, *Nicotiana Tabacum: The History of Tobacco and Tobacco Smoking in the Netherlands*, Gronigen, Niemeyer, 1964, pp. 107–13, 157–62.

94 W. Schivelbusch, *Tastes of Paradise: A Social History of Spices, Stimulants and Intoxicants*, New York, Pantheon, 1992, pp. 53–5, 99–106, 133–9.

95 See the comments in Shammas, op. cit., p. 14 and Schivelbusch, op. cit., pp. 61–6. Also see D. U. Ball, 'Introduction', in Ball, op. cit. and the sources on coffee consumption listed in note 7.

96 Lettsom, op. cit., pp. 52–3.

97 Ibid.

98 See Shammas, op. cit., and C. Shammas, 'The eighteenth-century English diet and economic change', *Explorations in Economic History*, 1984, vol. 21, pp. 254–69 for information on England. In Ulster, the change in breakfast habits to tea and sugar plus baker's bread occurred later, towards the end of the eighteenth and into the nineteenth century – see Lysaght, op. cit., pp. 45, 48–51.

99 See Braudel, op. cit., p. 258; Desmet-Grégoire, op. cit., p. 109; Bödecker, op. cit., p. 571; G. Wiegelmann, *Alltags und Festspeisen: Wandel und gegenwärtige Stellung*, Marburg, N. G. Elwert, 1967, pp. 235–44; G. Wiegelmann, 'Innovations in food and meals', *Folklife*, 1974, vol. 12, pp. 20–9; and Schivelbusch, op. cit., pp. 23, 61. Recent research on Finland shows a similar transformation of breakfast but at a later date than the continent of Europe or England – see D. Kirby, ' "Noble nourishment for the body", or a "hole in the purse"? Coffee consumption and the peasantry of northern Europe', paper presented at Social History Society Conference, London 1993.

100 Labat, op. cit., p. 342.

101 Moseley, op. cit., p. 73.

102 Goodman, op. cit., pp. 42–3; Moseley, op. cit., p. 58; Ovington, op. cit., pp. 26–8.

103 Schivelbusch, op. cit., pp. 147–203; T. Brennan, 'Social drinking in Old Régime Paris', in S. Barrows and R. Room (eds), *Drinking: Behavior and Belief in Modern History*, Berkeley, California, University of California Press, 1991; R. Porter, 'The drinking man's disease: the "pre-history" of alcoholism in Georgian Britain', *British Journal of Addiction*, 1985, vol. 80, pp. 385–96;

P. Clark, *The English Alehouse: A Social History 1200–1830*, London, Longman, 1983; P. Clark, 'The "Mother Gin" controversy in the early eighteenth century', *Transactions of the Royal Historical Society*, 1988, 5th series, vol. 38, pp. 63–84; J. Warner, 'The sanctuary of sobriety: images of women and alcohol in seventeenth-century England', paper presented at Social History Society Conference, London, 1993; and Lysaght, op. cit., p. 48. See also the parallels with Smith's notion of eighteenth-century respectability, as he uses it in his essay in this volume and his published work on the subject cited therein.

104 See, for example, Ovington, op. cit., p. 28.

105 See Mintz, 'The changing role of foods', op. cit.; and T. McKenna, *Food of the Gods*, London, Rider, 1992, pp. 169–206.

106 Lettsom, op. cit., p. 50.

7

FROM COFFEEHOUSE TO PARLOUR

The consumption of coffee, tea and sugar in north-western Europe in the seventeenth and eighteenth centuries

Woodruff D. Smith

Between the mid-seventeenth century and the early nineteenth century, tea and coffee, both taken with sugar and usually with milk, came to be consumed by people of almost all social classes in Western Europe. Not only did these products emerge as mainstays of world trade, but their consumption became a central feature of some of the most significant social rituals of European culture.[1] Among the prime reasons that their use expanded, that they replaced domestic European substances as the licit 'soft drugs' of choice in the Western world, were the roles they played and the social and cultural meanings they possessed within the framework of these rituals. Of course, the psychoactive properties of tea and coffee as stimulants helped to promote consumption. The ability of tea and coffee to reduce the physical sensation of hunger, and of sugar taken with tea and coffee to provide cheap calories to the poor, also encouraged their adoption in Europe.[2] But the main reason for the triumphal progress of coffee and tea described in the preceding article lay in their relationship to developing social and cultural contexts in the West.

Although coffee had been known in Europe (especially in Mediterranean areas) in the sixteenth century and although small amounts of tea had entered Europe from China and Japan as a medicine in the same century, substantial amounts of either product were consumed and a fashion for drinking them appeared only in the 1650s. Both coffee and tea were first introduced into the homes of fashionable aristocrats and intellectuals, initially in France and then in England and the Netherlands, during the middle decades of the seventeenth century, but they soon reached a wider public with the establishment of commercial coffeehouses and teahouses.[3] By the 1660s these new establishments had become common in Paris, Amsterdam and London. The popularity and price of tea and coffee varied greatly during the next few decades, but by 1700 demand had risen substantially. The scale of imports continued to increase thereafter.[4]

By the first quarter of the eighteenth century most of the cultural framework specifically associated with coffee drinking and tea drinking had been firmly established. The addition of sugar had become customary; the consumption of tea and coffee at particular meals and in particular settings, both inside and outside the home, had become commonplace.[5] The culture of the teahouse and coffeehouse was fully developed in England, the Netherlands and urban areas of Scotland, Ireland, Germany and Scandinavia. The pattern differed somewhat in France: sugaring was less important, and domestic tea and coffee taking spread more slowly beyond aristocratic circles.[6]

From the standpoint of the cultural and social contexts within which tea and coffee were consumed, their spread in north-western Europe took place in three phases. In the first phase, which lasted from the initial introduction of tea and coffee until the early eighteenth century, they found their places in rituals of gentility patterned (distantly) on tea rituals in China – a country whose upper classes still seemed to Europeans to be more refined than their own. Tea and coffee were exotic and fashionable luxuries, as likely to come into vogue as to pass out of it, but protected against extinction as fashions by being associated with the maintenance of physical health. In this elite context, the high prices of tea and coffee were significant parts of their appeal, although they limited the extent of the market. The first phase overlapped considerably in time with the second phase – especially in Britain.[7]

The second phase (on which this chapter concentrates) featured two closely related but quite distinct cultural elements: the formation of the coffeehouse and teahouse, and the development of the rituals of domestic consumption of tea and coffee. The second phase originated shortly after the beginning of the first – in the 1650s and 1660s – but outlasted it by nearly a century. The coffeehouse aspect appeared first. Regular domestic consumption of tea and coffee at particular times of day and outside aristocratic circles was in evidence by 1700 in England.[8] Tea and coffee had ceased to be elite fashions. They were transformed into central features of the social and cultural lives of the middle classes in north-western Europe and into significant elements of bourgeois culture.

The third phase began around the end of the eighteenth century. In Britain coffeehouses and teahouses disappeared in their classic forms and metamorphosed into restaurants, private clubs, even (in the case of Lloyd's) business institutions unrelated to the consumption of tea and coffee.[9] The traditions of the coffeehouse remained stronger in urban areas of continental Europe, but there, too, coffeehouses tended to become more general establishments serving a wider variety of drinks and foods. Vastly more important, however, was the tremendous spread of domestic coffee and tea taking in connection with certain meals (breakfast, teatime, etc.). The practice diffused socially to practically all classes in north-western Europe in the first half of the nineteenth century, and geographically to all parts of the world that adopted or followed north-western European cultural patterns. For the most part, however, the domestic rituals of tea and coffee taking remained essentially similar to those that had developed during the second phase in the eighteenth century.[10]

There is a common thread that binds the two elements of the second phase together and runs from the second phase into the third: the emergence of *respectability* as a significant cultural pattern in the Western world in the eighteenth century, as one of the foundations of bourgeois society. Taking tea or coffee in the setting of the coffeehouse or parlour showed that a person was respectable. Respectability, like most broad cultural patterns that frame social life, included cognitive, structural, behavioural and material elements. Many of the specific items encompassed in these categories were borrowed or adapted from earlier patterns – mainly from the aristocratic culture that centred around the concept of *gentility* (and within which coffee and tea had initially found their meanings). The items were reorganized, however, and given new meanings, ones that we recognize as aspects of bourgeois culture.[11]

The central cognitive elements were a set of attitudes that people who considered themselves respectable characteristically took towards their relationships with other people in the social hierarchy, and a set of demands that corresponded to those attitudes. A person who claimed to be respectable was in essence demanding deference from social inferiors and respect from equals and superiors. The demand was based (at least ostensibly) on demonstrated moral standing, not (as was the case with gentility) on birth. Again ostensibly, the individual displayed his or her virtue; the social group to which the individual belonged did not (as with gentility) bestow standing so much as it provided the environment in which it was more or less likely that the appropriate individual virtues would be developed. Middle-class people with adequate incomes were more likely to display respectability than lower-class people (or, according to some, than the wicked aristocracy), but in principle, anyone could be respectable. One of the reasons for the vast appeal of respectability as a cultural pattern was that it was not conceptually class bound. It spread among the middle classes of Western Europe broadly defined, but there could be (and were) self-consciously respectable working-class and upper-class people. The ability of bourgeois culture to extend beyond the limits of the middle classes in the nineteenth and twentieth centuries was partly due to the fact that it incorporated the idea of respectability.[12] The key to respectability was behaviour. Certain patterns of public behaviour – including modes of dressing, rules of politeness and gender relations, eating and drinking customs – signified respectability because they were interpreted as manifesting individual virtues: balance in temperament, respect for individuals on the basis of their merits, sobriety and reliability, and so forth.[13] Private behaviour was also important within the cultural pattern of respectability, in part because it was thought that the foundation of public morality lay in private life, in the home. Respectable patterns of domestic behaviour taught and reinforced the virtues that underlay respectable behaviour in public. Discrepancies between respectable public behaviour and less-than-respectable private behaviour were evidence that the former was a sham.

Respectability was also manifested in the use of particular physical objects, particularly consumer goods employed in social rituals. In the eighteenth century, tea and coffee, taken with sugar, came to be central material features of the emerging pattern of respectability – not merely symbols of respectability, but part of the meaning of respectability itself. We can follow this process and consider some of its effects by looking more closely at the two main social contexts within which coffee and tea were consumed in the eighteenth century: the coffeehouse or teahouse, and the parlours of respectable homes.

THE COFFEEHOUSE: A CONTEXT OF RESPECTABLE MALE PUBLIC ASSOCIATION

The first reports of coffeehouses in Western Europe come from the 1650s. Many appear to have been in operation in London in the 1660s. Samuel Pepys reports several visits to coffeehouses while engaged in two of his main hobbies: exchanging information and social climbing.[14] Coffeehouses were sufficiently numerous and sufficiently attractive as venues for political discussion in the 1660s that the English and French governments tried to regulate them – apparently without permanent effect.[15] Teahouses were also popular in urban areas of north-western Europe in the late seventeenth century. The heyday of the coffeehouse and teahouse, however, was the eighteenth century, when Paris and London were reported to possess 600 coffeehouses each.[16] (Because coffeehouses were more numerous than teahouses, we shall refer to both types henceforward as 'coffeehouses'.)

As a type of public business establishment, the coffeehouse followed the older model of the tavern. It provided a particular range of beverages and a place for people to meet, to do business, to talk about ideas and politics. Just as merchants and brokers had advertised their presence at certain times of day at particular taverns, so some of them began in the late seventeenth century to do business at coffeehouses.[17] Just as certain taverns and wine shops had become the favoured gathering places of circles of urban professionals and intellectuals in the sixteenth century, so in the seventeenth and eighteenth centuries, similar groups met in particular coffeehouses. Like the tavern, the coffeehouse catered to a mixed social clientele, although taverns had a much wider appeal. Before the nineteenth century, coffeehouses were not very attractive below the middling level of society.

Despite similarities to the tavern, however, the coffeehouse developed its own pattern and its own cultural significance almost immediately after its appearance. Most of the reason for its distinctiveness derived directly from the nature of the beverages consumed in coffeehouses and the construction that was placed on them.[18] Part of the initial appeal of coffee and tea was that they were novel, exotic and thus fashionable. They could therefore find a place within the culture of gentility, in which the following of new fashions in consumption played an extremely important role in the seventeenth century. The coffeehouse was a place where persons at the fringes of fashionability (people like Pepys, for instance) could publicly display the manners of the gentry while participating in fashionable rituals of consumption. But other qualities besides fashionability took tea and coffee out of the cultural framework of gentility and made them part of the culture of respectability: their promotion of health, sobriety, moderation and rationality.

Coffee and tea were initially publicized in Europe as supports for health, and despite the appearance in the eighteenth century of a literature arguing the contrary, the association stuck.[19] The key factor that made the supposed healthfulness of tea and coffee part of the cultural pattern of respectability was a connection between the individual pursuit of health and the possession of manifest virtue. Steven Blankaart, an Amsterdam physician and the author of a classic book on diet, wrote in 1683 that 'the health of the body is the greatest treasure men can have on earth'.[20] Health is achieved by balance and measure in diet, by limiting the intake of unhealthy foods (such as sugar, soft foods and foods with excessive salt or fat), and by consuming substances that counteract the effects of such unhealthy foods through maintaining the balance of humours in the body. Individuals who possess sufficient self-control to protect their bodily 'treasure' in this way are, by implication, those also capable of maintaining their moral standing through measure and balance, and therefore are the best citizens. Blankaart, following the prescription of the famous Dutch 'tea-doctor' Cornelis Bontekoe, advised his readers to drink coffee and very large quantities of tea as a means of achieving a balance of humours.[21] He did not advocate mixing them with sugar, but he lay down the basic principle according to which bitter liquids such as tea and coffee are seen as counterbalances to sweet, dangerous solids.

This principle, together with a much more detailed consideration of the moral, social and religious implications of maintaining a healthy diet, are included in several of the books of Thomas Tryon (1634–1703). Tryon was one of the most influential English writers of self-improvement literature in the late seventeenth and early eighteenth centuries and a source of the kind of moralistic materialism associated with Benjamin Franklin.[22] Tryon worried in particular about the threat of excessive sweetness in foods and drinks:

> . . . let them refrain All or most sorts of Food made sweet with Sugar, for the frequent use of such Meats and Drinks do prove very prejudicial to most Peoples health, but most especially such as are subject to the forementioned Diseases [stone and gravel]; for over-sweetness in Foods and Drinks, does not only thicken the Blood, and hinder its free Circulation, but it indues it with a watery phlegmatick quality, and turns the Humours to the highest degree of souerness, most especially if fats and sweetness be compounded together, as they are for the most part (as the sweetest Wines make the sharpest Vinegar) which immediately tends toward Putrifaction, whence proceeds various Diseases, according to each mans Constitution and Complexion, viz. Scabs, Boyls, Leprosies, Consumptions, Gout and Stone, all Stoppages of the Breast, ill Digestion, Nautiousness, rotten Teeth, offensive Breath, all which distempers have of late years been more brief and frequent, since the common eating of sugared Foods and Drinks.[23]

Tryon's strictures against mixing sugar in drinks did not extend to 'herbal infusions' in which the bitterness of the herbs counterbalances the sweetness of the sugar. He did not specifically mention tea as such an infusion, but this was one of the bases for the eighteenth-century argument in favour of taking sugar with tea. If a person could not do without sugar altogether and obtain sweetness from other sources, such as fruit, he or she could still maintain health and demonstrate moral character by taking sugar in an appropriately balanced manner. Consuming excessive amounts of sugar was not, according to Tryon, just a threat to the body or merely a sign of weak self-control; he also found sugar morally suspect because of its close association with West Indian slavery.[24] Herbal infusions did nothing directly about that, of course, but it could be at least assumed that if sugar were taken only in infusions, the overall demand for it would decline.

The drinking of tea and coffee as a support for health was not limited to the setting of coffeehouses, although such establishments undoubtedly derived part of their public attraction from the fact that people who frequented them could lay claim to being more health conscious, and therefore more virtuous and reliable, than people at taverns or other places where alcohol was consumed. Some of the other qualities of coffee and tea that connected them with respectability – their promotion of sobriety, moderation and rationality – also extended beyond the coffeehouse: 'Then consider how many sober Companies it [tea] assembles both in Coffee-Houses . . . and private Houses. Observe the Business, Conversation, and Intelligence it promotes, the Expence and Debauchery it prevents.'[25] These additional virtues became specific to the coffeehouse when they were given a distinctive gender construction, because the culture and society of the coffeehouse were overwhelmingly masculine. Women are seldom mentioned (except as servants) in descriptions of coffeehouses in Britain and the Netherlands, and only slightly more frequently in France.[26] There were plenty of places at which men and women of the upper and middling classes regularly mingled (the theatre, pleasure gardens, public buildings), but not coffeehouses. The masculinity of coffeehouses was linked to their behavioural imagery, to the purposiveness and seriousness of the associations formed there and the kinds of behaviour men were expected to display. Within the earlier pattern of gentility, boisterous and often violent behaviour was accepted, even expected, in places where men gathered informally. The coffeehouse, by promoting a very different model of male behaviour, contributed to a redefinition of masculinity in a bourgeois world – a redefinition connected to several vitally important changes in eighteenth-century economic, cultural and political life.[27]

One reason that bourgeois men went to coffeehouses was to do business. Coffeehouses played an important part in the appearance in the eighteenth century of new types of flexible business institution, formed on the basis of short-term associations for particular purposes. For example, the insurance brokers who frequented Lloyd's coffeehouse in London used their proximity to one another to create insurance pools to cover particular ships and ventures, thereby turning Lloyd's into an insurance exchange. Brokers in various commodities, not wanting to be limited by the hours and the rules of incorporated exchanges, made it a custom to be present at particular coffeehouses at particular times of day. In this way, the coffeehouse became a significant part of the infrastructure of commercial capitalism and a real, observable element of what the classical economists described abstractly as 'the market'.[28]

Why did coffeehouses replace taverns as preferred sites for the establishment of informal business associations? One reason given in the eighteenth century was that alcoholic beverages dulled the mental faculties, whereas tea and coffee increased mental acuity, thereby promoting better business.[29] But this has to be understood within a larger cognitive framework, in which business was seen as something that required not only mental alertness but also a mutual assumption of honesty, reliability and moderation among the participants in commercial interchanges. The coffeehouse projected an image that embodied such qualities, especially when compared to establishments that served alcohol, and that image was conveyed to the transactions accomplished there. At the same time, the coffeehouse, with its atmosphere of moderate fashionability and unhurried calm, was more attractive than old-fashioned (and practically moribund) institutions of traditional urban commerce, such as guilds, and less frenetic than the exchanges.

Men also went to coffeehouses to exchange ideas. Even in the 1660s, men's clubs devoted to the discussion of serious intellectual subjects (and politics) met in coffeehouses. Pepys attended meetings of a famous club called the 'Rota' in which the central figure was James Harrington.[30] In eighteenth-century cities throughout north-western Europe, coffeehouses were central locations for the interchanges among intellectuals that constituted much of the structure of the Enlightenment.[31] The setting of the coffeehouse was consciously contrasted by observers with that of the salon, where intellectuals met potential patrons and engaged a wider elite public, but where the level of conversation was supposedly more frivolous. Again, why coffeehouses? In part, because the consumption of coffee and tea promoted the sobriety appropriate for the discussion of important subjects. At the same time, the coffeehouse permitted an informal intercourse, without elaborate rules of procedure or precedence. In circumstances of unforced good fellowship, without the impetus to violent or irrational behaviour that alcohol promoted, a natural order among intelligent men appeared, a kind of living, present example of the ideal civil society about which Enlightenment thinkers wrote. Intelligent men, not women. One of the reasons that salon discourse was thought to be more frivolous than coffeehouse conversation was that the former had to be directed in part towards women, and most women were believed by men to be incapable of the kind of sustained rational activity that was required for consideration of significant subjects.

One of the significant subjects discussed in coffeehouses was politics. Although Montesquieu complained that in early eighteenth-century Paris, intellectuals in coffeehouses preferred to deal with trivial issues, the coffeehouse increasingly became the prime location for political conversation (outside the government) and the formation of public opinion in France – a society not well equipped with public institutions for the discussion of politics.[32] When the Revolution came, coffeehouses took on an additional role as centres of political action, as political clubs and parties chose particular coffeehouses as informal headquarters. This pattern was repeated in Germany as late as the 1848 Revolution.[33]

The coffeehouse appealed as a place for political discussion and organization for many of the same reasons that attracted businessmen and intellectuals: coffee and tea were supposed to promote rational discourse in an atmosphere of sobriety and balance, without formal distinctions among participants. It is not unlikely that coffeehouses became centres particularly of *liberal* political activity on the continent in the late eighteenth century and the first half of the nineteenth because in some sense the values associated with tea and coffee, the cultural patterns and social rituals constructed around their public consumption in coffeehouses, made up a kind of living model of the ideal of the civil society to which liberals subscribed.[34] This role for coffeehouses was more important in Old Regime France and in autocratic German states than in Britain because of the lack of public political institutions from which alternative models could be derived. In coffeehouses, men supposedly behaved themselves without being forced to do so by rigid rules or by an application of authority, as contrasted with taverns where the authorities had to intervene frequently. Men acted civilly towards one another even while disagreeing. In other words, liberals who frequented coffeehouses could, if they wished, look around them and see a natural order in place, which gave the lie to the authoritarian assertion that order could be maintained and rational action afforded only by external direction and force. There was a close connection between images of the coffeehouse and images which permeated liberal ideology, a connection that extended even to exclusionary implications. The kinds of people who voluntarily patronized coffeehouses were the kinds of people whom liberals tended to envision as the 'active citizens' of a civil society: educated, respectable men with sufficient means to be able to act independently in politics (and to afford regular attendance at coffeehouses). The poor, the economically dependent, and women were excluded.[35]

The link between the respectability of the coffeehouse and the consumption of coffee and tea within it was, therefore, a not insignificant element of the economic, cultural and political history of Europe in the eighteenth century. To the extent that the modern capitalist world (as a real social structure and as a set of images underpinning abstract economic theory) expanded, recourse to the coffeehouse as a place of business and as a setting which reinforced the moral value of business increased. To the extent that intellectual exchange became more public and generally participatory in the eighteenth century, patronage of coffeehouses rose. And to the extent that public discussion of politics increased and liberal notions of what ought to constitute politics spread, the significance of coffeehouses as centres of politics and legitimating examples of liberal ideals broadened. Eventually, at different times in different countries, these activities outgrew the confines of the coffeehouse.[36] In London by the early nineteenth century, the market had bypassed the coffeehouse and other, older institutions and distributed itself among a plethora of more specialized establishments. Intellectual discussion had moved on to the pages of the literary reviews. And politics had moved elsewhere, particularly into the rooms of the Westminster clubs (some of which had started in coffeehouses). In France, Germany and the Netherlands, this process took place more slowly, especially in the intellectual and political spheres. In France, the café remained a significant (male) institution throughout the nineteenth century;[37] but elsewhere, it is fair to say that the coffeehouse did not maintain the importance it possessed in the eighteenth century into the third phase in the evolution of coffee and tea consumption in Europe which occurred in the nineteenth and twentieth centuries.

In this respect, the other typical context of tea and coffee consumption in the eighteenth century was quite different. Strong in the second phase, it became even stronger and more prevalent in the third.

THE PARLOUR: A CONTEXT OF FEMININITY AND DOMESTIC RESPECTABILITY

Early in *Clarissa* (1747–8), Richardson's heroine is called to tea with her family in the parlour, where she finds her parents, aunt, brother and sister in their accustomed places but not in their usual spirits.[38] It transpires that the brother and sister have informed the parents of Clarissa's innocent acquaintance with the unworthy Lovelace. Matters have been arranged so that Clarissa will eventually be alone with her father, who wishes her to marry the even more unworthy Solmes and will forbid further occasions for contact with Lovelace. But before that can happen, the ritual of tea must be performed, with the entire family present. The mother is the centre of the action and the primary person to whom the others defer. She decides that she will herself make the tea instead of Clarissa, who usually performs the task – an obvious, but indirect, sign of displeasure. The silence of the gathering is notable, presumably because conversation is the norm. But even though the parents are angry and the brother and sister are gloating at Clarissa's distress, no one brings up the unpleasant point at issue while the ritual is under way. Only when everyone but Clarissa and her father have found excuses to leave (after the second dish of tea) does the practical work of bullying Clarissa begin.

The situation is a fictional one, but it is consistent with non-fictional eighteenth-century accounts and with published advice on manners.[39] Similar scenes of formalized, meaningful social intercourse are described throughout Richardson's novels.[40] Richardson, like many others in his time, was deeply concerned with the moral meanings implicit in manners, with the symbolic language in which the meanings were expressed, and with the relationships among morality, manners and the actual behaviour of people.[41] The fact that attention was so often focused on such matters in the context of the domestic consumption of tea and coffee suggests connections between those products and the larger socio-cultural history of the eighteenth century that parallel the ones we analysed in the case of coffeehouses. Although tea and coffee became central features of several recognized meals, we shall concentrate for convenience on afternoon tea in Britain and northern Europe.

By the time Richardson wrote in the 1740s, afternoon tea had been established for nearly two generations as a custom of families of good standing in Britain and was very common in the Netherlands. The physical context was, of course, quite different from that of the coffeehouse. Tea was taken at home, not in a public place. In the eighteenth century, when tea and the other accompaniments of the tea meal were fairly expensive, the custom was effectively limited to people in the middle and upper ranges of society – rather like the clientele of the coffeehouse. But even at mid-century there were no obvious class preferences with respect to tea within those limits. It was practised in the very highest circles and it had become, both in north-western Europe and in English America, a badge of the respectable tradesman.[42] The custom was readily adopted by working-class and peasant families when prices came down in the nineteenth century. Tea was not so much a symbol of the social class to which one belonged as it was, like patronising coffeehouses, a means of claiming respectability.[43]

Tea was not only a meal taken at home; it was even more a meal taken with the *family*, as we can see from Richardson's description. It was not an entirely closed family occasion. Guests could be invited, but they acquired temporary status within the structure of the family while the meal lasted. Some permanent non-family residents of the household might take tea with the family (governesses or tutors in some families, apprentices in others), but in general people with the status of servants took tea separately, with the often-artificial service family downstairs. Tea was not an outwardly directed activity like a banquet or a party, nor was it primarily an occasion to form associations. It was in a sense a celebration of the fundamental permanent association: the family.[44]

Like most meals, tea was a ritual occasion. It was not just the structural nature of the ritual, however (who took part and what their functions were) that had meaning, but also the attitudes and demeanour that were supposed to be displayed. Although matters pertaining to the family were supposed to be discussed, conflict and division were to be avoided – hence the unwillingness of Clarissa's family to speak of the subject foremost in their minds while tea is going on, even though tea is the formal occasion that in some sense sanctions the action her father takes afterwards. Tea was intended to manifest family solidarity. It was the duty of the presiding woman to make sure it did so, and the duty of the other participants to defer to her leadership in this regard. In other words, tea was not just a symbol of the family; it was part of what it meant to *be* a family, a ritual that gave a family as a whole a psychological meaning apart from the dual relationships among individuals in it.[45]

Teatime manners were significant as well. There was, in addition to the specific ritual actions of making, pouring and distributing the tea and other comestibles, a well-understood pattern of appropriate behaviour for participants. It involved mutual deference between the sexes, general politeness and natural decorum. The pattern did not, however, include the rigid rules of courtesy that had been developed for upper-class public behaviour in the seventeenth century and that were adapted for more general use on festive occasions in the eighteenth century. In this respect, parlour behaviour resembled coffeehouse behaviour, and it bore a related set of meanings. Human sociability was a natural phenomenon, closely allied to reason and moderation. Within the family (portrayed as the basic institution for fostering sociability), reason and moderation in social relations were promoted by such activities as tea, which was to some extent a training process for adolescents and a reminder to adults about how to behave in the world at large. The coffeehouse performed a similar function in a non-domestic, public context.

The fact that tea was a family affair was related to another of its prominent features: women not only took part in the meal along with men, but they were also the central actors in the ritual of tea itself. The senior woman in the household (usually the wife of the householder) oversaw the making of the tea and assigned service tasks to various members of the family, with the assistance of servants if the latter were present. The centrality of women in the ritual of tea – at once ministering to the needs of the family and receiving the deference that their roles demanded – constituted a substantial difference from the masculinity of the coffeehouse. The specific nature of women's roles at tea had meaning as well.[46] A woman presided, directing the division of labour; women generally poured, thus symbolically providing sustenance and health. Topics and the manner of conversation were limited by the presumed sensibilities of ladies, and the women (especially the presiding woman) were expected politely to ensure that transgressions of this rule were immediately brought to the attention of the transgressors. In other words, women acted out roles as 'civilizers'. Also, the symbolic exchange of service on the part of women (pouring and usually distributing the tea) for deference on the parts of male participants reflected an ideal vision of the dynamics of gender interaction, the appeal of which was growing rapidly in the eighteenth century.[47]

The phenomena we have discussed – the domestic location of the tea meal, its social siting in the upper and middle ranges of society and growing appeal below them, its inward focus on the family, and its emphasis on the centrality of women in the family – can all be connected to wider trends in north-western European society. The so-called 'invention' of private life and domesticity in the seventeenth and eighteenth centuries is the most obvious of these, but there are others, particularly the emergence of respectability as a cultural pattern and of femininity within that pattern.[48]

The practice of the tea ritual (and its equivalents at other meals) was one of the many criteria that determined whether a family and its individual members were respectable. The public side of respectability can be seen in the coffeehouse. A more subtle, private side can be seen in the parlour, at teatime. To some extent families that adopted the tea custom were announcing to the world their respectability (and thus their qualifications for full participation in society).[49] But even more, they were confirming their respectability to themselves by taking part in rituals that demonstrated their civilized patterns of behaviour and their intention of promoting them through future generations. Access to such material complements of domestic respectability as tea, coffee and sugar had at least as many political implications as access to coffeehouses did. The protests against inflated prices of tea, coffee and sugar in Paris in 1792, like the reaction to the Tea Act in British North America nearly two decades before, suggest that these products had implications for the self-respect of substantial numbers of people – implications that could be readily exploited by radical politicians.[50]

The central role of women in the afternoon tea ritual (which was probably developed by women in the first place) was evidently connected to the emergence in the eighteenth century of an ideal of gender relations that eventually became the 'separate spheres' ideology of the Victorian era.[51] Men had the duty, so the usual line went, of negotiating for the family with the outside world, especially with the external institutions of power and public decision-making. The nature of those duties and the need to perform them respectably were symbolized by the coffeehouse. Women had responsibility for organizing the home, managing it as a source of moral support and physical sustenance, and maintaining it as an instrument of moral education. Although men's externally oriented roles (and, supposedly, their greater aptitude for rational analysis) gave them a legitimate preponderance of influence in family decision processes, the roles of women had to be respected and their authority within the domestic sphere had to be upheld.[52] The division of power was clearly unequal, and eventually, in the nineteenth and twentieth centuries, many people came to recognize the 'separate spheres' and the whole ideal of feminine respectability represented by afternoon tea as a trap. But initially, in the eighteenth century, the ideal was extremely popular, and women in widely varied social strata adopted and (through such rituals as afternoon tea) promoted it when their means permitted. It reinforced a role for women that was respectable, that afforded them deference for their performance of social and cultural functions that were recognized as vital. The ideal portrayed them as managers within the household, not (as had often been the case even among the higher ranks of the middle classes) as domestic functionaries who performed hard physical labour.[53]

Tea and coffee, with their concomitant of sugar, constituted one of the most important and dynamic ensembles of consumer goods in eighteenth-century Europe. They did so in large part because they were connected in a complex way to some of the most significant changes that took place in Western culture and society. Tea, coffee and sugar were essential to the display, and even more to the self-perception, of respectability, which was in turn a very important, possibly definitive, element of bourgeois consciousness. The more difficult it becomes for historians to identify the 'bourgeoisie' exclusively with social groups defined by income, occupation, or even structural relationship to capital as a means of production, the more we are led to focus on behavioural, attitudinal and intellectual phenomena like respectability in order to identify the bourgeoisie. If we want to know whether or not a particular eighteenth-century family was bourgeois in a meaningful sense, it may be at least as important to find out whether it regularly took afternoon tea as to know the occupation of the head of household. Sugared tea and coffee thus became the preferred 'soft drugs' of Western Europe because they afforded access to respectability and bourgeois standing – a function completely different from those performed by indigenous European psychoactive substances.

NOTES

1 S. Mintz, *Sweetness and Power: The Place of Sugar in Modern History*, New York, Penguin, 1985, pp. 108–17.
2 See the contribution to this volume by Jordan Goodman.
3 W. Ukers, *All About Tea*, New York, Tea and Coffee Trade Journal Company, 1935, vol. 1, pp. 23–48; *Thema Thee. De geschiedenis van de thee en het theegebruik in Nederland*, Rotterdam, Museum Boymans-van Beuningen, 1978, pp. 36–8. *The Diary of John Evelyn*, ed. E. de Beer, Oxford, Clarendon Press, 1955, vol. 1, pp. 14–15, reports coffee as a novelty at Oxford around 1637.
4 See the figures for consumption (imports) in Jordan Goodman's essay in this volume, p. 126.
5 W. Smith, 'Complications of the commonplace: tea, sugar and imperialism', *Journal of Interdisciplinary History*, 1992, vol. 23(2), pp. 259–78.
6 R. Stein, *The French Sugar Business in the Eighteenth Century*, Baton Rouge, Louisiana State University Press, 1988, pp. 93–105, 120.

7 *Thema Thee*, op. cit., pp. 13–19; P. Dufour, *Traitez nouveaux et curieux du cafe, du thee et du chocolat*, The Hague, A. Moetjens, 1685, pp. 101–58.

8 Evidence for this assertion can be found, among other places, in the account books of a well-to-do English spinster between 1697 and 1704, located in Chancery Masters' Exhibits, Public Record Office, London (PRO) C114/182. See also F. Braudel, *Civilization and Capitalism 15th–18th Century*, vol. 1: *The Limits of the Possible*, New York, Harper & Row, 1981, pp. 256–8.

9 Ukers, op. cit., vol. 1, p. 46; E. Robinson, *The Early History of Coffee Houses in England*, London, Routledge & Kegan Paul, 1893.

10 C. Shammas, 'The eighteenth century diet and economic change', *Explorations in Economic History*, 1984, vol. 21, pp. 254–69.

11 Mintz, op. cit., pp. 140–2; R. Porter, *English Society in the Eighteenth Century*, Harmondsworth, Penguin, 1982, pp. 324–5.

12 See Geoffrey Best, *Mid-Victorian Britain 1851–1875*, New York, Schocken, 1971, pp. 256–63.

13 The significance in this respect of the custom of wearing cotton garments is discussed by C. Mukerji, *From Graven Images: Patterns of Modern Materialism*, New York, Columbia University Press, 1983, p. 192.

14 S. Pepys, *The Diary of Samuel Pepys*, ed. R. Latham and W. Matthews, Berkeley and Los Angeles, University of California Press, 1970–83, vol. 1, pp. 14, 20–1, 61; vol. 2, pp. 108, 111.

15 *A Proclamation for the Suppression of Coffee-Houses*, Broadside, London, 29 December 1675; Braudel, op. cit., vol. 1, pp. 256–8.

16 T. Short, *Discourses on Tea, Sugar, Milk, Made-Wines, Spirits, Punch, Tobacco, etc., With Plain and Useful Rules for Gouty People*, London, Longman, 1750, p. 32; Braudel, op. cit., vol. 1, p. 258.

17 See the description of a coffeehouse in D. de la Feuille, *Le Guide d'Amsterdam*, Amsterdam, D. de la Feuille, 1701, pp. 65–6.

18 Short, op cit., p. 32.

19 Ibid., pp. 1–76; J. Chamberlain, *The Manner of Making of Coffee, Tea, and Chocolate*, London, William Crook, 1685, pp. 48–52.

20 S. Blankaart, *De Borgerlyke Tafel. Om lang gesond sonder ziekten te leven*, Amsterdam, Jan ten Hoorn, 1683, preface, n.p.

21 Ibid.; C. Bontekoe, *Tractaat Van het Excellenste Kruyd Thee, Coffi en Chocolate*, Amsterdam, Jan ten Hoorn, 1689.

22 L. Labaree et al., *The Autobiography of Benjamin Franklin*, New York and London, Yale University Press, 1964, pp. 63, 87–8.

23 [T. Tryon], *A New Art of Brewing*, London, T. Salusbury, 1690, pp. 68–70.

24 Ibid., pp. 52–3, 79–80, 85–6.

25 Short, op. cit., p. 32.

26 De la Feuille, op. cit., pp. 65–6. Braudel (op. cit., vol. 1, p. 258) mentions 'beautiful women' at fashionable coffeehouses in the seventeenth century, but most portrayals of coffeehouses (including the one reproduced in Braudel, vol. 1, p. 259) show only men as patrons.

27 The development of 'civilized' male behaviour based on self-restraint in the seventeenth and eighteenth centuries is emphasized by Norbert Elias. The relationship between this development and the emergence of culinary 'taste' is discussed in S. Mennell, *All Manners of Food: Eating and Taste in England and France from the Middle Ages to the Present*, Oxford, Blackwell, 1985.

28 Among countless examples that illustrate this process, two may be cited. See Chancery Masters' Exhibits, PRO 112/62, papers of W. and G. Panter, brokers operating out of Lloyd's, and a bill of sale for coffee sold at auction at Garroway's Coffee House, 4 May 1738, in Chancery Masters' Exhibits, PRO

113/11, no. 20: re Philips.

29 Short, op. cit., p. 32.

30 Pepys, op. cit., vol. 1, p. 14.

31 Braudel, op. cit., vol. 1, pp. 258–9.

32 Ibid. See Montesquieu, *The Persian Letters*, tr. and ed. J. Loy, New York, Meridian, 1961, pp. 94–5 (Letter XXXVI).

33 M. Kennedy, *The Jacobin Clubs in the French Revolution: The First Years*, Princeton, Princeton University Press, 1982, pp. 3–30; D. Mattheisen, 'Liberal constitutionalism in the Frankfurt Parliament of 1848: an inquiry based on roll-call analysis', *Central European History*, 1979, vol. 12, pp. 124–42.

34 P. Albrecht, 'Coffee-drinking as a symbol of social change in continental Europe in the seventeenth and eighteenth centuries', *Studies in Eighteenth-Century Culture*, 1988, vol. 18, pp. 91–103; M. Aymard, 'Friends and neighbors', in R. Chartier (ed.), *A History of Private Life: III. Passions of the Renaissance*, Cambridge (USA), Belknap, 1989, pp. 470–7.

35 The connection between manifest respectability as a differentiator of persons and the operation of the nineteenth-century English legal system is analysed in C. Conley, *The Unwritten Law: Criminal Justice in Victorian Kent*, New York, Oxford University Press, 1991, pp. 4–6, 173–201.

36 Ukers, op. cit., vol. 1, p. 46.

37 M. Perrot (ed.), *A History of Private Life: IV. From the Fires of Revolution to the Great War*, Cambridge (USA), Belknap, 1990, pp. 28, 136, 174, 341.

38 S. Richardson, *Clarissa or the History of a Young Lady*, abr. by G. Sherburne, Boston, Houghton Mifflin, 1962, pp. 16–18.

39 Short, op. cit., p. 32.

40 See, for instance, Richardson, op. cit., pp. 26–7, 240–1.

41 Ibid., pp. v–xiv.

42 *Thema Thee*, op. cit., pp. 26–36. Tea merchants were highly aware of the social spread of the tea custom. See, for instance, the records of Thomas Hall, a London merchant, in Chancery Records (PRO), C103/132, Exhibit 49 (correspondence of Hall and A. Crop of Amsterdam, letters 18 May 1736 and 28 October 1738).

43 Mintz, op. cit., pp. 140–2.

44 L. Weatherill, *Consumer Behavior and Material Culture in Britain 1660–1760*, London and New York, Routledge, 1988, pp. 157–9.

45 Ibid., pp. 152–9; A. Martin-Fugier, 'Bourgeois rituals', in Perrot, op. cit., pp. 261–337.

46 Martin-Fugier, op. cit., pp. 274–7.

47 See *A Treatise on the Inherent Qualities of the Tea-Herb*, London, C. Corbett, 1750, ii–iii.

48 Chartier, op. cit., pp. 161–395.

49 For a discussion of respectability as a criterion for full civic participation, see Macaulay's 1831 speech in favour of parliamentary reform in T. Macaulay, *Selected Writings*, Chicago, University of Chicago Press, 1972, pp. 165–80.

50 G. Rude, *The Crowd in the French Revolution*, Oxford, Clarendon Press, 1959, pp. 96–7; B. Labaree, *The Boston Tea Party*, New York, Oxford University Press, 1964.

51 C. Hall, 'The sweet delights of home', in Perrot, op. cit., pp. 47–93.

52 M. Perrot, 'Roles and Characters', in Perrot, op. cit., pp. 190–2.

53 In the 1660s, Samuel Pepys' wife Elizabeth not only directed her servants in their housework, but did a great deal of the work herself (including some of the hardest and dirtiest tasks). Samuel Pepys, who was quick to react to anything that might lower his standing in the eyes of fellow state officials, does

not appear to have regarded his wife's role as anything but normal. A century later, such behaviour on the part of the wife of the secretary to the Navy Board would have been unthinkable. Pepys, op. cit., vol. 1, p. 301. See also Weatherill, op. cit., p. 150.

8

TOBACCO USE AND TOBACCO TAXATION

A battle of interests in early modern Europe

Jacob M. Price

Adam Smith saw the economic world in which he lived as engaged in an ongoing process of creation and adaptation set in motion initially by the discovery of America and the ocean routes to Asia.[1] In the centuries between Columbus and Smith, the lives of diverse sectors of the European population were touched and changed by the introduction of new botanical items from overseas. One of these, tobacco, was particularly well known in Smith's world. He, of course, lived and worked in Glasgow, a major tobacco port. By his day the new leaf, however used, not only impinged on the daily routines, health and pocketbooks of millions, but had also confronted their governments with the ever pressing need to set policy priorities and arbitrate between the inharmonious interests of planters, merchants, manufacturers, tax farmers, state treasuries and consumers. To understand the differing ways in which these discordant demands were harmonized or at least mollified in different countries, we must keep in mind both the geography and the chronology of the tobacco question in the three centuries following Columbus' voyages.

In the sixteenth century, tobacco as a curiosity attracted the attention of botantists, gardeners, physicians, travellers and men of letters.[2] In the popular history of tobacco, the sixteenth century means anecdotes about Jean Nicot, Catherine de Medici, or Sir Walter Raleigh. Serious discussion of weighty social or economic questions had to await the seventeenth century. From an exotic curiosity known primarily to botanists, physicians, sailors and a few raffish novelty-mongers about court, tobacco was to become an item of ubiquitous if not universal consumption inevitably attracting the most serious attention of tax strategists.

This transformation was not without its critics. Both the clergy and the medical profession had serious doubts about the harmlessness of the fad;

James I was only the most prominent author to attack its use. However, demand in the expanding circles habituated to the weed created revenue possibilities which soon persuaded statesmen that they would have to accept tobacco taking as part of a changing social order. Russia was the last European country where religious hostility was strong enough to proscribe the use of tobacco, but in this too Peter the Great was determined to 'Westernize'. About the time of his visit to the West in 1697, he not only legalized the use and importation of tobacco but also set up Russia's first state monopoly for that trade.[3]

By the 1620s tobacco had entered the public culture of Western Europe. In that decade the cultivation of tobacco became firmly established in Virginia and, with the abolition of the Virginia Company in 1624, became much more attractive for both planter and trader. In the West Indies, that same decade saw the spread of tobacco cultivation to the new English and French settlements from the Spanish and Portuguese colonies where it had long been known. Those same years also saw the first heavy duties in France on imported tobacco as well as the beginning of tobacco cultivation in the south-west of France, Alsace, the Low Countries and adjacent areas – even in England. The Thirty Years War may have had an important part to play in the diffusion of tobacco consumption. In seventeenth-century France, consumption was particularly noticeable in Paris, a few other populous centres and port towns. Military service would have introduced many young rustics to this urban habit, while marching armies would have carried the weed into hitherto untouched rural areas. Contemporaries noted that tobacco was peculiarly well suited to assuage the cold, hunger and weariness of troops in the field.[4]

If tobacco was a common aspect of social life in most parts of Western Europe by the end of the seventeenth century, its consumption was not heavy by modern standards, not even after substantial growth in its use in the eighteenth century. For example, British imports from the Chesapeake, the most important source of European supply, tripled between the early 1720s and early 1770s, with up to 85 per cent of imports re-exported to the continent where demand was climbing slowly but steadily.[5] The use of tobacco was becoming widespread, but not yet intense. By the end of the eighteenth century, per capita consumption was about 1½ lbs per head in Britain and 1 lb in France. Such moderation stands in marked contrast to recent experience, with consumption per head per annum of about 3 lbs for France, 4½ to 6 lbs for the United Kingdom, the Netherlands, Belgium, Denmark and Canada and 7½ lbs for the United States.[6]

Part of this slow growth in consumption in early modern Europe must be ascribed to poverty and to the significant burden of tobacco taxation on the poorer would-be consumer. The apparent decline in per capita tobacco consumption in England during the 'gin craze' of the 1730s and

1740s suggests budgetary constraints on the poor.[7] Much must also be allowed for the cultural isolation of the rural population suggested by the limited penetration of tobacco taking in rural areas poorly supplied with authorized retail outlets, particularly in France. But something must also be allowed for the dominant fashion of snuff-taking in the eighteenth century. Snuff could be taken in working areas where smoking was dangerous or unacceptable; and women could take nasal snuff without appearing unladylike. (Both smoking and chewing were associated with the outdoors or with the coarser sort of public house.) Even so, impressions suggest that the average snuff-taker did not consume as much tobacco per day as the average smoker or chewer.

Despite still low consumption per head, eighteenth-century European finance ministers were very serious in their efforts to derive as much revenue as possible from this suspect luxury. In Great Britain and the United Provinces, state income was sought through ordinary customs and excise impositions. In England and later Britain, the ratio of the total net duty to the price 'at the mast' (i.e. before customs entry) rose from about 100 per cent following the adoption of the Tobacco Impost of 1685 to well over 200 per cent during 1760–75.[8] However, in most contemporary European countries, either customs duties of this level were not considered feasible or higher yields were desired. Thus a tobacco monopoly was deemed a necessary or preferable means to extract the revenue sought. Such a monopoly could be a department of state but more commonly was a privilege farmed to private interests. In France it proved efficient, particularly after 1730, to farm the tobacco monopoly to the same interests contracting with the central government for the collection of other indiret taxes (i.e. the United General Farms).[9] Monopolies of one kind or another could be found in France, Spain, Portugal, the Hapsburg dominions in central Europe and many of the smaller German and Italian states.[10]

The extra yields obtained by monopolies were not insignificant. In the age of Walpole's excise scheme (1733) Britain found it very difficult to increase significantly the net yield of the tobacco duties. Even after the substantial increases in rates during the American Revolution, the total yield of the British customs and excise duties on tobacco came to only 3.6 per cent of total state revenues in the 1790s.[11] In France, despite lower per capita consumption, the tobacco monopoly yielded from 6.4 to 7.3 per cent of total state revenues between 1763 and 1789, while in contemporary Spain, the monopoly produced at least 25 per cent of such revenues.[12] What weight should such figures carry? For students of *ancien régime* finance, 7 per cent of French state revenues was a very weighty figure: weighty in that it created both a state interest and private interests that could not readily be ignored when relevant policy questions came to be decided.

In the eighteenth century, one could still find medical dissertations and treatises investigating the healthfulness of tobacco.[13] Such concerns, however, scarcely intruded upon the consciousness of eighteenth-century statesmen. For them the public history of tobacco was focused on a different set of questions: how much revenue could the state extract from this suspect weed? How much attention must the state pay to the preferences of consumers? At what level of duties are smuggling and fraud likely to move yields beyond the point of diminishing returns? Should the state encourage tobacco production at home or in the colonies? How important is tobacco for the navigation of the realm? Should the state even ban the domestic production of tobacco in the interest of the fisc and the colonies? Must such concerns also oblige the state to regulate tobacco manufacture closely? How much attention must statesmen pay to the economic and political weight of tobacco merchants, manufacturers, distributors and revenue farmers?

These questions drew forth quite different responses from statesmen in Britain and France, the countries to be examined most fully in this chapter. Whether or not a land had a tobacco monopoly, the local cultivation of tobacco could create serious problems for those trying to extract a state revenue from its consumption. Since tobacco can be processed and sold in small quantities, cultivators seeking buyers could easily avoid the supervision of the the tax collector. In England the interest of the fisc and the interest of overseas traders coincided in preferring colonial production to domestic. From the time of James I successive regimes issued laws, orders and ordinances prohibiting the cultivation of tobacco in England and Wales. Yet the political upheaval of the middle decades of the century made such restrictions virtually unenforceable so that the Restoration Parliament and government had almost to begin again in the campaign against domestic cultivation. The centre of disobedience proved to be northern Gloucestershire around Tewkesbury where the husbandmen of the Cotswolds found tobacco a most remunerative crop on small holdings. Even so, the repeated and unrelenting use of force, including the royal cavalry, eventually weaned the hill-dwellers from their once profitable sideline. By the time of the Revolution of 1688, domestic cultivation was no longer a problem for English governments.[14]

The French government, slower to seek a substantial tobacco revenue, was under less pressure to develop a planting policy. However, when the tobacco monopoly and farm were established by Colbert in 1674, the monopolists obtained clauses prohibiting cultivation in France proper. Exceptions were made, though, for certain specified parishes in the modern departments of Lot-et-Garonne and Tarn-et-Garonne in the south-west and a few places in Normandy.[15] In 1719, during the brief ascendancy of John Law, French policy temporarily followed the British model: a customs duty was established in place of the monopoly and all cultivation in France proper prohibited.[16] When the monopoly was re-established on Law's downfall, the new farmers insisted on keeping the ban on domestic cultivation, at least in inner France. The frontier provinces, of course, had long been shown greater leniency by the French crown, and, even after the restoration of the monopoly, cultivation was permitted in French Flanders, Artois, Alsace, Franche Comté and the Pays de Labourd around Bayonne. These privileges continued until the French Revolution, though cultivation was progressively restricted in the parts of the frontier provinces contiguous to France proper, particularly lands within three leagues (7.27 English miles) of the borders of the monopoly's jurisdiction.[17]

Prohibition of domestic cultivation was by no means only characteristic of countries with alternative sources of supply in their own colonies. Other European countries also prohibited domestic cultivation, including both those with colonial supplies – particularly Spain and Portugal – and those without useful colonies, including the Hapsburg crown lands and many of the smaller states in Italy and Germany. For them the interest of the fisc was reason enough.[18]

There was less difference of opinion about the desirability of encouraging colonial production. For statesmen who had experienced the long depression of the mid-seventeenth century, colonies were attractive abstractly as havens for surplus population, markets for domestic manufactures, employers of the national mercantile fleet, and sources of needed imports – including even tobacco – that otherwise would have had to be purchased from foreigners. England was particularly fortunate in having in North America the colonies of Virginia, Maryland and North Carolina, with soils well suited to the production of vendible varieties of tobacco.[19] The English and later British government encouraged the production of tobacco in the colonies by duties discriminating against Spanish and Portuguese tobacco and by total prohibition of the importation of tobacco from Germany and the Low Countries where by the end of the seventeenth century there was competing tobacco cultivation and exportation.[20] Counter-balancing these encouragements was the legal obligation under the acts of trade to ship tobacco from the colonies to Europe only via the mother country and only in national vessels.[21] These restrictions were undoubtedly burdensome when adopted in the mid-seventeenth century, but by the eighteenth century, given the structure of the market, their costs were very likely shifted in large part to the continental buyer.[22]

France too had colonies that could and did produce tobacco – particularly Martinique, Guadeloupe and St Domingue. The first two, like the nearby British Leeward and Windward Islands, soon found it much more in their interest to concentrate on sugar and later coffee as well.

On St Domingue, however, there was plenty of suitable land available, and tobacco cultivation was quite economic for the small planters more numerous in that colony. Production of tobacco on St Domingue continued even after the establishment of the monopoly in France in 1674. However, the monopolists were reluctant to pay enough above the European market price to sustain production in that colony. Their interests and those of the small planters were incompatible; and cultivation on St Domingue almost inevitably collapsed by 1700.[23] There too sugar proved more attractive. Later, under Law, a serious effort was made to obtain a colonial supply for France by encouraging tobacco cultivation in Louisiana. But the same difficulties which afflicted St Domingue a half-century before reappeared here – particularly after the restored tobacco monopoly was taken away from the Indies Company in 1730 and entrusted once more to the United General Farms. Because Louisiana was even further from France than St Domingue and had an ongoing acute shortage of labour, here too the monopoly would have had to pay an artificially high price to make tobacco cultivation attractive to the settlers. This the monopoly was reluctant to do, particularly as there was no noticeable demand for Louisiana tobacco among French consumers. Even though successive secretaries of state for the navy induced the monopoly to pay enough to procure some tobacco from the colony, Louisiana had not yet become a significant supplier of leaf to France when the colony was lost at the end of the Seven Years War.[24] In the following years the government tried to repeat much the same experiment in French Guiana with even less success.[25] Governments could have colonial objectives as well as fiscal, but in making revenue contracts usually placed the fisc first. Consequently a monopoly, with a fixed contract price and more or less fixed retail prices, did not have the leeway to pay much above world prices simply to help a colony that was not otherwise an absolute priority for the government.

Portugal and Spain had equivalent problems but were rather more successful than France in reconciling colonial and fiscal objectives. Both had domestic tobacco monopolies from the 1630s onwards, and both had problem-plagued colonial supplies. Brazil, particularly in the area around Bahia (Salvador), was Portugal's major source of tobacco, valued not only for domestic consumption but also for export to other European countries and to Africa. These quite distinct markets created conflicts of interest. After Portuguese independence from Spain was restored in 1640, the government re-established the domestic tobacco monopoly but gave permission to the Bahians to export tobacco directly to Africa in exchange for slaves. An attempt was made to reconcile Bahian and metropolitan interests by requiring that all supplies of the better qualities of tobacco be shipped home and only the inferior grades sent to West Africa. Even 'third class' Brazilian leaf, spun and heavily coated with molasses, sold well on the African coast. In fact, it became a necessary trading commodity for the slave trade in the Bight of Benin,[26] even after the Portuguese lost their trading stations on the Gold Coast and Slave Coast to the Dutch in the 1630s. The Dutch West India Company obliged all vessels from Brazil wishing to trade on this coast to bring tobacco and stop first at Elmina to pay a toll of 10 per cent of their leaf for permission to trade. The toll plus the trading opportunities created by the stop at Elmina gave the Dutch a supply of Bahian tobacco for their own slave and gold trades. The Brazilian vessels then proceeded eastwards where they could trade for slaves. The value of Bahian tobacco in the African trade was significantly enhanced by the discovery of gold in Brazil in the 1690s, which swelled the demand there for the sturdier slaves from the Bight of Benin. Realizing that Brazilian tobacco was necessary in the slave trade, the Lisbon government brought pressure on the Portuguese monopoly not to sell any to foreign slave traders, though the French were able to obtain some at Lisbon by subterfuge.[27]

The British developed a market in West Africa for their own Chesapeake tobacco, with leaf exports to there increasing tenfold between the beginnning of the century and the early 1770s.[28] Even so, Britain still needed Brazilian tobacco for its slave trade on the coast. This they obtained by 'clandestine trade' with vessels from Bahia. Such traffic was tolerated by a 1708 agreement between senior British and Dutch officials on the coast. This trade increased in the following decades, perhaps because the Brazilians' own trade there was encumbered by a difficult set of regulations promulgated by the Pombal regime after 1751. In the 1760s the Dutch Company, wishing to obtain more Bahian tobacco, tried to impede the Bahian traffic with the British and seized several Brazilian vessels. The British ministry responded to the complaints of the Company of Merchants Trading to Africa by exerting diplomatic pressure on the United Provinces, which conceded in 1771 that, once toll had been paid at Elmina, Brazilian vessels could trade as they wished on that coast.[29]

The Spanish were less successful than the Portuguese in developing a tobacco supply that could at once satisfy domestic demand and provide a major export or re-export. They too had had a domestic tobacco monopoly since the 1630s, which by the mid-eighteenth century was producing over £1½ million per annum, several times the yield of a much higher consumption in Britain.[30] This income represented a proportion of state revenues even higher than that realized in France. The tobacco monopoly's share in the total domestic revenues of the Spanish crown (excluding the colonies) rose from about 10 per cent at the beginning of the eighteenth century to 25–33 per cent by the 1760s.[31]

Because such a large proportion of state revenues came from the tobacco *estanco*, the Spanish government insisted colonial production be sent home and sold to the monopoly at prices usually unattractive to the producers. As early as 1614, a royal *cedula* ordered that all tobacco not consumed in the province of production must be shipped directly to Seville – on pain of death![32] Tobacco was grown for local consumption in many of the Spanish provinces in America, but, from a European perspective, the important exporting areas were Venezuela and Cuba. A zone of noted export production lay in the western extremities of modern Venezuela to the east of Lake Maracaibo and ultimately extending as far south as the valley of the Arauca. From Baranas (Barinas) in the centre of this zone came the European commercial name for this tobacco: Verinas tobacco or *tabac de Vérine,* a rather exotic and recherché product in Europe selling at up to ten times the price of Virginia, European and other ordinary varieties. In Venezuela such tobacco was generally cultivated on the small holdings of both indigenes and settlers. (The larger planters of the area preferred sugar or cacao.) The area was closely linked by illicit trade to Dutch Curaçao, off the north-west Venezuelan coast. In the seventeenth century more Verinas tobacco was probably sent from Curaçao to Holland than from Venezuela to Cadiz and Seville. In the eighteenth century the irregular Curaçao trade was greater than the authorized trade, except in the late 1730s, when for a few years the new Caracas Company, a regional trade monopoly, raised legitimate shipments to Spain to levels far above the Curaçao–Amsterdam flow. However, this happy interlude came to an end with the outbreak of the British–Spanish War in 1739, after which Curaçao shipments exceeded those of the company by as much as eightfold or more.[33]

In the eighteenth century, the Spanish administration was more successful (if not completely so) in developing a major source of tobacco in Cuba. Its relative proximity to Europe and the route of the fleet from Mexico, which stopped regularly at Havana, meant that transportation need not have been a problem. Moreover, even before the days of the cigar, Cuban or Havana leaf was recognized as a superior product justifying a higher price to producers even from a monopoly. It was also particularly well suited for snuff, the most fashionable form of tobacco taking in the eighteenth century.[34] But, even though tobacco was Cuba's major export by 1650, the Spanish monopoly had continuing difficulties getting as much of the 'Havana leaf' as it desired in the later seventeenth and the early eighteenth centuries. Much of what was grown was smuggled out of the island to Dutch, French or British colonies and transshipped to Europe where Havana leaf and snuff appeared regularly in the Hamburg and Amsterdam markets.[35]

Since private traders were not bringing enough Cuban tobacco to Cadiz, the Spanish monopoly sent a purchasing agent to Havana in 1708. The new arrangement procured more leaf for Spain but not all that was desired, particularly of the better qualities. In 1717 new royal instructions designated the agent of the monopoly as the sole legal buyer of all tobacco produced on the island. The law also prohibited the construction of any further snuff mills there. Hundreds of such mills already existed in the colony, and snuff was the preferred export in the illicit trade. This effort to pre-empt supplies combined with the less-than-attractive price offered by the monopoly's agent led in the early 1720s to a revolt by Cuban growers and traders that had to be suppressed by royal troops. Such heavy-handedness did not procure all the supplies desired by the monopoly and from 1734 the privilege of buying Cuban tobacco was farmed out. Some private trade was permitted after the agent procured the quantity needed in Seville.[36]

Under these arrangements, slightly over 2 million lbs of tobacco were sent annually from Cuba to Spain during 1740–61.[37] As the monopoly reportedly needed 3½ million lbs per annum, this left a significant margin to be made up by imports from Venezuela and from foreign sources – particularly Brazil tobacco from Lisbon and Chesapeake tobacco from London. Some idea of the under-performance of Spanish monopoly-monopsony arrangements is suggested by figures for English and later British exports of tobacco to Spain (Table 2).

Table 2 English/British tobacco exports to Spain, 1696–1775[38]

Date	*lbs per annum*
1696–1700 (from England)	1,988,000
1714–18	849,000
1720–8	1,098,000
1729–38	1,175,000
1749–54	494,000
1755–61 (from Britain)	846,000
1762–8	1,093,000
1769–75	619,000

These figures suggest that at the end of the seventeenth century the Spanish tobacco monopoly had egregiously failed to develop a dependable supply from the Spanish colonies and that more than half of its tobacco inputs were seemingly met by imports from England. Conditions changed with the advent of the new dynasty, as was soon manifest in the legislation of 1701 prohibiting the importation of foreign tobacco. A significant part of the previous English exports to Spain would appear to have gone to the fiscally separate kingdom of Valencia but the Bourbon integration of that jurisdiction into Castile ended that anomaly.[39] The resumption of substantial exports to Spain in the 1720s and

1730s can only have meant that even the reformed monopoly there wasn't getting as much tobacco as it needed from Spain's colonies, particularly Cuba. An experienced merchant explained to the British Board of Trade:

> In Spain, by means of [i.e. by orders from] those Estankers or Farmers, I have known considerable parcels [to] have been vended at Allicant [in Valencia] and Barcellona, when their own has been dear or lay under some difficulties as in time of War, or by the long delay of their ships returning from the West Indies, and whenever that happens, they will again furnish themselves from Us.[40]

In fact, during the Spanish and Austrian Succession Wars and in 1719 (also a war year), there was a marked reduction but not total suspension of British tobacco exports to Spain. But during the wars of 1726–8 and 1762 there was no decline in such exports at all. In 1762 the British and Spanish governments licensed the trade (from London to Cadiz and Seville) despite the war, just as was being done at the time for British exports to France.[41]

Looking at the Spanish experience as a whole, we see that the Spanish colonies produced tobaccos with quite different market strengths. If Havana leaf and snuff sold in neutral markets for only a little more than the Virginia equivalent, Verinas tobacco had a more erratic price history. At the beginning of the century it sold at prices comparable to those paid for Havana or Virginia. By the 1730s, however, at the height of the success of the Caracas Company, it realized open market prices up to ten times those of Chesapeake leaf. This would appear to reflect the temporary success of the Spanish monopoly in pre-empting an increasing share of a stagnant production.[42] Yet, whatever their fiscal achievements, the Spanish cannot be said to have exploited fully the commercial possibilities of these colonial crops.

Different countries worked out their own distinctive formulas for reconciling the desire for both revenue and agricultural/commercial development. At one extreme, the British, even while taxing tobacco heavily, were prepared to sacrifice revenue for agricultural and commercial growth. At the other extreme, the French let their colonial tobacco production shrivel almost to nothing to defend the revenue. The Spanish state derived even more from the monopoly than the French but tried with partial success to encourage colonial production within a tightly regulated regime.[43] Much of the tobacco production of both Cuba and Venezuela slipped surreptitiously out of Spanish hands so that the monopoly at home had continually to rely on 'emergency' supplies from England to keep their manufacture operating at the desired level. Only the Portuguese were able to combine a substantial revenue with looser regulation and significant exports to both Africa and Europe.

In all countries where there was a monopoly farmed by private interests, the farmers of the privilege obviously constituted a most powerful pressure group. In negotiations with the government, such an entrenched interest was more often than not able to triumph in disputes with cultivators (colonial and domestic), merchants and manufacturers. In Britain, where there was no monopoly, a role almost as influential was played by the import merchants who paid large amounts to the state in customs. The high level of import duties and the elaborate regulations that went with them were among the factors that tended to discourage smaller importers, leaving the trade increasingly in the hands of fewer and larger houses, firms that could make their needs known to government.[44] Their greatest achievement was persuading successive London governments that there was a substantial state interest in encouraging the tobacco re-export trade to the continent. From 1660 all duties paid on tobacco at importation were refunded or 'drawn back' except for a 'halfpenny' (actually 0.375 d.) per pound. To relieve the liquidity problems of tobacco merchants, all the other duties could be bonded with the bonds to be cancelled by the 'drawback' credits at exportation.[45] In the 1720s, when English merchants became upset by 'unfair' Scottish competition, Walpole appeased the English without offending the Scots by conceding the refunding of the last 'halfpenny' per pound. When prices were low (i.e. in the vicinity of 2 to 2.5 d. per pound), the total drawback of duties made British colonial tobaccos much more competitive in Europe against German, Dutch and other inexpensive continental rivals. Attractive prices help explain the tripling of the British tobacco trade between the early 1720s and the early 1770s, by which time re-exports constituted 85 per cent of imports.[46]

When big British merchants and continental courtier-monopolists co-operated, they could on occasion move political mountains. A group of London merchants, including directors of both the Bank of England and the new East India Company, obtained from Peter the Great the monopoly of supplying Russia with foreign tobacco. To exploit this opportunity, they had both to get Parliament to end the exclusivity of the London Muscovy Company and to persuade Queen Anne's ministers to send the first English minister to Moscow. In the end the 'tobacco adventurers' were more successful politically than commercially for their monopoly proved unenforceable in Russia.[47]

Even before the Russian experiment, leaf tobacco was purchased in England by several continental monopolies, including the Spanish and Swedish[48] but not the French at first. During the war of the 1690s, however, French privateers captured a large number of vessels carrying tobacco from Virginia and Maryland. When brought into French ports these prize cargoes were purchased cheaply by the monopoly which soon found tobacco products made from Chesapeake leaf most acceptable to French consumers. With the return of peace in 1697, the French monopoly began for the first time to purchase over a million pounds a year from England. In the peak year 1701, 2.24 million lbs went from England to the territories of the French monopoly.[49]

The War of the Spanish Succession created great difficulties for both the French tobacco monopoly and the Chesapeake traders of England. Towards the end of the conflict, overcoming great political obstacles, the two interests persuaded their respective governments to permit British tobacco to be sent to France in exchange for French wine. The state treasuries of both sides were expected to benefit.[50] During the subsequent wars of 1744–63, the tobacco interests on both sides were in a much stronger negotiating position *vis-à-vis* their respective governments, for in the intervening years the monopoly's yield to the French government had increased tenfold and Britain had become the major supplier of leaf to that monopoly. In both the War of the Austrian Succession and the Seven Years War, the export of British tobacco to France was licensed without any compensating importation of French wines. The British merchants had been able to persuade their government that they could thereby help the tobacco colonies without conceding anything to the French. The French farmers-general obviously persuaded their government that they could only continue paying their substantial rent for the tobacco monopoly in wartime if they could obtain British leaf. During the Seven Years War, their special licensed imports came to 11.7 million lbs per annum – impressive when compared with the figures a half-century before but only half what shipments were to be in 1771–5.[51]

One important influence on such decisions was knowledge of the preferences of the French consumer. If the monopoly could not supply tobacco products made from the now familiar Chesapeake leaf, the consumer would be tempted to look elsewhere for what he wanted. France, like Spain, had exposed seacoasts and British territories close at hand. It also had hundreds of miles of poorly secured land frontiers, a vastly greater challenge than that faced by Spain around Gibraltar. It was relatively easy to smuggle British tobacco into Normandy or Brittany from the Channel Islands and substantial quantities took that route.[52] In peacetime much British tobacco also went to Dunkirk for sale to manufacturers there and at nearby St Omer. The border between Picardy within the tobacco monopoly's jurisdiction and Artois outside was one of the greatest smuggling frontiers in Europe.[53] The prejudices of the domestic consumer could not be forgotten as the French monopoly learned very quickly when they tried unsuccessfully to substitute Ukrainian leaf during the Seven Years War.[54]

Because licit and illicit leaf could so easily be mixed together during manufacture, both monopolists and tax collectors thought it highly desirable to control or at least monitor the flow of tobacco through the manufacturing process. Tobacco generally reached Europe from America in one of two forms.[55] In Brazil and the French Caribbean colonies, the tobacco leaves were usually spun into crude ropes, wetted with a preservative generally containing molasses and then wound round a rod to form a great roll of up to 1,000 lbs weight. Quite different was the procedure in the Chesapeake where the leaf was dried and packed under pressure into hogheads weighing about 450 lbs at the end of the seventeenth century and over 1,000 lbs on the eve of the American Revolution. Such packing required an abundant supply of barrel staves and hoops and the services of skilled packing workmen or prisers. In Europe the spun tobacco could be unwound from the roll and sold as it was to smokers, or further processed into twists or plugs (called *briquets* in France). These could be cut up by the consumer for either chewing or smoking.

When snuff became more popular in the eighteenth century, strands of spun tobacco about a foot long were pressed together and then wound round with string for sale to snuff-takers who could rasp or grate these *carottes* to make their own course snuff or *râpé* better suited for use as an oral rather than as a nasal snuff. For the latter, consumers increasingly preferred the finer, drier snuff ground with mortar and pestle. In Britain, by the mid-eighteenth century, nasal or 'Scottish' snuff was generally ground in the watermills of large wholesale tobacconists and then sold to retailers (snuffmen) who usually added perfumes or other scents to make the product more distinctive and saleable. In France grinding was generally done by hand, either in the workshops of the monopoly or by the retailer. In Cuba hundreds of small grinders, primarily in the vicinity of Havana, converted tobacco into snuff. Most used handmills – as in France – but some relied on horsepower, and a few had watermills.[56]

In all systems, the retailer was regarded as the obvious gap in the security of the revenue. Until the 1780s the collection of British duties on tobacco was the responsibility of customs officials who lacked the search powers that British excise enjoyed *vis-à-vis* brewers and distillers.[57] In an effort to correct this deficiency Sir Robert Walpole sought in 1733 to transfer part of the responsibility for the tobacco duties from customs to excise. The big port merchants and manufacturers, allied with the Parliamentary opposition, were able to mobilize thousands of small retailers and manufacturers all over the country, and the resulting political pressure persuaded Walpole to withdraw his proposal.[58] The scheme was later enacted by the younger Pitt in 1789–90 but met with only partial success.[59] Because tobacco can gain or lose weight in storage, transit or manufacture, depending on exposure to heat and moisture, greater scientific knowledge and measuring skills were needed before modern methods of inventory auditing could be implemented.

On the continent almost all effective monopolies in the eighteenth century operated their own 'manufactories'.[60] These were frequently large establishments employing hundreds of workers. In France the farm's security arrangements could lead to difficult labour relations and strikes in the works.[61] These were minor problems though compared with those associated with the 10,000 licensed retailers scattered over the country. In the first two-thirds of the eighteenth century the French monopoly was able to contain the fraudulent proclivities of many of its licensed retailers by its normal system of supervision, but the growing popularity of dry nasal snuff (*tabac en poudre*) made the task of inspection more difficult. When the French snuff-taker had been content to buy the monopoly's *carottes* and rasp or grate his own snuff, the monopoly could guard against fraud by wrapping around the *carotte* a distinctive string, one end of which carried the company's seal. However, in the later eighteenth century consumers increasingly demanded preground fine dry snuff which retailers more and more ground in their own shops. It was obviously too easy for the retailer preparing snuff to mix in smuggled leaf with the *carottes* obtained from the monopoly. One solution was to grind snuff only in the big workshops or *manufactures* of the monopoly and forbid retailers even to have grinding equipment. Such an innovation irritated not only the thousands of retailers within the monopoly's jurisdiction, but consumers there as well. Because the monopoly did all its manufacturing in a few large establishments, some of its snuff had to travel hundreds of miles from point of manufacture to point of sale: for example, from Toulouse overland to Lyon or Grenoble. During these long wagon hauls, the snuff might begin to spoil. The retailers turned the resulting dissatisfaction of their customers against the monopoly. On the eve of the Revolution, sovereign courts in Dauphiné, Brittany and elsewhere felt the need to protect public health and began for the first time to interfere with impunity in the internal affairs of the monopoly. The company was forced by the courts to discontinue snuff-making and return grinding equipment to the retailers.[62]

Both Walpole's defeat on the excise scheme and the French monopoly's defeat on snuff-grinding can be seen as rare successes for the small man, here the retailer, against the 'system' of *ancien régime* finance. But there were significant differences between the two tales. The merchants, manufacturers and retailers who fought Walpole worked through established political institutions, persuading town councils and similar bodies to write to their members of Parliament. The retailers made no effort to panic consumers who were, if anything, rather suspicious of them. By contrast, the success of the French retailers clearly involved directing the hostility of the consumer towards the monopoly to the point where the courts were induced to intervene in an unprecedented way. The courts' effective attack on the monopoly can be viewed as an important step in the breakdown of *ancien régime* institutions on the eve of the Revolution.

In summary, the broad diffusion of the tobacco-using habit in Europe was a slow process spread over several centuries, with per capita consumption before 1800 still well below later levels. Yet, among those who had acquired the habit, demand was highly inelastic – as was clearly demonstrated by the tenfold increase in leaf prices when the American Revolution temporarily cut Europe off from its most significant tobacco source in the Chesapeake.[63] This inelasticity of demand gave governments the opportunity to experiment with levels of taxation quite exceptional for the seventeenth and eighteenth centuries. In many countries the yields sought were held to require a monopoly usually farmed by private interests. In Britain, Holland and a few other places, commercial interests were strong enough to keep out monopolies and to prevent the state's fiscal demands from interfering with transit trades.

The contrasting examples of Britain and France suggest that the widespread preference for monopoly was not unreasonable, and that the administrative apparatus and skills of monopolies could yield more to the state than simple customs or excise duties as then collected. The Spanish example is even more striking. Under both monopoly and non-monopoly systems, the interests of the domestic cultivator were sacrificed to the priorities of the revenue, though the overseas cultivator had to be offered at least the open market price if the monopoly was to get its desired supply without dysfunctional strain. Where this was not so (Spain being the conspicuous example) the monopoly did not get all it needed and had to supplement its colonial supplies with purchases from foreigners.

Since the purse of the consumer was the target of both monopoly and open market systems, his tastes and his preferences limited the options available to legislator and monopolist. Even where the monopoly provided tobacco products of a quality and variety acceptable to the consumer, the monopolists could undermine their own position by their pricing policy. Given the inelasticity of demand for tobacco, it is unlikely that any state, particularly before 1776, raised the retail price of tobacco high enough to reduce net state income, (i.e. to pass beyond the point of diminishing returns). Higher prices did, of course, create ever more attractive prospects for smugglers and in response governments or monopolists had to increase expenditures on inspection and patrols by land and sea.

None of these problems disappeared with the *ancien régime*. Future governments were to have revenue needs at least as acute and, in the long run, revenue maximization was to require even more elaborate inspections and controls. In the seventeenth and eighteenth centuries, the state fiscs had to make do with the scientific knowledge, administrative skills and support services available. Policy-makers had to contend with the conflicting interest of the fisc, commerce and colonies, and domestic agriculture. If most states in Western Europe were prepared to sacrifice domestic cultivators to fiscal need, balancing the interests of the colonies against those of the treasury varied significantly from state to state.

NOTES

1 Adam Smith, *An Inquiry into the Nature and Causes of the Wealth of Nations*, R. H. Campbell, A. S. Skinner and W. B. Todd (eds), Oxford, Clarendon Press 1976, vol. 2, pp. 625–35.

2 For tobacco in sixteenth-century consciousness, cf. Sarah Augusta Dickson, *Panacea or Precious Bane: Tobacco in Sixteenth Century Literature*, New York, New York Public Library, 1954, (reprinted from the *Bulletin of the New York Public Library*, 1953–4). Cf. also C. M. MacInnes, *The Early English Tobacco Trade*, London, Kegan Paul, Trench, Trubner, 1926, Ch. 1; Marc and Muriel Vigié, *L'herbe à Nicot: Amateurs de tabac, fermiers généraux et contrebandiers sous l'Ancien Régime*, Paris, Fayard, 1989, Chs 1–3; and Orazio Comes, *Histoire, géographie, statistique du tabac . . .*, Naples, 1900, pp. 5–40.

3 Jacob M. Price, *The Tobacco Adventure to Russia: Enterprise, Politics, and Diplomacy in the Quest for a Northern Market for English Colonial Tobacco, 1676–1722 (Transactions of the American Philosophical Society*, n. s., vol. 51, pt. 1), Philadelphia, 1961, Ch. 2.

4 Jacob M. Price, *France and the Chesapeake: A History of the French Tobacco Monopoly, 1674–1791, and of Its Relationship to the British and American Tobacco Trades*, Ann Arbor, Michigan, University of Michigan Press, 1973, Ch. 1; Lewis Cecil Gray, *History of Agriculture in the Southern United States to 1860* (Carnegie Institution of Washington, publ. no. 430), Washington, DC, 1933, vol. 1, pp. 21–2.

5 United States Bureau of the Census, *Historical Statistics of the United States, Colonial Times to 1970, Bicentennial Edition*, Washington, DC, US Government Printing Office, 1975, vol. 2, pp. 1189–91.

6 Jan Rogoziński, *Smokeless Tobacco in the Western World 1550–1950*, New York, Praeger, 1990, p. 113.

7 Jacob M. Price, 'The tobacco trade and the treasury, 1685–1733: British mercantilism in its fiscal aspects', unpublished PhD thesis, Cambridge, Mass., Harvard University, 1954, vol. 1, pp. 89–92.

8 Ibid., p. 2.

9 Price, *France and the Chesapeake* op. cit., Ch. 14 et seq.

10 Rogoziński, op. cit., p. 63; Comes, op. cit., pp. 88–97, 106–12.

11 'Customs tariffs of the United Kingdom from 1800 . . .', *British Parliamentary Papers, 1898*, vol. 85, pp. 193–5; B. R. Mitchell, *Abstract of British Historical*

Statistics, Cambridge, Cambridge University Press, 1962, pp. 386–8. For difficulties faced by the revenue in Walpole's time, cf. Jacob M. Price, 'The Excise Affair revisited: the administrative and colonial dimensions of a parliamentary crisis', in Stephen B. Baxter (ed.), *England's Rise to Greatness, 1660–1763*, Berkeley and Los Angeles, University of California Press, 1983, pp. 257–321, esp. pp. 260–71.

12 Price, *France and the Chesapeake*, op. cit., vol. 1, pp. 374–5; Vigié and Vigié, op. cit., p. 532. For Spain, see note 31 below.

13 Many of them are listed and described in Jerome E. Brooks (ed.), *Tobacco, Its History Illustrated by the Books, Manuscripts and Engravings in the Library of George Arents, Jr.*, 5 vols, New York, The Rosenbach Company, 1937–52.

14 George Louis Beer, *The Origins of the British Colonial System 1578–1660*, New York, Macmillan, 1922, pp. 126, 136, 152, 165–8, 403–8; idem, *The Old Colonial System 1660–1754*, 2 vols, New York, Macmillan, 1913, vol. 1, pp. 92n, 138–46; MacInnes, op. cit., pp. 79–129; Price, 'The tobacco trade and the treasury', op. cit., Ch. 3; Joan Thirsk, 'New crops and their diffusion: tobacco-growing in seventeenth-century England', in *The Rural Economy of England: Collected Essays*, London, Hambledon, 1984, pp. 259–85 [originally published in C. W. Chalkin and M. A. Havinden (eds), *Rural Change and Urban Growth, 1500–1800: Essays in Honour of W. G. Hoskins*, London, Longman, 1974].

15 Price, *France and the Chesapeake*, op. cit., vol. 1, pp. 143–72.

16 Ibid., vol. 1, pp. 255–7.

17 Ibid., vol. 1, pp. 294–301, 454–62, 477–506.

18 Rogoziński, op. cit., p. 63; Catherine Lugar, 'The Portuguese tobacco trade and tobacco growers of Bahia in the late colonial period', in Dauril Alden and Warren Dean (eds), *Essays Concerning the Socioeconomic History of Brazil and Portuguese India*, Gainesville, Fla., University Presses of Florida, 1977, p. 35.

19 For the sources of English/British imports of tobacco, see *Historical Statistics of the United States*, vol. 1, pp. 1189–90; for the high relative importance of tobacco in the exports of the Thirteen Colonies, see ibid., p. 1184 and James F. Shepherd and Gary M. Walton, *Shipping, Maritime Trade, and the Economic Development of Colonial North America*, Cambridge, Cambridge University Press, 1972, pp. 211–16.

20 For tobacco cultivation in the Netherlands, see H. K. Roessingh, *Inlandse Tabak: Expansie en contractie van een handelsgewas in de 17e en 18e eeuw in Nederland*, Wageningen, H. Veenman & Zonen, 1976, with an English summary on pp. 498–503; and a fuller summary by idem, 'Tobacco growing in Holland in the seventeenth and eighteenth centuries: a case study of the innovative spirit of Dutch peasants', *The Low Countries History Yearbook/Acta Historiae Neerlandicae*, 1978, vol. 12, pp. 18–54.

21 For the regulation of the maritime aspects of the tobacco trade, see Lawrence A. Harper, *The English Navigation Laws: A Seventeenth-Century Experiment in Social Engineering*, New York, Columbia University Press, 1939.

22 There was not a 'perfect market' for tobacco in Europe. Chesapeake tobaccos were distinctive and other tobaccos were only partially acceptable as substitutes. In addition, only the largest merchant houses could supply the continental monopolies. These large houses appear to have had a position sufficiently strong to enable them to shift most of their transit costs on to continental buyers. Their market strength persisted after the American Revolution when more American tobacco was sent to the Low Countries, Germany and Scandinavia via Britain than directly from the United States. Price, *France and the Chesapeake*, op. cit., vol. 2, pp. 731–7.

23 Price, *France and the Chesapeake*, op. cit., vol. 1, pp. 73–114. Cf. Médéric-Louis-Élie Moreau de Saint-Méry, *A Topographical Description of the Spanish Part of Saint-Domingo*, 2 vols, tr. William Cobbett, Philadelphia, 1798, p. 63. 'Saint Domingo' tobacco can be found in European price currents from the 1690s. See note 35.

24 Price, *France and the Chesapeake*, op. cit., vol. 1, pp. 302–58.

25 Ibid., vol. 1, pp. 358–60.

26 Carl A. Hanson, 'Monopoly and contraband in the Portuguese tobacco trade 1624–1702', *Luso-Brazilian Review*, 1982, vol. 19, pp. 149–68; Lugar, op. cit.; Stuart B. Schwartz, 'Colonial Brazil, *c.* 1580–1750', in Leslie Bethell (ed.), *The Cambridge History of Latin America*, Cambridge, Cambridge University Press, 1984, vol. 2, pp. 455–9; Dauril Alden, 'Late Colonial Brazil, 1750–1808', in ibid., vol. 2, pp. 631–5; Pierre Verger, 'Rôle joué par le tabac de Bahia dans la traité des esclaves au Golfe du Bénin', *Cahiers d'Études Africaines*, 1964, vol. 4(15), pp. 349–69; Robin Law, *The Slave-Coast of West Africa: The Impact of the Atlantic Slave Trade on African Society*, Oxford, Oxford University Press, 1991, pp. 135–6.

27 Hanson, op. cit., p. 160; idem, *Economy and Society in Baroque Portugal, 1668–1703*, Minneapolis, University of Minnesota Press, 1981, pp. 222, 229–32, 235–6, 239–40, 242, 254–9; Verger, op. cit., pp. 359–63; A. F. C. Ryder, 'The Re-establishment of Portuguese factories on the Costa da Mina to the mid-eighteenth century', *Journal of the Historical Society of Nigeria*, 1958, vol. 1, pp. 157–83; Elizabeth Donnan (ed.), *Documents Illustrative of the History of the Slave Trade to America*, 4 vols (Carnegie Institution of Washington, Publication no. 409), Washington, DC, 1930–5, vol. 2, pp. xix, 124, 130, 291, 540–1; Vitorino Magalhães Godinho, *Prix et monnaies au Portugal 1750–1850 (Monnaie-Prix-Conjoncture*, no. 2), Paris, SEVPEN, 1955, pp. 336–41. Both the British and the French tried without much success to prepare Chesapeake tobacco in the Brazilian fashion. [Pierre André O'Heguerty, comte de Magnières], *Essai sur les intérets du commerce maritime*, The Hague, 1754, pp. 106–10; Public Record Office, London, hereafter PRO CO5/1324 ff. 5–8, 49–50; CO5/1337 f. 181; CO5/1366, pp. 137–9.

28 English tobacco exports to Africa rose from 59,349 lbs per annum during 1699–1701 to 584,321 lbs per annum during 1771–3. PRO Customs 2 and 3. However, during 1782–6 almost 10 million lbs of tobacco were exported annually from Bahia to the Mina Coast. Alden, op. cit., vol. 2, p. 630.

29 Some material on this interminable dispute can be found in Clements Library (University of Michigan) Shelburne Papers, vol. 111, p. 249; PRO CO388/56/Oo.6, 44; CO 388/57/Pp. 16–21, 23, 56, 57; CO388/58/Qq. 33–40; CO389/32, pp. 231–2, 238, 251–60, 265–72; SP89/75 ff. 116–18, 152–6, 160–3, 171–2; British Library, hereafter BL Add. MS. 14,035 ff. 356–63. Cf. also C. R. Boxer, *The Dutch Seaborne Empire 1600–1800*, London, Hutchinson, 1965, p. 101.

30 John Robert McNeill, *Atlantic Empires of France and Spain: Louisbourg and Havana 1700–1763*, Chapel Hill, NC, University of North Carolina Press, 1985, p. 159. The peso was calculated at 40 *d*. See John J. McCusker, *Money and Exchange in Europe and America 1600–1775*, Chapel Hill, NC, University of North Carolina Press, 1978, p. 99; Patrick Kelly, *Universal Cambist and Commercial Instructor*, 2 vols, London, 1811, vol. 2, p. 243. For the yield of the English/British tobacco duties, see Price, 'The tobacco trade and the treasury', op. cit., vol. 1, p. 108.

31 According to Uztariz, the tobacco revenues accounted for 10.3 per cent of Spanish state revenues in 1722: Don Geronymo de Uztariz, *The Theory and*

Practice of Commerce and Maritime Affairs, tr. John Kippax, Dublin, 1752, p. 61. An account for 1740 shows the monopoly contributing 19.2 per cent of state revenues then: *Journal Oeconomique* (Paris), 1766, pp. 46–8. A similar percentage (19.8) is given in an account for 1760 in the papers of Lord North: Bodleian Library (Oxford) MS. North.a.6 f. 241. This is consistent with an undated account published in 1769 placing the share at 22.5 per cent: [William Knox], *The Present State of the Nation: Particularly with Respect to its Trade, Finances, &c.*, 4th edn, London, 1769, p. 32. However, an account for 1763 procured by British intelligence puts the monopoly's share at 32.1 per cent: PRO SP84/506 (Madrid, 25 June 1764). McNeill, who has published detailed accounts of the revenue and profits of the tobacco monopoly, 1740–64, concludes that these profits came to 'between one-fourth and one-third of the income of the Spanish fisc': McNeill, op. cit., pp. 158–9.

32 Roland Dennis Hussey, *The Caracas Company 1728–1784: A History of Spanish Monopolistic Trade*, Cambridge, Mass., Harvard University Press, 1934. p. 207.

33 Among the places mentioned as significant centres of tobacco cultivation in Venezuela were Barquisimeto, Guanare and San Felipe, all to the north of Baranas. Comes, op. cit., pp. 16–28; Hussey, op. cit., pp. 54, 56, 84–5, 87, 101–3, 164, 175–6, 181, 184. In an appendix on pp. 305–17, Hussey lists shipments to Spain by the Caracas Company. I have compared these with unpublished accounts (from the records of the Dutch West India Company) of shipments from Curaçao to Amsterdam, 1700–60, presented by Professor Miquel Izard of the University of Barcelona to a conference at the Library of Congress in May 1986. Other papers given at this conference were published in Franklin W. Knight and Peggy K. Liss (eds), *Atlantic Port Cities: Economy, Culture, and Society in the Atlantic World, 1650–1850*, Knoxville TN, University of Tennessee Press, 1991. It is, of course, possible that some of the tobacco shipped to Holland from Curaçao came from Cuba or elsewhere in the Caribbean. For price quotations of Verinas tobacco in price-currents printed at Amsterdam and Hamburg as early as 1696, see PRO C104/128/68; and Nicolaas Wilhelmus Posthumus, *Inquiry into the History of Prices in Holland: Vol. 1: Wholesale Prices at the Exchange of Amsterdam 1609–1914*, Leiden, E. J. Brill, 1946, pp. 199–206. See also BL Egerton MS. 507 ff. 191–5.

34 For the high proportion of snuff in tobacco coming from America to Spain, see Antonio Garcia-Baquero Gonzalez, *Cadiz y el Atlantico (1717–1778)*, 2 vols (Publicaciones de la Escuela de Estudios Hispano-Americanos de Sevilla, no. 237), Cadiz, 1976, vol. 1, pp. 338–40; vol. 2, pp. 222–46.

35 Before 1720, British and presumably other foreign traders had been able to buy Cuban snuff in the Canary Islands. PRO CO 388/22/Q42, 43, 52, 91. A Hamburg price-current of 1696 includes Santo Domingo tobacco. PRO C 104/128/68. This may have been a trade convention to cover Cuban tobacco, just as 'St. Vincent' was used to describe Virginia tobacco where the latter was prohibited. An Amsterdam price-current of 17 November 1760 shows Virginia leaf at around four stivers per pound and Havana at the equivalent of about 17 stivers per pound. Amsterdam price-currents for 1759–63 are reprinted in the *Journal de Commerce* (Brussels).

36 McNeill, op. cit., pp. 42–3, 115–21.

37 Ibid., pp. 154–8.

38 PRO Customs 2 and 3. It is unlikely that any significant amounts were sent from Scotland to Spain before 1755; none was sent in 1757–66.

39 PRO SP104/196 Vernon to Aglionby, 20 May 1701 with enclosure; CO 388/16/52 N. Herne to Bolingbroke, 16 October 1713; CO388/19/O:167 (1717).

40 PRO SP35/51/8 ff. 23–30 N. Torriano to board, 8 August 1724 (copy in CO 388/24/163).

41 PRO PC 2/109, pp. 13–14, 21–2, 25, 388–9, 391, 397, 401; T11/27, pp. 214–16: order-in-council of 3 November 1762 and pass.

42 Posthumus, op. cit., vol. 1, pp. 199–208. For example, in 1738 the prices of tobacco per 100 lbs on the Amsterdam market were: Dutch local *f*11.50; Virginia *f*23; Havana leaf *f*25; snuff (probably Cuban) *f*29; and Varinas *f*268. By contrast, the French monopoly *c*. 1708 calculated on paying no more for Verinas tobacco than they did for Havana. Price, *France and the Chesapeake*, op. cit., vol. 1, p. 187.

43 As noted above, the Spanish tobacco monopoly is reported to have produced the equivalent of £1.5 million per annum. By contrast, in its best year, the French tobacco monopoly produced 31.25 million *livres tournois* or (at 25:1) £1.25 million. Price, *France and the Chesapeake*, op. cit., vol. 1, p. 373.

44 The diminution of the number of firms in the trade is analysed in Jacob M. Price and Paul G. E. Clemens, 'A revolution of scale in overseas trade: British firms in the Chesapeake trade, 1675–1775', *Journal of Economic History*, 1987, vol. 47, pp. 1–43.

45 Details of the successive duties on tobacco (to 1775) and the drawback and bonding systems can be found in Price, 'The tobacco trade and the treasury', op. cit., Chs 1 and 10.

46 Jacob M. Price, 'Glasgow, the tobacco trade, and the Scottish customs, 1707–1730: Some commercial, administrative and political implications of the Union', *Scottish Historical Review*, 1984, vol. 63, pp. 1–36; Price, *France and the Chesapeake*, op. cit., vol. 2, pp. 843–9; *United States Historical Statistics*, vol. 2, pp. 46, 1189–91.

47 Price, *The Tobacco Adventure to Russia*, op. cit., Chs 2–8.

48 For purchases by the Swedish monopoly in England, Holland and Hamburg, see ibid., pp. 11–14.

49 Price, *France and the Chesapeake*, op. cit., vol. 1, pp. 178–82.

50 Ibid., vol. 1, pp. 184–9.

51 Ibid., vol. 1, pp. 54, 68, 71, 373, 563–85; vol. 2, p. 849.

52 Ibid., vol. 1, pp. 130–3, 447–51.

53 Ibid., vol. 1, pp. 134–6, 454–6.

54 Ibid., vol. 1, pp. 392–406, esp. 405.

55 Rogoziński, op. cit., Ch. 3; Jerome E. Brooks, *The Mighty Leaf: Tobacco Through the Centuries*, Boston, Little, Brown, 1952, Ch. 7; Vigié and Vigié, op. cit., part I.

56 Price, *France and the Chesapeake*, op. cit., vol. 1, pp. 189–95, 411–27; Joseph Collyer, *The Parent's and Guardian's Directory, and the Youth's Guide in the Choice of a Profession or Trade*, London, 1761, pp. 256–7, 279; Charles Lillie, *The British Perfumer, Snuff-Manufacturer, and Colourman's Guide*, London, 1822, pp. 293–330, written in the 1730s; Thomas Mortimer, *A New and Complete Dictionary of Trade and Commerce*, London, 1766: s.v. 'snuff-shop' and 'tobacconist'.

57 For customs, see Elizabeth Evelynola Hoon, *The Organization of the English Customs System 1696–1786*, New York and London, D. Appleton-Century, 1938, and Price, 'The tobacco trade and the treasury', op. cit. For excise, see John Brewer, *The Sinews of Power: War, Money and the English State, 1688–1783*, New York, Knopf, 1989, pp. 67–9, 101–14.

58 Paul Langford, *The Excise Crisis: Society and Politics in the Age of Walpole*, Oxford, Oxford University Press, 1975; Jacob M. Price, 'The Excise Affair revisited', op. cit, pp. 257–321.

59 John Ehrman, *The Younger Pitt: the Years of Acclaim*, London, Constable, 1969, p. 246.
60 Rogoziński, op. cit., pp. 61–73.
61 Price, *France and the Chesapeake*, op. cit.; vol. 1, pp. 189–95, 411–27.
62 Ibid., vol. 1, pp. 463–76.
63 Ibid., vol. 2, pp. 681–3.

9

JAPAN AND THE WORLD NARCOTICS TRAFFIC[1]

Kathryn Meyer

In November 1986 a small Lebanese journal scooped the international press when it revealed that the Reagan White House, long a vocal antagonist of Iran, had been selling arms to that country in exchange for hostages. Subsequent enquiries uncovered diversions of funds to the Nicaragua Contras at the same time as a congressional ban against such aid was in place. Further investigations revealed Contra ties to cocaine smuggling which coincided with a much publicized American war against drugs. This complicated international intrigue became known to the world as Iran-Contragate.

The White House, in its own defence, described the embroglio as a covert operation run out of the basement by Oliver North and a few cohorts. Congressional opposition jumped at the opportunity to implicate a popular president, yet the Tower Commission, after three months of Senate hearings, came up with the same conclusion: a president with an easy management style had allowed the National Security Council to carry out a renegade operation. Some among the popular press, a bit harsher on Reagan, suggested the managerial laxity might stem from his physical deterioration. Nevertheless, the image that the operation was somehow an aberration or a procedural abnormality remained.[2]

Oliver North's operation was not a fluke. He tapped into an international system of arms and narcotics traders with information to sell and the financial means to implement secretly a private foreign policy. This system was global in scope and many are the nations that contributed to its building. Created by the structural needs of drug traffickers to meet conditions imposed by increasingly stringent international prohibitions that have failed to stem consumer demand, this network traces its roots to the 1910s and 1920s when the League of Nations introduced mechanisms aimed at the elimination of the illicit narcotics trade.[3]

This system came into being through multi-national conferences which established an international certificate programme to register legitimate narcotics sales. Global bodies, like the Opium Advisory Commission, were established to aid in enforcement. Drug traffickers adapted. They regarded narcotics legislation and control policies as business problems to be confronted and solved. The most successful found niches in the system. The traders who thrived then and now did so when they made political connections. Because their business demanded that they cross borders, they often had access to information which could be strategically useful to men in power. They always had money unfettered by budgets and accountings. They therefore become hidden, but significant, players in foreign and domestic policy manoeuvres. Over the course of this century they collectively created a network through which covert activities could be funded.

It was Japanese adventurers in conjunction with expansionist-minded army officers in North China who perfected this underground system during the 1920s and 1930s. These men, like North, felt that the policy of their own government was misguided. Unlike North, they were able to use a legitimate, bureaucratically controlled opium monopoly to cover their covert actions. They were, therefore, more immediately successful in attaining their goals than was North.

OPIUM AND EMPIRE

Japan did not set out to foster a successful narcotics industry. Japan's initial reaction to the Asian opium traffic was hostile. In the 1830s, the British Empire was home to the great opium traffickers. When Japan finally accepted a similar role, it was in imitation of a colonial model already in place. Like other programmes of early modernization, the opium monopoly began as a government-sponsored enterprise, copied and adapted from existing models.

Japan remained closed to foreign trade and residence until forced to open to the world by the arrival of Commodore Perry in 1853. By 1868 new leaders emerged after what was, by world standards, a bloodless *coup d'état*. They began the revolutionary work of creating a modern state, based on trade and a strong defence, to preserve Japan's independence in a dangerous world. They negotiated commercial treaties with the Western nations, allowing trade in designated ports under certain conditions unfavourable to Japan. They did so, not out of trust, but to gain time to establish themselves at home and to learn the secrets of the West. While they yielded on many points when drafting these early treaties, they remained firm on one: opium was forbidden on Japanese soil.[4]

'Rich Country, Strong Army' well describes the domestic policy pursued by Japan's leaders from 1868 into the 1890s. Modern industry and commerce most interested them especially in so far as they had military applications. Model factories were purchased from abroad and managed by foreigners, while Japanese learned the jobs. Once the nascent industries became operative, they were sold to friends and backers who had supported the leadership during the difficult years of revolt. Their organizations included Mitsui, Mitsubishi and Sumitomo, which prospered through the continued patronage of the oligarchs. The economy, led by these profitable companies, enriched the country and the government sufficiently to finance an impressive army and navy.

The policy was spectacularly successful. By the turn of the century Japan seemed to have thrown off its feudal past. Its governors joined the Western nations by acquiring the *sine qua non* of a great power: a strong military with an empire to protect. In 1895 the military defeat of China led to Japan's acquisition of its first colony, Taiwan. In 1905 Japan defeated Russia, receiving as concessions Dairen and significant economic interests in Korea and Manchuria, including the South Manchuria Railway. By 1910 Korea had become a formal colony. When the First World War erupted in 1914 Japan joined the allies and thus acquired Germany's interests in China's Shantung province.

Involvement with opium was an integral part of the Asian enterprise. Great Britain and France had developed colonial monopolies which were quite profitable, and imperial success forced Japan to re-evaluate its own policy on opium. In 1895 the Japanese population had little experience with the drug, but Taiwan, which had experienced the earliest contacts with Europeans, had a population long acquainted with the pleasures of smoking opium. After 1895, as the island became the first Japanese colony, the conquerors had to confront an opium habit that had been entrenched for more than two hundred years. Opium suddenly became a matter of intense debate in Japan. Fearful that the Taiwanese habit would spread to the home islands, most Japanese in government and in the press assumed that opium would be prohibited in the new empire. Initially, only a handful of men advocated legalization of opium in Taiwan. Gotō Shimpei was the most notable of this group.[5]

Gotō was a man who flourished during Japan's spectacular transition. Born during the last days of the old order to a poor *samurai* family, Gotō embraced modernization, choosing to attend a Western medical school and later studying in Germany. He was politically ambitious. He made contacts in the government by writing strongly worded articles on the benefits of a public health policy to a modern nation, which earned him an appointment in the cabinet through the public health service. Once he entered politics, he remained among the upper echelons of policy-makers until his death in 1929.[6]

When Gotō Shimpei advocated the legalization of opium in Taiwan as a prelude to gradual withdrawal from the drug, his voice carried weight. His arguments for allowing legal opium initially came from an informed medical concern for the well-being of opium addicts among the Taiwanese. Gotō did not think it was possible for serious opium users to withdraw from their habits overnight without seriously harming themselves. Initially his proposal met with opposition, but Gotō was not a man to change his stand easily and time was on his side.

In 1895, when Gotō proposed a second time that a policy for gradual opium withdrawal be introduced, he argued that a revenue-producing opium monopoly should be adopted as an interim measure. His proposal was quickly accepted. Gotō spoke to the concerns of the Meiji oligarchs and presented a concrete proposal for the rigorous control of supply and sales. He advocated a controlled system with police supervision of licenced opium dens and dealers and doctors' examinations of registered addicts. He estimated that the income from the monopoly would reach ¥1,600,000, which he wanted to see used for public health programmes and for the education of youth to keep them from acquiring the habit.[7]

In February 1896 the Japanese Home Ministry assigned Gotō the task of putting his proposed monopoly into operation. He assumed the title of Colonial Health Adviser and eventually went to Taiwan to advance his own career by expanding his administrative experience beyond opium and public health into colonial affairs. Along with General Kodama Gentarō, he was responsible for formulating Japanese colonial policy in Taiwan. After the Japanese–Russian war in 1905, the same two men shifted their attention to Manchuria.[8]

At the core of Gotō's colonial system was a set of government monopolies, one of which was for opium, which soon covered the costs of occupation. The system also included information-gathering agencies. In Taiwan the Bureau for the Investigation of Traditional Customs studied all aspects of Chinese life, seeking information that would facilitate Japanese control. Later, in Manchuria, as president of the South Manchuria Railway Company, Gotō established a similar research bureau, which among other things engaged in espionage, population studies and economic planning. The research bureau became a standard feature of joint official/merchant ventures and played a role in service institutions created under war conditions in the late 1930s and 1940s. Although Gotō created these research bureaux to facilitate colonial control, they became instrumental to the Japanese narcotics industry as well.[9]

Once a monopoly existed, Taiwan authorities needed a steady supply of raw opium. At first this was easy. Until 1911, when international restrictions began to interupt supplies, the monopoly purchased opium as needed on the Hong Kong market. Authorities experimented with different shippers at different times, although Mitsui Bussan remained the backbone of the overseas supply lines. The Japanese soon began to develop domestic production with the hope of attaining self-sufficiency. In May of 1896 Nitanosa Otozō, a peasant youth from Osaka, barely twenty-one years of age, appeared in the offices of the Home Ministry with a petition to begin growing opium in Japan. Instead of being rejected, his proposal was forwarded to Gotō Shimpei, who received it enthusiastically.[10]

Nitanosa became the first of a handful of farmers in the home islands licensed by the government to grow opium under strict control. For forty years he and his colleagues worked to improve the quality of locally-grown poppies. Nitanosa occasionally faced difficult times, such as during the first years of his experiment when poor weather destroyed his crop. Yet he continued to study the qualities of soil and climate that produced the finest poppies.[11]

At times he and his colleagues prospered, especially during the First World War when combat conditions cut off German morphine supplies. At that time Nitanosa increased the morphia content of his poppies from the usual 6 to 12 per cent to as high as 25 per cent. He became so expert that he could judge quality by the smell and colour of the blossom. During the 1920s, when Japan yielded to international pressures and signed the League of Nations' prohibitions against opium, support for Nitanosa waned, only to reappear in the 1930s when he made several trips through Manchuria to advise the Japanese Army about its opium-growing operations. At this later time he came to be known as the Opium King.[12]

Association with a man of the status of Gotō Shimpei brought the young peasant a social prestige he could not have otherwise achieved, although Nitanosa did not live the flamboyant life that one might expect of an opium king. He was a family man, concerned with his status and security, sharing the deep patriotic feelings of his age. He was a farmer and through his life maintained the rough manners of the countryside. None the less, his connections with the government afforded him a better income than most rural Japanese enjoyed at the time; it also brought him into influential industrial and political circles in the Osaka area. He received awards and citations for his contribution to the nation.[13]

Nitanosa always assumed that he was engaged in a legitimate enterprise. After all, someone of the stature of Gotō Shimpei could not be associated with illicit affairs. Whenever allegations appeared in the press that the opium monopoly had its shadowy side, Nitanosa was shocked. The hidden side existed; in fact, it thrived. Had Japan's opium monopoly remained confined to Taiwan, perhaps it would have been the model it was touted to be. When it spread with the Japanese empire into Manchuria and China, where territorial boundaries were uncertain and civil war endemic, opportunities for undercover adventure and illicit profit were all too plentiful.

BETWEEN THE MONOPOLY AND THE ILLICIT MARKET

By 1911, the year of the Chinese Revolution, Japan already had a considerable economic and military presence in Asia. Nevertheless, this only drew Japan into an area of increasing geo-political importance, and so a potentially dangerous area. As the decade wore on, the weakness of the new Chinese Republic plunged the country into chronic civil war. Like other powers the Japanese took advantage of the situation, backing certain Chinese warlords with advice, money and weapons. The presence of such a state of turmoil, coupled with growing Japanese economic interests in the area, made the situation seem critical.

During these same years, as the Chinese political situation deteriorated, the drug traffic changed because of one little-known success. In spite of the chaos attending the birth of the Republic in the early 1910s the Chinese government, with British co-operation, conducted a fairly successful campaign to prohibit opium distribution. However, this campaign had its long-term consequences for, by the time prohibition lost its effectiveness in the 1920s, the anti-opium movement had created a new demand for morphine, heroin and codeine – any derivative of opium that could be rendered more portable and consumed in a less obvious manner than by smoking. Sales of these opiates increased among the poor, who were suddenly cut off from the increasingly scarce and expensive smoking opium. At first these new narcotics reached China from European pharmaceutical houses, although Japanese morphine was present from the first. By the 1930s, Japan had captured the China market.[14]

Hoshi Hajime was the pioneer of the Japanese morphine industry. He was born to a poor family in the Fukuoka area. In 1898, at the age of 18, he travelled on his own to New York City, where he studied politics at Columbia University. Twelve years later, when he returned from his study abroad, after a brief stint in journalism, he went into the pharmaceutical business. Hoshi began with an idea that merged profits and patriotism. Observing that German firms dominated the Japanese patent medicine market, he sought to make Japan medicinally self-sufficient. Using borrowed funds to found the Hoshi Pharmaceutical Company, he hired chemists to produce a line of patent medicines. Once his company began to prosper he expanded into alkaloids. Because Japan was dependent on German-made morphine, he targeted that drug as his next product. He contacted Gotō Shimpei, whom he knew from his journalist days, and Gotō provided the proper introductions to the Taiwan Opium Monopoly.[15]

In 1913 Hoshi approached the opium monopoly with a well-researched and well-argued proposal. Pointing out the benefits to Japan of self-sufficiency in such an important medical commodity as morphine, he argued that the Taiwan monopoly itself could become more efficient by substituting morphine for opium it supplied to registered smokers. He demonstrated that money could be saved by switching from Indian opium, which only contained 6 per cent morphia, to Persian and Turkish poppies, sold at much the same cost but with a morphia content close to 12 per cent. Although smokers preferred the gentler Indian opium, chemistry would render the Persian variety more profitable.[16]

Hoshi liked the role of entrepreneur. He brought to his business an open style he had picked up in America. He treated his employees in a familiar fashion, defying the rigidly hierarchical structure of most Japanese companies. As an advocate of American individualism, he translated Herbert Hoover's *American Individualism* into Japanese, and in 1919 his newspaper advertisements featured a picture of the Statue of Liberty. He supported practical scientific research through his company and through philanthropy. The Hoshi Pharmaceutical Building – seven stories of concrete and glass in the Kyobashi area – completed in 1920, was considered quite modern. The building had a showroom on the first floor along with an American-style cafeteria and an ice-cream parlour.[17]

Morphine made Hoshi a rich man. Wartime inflation made him even richer. Between 1914 and 1918, when he held the morphine franchise, he produced 20,000 lbs of morphine a year. During that time the world price of morphine rose from ¥500–600 to ¥1,000 per pound. Wealth brought him into influential circles: he joined prestigious clubs and helped form the Opium Growers Encouragement Association. In this latter organization he befriended Nitanosa Otozō whose superior poppies he appreciated.

But success brought Hoshi's enterprise under scrutiny. Politically important companies naturally wanted a share of his profitable monopoly. From 1919 to 1925, when his company collapsed under the weight of litigation and legal fees, he was attacked in the Diet and brought before the courts under allegations of wrongdoing. During these attacks embarassing information became public. Hoshi's shareholders included certain Taiwan officials and their wives, and the implication that Hoshi and the Taiwan colonial government were growing rich together was hard to miss.[18]

Investigations also identified Hoshi as a source of illicit drugs. At the war's end, when the price of raw opium dropped, Hoshi bought a large supply of the drug from the Middle East. Although the amount of opium he could bring into Japan in one year was restricted, he found a legal loophole which allowed him to use bonded customs warehouses where his goods remained until he needed them. Thus he took advantage of a buyers' market which he assumed would not last. In 1920 he bought 2,000 chests of Turkish opium through the R. L. Fuller Drug Company of New York and stored them in Yokohama.

Suddenly and unexpectedly, in the summer of 1921, all customs warehouses received an urgent message to clear their opium stores immediately. Hoshi had to dispose of his Yokohama opium at once. The timing of the order created a problem, since he had hoped to wait for a rise in the world price. Upon enquiry he learned that a British consul in Kobe had seen bonded opium being moved out of a warehouse illegally one night. The consul protested to the Japanese government, and the Japanese government responded by demanding a house-cleaning of all bonded warehouses.

Hoshi had to move fast. He asked for help from a friend, Sekito Shinji, an American-educated businessman who owned a shipping company in Yokohama. Immediately Sekito began to move Hoshi's opium from Yokohama to Siberia. On his second run, while his ship was docked at Otaru in Hokkaido, it was searched by harbour police and the opium impounded. Hoshi claimed the shipment was in order. The opium was going to Vladivostok and had proper documents from the government there, that is, from the Merkulov government, which was fighting the Bolsheviks with support from the Japanese army. At the same time Hoshi began transferring even larger amounts of opium to Keelung, the port just north of Taipei, Taiwan. Hoshi claimed that the entire manoeuvre was legal and that it made good business sense. Nevertheless, Shanghai police named the Vladivostok route as a source of illicit drugs.[19]

British officials, in concert with their own government's policy against narcotics trafficking, kept watchful and suspicious eyes on the Taiwan Opium Monopoly. They were not convinced of its benevolence and cited the bonded warehouses in Japan and Taiwan as sources of smuggled drugs in China. They also knew that the Vladivostok route followed by Hoshi's friend was a common means of importing illegal drugs into China in the 1920s.[20] The Eric Moller Company, for example, was one firm involved in the trade. Ostensibly in the business of transporting fish, the vessels *Minnie Moller* and *Nancy Moller* sailed from Taiwan to Vladivostok and along the China coast picking up and discharging quantities of opium. Once in China, the drugs were sold by soldiers of fortune or by Japanese merchants. One Japanese consul, in a report on the monopoly system, estimated that 70 per cent of the Japanese residing in Tientsin were somehow involved in the illicit trade.[21]

FINANCE FOR ADVENTURE

With the demise of Hoshi Pharmaceutical, Japanese opiate production assumed a different form. The production of morphine and heroin drifted into the hands of adventurers and small producers located on the Asian mainland closer to the market. Japanese soldiers of fortune who had forged the channels where opium leaked from the legal monopoly bureaux into the China market during the 1910s, continued to operate in the 1920s. When the Chinese government tried to enforce its ban on opium, morphine and heroin began to move through these same channels. Small producers, the heirs of Hoshi's operation, improved the product, rationalized the processing, and streamlined the distribution to such an extent that they managed to all but eliminate European competition in China.[22]

One heroin chemist, Yamauchi Saburō, recorded his business history. Yamauchi moved to Tsingtao in 1930, where he worked in a heroin factory. In 1934 he relocated to Dairen, founding the South Manchuria Pharmaceutical Company, capitalized at ¥50, 000. He did not have a factory but instead set up clandestine operations in an apple orchard where ten teams of three men each worked at night distilling heroin. Each of his groups could produce 10 kgs in an evening, which yielded gross profits of between ¥5 and ¥10 million yen each year. Nevertheless, Yamauchi had expenses: necessities like ether and alcohol were acquired cheaply enough through Mitsubishi Company; more significant were the payments he made to his suppliers of crude morphine and the army officers who protected them. He claimed that some of his fellow heroin manufacturers (and we may assume Yamauchi himself) donated as much as ¥50,000 to the Japanese imperial army, for which they received decorations presented in formal military ceremonies.

Chemists like Yamauchi produced a good, cheap product. They even improved the quality of the heroin by substituting acetone for ether in the distilling process, giving the resulting residue less bulk and producing a lower burning point in their heroin that smokers appreciated. Japanese brand names, such as 'Tientsin LowBulk', advertised this trait. By the 1930s, Japanese morphine- and heroin-makers had driven out the last European firms.[23]

Yamauchi and other heroin-makers, like Hoshi before them, often used Japanese soldiers of fortune, or *rōnin*, as distributors: independent, resourceful, romantic, often brave, rebels in the highly structured Japanese society. Unwilling or unable to fulfil the expectations of a static society, they drifted through China riding the tide of adventure. Through their manner of living they seemed to reject Japanese values; yet they considered themselves the essence of everything fundamental about Japan. They lived their lives as they did to preserve the basis of the Japanese spirit which, they claimed, was being eroded by the intrusion of corrupting Western institutions: liberalism, capitalism, communism, jazz, women who smoked.

In Japan of the 1920s this liberalism seemed to be the dominant political force. Yet there were individuals in the government, and especially in the armed services, who, like the *rōnin*, privately considered such weakness as a sign of corruption, especially when it came in foreign affairs. In their eyes both major Japanese parties seemed to be stymied by the situation in China. Therefore, as the *rōnin* took Japan's foreign policy into their own hands, or rather, as they acted for better-placed men with positions to protect who cherished these same causes, they could claim loyalty to a higher form of patriotic morality, even as they lived their lives of adventure. Their connections gave them legitimacy, and the treaty situation in China provided them with the legal immunity of extraterritoriality that made them uncontrollable.

These soldiers of fortune often made tacit arrangements with the Japanese army, with men in government as well as with right-wing political activists and ultra-nationalists who formed organizations to promote reform at home. The *rōnin* could help those who might disagree with foreign policy. They were not as conspicuous as army personnel were, and through their mercenary activities, they came to know the political terrain of China. They had access to useful information, many had Chinese connections who were well placed if not always powerful, and their unofficial actions encouraged Japanese expansion in China, while the government at home floundered in liberal hands. When they were exposed, their actions were officially denied.[24] Not surprisingly, their activities were also connected with drug trafficking.

Rōnin, in collusion with individual army officers, interfered in the civil wars in China. They were especially active in the north and in Manchuria, where Japanese interests were the strongest, further straining an already tense situation. Their home government responded to their disturbances in a manner they considered appeasement. Some came to feel that the only solution to the question of north China was to detach the territory from Chinese sovereignty altogether and place it under Japanese control.

The opportunity came on 18 September 1931. That evening young officers in the Kwantung Army abruptly ended the tense stand-off in Manchuria by secretly placing a bomb on the tracks of the Southern Manchurian Railway. They blamed this sabotage of their own doing on Chinese bandits and used the incident as an excuse to create the puppet state of Manchukuo. This incident had been planned well in advance, not by the general staff in Tokyo, but by a group of radical young officers in the Kwantung army. Immediate military action followed the bomb blast and Manchuria was occupied by the Japanese army before the civil government had time to respond to international complaints. By February 1932 the state of Manchukuo replaced the three north-eastern provinces of China. By 1933 Japan left the League of Nations. Soon after the neighbouring province of Jehol was incorporated into Manchukuo.

A military action of such scope required substantial funding. The nature of the plot called for the utmost secrecy, of course, and no money could be derived from the Japanese government without alerting the wrong people. Therefore the conspirators turned to one Fujita Osamu for a solution to their financial worries. Fujita was a journalist and an adventurer with connections to ultra-nationalist organizations. During the First World War he spent some time in north China, where he gained experience in the local narcotics traffic as well as having sponsored mercenary activities in south-east Asia.

In the 1920s he returned to Tokyo where he worked as a journalist, quickly acquiring a wide range of connections, including Gotō Shimpei. He soon gained something of a reputation as a behind-the-scene manipulator and problem-solver. One dilemma that he straightened out involved a major Japanese trading company. Facing bankruptcy because of the post-war business slump, the company bought a shipload of Indian opium hoping to sell it in China, make a windfall and so balance its books. But the company found it could do nothing in China without running afoul of local gangs. Fujita successfully managed their transaction, receiving a commission of ¥300,000.

Fujita was not only a fixer but an ardent ultra-nationalist. When Japanese army officers plotted the manoeuvres of September 1931, and found they could get no funding from legitimate channels, they turned to Colonel Hashimoto Kingorō, whose patriotic Cherry Blossom Society would attempt a *coup d'état* later in the same year. Hashimoto's right-wing connections brought him into contact with Fujita, who donated ¥50,000 to the cause. This sum proved to be enough to cover the expenses of the early operation, after which the Manchurian coffers fell under the control of the Japanese army. Yamauchi Saburō even claimed that Fujita financed the establishment of Manchukuo.[25] Thus Manchukuo came into being, not through foreign policy efforts or central military planning, but through the covert actions of field officers involved in drug trafficking.

NARCOTICS AND THE NEW ORDER IN ASIA

The establishment of Manchukuo changed the political dynamics in Japan. Between 1932 and 1937 influential men on the extreme right, who had been discontentedly watching from the sidelines during the 1920s, began to gain control. The puppet state of Manchukuo gave them a base for implementing a stronger policy in north China, while political assassinations by ultra-nationalist activists at home created a power vacuum which the military filled. In the six years before the beginning of the China War in July 1937 Japan and the territories under its control moved towards an economic fusion, creating what some on the right called a national defence state.

The co-ordination between the military, the bureaucracy and industry was mirrored in the narcotics industry. After 1933, the year Japan withdrew from the League of Nations, the development of the opium industry in Manchukuo was no longer constrained by Japanese concerns about international opinion. Indeed, in 1934 supervised poppy plantings, abandoned earlier in Korea, began in Manchuria. As an increasing number of foreign observers reported during the 1930s, Japanese army officials were using the idealistic rhetoric of opium control to eliminate independent competitors, not opium use. These competitors included Chinese businessmen such as Tang Yu-lin, who had been the head of Jehol provincial committee before the creation of Manchukuo. Until 1932, Tang ran his own heroin factory, but in that year he lost his concession to a Japanese syndicate.[26]

The Japanese plans for Manchurian economic development renewed the opium-growing programme. In the early 1930s, after ten years of obscurity, Nitanosa Otozō once again reigned as the opium king. This time it was not bureaucrats who called on his expertise but the army in Manchukuo. Previously, when he travelled to Korea to examine poppy-planting conditions, he had found the soil inferior, but he noted that Manchurian soil contained the proper combination of loam and sand. The Korean experiment never produced morphine-rich poppies, and because of international pressure, opium growing had been abandoned. In 1934, however, Nitanosa located excellent conditions in the county of Antung in Fengtien province of Manchuria.

Nitanosa's trip to Manchuria, one of three he made during the Japanese occupation of China, was the adventure of a lifetime. In 1934 the Manchurian countryside was not pacified, nor was transportation convenient or comfortable beyond the railway lines. For the first time Nitanosa, the farmer, rode a horse, not an experience he remembered fondly. The journey, filled with rumours of rebel movements, had to be made with a military guard. On the way Nitanosa befriended Miyazawa Shuji, a 28-year-old agent of the newly established Monopoly Bureau in Manchukuo. Soon after Nitanosa returned to his poppy farm in Osaka, Miyazawa became his apprentice. In 1936 Miyazawa returned to Manchukuo with a letter of recommendation from his mentor, and he himself became the new poppy expert of the expanding Japanese empire. He worked in Jehol and later in Mongolia, where extensive poppy fields blossomed as Japanese armies fanned out into north China.[27]

Heroin manufacturing also came under closer control in the 1930s. In the early days of Yamauchi's career, heroin-makers led precarious lives. If the Chinese police raided a factory, heroin-makers would often set the facility on fire causing the chemicals used in the process to explode, endangering both themselves and the police. At times heroin-makers preyed on one another, raiding one another's operations and fighting for shares of the market. As the 1930s wore on heroin manufacturers and distributors increasingly came under the control of the army, especially the *Kempeitai* (military police) and the Special Service Section (army intelligence). The heroin manufacturers who survived were the ones who came to terms with the army, thus assuring themselves and their distributors safe passage on railways and across borders. Japanese acted as the chemists and wholesalers, while Koreans or Chinese ran the retail shops.[28]

The organization of distribution tightened as well. In September 1936, for example, ten months before the Marco Polo Bridge incident triggered war with China, the Japanese garrison assisted a number of Japanese and Korean adventurers in Peking to organize the East Asia Club, to which they each paid 5 per cent of their profits. The structure which emerged had Japanese as manufacturers and major distributors, with Koreans and selected Chinese running the local opium shops and taking the risks of low-level distribution. Opium profits helped finance further military expansion along the borders of Manchuria, especially into the region of Inner Mongolia.[29]

THE FINAL PHASE OF THE MONOPOLY

The outbreak of full-scale war in north China in the summer of 1937 introduced a new phase in the Japanese narcotics industry. With the military advance into China, the monopoly organization begun in Taiwan spread into occupied territory and, after 1941, into South-East Asia as well. At the same time the organization reverted to its original purpose – the maintenance of a government monopoly to raise revenue while bringing some control to the problem of drug addiction.

The reasons for the change in policy were many. Once Japan was involved in a full-scale war in northern China there was no need for covert operations, nor did expansionists require unbudgeted funds. War hastened the consolidation of a national defence state, formalized in 1939 as the New Order in east Asia. The beginnings of full-scale war created an urgent need to rationalize and co-ordinate all aspects of the Japanese economy, especially as that economy spread into hostile territory. Thus a tendency already under way after 1931 became institutionalized policy. One agency created to meet this need was the Ko-A In (Asian Development Agency), formed in September 1939. With political, economic and propaganda branches, it served as a conduit for policy made by the Japanese military and included an opium supply agency.[30]

The policy shift was also associated with the emergence of Tōjō Hideki's faction. Tōjō and his comrades shared many of the right-wing ideals of the ultra-nationalists. They supported the aggression of 1931, but their goal was the creation of a national defence state. For this purpose they were not hostile to capital enterprises or the bureaucracy; instead they wanted to bring such agencies under military control. Between 1932 and 1936 Manchukuo experienced an influx of bureaucrats sent to co-ordinate the apparatus of the new colony with the government in Japan.

For four years the government of Manchukuo, as well as the Japanese military command, became a battleground for those idealists on the right who advocated an agrarian military state of Asian harmony and those who wanted to harness capitalist development for national defence. The ideals of the first group created Manchukuo, but the organization and political connections of the second group made the puppet state work. As Manchukuo became more organized the idealists came to be seen as troublesome and had to be brought under control.[31]

These tensions came to a head in Tokyo. On 26 February 1936 a group of young radical officers attempted a *coup d'état*. For three days two regiments calling for changes in the constitutional structure surrounded the imperial palace and occupied key government offices. The *coup* ended with the arrest and execution of the officers involved. A general purge of extremists in the military ranks followed. Since many of the adventurers had been involved in narcotics trafficking to fund their schemes, these activities were targeted as well.

Fujita Osamu was one man whose opium career ended with the new economic order. In 1937 the military sent him to Shanghai to oversee the disposal of a shipment of Persian opium brought in by Mitsui Bussan. Fujita handled the deal, but his commission was too high, and his continued contacts with the radical right in Tokyo also compromised his position. In 1938 he was replaced by Satomi Hajime, a reporter with connections to the Tōjō faction. Satomi organized the Shanghai opium operation along the model of the Manchurian monopoly, depositing the profits into a bank account created by the Special Service Section.[32]

Both the bureaucratization of narcotics trafficking in Japanese-occupied areas and the control of the adventurers gave the appearance that the opium monopoly was working. Some foreign observers claimed to see a marked reduction in the trade in the north, but Japanese records reveal massive poppy plantings in Manchuria and Inner Mongolia, with proceeds funnelled through the Mongolian Border Bank. While the opium monopoly also led to the creation of health clinics and a certain measure of control over the addicted population through registration, nevertheless, in the late 1930s, a large population of unemployed addicts wandered the streets of the large cities of Manchuria and north China, barely making ends meet by theft, trickery, picking pockets and prostitution.[33]

Addicts lived in tent cities or flophouses that catered to their kind and kept them off the main thoroughfares. Outside the West Gate in Mukden, adjacent to the rag pickers' market, there were about fifty hovels that had been built from scrap metal and old carpets. These were the residences of prostitutes and narcotics dealers. The Red Swastika Society regularly removed dead bodies from behind this campsite. Located in the Chinese slums of Harbin, the Garden of Grand Vision had once been a theatre. In the late 1930s, however, after having been gutted by fire, it harboured a warren of flophouses catering to addicts. Downstairs were shops, fortune-tellers, and the Harbin #34 Opium Office. Numerous unlicensed morphine dealers, generally described as Korean, occupied the building. It was also a haven for spies, *Kempeitai* informants, and at least one undercover police agent, who has left us with a detailed description.[34]

The story of Feng Teng-chun, a resident of the Garden who turned police informant, was typical of the kind of persons who supplied the addicted population in Manchuria. Feng came from a farm in Hopeh Province, where his family barely managed to feed itself by growing sorghum, beans and wheat. After a series of personal reversals, Feng went to Tientsin to earn money to pull his family through its difficulties. Through an employment agency, he found a job with the Tairiku Jinkō Co., which sent him to the new capital of Manchukuo, where he worked on a labour gang digging holes.

Feng survived on a diet of sorghum mash, living in a tent city for five months, during which time he was not paid. His crew was supervised with a whip, and members of his work crew died in mud slides. Feng finally escaped north to Harbin, a city the other coolies had described with enchantment. Eventually he ended up at the Garden of Great Vision, where he was cheated out of his clothes. Feng was not an addict, yet at one point in his saga he lied to the police, obtained a certificate of addiction and so was able to spend nine weeks in a state hospital for a cure. This gambit afforded him two months of free food and shelter, and a new set of clothes.[35]

This police report from Harbin, submitted in 1941, demonstrates that the consumption of opium and narcotics continued in Manchuria, even as the financial mechanisms of the Greater East Asian Co-prosperity Sphere centralized production, distribution and use. Addicts were not as visible as before, perhaps, and some clinics became available for those who wished to use them. But the result was to hide the problem rather than solve it. The real change came in the increased control that those who consolidated authority after 1936 had over the exploits of both the rōnin and the ultra-nationalists.

Adventurers in China came under tighter supervision, and many made their peace with the new order. After all, both sides respected military might and promoted expansion in Asia. Their similarities far outweighed the differences. These men easily went into espionage. Perhaps the most successful of these new soldiers of fortune was Kodama Yoshio.

Kodama began his career as an avid right-wing idealist. He had been involved with several ultra-nationalist groups during the Taishō and Shōwa years. Implicated in an assassination plot during the early 1930s, he spent time in prison, where he underwent a change of heart. After his release in 1937, he went to Manchuria, where his reputation as an activist assured him profitable contacts. Privately, though, he confided that only a fool would die for politics. Kodama concentrated on profits instead. When the Pacific War began in 1941 and supplies became tight Kodama went into the procurement business for himself. Friends introduced him to the proper naval personnel and he formed the Kodama Agency.

Supplying the Japanese war effort was a major problem even from the beginning of hostilities. As the war progressed, supplies grew tighter; inflation escalated throughout war-torn Asia. Under these conditions narcotics retained their value and so became not only an instrument of wealth but a medium of exchange. This function was especially convenient during the last days of the war, when the desperate Japanese army was forced to buy goods from the Chinese enemy.[36]

Kodama worked for naval intelligence in Shanghai, but he also made his name and fortune procuring supplies for the military. He was particularly important in acquiring tungsten, the strategic metal used in the manufacture of weapons. Its major source was located in areas controlled by the Nationalist Chinese. Kodama made contacts that enabled him to exchange narcotics for tungsten. At the war's end, he returned from Shanghai a rich man, but his reputation attracted the attention of the American authorities.

Kodama was arrested as a Class A war criminal and served some time in Sugamo Prison. Once again, however, he landed on his feet: he secured his release by exchanging his intelligence connections on the Asian mainland for personal freedom, a trade that seemed increasingly valuable to the United States which was concerned with the post-war resurgence of communism in China. Once free, Kodama became a powerful political force behind the scenes in post-war Japan. He became a household name in 1972 as a result of his connection with the Lockheed bribery scandal.[37]

CONCLUSION

Li Hung-chang, the Chinese statesman who negotiated the treaty transferring Taiwan from Chinese to Japanese control in 1895, reputedly warned the Japanese that they would run into trouble once they had to manage the opium problem themselves. Kodama Yoshio expressed the same feelings, but in language more befitting the ultra-nationalist patriot that he was. He likened the Japanese to pure water in a bucket, in contrast to the Chinese who were like the muddy Yangtze River. Should the smallest bit of dung get into the bucket, he said, the water would become contaminated. Since all the toilets in China emptied into the muddy Yangtze, it would forever remain unchanged. Japan's task was to remain pure.

The metaphor indicates that there was something about the situation in China that might bring out the worst in Japan. Li Hung-chang claimed that opium caused the problem, while Kodama, true to the Japanese spirit, was inclined to blame an indigenous moral weakness. If there was a corrupting influence in China, it was not caused by the land or the people, however, but by the environment created by international strategic and economic rivalries focused in the area during the first half of the twentieth century. Multinational competition produced opportunities for narcotics dealers. China provided havens for adventurers who were willing and able to sacrifice legality for expediency when their publicly placed superiors would not. Thus a land in which the traditional values were strict and formal turned into a moral cesspool.

The opium and narcotics trades follow the course of Japan's involvement in the power rivalries of east Asia like a shadow. Opium had long been an integral part of the foreign presence in Asia, and when Japan became a regional power, its leadership had to come to terms with a traffic that was already in place. In the days of the Meiji oligarchs the foundations of Japanese involvement in the trade were set by Gotō Shimpei in imitation of the established European trade. Japanese entry received firm bureaucratic support which gave the Japanese opium and narcotics industry an official status and outwardly benign image that secret realities betrayed. Official sponsorship allowed an underground system to develop and become competitive, cloaking the points of contact between officials with private agendas and *rōnin* with the wherewithal to carry out their imperialist and ultra-nationalist plots.

The *rōnin* then became the agents of a private foreign policy and their actions remained unaccountable to the constitutional body of the Japanese government. They could continue their activities because they had a lucrative source of funding in the narcotics trade. These adventurers foreshadowed people like Oliver North of the later Iran-Contra affair. Indeed the *rōnin* and North's cohorts were similar in many respects. Both groups were composed of restless men, addicted to action and ready to pick up arms for nationalistic causes. Both groups caught their own nation's imaginations as 'can-do heroes', even as they circumvented national laws. They both prosecuted their programmes through funds from illicit narcotics, short-circuiting their government's power of the purse. North and his Contra connections were the beneficiaries of the system developed in north China by radical elements of the Japanese army and the *rōnin* in the 1920s and 1930s. The end of the war in the Pacific and the drift of the world into the Cold War shifted the location of the narcotics market and the personnel, yet the potential of the business remained.

NOTES

1 Research for this essay has been made possible, in part, by a grant from the National Endowment for the Humanities.

2 *The Tower Commission Report*, New York, Bantam Books, 1987; J. Marshall and P. D. Scott, *The Iran Contra Connection; Secret Teams and Covert Operations in the Reagan Era*, Boston, South End Press, 1987; P. D. Scott and J. Marshall, *Cocaine Politics; Drugs, Armies, and the CIA in Central America*, Berkeley, University of California Press, 1991; Theodore Draper, *A Very Thin Line, The Iran Contra Affairs*, New York, Hill & Wang, 1991.

3 Bertil Renborg, *International Drug Control: A Study of International Administration by and through the League of Nations*, Washington, DC, Carnegie Endowment for International Peace, 1947, is the most scholarly and thorough publication on the League's efforts. See also Kettil Bruun, Lynn Pan and Ingemar Rexed, *The Gentlemen's Club: International Control of Drugs and Alcohol*, Chicago, University of Chicago Press, 1975; Arnold H. Taylor, *American Diplomacy and the Narcotics Traffic, 1900–1939*, Durham, NC, Duke University Press, 1969.

4 The first commercial treaty, signed with the United States in 1857, prohibited opium. The policy was reiterated in the new treaties redrawn in April, 1868. Ōkura Shō [Ministry of Finance], *Meiji Taishō Zaisei Shi Gaichi Zaisei* [*Financial History of the Meiji and Taishō years, 1868–1925, Overseas Finances*], Tokyo, Keizai Ōrai Sha, 1958, vol. 19, p. 826.

5 Ryū Meishu, *Taiwan Tōchi to Ahen Mondai* [*Control of Taiwan and the Opium Problem*], Tokyo, Yamakawa Publishing Co., 1983, pp. 5–10.

6 Kitaoka Shinichi, *Gotō Shimpei: Gaikō to Bijyon* [*Gotō Shimpei: Foreign Policy and Vision*], Tokyo, Chuō Kōron Sha, 1988.

7 Ryū, op. cit., pp. 50–4.

8 Kitaoka, op. cit., pp. 20–5; Ryū, op. cit., pp. 46–83.

9 Kitaoka, op. cit. Many of the essays in Ramon H. Meyers and Mark R. Peatie, *The Japanese Colonial Experience*, Princeton, Princeton University Press, 1984, discuss Gotō and his ideas as applied by the Japanese in the administration of their empire.

10 Nitanosa Nakaba, *Sensō to Nihon Ahen Shi; Ahen Ō Nitanosa Otozō no Shōgai* [*War and the History of Opium in Japan: The Life and Times of Nitanosa Otozo, the Opium King*], Tokyo, Subaru Shobo, 1977, pp. 1–23.

11 Ibid.

12 Minami Manshu Tetsudo Kabushiki Kaisha, Keizai Chōsakai, Daigobu [South Manchuria Railway Co., Economic Research Association, Fifth Division], *Chōsen Ahen Mayaku Seido Chōsa Hōkoku* [*Report on an investigation of opium and narcotics in Korea*], mimeographed report, 1932; Reports of Nitanosa's success with increasing the morphia content of poppies vary. This report claims that the average Korean poppies yielded a morphia content of 10 per cent.

13 Nitanosa, op. cit., pp. 124–35.

14 Ibid., pp. 94–100.

15 Hoshi Shinichi, *Jinmin wa Yowashi; Kanri wa Tsuyoshi* [*The People Are Weak; The Bureaucrats Are Strong*], Tokyo, Kadokawa Shoten, 1971, pp. 1–5.

16 Ibid., pp. 28–48; Hoshi Hajime, *Ahen Jiken* [*The Opium Incident*], Tokyo, Hoshi Pharmaceutical Business School, 1926. This document was Hoshi's printed apology to his shareholders after his business went bankrupt.

17 Hoshi Shinichi, op. cit., pp. 1, 86–90, 130–6.

18 Nitanosa, op. cit., pp. 68–70; *Asahi Shimbun*, 20–30 March 1919.

19 Hoshi Shinichi, op. cit.; Hoshi Hajime, op. cit., pp. 40–54; London, England,

Public Records Office, Foreign Office Records [hereafter PRO FO], 371/12527, Memorandum, pp. 108–12; 'Opium Scandal', *Japan Chronicle*, 17 May 1925; PRO FO371/11714, P. D. Butler to Sir John Tilley, 16 October 1926.

20 PRO FO371/9247, 'Resumé of Correspondence', undated but probably Fall 1923; PRO FO 371/13974, G. P. Paton, 'Report of the Japanese government for 1927 on the drug traffic', 20 September 1929.

21 Washington, DC National Archives, Shelf 76, Drawer 5, Records of the Shanghai Municipal Police Criminal Investigation Division, Reel 2, file D441, CID Office Notes, 22 August 1929; Fujiwara Tetsutarō, 'Ahen Seido Chōsa Hōkoku' [Report on Investigation of the Opium System], *Zoku: Gendaishi Shiryō, #12 Ahen Mondai* [*Continued: Modern History Resources, vol. 12, the Opium Problem*], Tokyo, Misuzu Shobo, 1986, p. 190.

22 Washington, DC, National Archives, Record Group 59, [hereafter RG 59], Box 4539, 893.114NARCOTICS/497, American Consulate General Tientsin to Secretary of State, 8 May 1933, pp. 20–2.

23 Yamauchi Saburō, 'Mayaku to Sensō; Nitchu Senso no Himitsu Heiki' [Narcotics and War; A Secret Weapon of the China War], *Jimbutsu Ōrai*, [*Personal Affairs*], October 1956.

24 Amakasu Masahiko, who worked in Harbin staging fake Chinese attacks against Japanese targets after the Manchurian Incident in 1931, always knew that if he was caught his ties to the army would be denied. He was prepared to take his own life should he run into unexpected difficulties. In this he shows more honour, or perhaps, more understanding of the nature of his situation, than North, who turned on his superiors during his defence. Tsunoda Fusako, *Amakasu Tai-i* [*Captain Amakasu*], Tokyo, Chukō Bunkō, 1976, pp. 146–56.

25 Senda Kako, *Kōgun Ahen Bōryaku* [*The Opium Encroachment of the Imperial Army*], Tokyo, Chobunsha, 1980, pp. 25–31; Fujise Kazuya, *Shōwa Rikugun Ahen Bōryaku no Taizai* [*The Opium Encroachment Crimes of the Shōwa Army*], Tokyo, Yamanote Shobō, 1992, pp. 110–20.

26 Tokyo, National Diet Library, International Military Tribune [hereafter IMT], exhibit 391, doc. 9517, Shanghai to Treasury Department, 9 May 1936.

27 Nitanosa, op. cit., pp. 142–52.

28 Yamauchi, op. cit.; the Japanese intelligence services were complex and never centrally organized. The *Kempeitai* was a military police, primarily charged with controlling the services and counter-espionage. The *Tokumubu*, or Special Service Section, supplied information to the military and each section of the army had its own. Then, of course, there were the research bureaux established by Gotō Shimpei and others set up later after the same model.

29 IMT, exhibit 399, doc. 9519, N. C. Nicholson to Treasury, 13 January 1937.

30 Satomi Hajime, 'Satomi Hajime Sensei Kōjutsu Sho' ['Satomi Hajime's Oral Deposition'], in Eguchi Keiichi, *Shiryō: Nitchu Sensōki Ahen Seisaku* [*Sources: Opium Policy during the China–Japan War*], Tokyo, Iwanami Shoten, 1985, pp. 623–6.

31 This process is described in almost any book on the Japanese army in the 1930s but Tanaka Ryukichi, *Nihon Gunbatsu Antō Shi* [*History of the Secret Struggles of the Japanese Army Factions*], Tokyo, Chuō Kōronsha, 1990, gives a personal account.

32 Fujise, op. cit., 121–37, 184–6.

33 William O. Walker, *Opium and Foreign Policy*, Chapel Hill, NC, University of North Carolina Press, 1991, 121–31.

34 Tokyo, National Diet Library, Hinkōshō Chihō Hōankyoku [Hinkō Prefecture Regional Public Safety Bureau], Keimu Sōkyoku [Manchurian Police Bureau],

Daikan-en no Kaibō [*An Autopsy of the Garden of Great Vision*], Kanminzoku Shakai Jittai Chōsa [Investigations of the Conditions of Chinese Society], 1941, pp. 1–7.

35 Ibid., pp. 63–6.

36 Yamamoto Tsuneo, *Ahen to Taihō* [*Opium and Canons*], Tokyo, P. M. C. Shuppan, 1985, describes the breakdown of supplies on the China front and the use of opium in barter for information and commodities.

37 Takemori Hisaakira, *Miezaru Seifu: Kodama Yoshio to Sono Kuro no Jimmyaku* [*The Invisible Government: Kodama Yoshio and His Dark Connections*], Tokyo, Shiraishi Shoten, 1976, 39–59; Jonathan Marshall, 'Opium, Tungsten, and the search for national security, 1940–1952', in William Walker (ed.), *Drug Control Policy*, University Park, PA, The Pennsylvania State University Press, 1992, pp. 89–116.

10

THE RISE AND FALL AND RISE OF COCAINE IN THE UNITED STATES

David T. Courtwright

I

Cocaine epidemics have twice figured in American history. The first sustained episode of cocaine use and addiction began in the 1880s and lasted into the 1920s. The second began about 1970 and peaked in the late 1980s. Together the two epidemics illustrate a cardinal principle of drug history: what we think about and how we regulate 'consuming habits' depends very much upon the characteristics of those who consume them.

The widespread use of cocaine in the United States, like the widespread use of narcotics, originated in the nineteenth century as a by-product of medical research and practice. In 1860 a graduate student at the University of Göttingen named Albert Niemann devised a technique for isolating cocaine, the active alkaloid of the coca leaf. Niemann's work made it possible for European and North American medical investigators to carry out human and animal experiments with the new alkaloid. The success of Vin Mariani, a coca tonic introduced in 1863, encouraged research in the field. Vin Mariani was a comparatively mild product, made by steeping blended coca leaves in Bordeaux wine, but its great popularity underscored the likelihood that the coca alkaloid might have therapeutic applications.[1]

American physicians learned of the pharmacological possibilities of coca and cocaine in the late 1870s and early 1880s. Articles in medical journals recommended cocaine as an all-purpose stimulant, a cure for depression, a specific for hay fever and asthma and other conditions. Especially encouraging were reports that the new drug was useful in treating alcoholism and opiate addiction, then widespread problems.[2]

American optimism about coca and cocaine therapies quickly spread to Europe. In 1884 Sigmund Freud, an ambitious young physician at the Vienna General Hospital, published 'Über Coca', a literature review which he brashly described as a compendium of all existing information on the drug. It was closer, in the tactful words of Freud biographer Peter

Gay, to 'a compound of scientific reporting and strenuous advocacy'. Freud recommended the drug as a general stimulant; for treating indigestion; for cachexia (wasting and malnutrition) associated with such diseases as tuberculosis; for addiction to morphine and alcohol; as an aphrodisiac; and as a local anaesthetic.[3] This last suggestion was quickly confirmed by Carl Koller, Freud's friend and colleague, who demonstrated the drug's anaesthetic potential by touching the head of a pin to his own cocaine-numbed cornea.

Cocaine revolutionized eye, nose and mouth surgery. Operations that had been exceedingly difficult or painful were made routine by the topical application or injection of cocaine solution. The anaesthetizing properties of the drug also proved a boon to the operatic world. As early as 1865 professional singers, at the suggestion of Paris laryngologist Charles Fauvell, began sipping Vin Mariani during rehearsals and recitals to ease the pain of sore throats. Singers sometimes sniffed cocaine to shrink nasal mucous membranes and drain sinuses, better enabling them to resonate their voices through their facial cavities. 'Kindly send to me', the great basso Edouard de Reszke wrote during a 1902 stint at the Metropolitan Opera, 'some of the white pills and powder which do me so good.' A few days later he sent another note to the same obliging physician, asking for 'a good package of your powders which are taken while singing' to be sent to his tenor brother, Jean de Reszke, then performing in Paris.[4]

Had cocaine's uses been restricted to local anaesthesia and the enhancement of opera-singing, it would be remembered as an unqualified triumph of nineteenth-century scientific medicine, rather like William Morton's demonstration of ether anaesthesia. The problem was the excessive enthusiasm of cocaine's medical proponents. As had happened earlier with brandy, tobacco, morphine and other novel psychoactive drugs, some physicians and manufacturers recommended cocaine too indiscriminately and with too few precautions for its toxic and habit-forming properties, which were either unknown or simply dismissed. In 1886 William Hammond, the former US Army Surgeon General, assured an audience of New York physicians that there was no such thing as cocaine addiction. Based on self-experimentation, he concluded that regular use of the drug was comparatively easy to break off, like quitting coffee or tea, and not at all like enslavement to the opiates. In fact, Hammond related, he had given cocaine for some months to a woman addicted to the opium habit, increasing the dose up to five grains (324 mg) injected once a day. 'It overcame the opium habit', he claimed, 'and the patient failed to acquire the so-called cocaine habit.'

When Hammond finished his remarks a Brooklyn physician and addiction specialist named Jansen Mattison rose to offer rebuttal. Hammond was wrong, he said – dangerously wrong. Seven cases of cocaine addiction had already come under his care, five physicians and two druggists. They had acquired the habit gradually, by making small injections several times a day. Cocaine could damage nerves and tissues, producing hallucinations, delusions and emaciation. Cocaine was undoubtedly toxic, and death by overdose was a real possibility. Mattison pointedly advised his listeners not to repeat Hammond's self-experiments.[5]

Mattison knew what he was talking about. Over the next seven years medical journals published or cited hundreds of case histories of 'cocainism'. As Mattison had anticipated, many of the cocaine addicts were medical practitioners who had injected themselves. Another common type was the opiate addict treated with cocaine. Some of these addicts switched to cocaine, others continued to use both drugs. In at least one famous case, that of American surgical pioneer William Halsted, a switch was made from cocaine to morphine as the lesser of two evils.[6]

In 1886, the year European and American physicians began to receive warnings of the possibility of addiction, reports began to appear of sudden death from cocaine-related cardiac arrests and strokes. In 1887 one researcher described more than fifty cases of cocaine toxicity, including four with fatal outcomes. Even the routine application of cocaine as an anaesthetic in genito-urinary procedures, or to numb the gums prior to the extraction of teeth, might result in convulsion and death.[7]

Despite these dangers, the authors of the cautionary articles that appeared in the medical literature between 1886 and 1893 did not contemplate the prohibition of cocaine, nor were they particularly interested in blaming the 'cocainists', as compulsive users came to be known. Those who had become addicted to the drug may have been ill-advised by physicians or druggists, or may have unwisely medicated themselves, but they were neither culpable nor vicious. As had happened with the hypodermic injection of morphine in the 1870s and early 1880s (and would happen again with heroin in the early 1900s) the debate over cocaine began as an intramural medical skirmish. Doctors wrangled over the indications, contraindications, dosages and precautions necessary for this new – and, in the right circumstances, undoubtedly useful – alkaloid. When the finger of blame was pointed, it was pointed at other, insufficiently chary doctors, like Freud or Hammond, and not at the cocainists themselves.

Then, beginning in the mid-1890s, the tone of articles in both the medical and popular press abruptly changed, becoming much more critical of the cocaine users and those who supplied them. Although medical addiction was still a threat, it was rapidly overtaken by the spread of cocaine sniffing and injection in the underworld, the traditional locus of vice in Victorian America. Drink, cigarettes and opium smoking were well established among the prostitutes, pimps and gamblers who catered to the lower-order males (and decadent rich ones) in America's cities and towns. Cocaine was portrayed as a new addition to the menu of depravity. Reports began to appear of white and black prostitutes stupefied by cocaine crystals, or of 'drug fiends' who went from smoking opium to injecting morphine, thence to cocaine and morphine in potent combination.[8] In Fort Worth, Texas, where prostitutes sported nicknames like 'Queen Coke Fiend', addiction to cocaine may actually have surpassed addiction to the more traditional opiates. In 1900 more than half of the prostitutes in the local gaol were cocaine addicts.[9]

Cocaine's popularity among vice figures and their patrons triggered a large increase in importation and manufacture. Consumption levels were fairly flat during 1885–93, when most use was therapeutically initiated. Over the next ten years, however, aggregate national consumption rose 500 per cent and remained on a high plateau until 1910. Medicine may have launched cocaine's career in America, but it was non-medical demand that drove the cocaine epidemic from the mid-1890s on.[10]

American urban culture has long served as a leading indicator of trends in international vice. Cocaine's descent into the American underworld anticipated what was about to happen in the rest of the industrialized world. In Canada cocaine was firmly linked to prostitution and crime by 1910.[11] In England recreational cocaine use flourished, albeit on a smaller scale than in the United States, in underworld and Bohemian circles from the First World War through the early 1920s.[12] In Germany illicit cocaine use became a notorious feature of Weimar nightlife.[13] Some of the German cocaine was shipped to France and Belgium, nations whose proximity made smuggling easy. Cocaine smuggling was also a problem in Austria, where an upsurge in cocaine use, notably in Vienna, occurred around 1923.[14] In 1931 Arthur Woods, a former New York City police commissioner and narcotics adviser to the League of Nations, observed that cocaine was still popular in certain underworld groups 'in practically every country', although the volume of its illicit traffic was less than that of heroin and morphine, the mainstays of the international underground market.[15]

II

If the American underworld pioneered recreational cocaine use, the American middle class characteristically led the way in its condemnation and repression. From 1896 on newspaper and periodical articles cast cocaine as an exhilarating but deadly new vice. The road to cocainism, like the road to hell, was wide and easy. By 1897 the price of cocaine was approaching $2 an ounce, making it increasingly affordable to the 'tramp and low criminal classes' of the cities. Small packages retailed for anywhere from 5 to 50 cts.[16] American and Canadian writers complained that profiteering druggists would sell pure cocaine to anyone, or that anyone could buy 'catarrh cures' and other patent medicines with a heavy cocaine content.[17] Packages of cocaine powder were also sent discreetly through the mails to customers like nurses or soldiers, who were anxious to conceal their habits.[18]

However come by, cocaine was easy to use. The common commercial form of the drug, cocaine hydrochloride, was a white powder that could be dissolved and injected, or simply sniffed up the nose. Sniffing avoided the hypodermic needle, which many erstwhile users instinctively feared. It also appealed to city boys whose craving for excitement was, as reformer Jane Addams put it, 'directed into forbidden channels by the social conditions under which they live. [They] are prone to experiment with drugs, as well as the other evils of drink and cigarettes.'[19] Addams was referring to the situation in Chicago, the site of her famous settlement house, but youthful cocaine use was a common occurrence on New York's Lower East Side and in tenement districts throughout the country.[20]

Non-medical cocaine users were considered dangerous to themselves and to society. Their enthusiasm for the exhilarating drug caused them to urge it upon others – pals in a gang, customers in a brothel, tent-mates in the army. They were likened to viruses in the body of the nation, spreading a deadly and compulsive disease. Though not addictive in the same way that opium and morphine were, cocaine could produce a different sort of dependence. The drug imparted a pervasive sense of well-being (one writer chose the word 'beatification' to describe its effect) but its absence could produce the opposite feeling. Habitual users deprived of cocaine felt 'a great emotional longing, a profound depression, a bitter homesickness which only more of the cocaine will relieve'. The cocainist was thus impelled to acquire more of the drug and would stop at nothing to do so. Cocaine was said to destroy the moral senses, turning women into prostitutes, boys into thieves and men into hardened killers. Notorious murders in the slums of New York, Chicago and other American cities were attributed to people under its malign influence.[21]

Particularly to Black people. In 1903 Colonel J. W. Watson of Georgia declared himself convinced 'that many of the horrible crimes committed in the Southern States by the colored people can be traced directly to the cocaine habit'.[22] In 1909 Harris Dickson, a municipal court judge in Vicksburg, Mississippi, complained that anyone who deliberately put cocaine into a Negro was more dangerous than a person who would inoculate a dog with hydrophobia.[23] The following year Dr Hamilton Wright, the chief instigator of federal narcotic laws, informed Congress that 'cocaine is often the direct incentive to the crime of rape by the negroes of the South and other sections of the country'.[24] 'Sexual desires are increased and perverted', Dr Edward Huntington Williams wrote in 1914, 'peaceful negroes become quarrelsome, and timid negroes develop a degree of "Dutch courage" that is sometimes almost incredible'.[25]

Whether and to what extent there was a cocaine-inspired crime wave among American Blacks has been disputed. The historical evidence clearly shows an increase of cocaine use among Blacks, particularly among Black labourers. Before the mechanization of construction and Southern agriculture, Black labour was employed for loading and unloading steamboats, building roads and levees, laying track, picking cotton and other physically demanding jobs, often carried out in primitive circumstances with no protection from the extremes of climate. Stevedores, construction workers and field-hands toiled for long hours if the schedule or contract or harvest crisis demanded. Some time around 1890 cocaine began to be used by, or was given to, Black labourers to help them cope with these conditions. There was ample precedent for this action. South American natives had for centuries chewed coca leaves to ameliorate fatigue and hunger, and in the eighteenth and nineteenth centuries American agricultural workers often interrupted their labours to imbibe another psychoactive drug, alcohol. 'It is said', reported the *British Medical Journal*, 'that some planters kept the drug in stock among the plantation supplies, and issued regular rations of cocaine just as they used to issue rations of whisky.'[26]

From the docks, construction sites and plantations cocaine spread to the Black underworld, where it flourished in the early twentieth century. A 1902 report from a Georgia correspondent to a special committee of the American Pharmaceutical Association declared that almost every coloured prostitute was addicted to cocaine.[27] Cocaine's use was 'confined to the immoral and lower classes of the community, both white and black', New Orleans Police Inspector W. J. O'Connor wrote in June 1909. 'The habitual use of this drug undoubtedly leads not only to the increase of crime, but weakens both the mental and physical strength of those who use it to that extent.'[28]

O'Connor's judgement epitomized the conventional wisdom. Cocaine had become widely associated with crime, above all with Black crime. But precisely how was it associated and what was the direction of the causality? One possibility is that the vice figures who used cocaine were already involved in criminal activity, rather than the other way around. When prostitutes and petty thieves were observed to snort cocaine, or landed in gaol, the inference was drawn that cocaine had caused the criminal behaviour. Another possibility is that cocaine users were driven to crime, not by the drug itself, but by their addiction to it. That is, they resorted to prostitution or theft to purchase a regular supply of the drug.

A third possibility is that cocaine was itself criminogenic. Crazed users robbed merchants, attacked police, raped women.

This last notion is at least plausible, given that scientific studies have shown a statistical link between regular cocaine use and episodes of violence and paranoia. There are two problems, however. One is that anti-social behaviour is most likely to result from the most drastic and toxic modes of administering cocaine (i.e. smoking or injecting the drug rather than sniffing it).[29] Smoking cocaine was uncommon[30] in the early twentieth century and few Blacks, criminal or otherwise, injected the drug. The second problem is that there is little concrete evidence of such crimes. Those who alleged a cocaine-inspired crime wave tended to be long on generalities and short on specifics.

In some instances they were also disingenuous. Dr Williams was an anti-prohibitionist who portrayed cocaine as the greater evil to which Blacks and poor Whites would turn if denied whiskey. Knoxville, he said, was experiencing a cocaine epidemic because the saloons had been closed. In Memphis, where no attempt had been made to stop the sale of liquor, only a 'moderate' increase in drug-taking had been observed.[31] Dr Wright's motives for exaggerating the cocaine crime connection were even more transparent: at the time he made his report to Congress in 1910, he was preparing narcotic control legislation that entailed a sizeable expansion of the federal police power. To emphasize the necessity of the legislation to southern congressmen, many of whom were states' rights conservatives opposed to the extension of federal power, Wright played the Black rape card.[32]

One other possible explanation is racial hypersensitivity. The condition of Blacks in the South after the Civil War was in several respects unchanged from the days of slavery. They remained a servile labour force, deeply distrusted by their White superiors and closely watched for signs of rebelliousness. Black-on-Black crime was expected and to an extent tolerated, but extreme vigilance was exercised against Black assaults on Whites, above all sexual assaults on White women, which became a virtual obsession.[33] Assuming that there were some genuine cocaine-inspired Black felonies, the natural tendency, in such a highly charged racial atmosphere, would be to magnify the threat posed to Whites. Southern newspapers in this period often republished accounts of black crimes and lynchings from other towns and cities. It is possible that isolated episodes, broadcast by newspaper stories and headlines, were conflated into a cocaine crime wave, and that fear of such a crime wave played into the hands of those who further exaggerated the cocaine menace for their own ends.[34]

The fact that a historical phenomenon was consciously or unconsciously exaggerated by contemporaries does not necessarily lessen its impact. Quite the contrary. Appearances, however deceptive, can translate into political pressure, and political pressure is what drives the history of drug laws. Whenever use of a psychoactive substance is perceived to entail significant personal and public health problems, to cause crime, to constitute a sinful indulgence (as opposed to necessary medication), and to be associated with disliked or deviant groups, a public outcry is likely to ensue, to which politicians generally respond by enacting restrictions or outright prohibition.

This is precisely what happened with cocaine: resentment of criminal and minority users combined with the fear that thousands of impressionable young men were ruining their lives with a cheap and accessible drug. Faced with strong expressions of public, professional and editorial concern,[35] legislators passed laws that, at a minimum, required a licensed physician's prescription to purchase cocaine. Illinois enacted one such measure in 1897, prompting the anxious makers of Vin Mariani to proclaim that their coca wine was not a cocaine preparation, and to offer a reward of $1,000 for information leading to the arrest and conviction of anyone spreading libelous reports to the contrary.[36] By 1915 practically every state in the Union had a statute similar to or stricter than that of Illinois.[37] New York enacted so many restrictions on cocaine that its legal distribution became nearly impossible.[38] The Harrison Narcotic Act, implemented in March 1915, was a federal statute designed in part to help state governments suppress the cocaine traffic within their borders by monitoring and controlling interstate shipments from without.[39]

The immediate consequence of these laws was to enlarge the underground market for cocaine and to increase its price sharply.[40] Initially this market was based on diversion from legitimate medical sources. Profiteering druggists and manufacturers sold the drug to intermediaries who resold it on the street.[41] In Philadelphia old Black men, ostensibly peddlers of roots, barks and herbs, would conceal cocaine beneath their wares and sell it in white envelopes or twisted newspaper packages, earning as much as $20 a day. In Des Moines, Iowa, one peddler was said to acquire his cocaine at a drugstore, and then sell it to teenagers, who sniffed it through rolled cigarette papers.[42] The profits to be made from such sales lured many into the illicit trade. In New Orleans, a police crackdown on violators of the state pharmacy law netted more than fifty cocaine vendors in one twenty-day period.[43] The risk of arrest, in turn, inflated the price of cocaine. In New York City decks, or small paper packages, of cocaine retailed on the street for 25 cts, but contained an average of only 1.3 grains (less than 85 mg) of the drug. The equivalent cost per gram was eleven times that of the legitimate wholesale price of cocaine during the years 1908–14.[44]

Many casual users undoubtedly responded to the price increases by cutting back their consumption of cocaine or stopping altogether. For those who would not, or could not, abstain there was a potent alternative, heroin. Prior to 1915 heroin was much cheaper than cocaine and more readily available.[45] Since the crusade against cocaine had reduced its supply in Boston, complained reformer J. Frank Chase in 1912, 'dope users have turned to [heroin], and as this drug is not so well known we find apothecaries who would not sell cocaine who are selling heroin apparently quite freely'.[46] It could be taken in the same manner, by sniffing, and did not require use of a needle and syringe. Heroin had the added attraction of alleviating the unpleasant effects of cocaine withdrawal, particularly depression. Heroin was a powerful tranquillizer – sometimes too powerful: in Philadelphia several switchers ended up on the coroner's slab, dead by overdose.[47] Those who survived often became compulsive heroin users. In the 1910s reports began to surface of heroin addicts in New York City, Philadelphia and other cities who had a prior history of cocaine use.[48] In 1923 Lawrence Kolb, a pioneer of addiction treatment in the United States, began a systematic study of 230 cases of narcotic addiction. His manuscript records show that forty of these cases were heroin addicts, and that fully twenty-six of the forty used cocaine prior to or concurrent with their first use of heroin.[49]

III

The first American cocaine epidemic ended with the 1920s. For the next four decades, from 1930 to 1969, cocaine was a triply marginal drug in the United States. It was of marginal concern to the police, of marginal concern to the public, and of marginal interest to the main addict sub-culture, which was geared towards heroin. I have recorded the life histories of older narcotic addicts who were active during this period and found among them a consistent attitude towards cocaine. 'When you have some cocaine, fine', summarized one man, who was a professional dancer. 'Beautiful. But it's a short-lived euphoria. . . . Cocaine is a lot more expensive than heroin. So when you mixed some cocaine with heroin, it was done sparingly.'[50] The use of speedballs (combinations of heroin and cocaine) was regarded by addicts as an expensive treat, rather like eating a hot fudge sundae instead of plain vanilla ice cream. Of sixty-five interviewees, only one could be described as primarily a cocaine addict, and eventually he had to switch to sniffing and then injecting heroin.

Some, in all probability the majority, of mid-twentieth-century cocaine users were not addicted, either to heroin or to cocaine itself. The dilettanti included entertainers and musicians, Bohemians, prostitutes and assorted underworld figures. Their numbers were not large. Cocaine seizures were tiny compared to seizures of the opiates and marijuana, which the Bureau of Narcotics regarded as the most common illicit drugs. During 1938, the year after the prohibitive Marijuana Tax Act was enacted, the federal government seized 558 kgs of bulk marijuana, nearly 18,000 marijuana cigarettes, and seized or destroyed 40,000 marijuana plants. In 1938 federal agents also confiscated 674 kgs of opium,[51] 12 kgs of morphine, and over 94 kgs of heroin. Federal cocaine seizures in 1938 totalled only 417 gms – less than a half of 1 per cent of the weight of the confiscated heroin.[52] Reports of annual seizures throughout the 1930s, 1940s, 1950s and 1960s revealed a similar distribution: cocaine seizures were but a fraction of the seizures of opiates.[53] Even in New York City, the national entrepôt of the illicit drug traffic, cocaine became scarce. A significant New York City police problem as late as 1926, cocaine was practically gone by 1940.[54] In 1957 Harry Anslinger, head of the Bureau of Narcotics, declared that cocaine addiction had disappeared in the United States.[55] He was exaggerating, but, if seizures are any indication, the problem was by then minuscule.

Minuscule is not the term that comes to mind to describe cocaine abuse and addiction in the United States during the 1970s, 1980s and 1990s, the decades of the second epidemic. The epidemic can be broken down into three stages: a sustained increase in cocaine use, mostly sniffing from an initially low level in 1969 through the early 1980s; the explosive growth of crack smoking in the mid-1980s; and a decline after 1988 among younger, casual and affluent users, though not among those already addicted.

The American cocaine revival had several different origins. One, curiously, was the growing availability of methadone programmes for heroin addicts in the late 1960s and early 1970s. At a sufficiently high maintenance dose, methadone blocked the euphoric effects of opiates while satisfying addicts' physical need for them. However, methadone patients soon discovered that non-opiate drugs, including cocaine, could still produce pleasure. To acquire cocaine they sometimes sold or traded part of their supply of methadone. By 1970 one Philadelphia methadone patient in five showed traces of cocaine in his urine.[56]

Restrictions on amphetamines also played a role in the cocaine revival. Introduced in the 1930s, the amphetamines were relatively inexpensive stimulants, widely and legally available. Some 200 million tablets were given to American troops during the Second World War, and by the 1950s amphetamine use had spread to college students, athletes, truck drivers and housewives in the United States. In fact, the growing popularity of the amphetamines may well have contributed to cocaine's mid-century eclipse.[57] By the early 1970s, however, amphetamines were becoming subject to tighter restrictions. 'Speed kills', the most concise and probably the most effective anti-drug slogan in American history, warned of amphetamines' toxic effects. Fear and shorter supplies of amphetamines made cocaine an attractive alternative. The illusion of cocaine's safety was widespread until 1986, when basketball star

Len Bias collapsed and died of an overdose. The widespread publicity following Bias' death – analogous in many ways to actor Rock Hudson's death from AIDS – served notice that cocaine could kill at any age.[58]

But the Len Bias tragedy lay in the future. In the late 1960s and 1970s the United States was experiencing a population bulge of 16- to 25-year-olds, the celebrated baby boom. Because experimentation with illicit drugs typically occurs during these years, the number of potential new users was unusually large. Political turmoil increased the likelihood of experimentation, especially with marijuana. Pot was a cheap, double-duty drug, smoked for the high and for symbolic protest against the forces of war and segregation.[59] Students who tried marijuana and who suffered no ill effects grew sceptical (if they were not already) of drug abuse warnings, dismissed as so much propaganda.

Cocaine was a logical next-step drug for baby boomers attuned to the recreational possibilities of illicit substances. It was subtly pleasurable, sexually stimulating, easy to use, considered to be safe and, though expensive, affordable for those with substantial allowances or good jobs. At some universities the percentage of undergraduates who experimented with cocaine increased tenfold between 1970 and 1980.[60] Bob Colacello, the editor of *Interview* magazine, recalled that 'cocaine suddenly was everywhere' in New York City by the mid-1970s.

> It went from something people tried to hide, except among close friends, to something people took for granted, and shared openly. . . . None of us thought cocaine was really dangerous, or even addictive, back then. Heroin was off limits in our crowd, but coke was like liquor or pot or poppers, fuel for fun, not self-destruction.[61]

The new fun fuel was openly indulged by some of the most famous celebrities in the world, from Mick Jagger to the glitterati who frequented New York's Studio 54 nightclub. Reports of celebrity use were, in an unintended way, like the written endorsements of eminent persons, such as Thomas Edison, which had helped to sell Vin Mariani a century before.[62]

The American mass media, slavering for trends among the young and famous, played up the cocaine renaissance. Cover stories on the drug and its (revised) history appeared in both conventional and countercultural magazines. *Easy Rider*, one of the most popular and profitable films of 1969, opened with a cocaine deal on the Mexican border. It was followed by a string of 1970s hits like *Superfly* or *Annie Hall* in which cocaine played at least a cameo role. Retailers capitalized on the trend by stocking cocaine handbooks and gilded paraphernalia, symbols of sexual prowess and conspicuous consumption. 'Everyone here has the Jordache look', wrote novelist Jay McInerney, describing the clientele of a fashionable Manhattan singles bar of the early 1980s. 'Hundreds of dollars' worth of cosmetics on the women and thousands in gold around the necks of the open-shirted men. Gold crucifixes, Stars of David and coke spoons hang from the chains.'[63]

IV

As the 1970s ended most Americans knew that cocaine use was spreading, but they were not unduly alarmed by the trend. The past having been forgotten or sanitized, the prevailing view was that cocaine sniffing was neither addictive nor *déclassé*, most users being affluent, White, sexy and successful. This benign view of the drug and the related commodification of its paraphernalia were to prove short-lived, however. By 1986 cocaine was no longer thought of as an accessory of the wealthy, nor was it necessarily associated with sniffing. Indeed, cocaine had by then acquired a reputation as America's most dangerous and addictive drug, linked, as it had been in the early 1900s, with poverty, crime, depravity and death.

What happened was a shift in the pattern of cocaine usage, triggered by an increase in supply, a lowering of wholesale and retail prices, and the introduction of new techniques of administration, freebasing and smoking crack. Colombian drug traffickers, who in the late 1970s realized that they could earn far more by smuggling cocaine than marijuana, developed an elaborate network for acquiring, processing, and transporting the drug. By 1982 these smugglers had become so sophisticated that they were air-dropping cocaine in watertight containers to waiting speedboats, which raced off to Miami at ninety miles per hour. They secured protection for their operations by means of systematic bribery and violence. In Colombia, where assassinations and car bombings became commonplace, uncooperative government officials were subjected to a reign of terror.[64]

Producers in Peru and Bolivia, whence most of the coca leaves came, expanded their acreage to take advantage of the rising demand. More cocaine entered the smuggling pipeline, driving down prices. Between 1980 and 1988 the wholesale price of the drug in the United States dropped from $60,000 to $10,000–15,000 a kilo.[65] Some of these savings were passed on to lower-level dealers and consumers. The standardized price, defined as the price paid per pure gram of cocaine in a 1-oz transaction, declined from over $120 at the beginning of 1981 to just $50 in late 1988.[66]

As cocaine became cheaper in bulk it also began to be sold in smaller and less expensive units. The key was the development and popularization of crack. Beginning in California in 1974, avant-garde users took to converting illicit powder cocaine, which was adulterated and noncombustible, into cocaine freebase. The method, which involved heating cocaine hydrochloride in a water solution with ammonia and ether, was complicated and time-consuming, but it produced pure crystalline flakes of cocaine that were suitable for vaporization and inhalation from a pipe. The vapour went from lung to arterial blood to heart to brain, jolting the user with a powerful rush. Just as smoking cigarettes was a more intensely pleasurable way of using tobacco than dipping snuff, freebasing was a more intensely pleasurable way of using cocaine than sniffing. By the late 1970s freebasing was in vogue in Hollywood and environs, though expense and complexity limited its appeal. The near-death in 1980 of comedian Richard Pryor, who caught fire while preparing freebase, served to warn that the process could be dangerous. What was needed, from a marketing standpoint, was a form of freebase that was cheap and ready to use.

The ultimate answer was crack. Heating cocaine hydrochloride in a simple baking-soda-and-water solution produced a residue of cocaine which was not as pure as freebase but which was none the less suitable for the pipe, and easy to sell in small chunks. Because these chunks made a crackling sound when smoked, they came to be called 'crack'.

Crack's big advantage was low unit cost. Cocaine powder generally retailed for $75 or more a gram, but crack could be sold in small vials for $5 or less, bringing it within reach of the poor. By 1984 the crack trade, fuelled by ever larger and purer shipments of smuggled cocaine, was flourishing in such impoverished districts as South Central Los Angeles or Miami's Overtown and Liberty City. By 1985 the crack revolution was transforming the cocaine business in Washington Heights, Harlem and other New York City neighbourhoods populated by Blacks and Latinos. Heroin, the inner-city drug-of-choice a decade before, was partially eclipsed by cocaine – in Miami, almost totally so. Pure heroin addicts became increasingly rare. In San Francisco and Oakland heroin addicts took advantage of the cocaine surfeit to speedball more often, and even began smoking crack after injecting heroin-cocaine solutions into their veins.[67]

The profile of the crack smokers of the mid-1980s was quite different from that of cocaine sniffers five years before. Although suburbanites would drive through the ghetto to purchase crack for home consumption, regular crack users were concentrated in poor Black and Latino neighbourhoods.[68] So were the street-level dealers. In Washington, DC, Black adolescents who sold crack could expect to earn an average of $30 an hour, more than four times the hourly wage of the legitimate jobs open to them.[69] The crack business had other advantages: no White bosses to placate, no strictures on language, dress, or demeanour, no forms to fill out, no taxes to pay. Chances for advancement were better than in the legitimate service sector. For those whose future prospects were otherwise bleak, hustling crack was an appealing job.[70]

If they survived. By 1986 and 1987 the crack trade was attracting heavily armed gangs like the Shower Posse, so named for showering automatic fire on their opponents. As the bodies and drugs stacked up in the metropolises, enterprising gang members began taking their abundant product elsewhere, branching out into second-tier cities like Seattle and Kansas City, and even Mississippi Delta towns like Clarksdale.[71] '[T]oo many dope dealers in Los Angeles', explained one gang member. 'So they take it out of town. The profits are better. Here you can sell an ounce for $600, over there you can sell it for $1,500.'[72]

Because crack was cheap and did not have to be injected, an unusually high percentage, in some places a majority, of its smokers were women.[73] Like their turn-of-the-century counterparts, they frequently resorted to prostitution or its equivalent, trading sex for drugs. The exchange often took place in 'freak houses' – a freak being a woman who would perform any form of intercourse, oral, anal and unprotected vaginal. Thus crack contributed to the other great American epidemic of the 1980s, the spread of HIV infection.[74]

It also gave rise to a new pathology, crack babies. Researchers have disputed the magnitude and source of crack babies' medical problems, but there is no doubt that *in utero* cocaine exposure increased after 1985. In that year 5.3 of every 1,000 New York City birth certificates reported cocaine or crack exposure; in 1990 the rate was 17.6. Of the 2,455 cocaine-exposed babies born in New York City in 1990, 66.3 per cent were Black and 20.3 were Puerto Rican. Similar data from other cities emphasized that the crack baby problem, like crack smoking itself, was concentrated among the non-White and the poor.[75]

The disturbing consequences of crack smoking were made known to the American public beginning in 1986, when the media seized upon the crack story, giving full play to its most sordid elements. Although mass-circulation newspapers and articles had not been alarmist about cocaine in the 1970s or early 1980s, crack was portrayed as extremely – indeed, uniquely – addictive, and a prolific source of urban crime.[76] Similar fears were voiced in Congressional hearings, where crack was compared to the Black Death.[77] Crack catalyzed what came to be known as the drug war, formally declared by President Reagan in August 1986. By 1993 the drug war had produced three nationally televised presidential addresses, two omnibus federal anti-drug laws, the creation of a national 'drug czar', and a fivefold increase in the federal drug control budget. It was easily the most dramatic, sustained and controversial governmental response to illicit drug abuse in American history.[78]

By 1988 it was apparent that cocaine was declining in popularity among middle-class and casual users, made wary by the negative publicity and new emphasis on its addictive potential. Crack was also becoming less popular among potential initiates.[79] The drug war had less impact on those who were already regular consumers, however. An ageing cohort of heavy users, who had begun their careers in the 1970s or 1980s, persisted in abusing cocaine in the early 1990s, developing serious health problems as a consequence. The number of such users has been disputed,[80] but it is widely agreed that since the late 1980s cocaine has been increasingly confined to a 'residual group of dysfunctional drug users' who are concentrated in urban minority groups.[81]

The transformation of cocaine from golden drug to ghetto drug was reinforced by the conduct of the drug war itself. Nationwide, Blacks were four times as likely – in some cities more than twenty times as likely – than Whites to be arrested on drug charges. The disproportionate arrest rate for Blacks has been variously attributed to racism, search tactics based on minority profiles, or to the fact that minority drug dealers and couriers are highly visible, easy targets for police.[82] Whatever the motivation for the large number of Black arrests, their ritualized presentation in newspapers and television news programmes intensified the impression that cocaine use and dealing were becoming the near-monopoly of the Black community.

Racial disparity was also built into the sentencing provisions of the 1986 federal anti-drug law. That statute specified a mandatory minimum sentence of ten years for a violation involving 50 gms of crack cocaine, but required a full 5 kgs (100 times the weight of crack) to warrant a comparable sentence for a powder cocaine violation.[83] The official justification of this disparity, known as the 100-to-1 ratio, was that crack is more dangerous and addictive than powdered cocaine. Those who have challenged the law have pointed out that powdered cocaine can be dissolved and injected, which is every bit as dangerous as smoking, probably more so, given the risk of needle-transmitted HIV infection. They have also charged that the real motivation and effect of this provision is to single out for harsher punishment Blacks who sell this particular form of cocaine. In 1992 nine out of ten defendants convicted of federal crack violations were Black, as compared to fewer than three of ten convicted of powder cocaine violations.[84] Because less crack was required to trigger a long mandatory sentence, convicted Black crack dealers were more likely to receive harsher punishment, despite the fact that they were usually only retailers in the drug distribution chain.

The sentencing double standard is not surprising. The background of users and sellers has always been an important determinant of the legal response, for cocaine or for any other psychoactive substance. The first anti-cigarette laws appeared in the United States in the 1890s, but there were no equivalent laws against cigars or pipe smoking. This seems irrational – tobacco smoke is tobacco smoke – but it makes social sense when we recall Jane Addams' observation that cigarettes were defiantly puffed by street urchins, while cigar and pipe smoking were habits of respectable men.[85] Anti-cocaine legislation, which also dates to the 1890s, was not enacted until it became clear that non-medical cocaine use was spreading among persons who were either considered anti-social or who might become so. Likewise, the high political drama and prison-mindedness of the drug war commenced only after it was apparent that compulsive cocaine use, especially crack smoking, was widespread in the urban underclass.

The *post hoc ergo propter hoc* fallacy is an old enemy of historians, and should be paid its due when we render causal judgements. I do not wish to argue that whenever the social and class characteristics of a particular drug-using population perceptibly worsen, stricter legislation will automatically follow. The formulation of drug policy is not simply the institutionalization of prejudice. It is a highly complex process shaped by experienced and, for the most part, rational actors who must respond to conflicting demands and forces, often with incomplete knowledge. Nevertheless, the history of the American cocaine epidemics reminds us that something more than reasoned debate shapes drug policy. Fear, anger, disgust and resentment have been the most common reactions to drug abuse by deviant members of society, above all by criminally inclined members of a racial minority. Moral and religious conservatives, more numerous and politically significant in the United States than in Europe, have been the most vociferous in their denunciations, but even the secular high priests of the *New York Times'* editorial page ('Mothers Turned Into Monsters') have been known to strike the shrill note.[86] Such deeply felt reactions have not escaped political strategists, preoccupied with polls and 'moving numbers'. American legislators have long faced an electoral temptation to go beyond what is necessary to deal with the public health aspect of the illicit drug problem, the very definition of which is shaped by user characteristics. In yielding to that temptation, they have created a regime for suppressing cocaine that is among the strictest in the world.

NOTES

1 Joseph Kennedy, *Coca Exotica: The Illustrated Story of Cocaine*, Rutherford, NJ, and New York, Farleigh Dickinson University Press and Cornwall Books, 1985, pp. 48–79. Another standard introduction to cocaine and its history is Lester Grinspoon and James B. Bakalar, *Cocaine: A Drug and Its Social Evolution*, New York, Basic Books, 1976.

2 E.g., John Q. Winfield, 'A case of opium habit of six or eight years' standing, treated successfully with the solid extract of coca', *Virginia Medical Monthly*, 1880, vol. 7, pp. 46–7, and H. F. Stimmel, 'Coca in the opium and alcohol habits', *Therapeutic Gazette*, 1881, vol. 5, p. 132.

3 'Über Coca', which first appeared in the *Centralblatt für die gesammte Therapie*, 1884, vol. 2, pp. 289–314, is translated into English in Robert Byck (ed.), *Cocaine Papers*, with notes by Anna Freud, New York, Stonehill, 1974, pp. 48–73. See also Peter Gay, *Freud: A Life for Our Time*, New York, W. W. Norton,

pp. 42–5, quotation at 43.

4 Kennedy, op. cit., pp. 63–4; Aida Favia-Artsay, 'White gold in the Golden Age: recalling the sound of the de Reszke brothers and one possible reason for its splendor', *Opera Quarterly*, Spring 1991, vol. 8, pp. 44–61. The letters quoted appear in facsimile on pp. 45 and 49.

5 Hammond's and Mattison's comments are both in 'Remarks on cocaine and the so-called cocaine habit', *Journal of Nervous and Mental Disease*, 1886, vol. 13, pp. 754–9. For more on the panacetic use of cocaine and Hammond's discounting of addiction see Byck, op. cit., pp. 119–50, 178–93.

6 H. G. Brainerd, 'Report of committee on diseases of the mind and nervous system: cocaine addiction', *Transactions of the Medical Society of the State of California*, 1891, n.s. vol. 20, pp. 193–201; J. B. Mattison, 'Cocainism', *Medical Record*, 1892 and 1893, vols. 42 and 43, pp. 474–7 and 34–6; David F. Musto, 'America's first cocaine epidemic', *Wilson Quarterly*, Summer 1989, vol. 13, p. 62; and Sherwin B. Nuland, *Doctors: The Biography of Medicine*, New York, Vintage Books, 1989, pp. 395–9.

7 Teri Randall, 'Cocaine deaths reported for century or more', *Journal of the American Medical Association*, 1992, vol. 267, pp. 1045–6; Robert W. Haynes, 'The dangers of cocain [*sic*]', *Medical News*, 1894, vol. 65, p. 14.

8 E. R. Waterhouse, 'Cocaine debauchery', *Eclectic Medical Journal of Cincinnati*, 1896, vol. 56, pp. 464–5; E. G. Eberle et al., 'Report of committee on the acquirement of drug habits', *Proceedings of the American Pharmaceutical Association*, 1903, vol. 51, pp. 468, 473. On the Victorian underworld as vice nexus see John C. Burnham, *Bad Habits: Drinking, Smoking, Taking Drugs, Gambling, Sexual Misbehavior, and Swearing in American History*, New York, New York University Press, 1993.

9 Richard F. Selcer, 'Fort Worth and the fraternity of strange women', *Southwestern Historical Quarterly*, 1992, vol. 96, pp. 74, 79.

10 Joseph Spillane, 'Modern drug, modern menace: the legal use and distribution of cocaine in the United States, 1880–1920', unpublished PhD dissertation, Carnegie Mellon University, 1993. Spillane read and commented on an earlier draft of this chapter, as did Jill Jonnes. I am grateful for their assistance.

11 Patricia G. Erickson et al., *The Steel Drug: Cocaine in Perspective*, Lexington, Mass., Lexington Books, 1987, p. 14.

12 Terry M. Parssinen, *Secret Passions, Secret Remedies: Narcotic Drugs in British Society, 1820–1930*, Philadelphia, Institute for the Study of Human Values, 1983, p. 216; Virginia Berridge and Griffith Edwards, *Opium and the People: Opiate Use in Nineteenth-Century England*, New Haven, Yale University Press, 1987, p. 224.

13 Louis Lewin, *Phantastica: Narcotic and Stimulating Drugs: Their Use and Abuse*, tr. P. H. A. Wirth, New York, E. P. Dutton & Company, 1931, p. 80.

14 Joël L. Phillips and Roland D. Wynne, *Cocaine: The Mystique and the Reality*, New York, Avon Books, 1980, pp. 82–5.

15 *Dangerous Drugs: The World Fight Against the Illicit Traffic in Narcotics*, New Haven, Yale University Press, 1931. Although Woods' name appears on the title page, *Dangerous Drugs* was researched and ghost-written by Kenneth Burke, later famous as a literary critic. Kenneth Burke to Lawrence B. Dunham, 4 June 1930, Bureau of Social Hygiene Papers, Series 3, Box 1, Folder 9, Rockefeller Archive Center, North Tarrytown, New York.

16 T. D. Crothers, 'Cocaine-Inebriety', *Quarterly Journal of Inebriety*, 1898, vol. 20, pp. 369–70, quotation at p. 370; ' "Cocaine Alley" ', *American Druggist and Pharmaceutical Record*, 1900, vol. 37, pp. 337–8; and Waterhouse, op. cit., pp.

464–5. Note that the $2-per-ounce figure given by Crothers may have been artificially low due to depressed economic conditions. In subsequent years the price rose and fluctuated around $4 an ounce – still much cheaper than it had been in the 1880s. Joseph Spillane, personal communication.

17 Eberle, op. cit., p. 476; Erickson, op. cit., pp. 8–13.

18 I. H. Kempner, *Recalled Recollections*, Dallas, Egan Company, 1961, pp. 48–9; W. B. Meister, 'Cocainism in the Army', *Military Surgeon*, 1914, vol. 34, p. 344.

19 Quoted in Charles W. Collins and John Day, 'Dope, the new vice', *Everyday Life*, 1909, vol. 5, no. 2, p. 4.

20 Alan A. Block, 'The snowman cometh: coke in progressive New York', *Criminology*, 1979, vol. 17, pp. 75–99.

21 Collins and Day, op. cit., vol. 4(10), pp. 3–4; (11), pp. 6–7; (12), pp. 4–5; and vol. 5(1), pp. 10–11; (2), pp. 4–5. The quotations are from vol. 4(12), p. 4. This series is a particularly good example of the sensationalized treatment accorded cocaine and other forms of drug use in the popular press in the decade prior to the First World War. For a well-researched but nontechnical account of how cocaine produces its pleasurable effects see John C. Flynn, *Cocaine: An In-Depth Look at the Facts, Science, History and Future of the World's Most Addictive Drug*, New York, Birch Lane Press, 1991.

22 'Cocaine sniffers', *New York Tribune*, 21 June 1903, p. 11.

23 Collins and Day, op. cit., vol. 4(10), p. 5.

24 US Senate, *Report on the International Opium Commission and on the Opium Problem as Seen Within the United States and Its Possessions*, 61st Cong., 2nd sess., Washington, DC, Government Printing Office, 1910, p. 50.

25 'The drug-habit menace in the South', *Medical Record*, 1914, vol. 85, p. 247.

26 'The cocaine habit among negroes', *British Medical Journal*, 1902, part 2, p. 1729.

27 Eberle et al., op. cit., p. 468. Although this article appeared in print in 1903, the local reports were solicited in the previous year, 1902.

28 O'Connor to Hamilton Wright, 22 June 1909, bound letter volume 1, 'Arkansas to Maryland', Records of the United States Delegation to the International Opium Commission and Conference, 1909–13, Record Group 43, National Archives, Washington, DC.

29 A. James Giannini et al., 'Cocaine-associated violence and relationship to route of administration', *Journal of Substance Abuse Treatment*, 1993, vol. 10, pp. 67–9.

30 In 1886 Parke, Davis & Co., a leading American manufacturer of coca and cocaine products, was producing coca cheroots and cigarettes and advertising their utility in treating throat affections. This means of using the drug seems not to have caught on, however. By the early 1900s the drug was generally obtained through patent medicines like Tucker's Asthma Specific or Crown Catarrh Powder, through medicated 'soft' drinks like Koca-Nola or Kola-Ade, or by outright purchase of cocaine hydrochloride, which could be injected or sniffed up the nose.

31 Williams, op. cit., p. 249. 'I am not an advocate of whiskey', the above-quoted Colonel Watson observed, 'but I am fully convinced that if a man feels he must have a stimulant, the best thing he can do is to get a bottle of liquor.' 'Cocaine sniffers', p. 11. See also David F. Musto, *The American Disease: Origins of Narcotic Control*, revised edn, New York, Oxford University Press, 1987, p. 284, n. 20.

32 In fact, Wright's entire report exaggerated the extent and danger of drug abuse in the United States as a goad to Congressional action. David T. Courtwright, *Dark Paradise: Opiate Addiction in America before 1940*,

Cambridge, Mass., Harvard University Press, 1982, Ch. 1, and Musto, *The American Disease*, op. cit., Ch. 2, esp. pp. 43–4.

33 Nicholas Lemann, *The Promised Land: The Great Black Migration and How It Changed America*, New York, Vintage Books, 1992, p. 27.

34 For more on Black cocaine use and its connection to crime see David T. Courtwright, 'The hidden epidemic: opiate addiction and cocaine use in the South, 1860–1920', *Journal of Southern History*, 1983, vol. 49, pp. 57–72.

35 E.g., 'The cocain [*sic*] habit', *Journal of the American Medical Association*, 1900, vol. 34, p. 1637, and ' "Cocaine Alley" ', op. cit., pp. 337–8.

36 Facsimile advertisement in Byck, op. cit., p. xxxviii.

37 Fifteen states also required that students in public schools receive instruction in the effects of alcohol and narcotic drugs – 'narcotic' then understood to include cocaine. Martin I. Wilbert, 'Efforts to curb the misuse of narcotic drugs: a comparative analysis of the federal and state laws designed to restrict or regulate the distribution and use of opium, coca, and other narcotic or habit-forming drugs', *Public Health Reports*, 1915, vol. 30, pp. 893–923.

38 Musto, *The American Disease*, op. cit., pp. 103–4.

39 US Senate, *Report on International Opium Commission*, op. cit., p. 50; Martin I. Wilbert, 'Sale and use of cocaine and narcotics', *Public Health Reports*, 1914, vol. 29, pp. 3180–1.

40 I say 'enlarge' because a small underground market actually existed before regulation, due to the fact that some retailers refused to sell to customers they deemed to be other than legitimate. Middlemen who had no such scruples would purchase and resell cocaine in the underworld, usually at inflated prices. Formal regulations had the effect of expanding this type of diversionary activity. Spillane, op. cit.

41 Even before the passage of state and federal laws the more professionally minded druggists voluntarily began restricting sales, a trend which also contributed to the rise of the underground market. Joseph Spillane, 'The retail druggists and the transformation of cocaine, 1885–1915', unpublished paper furnished by the author, 1992.

42 Harvey W. Wiley and Anne Lewis Pierce, 'The cocain [*sic*] crime', *Good Housekeeping*, 1914, vol. 58, pp. 393–4.

43 Undated clipping, 'Grand jury gets behind cocaine sellers', *New Orleans Item*, probably 1909 or 1910, Box 29, Records of the United States Delegation to the International Opium Commission and Conference, 1909–13, Record Group 43, National Archives, Washington, DC.

44 David F. Musto, 'Illicit price of cocaine in two eras: 1908–14 and 1982–89', *Connecticut Medicine*, 1990, vol. 54, 322–3.

45 A good description of the ease with which heroin could be obtained around 1910 is Leroy Street, in collaboration with David Loth, *I Was a Drug Addict*, New York, Random House, 1953, pp. 19, 29–30.

46 J. Frank Chase et al., *The Dope Evil*, Boston, New England Watch & Ward Society, 1912, p. 9.

47 Wilbert, 'Efforts to curb the misuse of narcotic drugs', op. cit., p. 898.

48 E.g., Charles F. Stokes, 'The problem of narcotic addiction of today', *Medical Record*, 1918, vol. 93, pp. 756–7, and Clifford B. Farr, 'The relative frequency of the morphine and heroin habits: based upon some observations at the Philadelphia General Hospital', *New York Medical Journal*, 1915, vol. 101, pp. 892–5.

49 Box 6, Kolb Papers, History of Medicine Division, National Library of Medicine, Bethesda, Maryland. For a fuller description of these records see Courtwright, *Dark Paradise*, op. cit., pp. 161–2, n. 9.

50 David T. Courtwright, Herman Joseph and Don Des Jarlais, *Addicts Who Survived: An Oral History of Narcotic Use in America, 1923–1965*, Knoxville, University of Tennessee Press, 1989, p. 235.

51 All forms, including crude, smoking, medicinal and tinctures and extracts.

52 US Treasury Department, Bureau of Narcotics, *Traffic in Opium and Other Dangerous Drugs*, Washington, DC, Government Printing Office, 1939, pp. 80–5.

53 A partial exception to this generalization would be the years 1948–9, when there was an influx of Peruvian cocaine and a dramatic, but temporary, increase in seizures. 'The white goddess', *Time*, 11 April 1949, vol. 53, p. 44.

54 'Cocaine used by most drug addicts', *New York Times*, 15 April 1926, p. 20; Garland Williams, New York District Supervisor, to Harry Anslinger, Commissioner of Narcotics, 9 February 1940, US Treasury Department File 0120–9, Drug Enforcement Administration, Washington, DC.

55 Harry Anslinger and Kenneth W. Chapman, 'Narcotic addictions', *Modern Medicine*, 1957, vol. 25, p. 179.

56 Gerald T. McLaughlin, 'Cocaine: The history and regulation of a dangerous drug', *Cornell Law Review*, 1973, vol. 58, pp. 555–6. See also James V. Spotts and Franklin C. Schontz, *The Life Styles of Nine American Cocaine Users: Trips to the Land of Cockaigne* [*sic*], National Institute on Drug Abuse Research Monograph 16, Washington, DC, Government Printing Office, 1976, p. 14, and Barry Spunt et al., 'Methadone diversion: a new look', *Journal of Drug Issues*, 1986, vol. 16, pp. 569–83. It should be emphasized that not all methadone patients continued to use illicit drugs and that there were and are large variations in 'cheating'. Research has shown that patients in programmes which administer higher doses of methadone, in the range of 60 to 100 mg a day, use fewer illicit narcotics and stimulants than do patients in low-dose programmes, who receive 30 to 50 mg a day. Dean R. Gerstein and Henrick J. Harwood (eds), (Committee for the Substance Abuse Coverage Study, Division of Health Care Services, Institute of Medicine), *Treating Drug Problems: A Study of the Evolution, Effectiveness, and Financing of Public and Private Drug Treatment Systems*, Washington, DC, National Academy Press, 1990, vol. 1, pp. 147–51.

57 Joseph L. Zentner, 'Cocaine and the criminal sanction', *Journal of Drug Issues*, 1977, vol. 7, p. 98, and Scott E. Lukas, *Amphetamines: Danger in the Fast Lane*, New York, Chelsea House, 1985, p. 21.

58 The thesis that increased cocaine consumption was partly a substitute for the amphetamines was developed by Edward Brecher et al., *Licit and Illicit Drugs*, Boston, Little, Brown, 1972, pp. 267–305. For further, empirical evidence that amphetamine use was declining as cocaine use was rising see Robert D. Budd, 'Drug use trends among Los Angeles county probationers over the last five years', *American Journal of Drug and Alcohol Abuse*, 1980, vol. 7, p. 59. For information on the amphetamines' legal restriction see Ch. 9 of Lukas, op. cit. The most detailed treatment of the Bias episode is Lewis Cole, *Never Too Young to Die: The Death of Len Bias*, New York, Pantheon Books, 1989.

59 See Todd Gitlin, *The Sixties: Years of Hope, Days of Rage*, New York, Bantam, 1987, esp. Ch. 8, on the political overtones of youthful drug use. The few radicals who shunned illicit drugs were mainly affiliated with the Progressive Labor Movement, a Maoist breakaway from the Communist Party (p. 209).

60 Thomas L. Dezelsky, Jack V. Toohey and Robert Kush, 'A ten-year analysis of non-medical drug use behavior at five American universities', *Journal of School Health*, 1981, vol. 51, pp. 52–3.

61 *Holy Terror: Andy Warhol Close Up*, New York, HarperCollins, 1990, p. 369.

62 Herbert D. Kleber, 'Epidemic cocaine abuse: America's present, Britain's

future?', *British Journal of Addiction*, 1988, vol. 83, p. 1362; William H. Helfand, 'Vin Mariani', *Pharmacy in History*, 1980, vol. 22, pp. 11–19.

63 *Bright Lights, Big City*, New York, Vintage, 1984, p. 153. See also Kennedy, op. cit., pp. 117–22.

64 Guy Gugliotta and Jeff Leen, *Kings of Cocaine: Inside the Medellín Cartel – An Astonishing True Story of Murder, Money, and International Corruption*, New York, Simon & Schuster, 1989.

65 Rensselaer W. Lee III, *The White Labyrinth: Cocaine and Political Power*, New Brunswick, NJ, Transaction Publishers, 1989, p. 100. See also Musto, 'Illicit price of cocaine', op. cit., p. 323.

66 US Office of National Drug Control Policy, Executive Office of the President, *Price and Purity of Cocaine: The Relationship to Emergency Room Visits and Deaths, and to Drug Use Among Arrestees*, Washington, DC, Office of National Drug Control Policy, 1992, pp. 5–6.

67 Dan Waldorf, Craig Reinarman and Sheigla Murphy, *Cocaine Changes: The Experience of Using and Quitting*, Philadelphia, Temple University Press, 1991, pp. 103–39; Kleber, op. cit., p. 1363; US House of Representatives, Select Committee on Narcotics Abuse and Control, *Cocaine: A Major Drug Issue of the Seventies: Hearings*, 96th Cong., 1st sess., Washington, DC, Government Printing Office, 1980, pp. 91, 120–1, 125; Gordon Witkin et al., 'The men who invented crack', *US News & World Report*, 19 August 1991, vol. 111, pp. 44–53; Douglas McDonnell, Jeanette Irwin and Marsha Rosenbaum, '"Hop and Hubbas": a tough new mix: a research note on cocaine use among methadone maintenance clients', *Contemporary Drug Problems*, 1990, vol. 17, pp. 147–51; and Beatrice A. Rouse, 'Trends in cocaine use in the general population', in Susan Schober and Charles Schade (eds), *The Epidemiology of Cocaine Use and Abuse*, National Institute on Drug Abuse Research Monograph 110, Washington, DC, Government Printing Office, 1991, p. 14. Two books by ethnographer Terry Williams that provide a vivid account of the transition from cocaine sniffing to smoking in New York City in the 1980s are *The Cocaine Kids: The Inside Story of a Teenage Drug Ring*, Reading, Mass., Addison-Wesley, 1989, and *Crackhouse: Notes from the End of the Line*, Reading, Mass., Addison-Wesley, 1992.

68 Ibid., pp. 3, 8–10; Cole, op. cit., pp. 150–1. Before the crack wave American Blacks were statistically less likely than Whites to initiate cocaine use, but north-eastern urban Black men who tried the drug were more likely than Whites to persist and to become heavily involved with it. North-eastern urban Hispanic men also tended to be more persistent users. Denise B. Kandel and Mark Davies, 'Cocaine use in a national sample of US Youth (NLSY): ethnic patterns, progression, and predictors', in Schober and Schade, op. cit., pp. 154–6.

69 Peter Reuter, Robert MacCoun and Patrick Murphy, *Money from Crime: A Study of the Economics of Drug Dealing in Washington, DC*, Santa Monica, RAND Corporation, 1990, pp. 56, 66.

70 Philippe Bourgois, 'Growing up', *American Enterprise*, May/June 1991, vol. 2, pp. 30–4. Bourgois, an ethnographer who has spent years studying the crack trade in East Harlem, thinks there is considerably less money in it than Reuter et al., op. cit. Bourgois estimates that most street-sellers earn only $6 to $8 an hour. He stresses the non-monetary advantages of selling crack over taking a low-skilled legitimate job with (White) rules, expectations, and requirements.

71 Witkin et al., op. cit., pp. 52–3; Lemann, op. cit., pp. 336–7.

72 Los Angeles County, Office of the District Attorney, *Gangs, Crime and Violence*

in Los Angeles, Los Angeles, Office of the District Attorney, 1992, pp. 60–81, quotation at 77.

73 New York City estimates indicated a female majority in early 1989. US General Accounting Office, *Drug Abuse: The Crack Cocaine Epidemic: Health Consequences and Treatment*, Washington, DC, Government Printing Office, 1991, p. 17. 'Many crack users', the report continues, 'are young, unemployed school dropouts who are socially disorganized and lack family support systems.'

74 Terry Williams, *Crackhouse*, op. cit., pp. 112–24; Alan Burdick, 'Looking for the high life', *The Sciences*, June 1991, vol. 31, pp. 14, 15; Paul J. Goldstein et al., 'Frequency of cocaine use and violence: a comparison between men and women', in Schober and Schade, op. cit., pp. 120–2; and Mindy Thompson Fullilove, E. Anne Lown, and Robert E. Fullilove, 'Crack 'Hos and Skeezers: traumatic experiences of women crack users', *Journal of Sex Research*, 1992, vol. 29, pp. 275–87. This last article errs in describing the sex-for-drugs trade as a unique feature of the crack subculture (p. 276). In the early 1980s, before the crack explosion, masseuses bartered powder cocaine for sex. Donald R. Wesson, 'Cocaine use by masseuses', *Journal of Psychoactive Drugs*, 1982, vol. 14, pp. 75–6. Bartering was also practised by female heroin addicts and, according to Goldstein, who is an authority on drugs and prostitution, has historically been commonplace in the illicit drug world: Goldstein, op. cit., p. 121.

75 Herman Joseph and Karla Damus, 'Prenatal cocaine/crack exposure in New York City', and Daniel R. Neuspiel and Sara C. Hamel, 'Cocaine and infant behavior', both in *Cocaine/Crack Research Working Group Newsletter*, October 1991, Issue 2, pp. 4–6 and pp. 14–25, respectively.

76 See, for example, Tom Morganthau et al., 'Crack and crime', *Newsweek*, 16 June 1986, vol. 107, pp. 16–22. It is striking that, fifteen years before, cocaine was described in the pages of the same periodical in a matter-of-fact, non-alarmist way. 'It's the real thing', *Newsweek*, 27 September 1971, vol. 78, p. 124. Drug authorities who had in the 1970s downplayed the dangers posed by cocaine also began changing their minds, sometimes reversing themselves in print. E.g., Waldorf et al., op. cit., pp. 8–9. Even professional ethnographers like Terry Williams, who ordinarily confine themselves to objective and value-neutral language, have deplored the crack revolution. See *The Cocaine Kids*, op. cit., pp. 107–11.

77 US Senate, Committee on Governmental Affairs, Permanent Subcommittee on Investigations, *'Crack' Cocaine: Hearing*, 99th Cong., 2nd sess., Washington, DC, Government Printing Office, 1986, p. 2.

78 For figures on the national drug control budget, 1981–93, see US Office of National Drug Control Policy, Executive Office of the President, *National Drug Control Strategy: Progress in the War on Drugs, 1989–1992*, Washington, DC, The White House, 1993, p. 4.

79 In 1991 Ansley Hamid, a veteran ethnographer of New York City's many drug sub-cultures, reported that it was hard to find crack users or distributors who had become involved after 1987. Burdick, op. cit., p. 15.

80 The National Institute on Drug Abuse's *Household Survey*, which did not cover such groups as prison inmates or the homeless, yielded an estimate of about 860,000 cocaine addicts. A different and more comprehensive study undertaken in 1990 estimated the total of addicts to be 2,200,000, or about one out of every 100 Americans. US Senate, Committee on the Judiciary, *Hard-Core Cocaine Addicts: Measuring – and Fighting – the Epidemic: A Staff Report*, 101st Cong., 2nd sess., Washington, DC, Government Printing Office, 1990.

81 Eric D. Wish, 'U.S. drug policy in the 1990s: insights from new data from arrestees', *International Journal of the Addictions*, 1990–1, vol. 25, pp. 377–409, quotation at p. 377. Data on cocaine-related emergencies showed a marked increase in patients who were Black, urban, and older in the early 1990s. 'Cocaine: the first decade', *Rand Drug Policy Research Center Issue Paper*, April 1992, vol. 1(1), p. 3, and US Department of Health and Human Services, Public Health Service, Substance Abuse and Mental Health Services Division, Office of Applied Studies, *Preliminary Estimates from the Drug Abuse Warning Network*, Rockville, Md., xeroxed advance report, April 1993, p. 5. What has happened with heavy cocaine users is reminiscent of the bulge of youthful heroin addicts who began their careers in the late 1960s and 1970s and who, as they aged, continued to show up in gaols, hospitals, and drug treatment programmes in the 1970s and 1980s.

82 Sam Vincent Meddis, 'Is the drug war racist?', series in *USA Today*, 23–25 July 1993, pp. 1A, 3A; 26 July 1993, p. 6A; and 27 July 1993, pp. 6A–7A. The centrepiece of Meddis' investigation is drug arrest data broken down city by city.

83 21 *United States Code* § 841(b).

84 US District Court, Eastern District of Missouri, Eastern Division, defense brief in *US* vs. *Clary*, no. 89–00167–CR(4), pp. 4–5.

85 Burnham, op. cit., pp. 90–2.

86 Sub-heading from an editorial, 'Crack', 28 May 1989, sec. 4, p. 14.

AFTERWORD

Jordan Goodman and Paul E. Lovejoy

Psychoactive substances are a rich analytical category for the study of historical and cultural processes. An understanding of their origins and patterns of use, whether transhistorical and comparative or within delimited historical periods and cultural settings, provides a unique insight into social and political life, as the essays in this volume demonstrate. We see these substances, first of all, as commodities that have similarities to other commodities studied by scholars; hence we have addressed issues relating to production, trade and consumption. Second, a better knowledge of these peculiar substances can contribute to the history of scientific and especially medicinal knowledge in different societies. Third, their study provides insights into the ritual and symbolic expressions of social and political order and thereby are related to issues of power and its distribution. Finally, the exploration of the history and anthropology of psychoactive substances opens a window into culture, especially religious expression and the process of secularization, as substances became popularized and disassociated from religion.

At various times in history, societies have evolved attitudes and predispositions towards psychoactive substances that can be labelled as 'drugphobic'. The contemporary Western world has moved along this path to a considerable degree, although not as far as Islamic societies have ventured. The increasing drugphobia of the Western world in particular has influenced scholarship adversely, distorting our understanding of the processes of cultural change as a result. Popular movements of reform as well as religious reaction have influenced those in power to reassess and redefine attitudes towards psychoactive substances. Consequently, distinctions are made between soft and hard 'drugs' and between licit and illicit 'habits' on the basis of a pharmacology that judges the physiological effects of substances to be good or bad. Addiction, when recognized, is the feature that makes psychoactive substances 'peculiar'.

These simplistic distinctions are intended to separate substances into categories of discourse: the vocabulary used to discuss coffee and tea, whose mild addiction is acceptable to most people, is fundamentally different from that of cocaine and heroin, addiction to which is not acceptable. Tobacco and alcohol are different again; their acceptability has varied considerably, especially in recent years, while cannabis has seldom achieved official respectability. These socially shaped distinctions not only obscure contemporary debates, but they have also had an impact on scholarship, with the result that the historical and cultural record is often distorted and poorly understood.

Until recently, for example, the consensus among historians of early modern Europe held that people were conservative, wary about plant substances in general. Only those on the margins of society, those engaged in nefarious activities, such as witchcraft, ingested plant substances to help them carry out their heinous practices and esoteric rituals. Ergot, mandrake root and deadly nightshade have been typically cast in this context. But the historical picture is both more complex and subtle than this. Early modern Europeans were far more knowledgeable about and consumed many more psychoactive plants than we have been led to believe.[1] Similarly, the study of shamanism, including Eliade's magisterial work, long portrayed the drug-taking shaman as an aberration of the true healer who resorted to no artificial aids in the search for the ecstatic state. By contrast, it is now generally accepted that ingesting plant substances, especially tobacco, was an essential component of shamanism.[2] Shamans used their privileged access to and knowledge of substances charged with symbolic significance to underpin their social standing and influence within their communities. Scholarship that is less drugphobic has revealed the widespread consumption of many plants for the psychoactive properties in the context of their medical and social consumption. The essays in this book help to erode further the constraints on analysis that are imposed by the drugphobia of contemporary society.

As Andrew Sherratt argues in his introductory essay, 'psychoactive substances can be seen as integral to the constitution of culture. They have been fundamental to the nature of sociality and an active element in the construction of religious experience, gender categories and the rituals of social life. No ethnographic or culture-historic account is complete without a consideration of these matters. They have been central to the formation of civilizations, the definition of cultural identities and the growth of the world economy.' The challenge for the future is to recover the history and anthropology of these substances in order to place them in the cognitive context in which they belong. This will not be an easy task since much of history, in particular, has been written and rewritten to delete evidence of the widespread use and importance of psychoactive substances.

Historians and anthropologists can uncover the extent to which psychoactive substances have been significant in several ways, thereby re-establishing their role in social and cultural settings. The first, and perhaps most important, is to enlarge the ethnographic and historical record with detailed studies of specific substances. Some of these substances are more in evidence than others.[3] There is, for example, an extensive literature on tobacco but virtually nothing on cannabis; more is known about *kava* and kola than *qat*; and coffee is better understood than chocolate and coca. Those substances that entered international commerce, especially trans-oceanic commerce, as a result of their appropriation by Europeans in the early modern period are especially visible, certainly more so than those whose circuits of exchange were small, such as betel, or those whose exchange was not organized by Europeans, as with kola. There has been a fair amount of ethnobotanical and ethnopharmacological work on psychoactive substances from central and south America but little historical study on their circuits of exchange and consumption. Similar work on other parts of the non-European world is relatively sparse.

The impact of technological and scientific change on the provision of psychoactive substances to consumers is an important area for future research. Until the beginning of the nineteenth century, there was little understanding of why some plants produced physiological effects and others did not and what it was in these plants that was responsible for psychoactive properties. Wilhelm Sertürner's isolation of an alkaloid in opium in 1804, which he called morphine, was a major breakthrough in identifying the scientific basis of psychoactive ingredients. On its own, morphine produced essentially the same physiological changes as did the crude opium latex. Thereafter, a substantial research programme, which paralleled the general scientific quest for knowledge about the plant world, went into action, principally in France and Germany, to isolate the active principles of other plants. By the end of the century, almost all the active ingredients in the most widely used plants in the European *materia medica* were isolated, including those in tobacco, coffee, tea, cocoa, *kava*, kola, and coca, to name but the most important. Indeed, the discoveries had profound medical implications as well. While these discoveries themselves have been well documented, the impact on production, distribution and consumption of the peculiar commodities from which these alkaloids derive has been neglected.[4] We have very little idea of how social contexts of consumption were affected by the availability first of the natural extracts (usually one or more alkaloid), such as cocaine, and then of synthetically manufactured substances, such as heroin, in the late nineteenth, and LSD, in the twentieth centuries.[5]

Even as commodities of exchange, there is scope for increasing our understanding of the production and distribution of psychoactive substances, whether in plant form, as natural extracts, or as synthetic manufactures. Our agenda is to uncover the mechanisms and circuits of exchange and their political and social contexts to learn what happens when these substances cross cultural boundaries. Why, for example, have some substances, such as tobacco, tea and coffee, diffused relatively easily, despite some initial constraints, while others, such as kola, *qat* and *kava*, have had a much more limited range of production and consumption? Even cocoa, which might appear to be well understood in its historical context, remains a remote subject. Like tobacco, its New World provenance is known, but unlike tobacco, its diffusion has not been studied as thoroughly. Cannabis presents an even more complex problem: its antiquity is known, as is its wide dispersion in the twentieth century, but beyond the barest outline virtually nothing is known about the history of cannabis.

Finally, we turn to what are perhaps the most vexing issues about psychoactive substances: why is it that at certain times and in certain places, some substances have become illicit while others remain acceptable, both legally and socially? What explains the shifts in attitudes that affect political and cultural decisions? The boundary between licit and illicit has been permeable, as opium and tobacco both demonstrate, but how can we analyse the space for negotiation in the signification of substances as one type or the other? This complex question is one that historians and anthropologists have not usually addressed, though their sensitivity to context makes them especially qualified to contribute to the debate over these issues.[6] The boundary separating legal and illegal cannot be taken for granted, as is generally the case in society as a whole and among far too many policy-makers, despite appeals from some quarters for caution in distinguishing among psychoactive substances. Whether or not to decriminalize some substances is a debate that should be taken seriously. Mind-altering chemicals like tranquillizers and Prozac achieve wide acceptance in some scientific circles without full discussion in society as a whole; consuming cannabis does not.

Anthropologists, historians and others interested in the pursuit of knowledge should recognize the danger in leaving the debate over what is acceptable and respectable and what is not solely in the hands of researchers who approach the study of psychoactive substances through reductive models, be they pharmacological, psychological or physiological. Researchers, whose model of social context is deviance, need to reconsider the willingness to accept psychoactive substances that are chemically derived without recognizing the long history of plant-based substances that also affect the mind and the lessons that might be learned from the anthropological implications of such a history. Policy-makers bound up in the discourse and metaphors of the military, exemplified best in the phrase 'War on Drugs', might well recognize that many substances that are presently 'acceptable' may have properties that border on thought control which are as dangerous in their own way as the most potent 'peculiar' substances examined in this volume. Either by stripping away the social context or by engineering it in a different frame, most of the debate on the 'drug problem' has distanced the substance from the context.[7]

The study of psychoactive substances along the lines suggested in this collection of essays can provide historians and anthropologists with a fresh perspective on the functioning of social relations, on economic systems of exchange and on political power and privilege. The Bibliography of the most important and, in many cases, most recent work in the general field that follows is intended to assist in moving these disciplines in the direction of meaningful research which, hopefully, will inform the debate over the effects of psychoactive substances on individuals and society at large, both in the contemporary world and historically.

NOTES

1 See, for example, the path-breaking work on the role of psychoactive plants in the diets of early modern Europeans – P. Camporesi, *Bread of Dreams: Food and Fantasy in Early Modern Europe*, Oxford, Polity Press, 1989. See also the essay by Jordan Goodman in this volume.

2 This is a large research area. For an appreciation of the use of psychoactive plants in shamanism see, for example, the following: W. La Barre, *Culture in Context*, Durham, North Carolina, Duke University Press, 1980; M. Dobkin de Rios, *Hallucinogens: Cross-Cultural Perspectives*, Albuquerque, New Mexico, University of New Mexico Press, 1984; R. G. Wasson, S. Kramrisch, J. Ott and C. A. P. Ruck, *Persephone's Quest: Entheogens and the Origins of Religion*, New Haven, Connecticut, Yale University Press, 1986; J. Wilbert, *Tobacco and Shamanism*, New Haven, Connecticut, Yale University Press, 1987; R. E. Schultes and A. Hofmann, *Plants of the Gods*, Rochester, Vermont, Healing Arts Press, 1992; and R. Rudgley, *The Alchemy of Culture: Intoxicants in Society*, London, British Museum Press, 1993.

3 Examples of the literature referred to in the rest of this paragraph may be found in the Bibliography accompanying this Afterword.

4 On the discovery of alkaloids, that is salifiable nitrogenous bases, as being the active principles of psychoactive (and other) plants see the following works – J. E. Lesch, 'Conceptual change in an empirical science: the discovery of the first alkaloids', *Historical Studies in the Physical Sciences*, 1981, vol. II, pp. 305–28, and his *Science and Medicine in France: The Emergence of Experimental Physiology, 1790–1855*, Cambridge, Mass., Harvard University Press, 1984; and L. Lewin, *Phantastica: Narcotic and Stimulating Drugs*, London, Kegan Paul, Trench, Trubner & Co., 1931. A number of psychoactive plants have many alkaloids as well as other pharmacologically active and inactive compounds. A list of some of the most important principles of many psychoactive plants can be found in Schultes and Hofmann, op. cit., pp. 65–79. *Kava* chemistry is particularly complex and has only recently attracted renewed attention after Louis Lewin first began his scientific research on the plant culminat-ing in his monograph on the subject in 1886. For a recent overview of *kava* chemistry, in a fascinating book on all aspects of this drug, see V. Lebot, M. Merlin, and L. Lindstrom, *Kava: The Pacific Drug*, New Haven,

Connecticut, Yale University Press, 1992.

5 The problem of technology and science being applied to psychoactive substances in delivering pure forms and designed compounds has been raised in R. K. Siegel, *Intoxication: Life in Pursuit of Artificial Paradise*, New York, E. P. Dutton, 1989. Some insight can be gained from the following works: D. T. Courtwright, *Dark Paradise: Opiate Addiction in America before 1940*, Cambridge, Mass., Harvard University Press, 1982, and his contribution to this volume; also G. J. Higby, 'Heroin and medical reasoning: the power of analogy', *New York State Journal of Medicine*, 1986, vol. 20, pp. 137–42.

6 There are some notable though few exceptions. A recent, albeit sketchy, attempt to raise the problem of how societies change in their attitude to psychoactive substances over a long historical period can be found in D. F. Musto, 'Opium, cocaine and marijuana in American history', *Scientific American*, 1991, vol. 265, pp. 20–7. Other bibliographical information is contained in Courtwright's essay in this volume. One of the best analyses of the debate over a substance leading to proscriptions has been done for coffee in Islam in the sixteenth century – see R. S. Hattox, *Coffee and Coffeehouses: The Origins of a Social Beverage in the Medieval Near East*, Seattle, University of Washington Press, 1985. For a recent reassessment of the 'tobacco controversy' in late sixteenth- and seventeenth-century England, see D. Harley, 'The beginnings of the tobacco controversy: puritanism, James I, and the royal physicians', *Bulletin of the History of Medicine*, 1993, vol. 67, pp. 28–50. Finally, there is the excellent analysis of the political contests leading to the Marijuana Tax Act of 1937 in the United States: see P. A. Morgan, 'The making of a public problem: Mexican labor in California and the Marijuana Law of 1937', in R. Glick and J. Moore (eds), *Drugs in Hispanic Communities*, New Brunswick, New Jersey, Rutgers University Press, 1990. For an interesting discussion of the policy of the League of Nations to drugs and the difficulty encountered in enforcing its policies, see A. A. Block, 'European drug traffic and traffickers between the wars: the policy of suppression and its consequences', *Journal of Social History*, 1989, vol. 23, pp. 315–37.

7 A notable exception was the publication of a special issue of *Daedalus* entitled 'Political Pharmacology: Thinking About Drugs'. This issue has two particularly important articles. They are: D. B. Heath, 'US drug control policy: a cultural perspective', *Daedalus*, 1992, vol. 121, pp. 269–91, and J. A. Husch, 'Culture and US drug policy: toward a new conceptual framework', *Daedalus*, 1992, vol. 121, pp. 293–304. For criticisms of the 'War on Drugs' in the United States, see P. R. Andreas, E. C. Bertram, M. J. Blachman and K. E. Sharpe, 'Dead-end drug wars', *Foreign Policy*, 1991–2, vol. 85, pp. 106–28; E. A. Nadelmann, 'Drug prohibition in the United States: costs, consequences, and alternatives', *Science*, 1989, vol. 245, pp. 939–46. Dwight Heath's work on the cultural context of drug use in the United States can very well act as a model for further anthropological (and historical) work on psychoactive substances. Besides his article mentioned above, see also 'Cultural factors in the choice of drugs', in M. Galanter (ed.), *Recent Developments in Alcoholism*, vol. 8, New York, Plenum Press, 1990, and 'Prohibition or liberalization of alcohol and drugs? A sociocultural perspective', in M. Galanter (ed.), *Recent Developments in Alcoholism*, vol. 10, New York, Plenum Press, 1992. Compare these 'cultural' approaches to the 'pharmacological' approach reflected in A. Goldstein, *Addiction: From Biology to Drug Policy*, New York, W. H. Freeman & Co., 1994.

SELECTED BIBLIOGRAPHY

Abel, E. L., *Marihuana: The First Twelve Thousand Years*, New York, Plenum Press, 1980.

Adler, P., *Wheeling and Dealing*, New York, Columbia University Press, 1993.

Alden, D., 'The significance of cacao production in the Amazon region during the late colonial period: an essay in comparative economic history', *Proceedings of the American Philosophical Society*, 1976, vol 120, pp. 103–35.

Appadurai, A. (ed.), *The Social Life of Things: Commodities in Cultural Perspective*, Cambridge, Cambridge University Press, 1986.

Austen, R. A. and Smith, W. D., 'Private tooth decay as economic virtue, the slave-sugar triangle, consumerism and European industrialization', in J. E. Inikori and S. L. Engerman (eds), *The Atlantic Slave Trade: Effects on Economies, Societies, and Peoples in Africa, the Americas and Europe*, Durham, NC, Duke University Press, 1992.

Austin, G. A., *Perspectives on the History of Psychoactive Substance Use*, Washington, DC, Government Printing Office, 1978.

Ball, D.U. (ed.), *Kaffee im Spiegel europäischer Trinksitten/Coffee in the Context of European Drinking Habits*, Zurich, Johann Jacobs Museum, 1991.

Barrows, S. and Room, R. (eds), *Drinking: Behavior and Belief in Modern History*, Berkeley, University of California Press, 1991.

Barthes, R., 'Towards a psychosociology of contemporary food consumption', in R. Forster and O. Ranum (eds), *Food and Drink in History: Selections from the Annales ESC*, Baltimore, Johns Hopkins University Press, 1979.

Berridge, V. and Edwards, G., *Opium and the People: Opiate Use in Nineteenth Century England*, London, Allen Lane, 1981.

Bonnie, R. J. and Whitebread, C.H. II, *The Marijuana Conviction: A History of Marijuana Prohibition in the United States*, Charlottesville, Va., University Press of Virginia, 1974.

Bourdieu, P., *Distinction: A Social Critique of the Judgement of Taste*, London, Routledge, 1984.

Bourguignon, E. (ed.), *Religion, Altered States of Consciousness, and Social Change*, Columbus, Ohio State University Press, 1973.

Brecher, E., et. al., *Licit and Illicit Drugs*, Boston, Little, Brown, 1972.

Brewer, J. and Porter, R. (eds), *Consumption and the World of Goods*, London, Routledge, 1993.

Brunton R., *The Abandoned Narcotic: Kava and Cultural Instability in Melanesia*, Cambridge, Cambridge University Press, 1989.

Burnham, J. C., *Bad Habits: Drinking, Smoking, Taking Drugs, Gambling, Sexual Misbehavior, and Swearing in American History*, New York, New York University

Press, 1993.

Burton-Bradley, B. G., 'Arecaidinism: betel chewing in transcultural perspective', *Canadian Journal of Psychiatry*, 1979, vol. 24, pp. 481–8.

Butel, P., *Histoire du thé*, Paris, Editions Desjonquères, 1989.

Camporesi, P., *Bread of Dreams: Food and Fantasy in Early Modern Europe*, Oxford, Polity Press, 1989.

——*Exotic Brew: The Art of Living in the Age of Enlightenment*, Oxford, Polity Press, 1994.

Carlson, B. R. and Edwards, W. H., 'Human values and marijuana use', *International Journal of the Addictions*, 1990, vol. 25, pp. 1393–401.

Cohn, M., *Dope-Girls*, London, Lawrence & Wishart, 1992.

Courtwright, D. T., *Dark Paradise: Opiate Addiction in America before 1940*, Cambridge, Mass., Harvard University Press, 1982.

——'The hidden epidemic: opiate addiction and cocaine use in the South, 1860–1920', *Journal of Southern History*, 1983, vol. 49, pp. 57–72.

Courtwright, D. T., Joseph, H. and Des Jarlais, D., *Addicts Who Survived: An Oral History of Narcotic Use in America, 1923–1965*, Knoxville, University of Tennessee Press, 1989.

Daedalus, special issue, 'Political Pharmacology: Thinking About Drugs', 1992, vol. 121.

Dickson, S. A., *Panacea or Precious Bane: Tobacco in Sixteenth Century Literature*, New York, New York Public Library, 1954.

Dietler, M., 'Driven by drink: the role of drinking in the political economy and the case of Early Iron Age France', *Journal of Anthropological Archaeology*, 1990, vol. 9(4), pp. 352–406.

Dobkin de Rios, M., *Visionary Vine*, Prospect Heights, Ill., Waveland Press, 1984.

——*Hallucinogens: Cross-Cultural Perspectives*, Bridport, Prism Press, 1990.

Douglas, M. (ed.), *Constructive Drinking: Perspectives on Drink from Anthropology*, Cambridge, Cambridge University Press, 1987.

Douglas, M. and Isherwood, B., *The World of Goods: Towards an Anthropology of Consumption*, Harmondsworth, Penguin, 1978.

Du Toit, B. M. (ed.), *Drugs, Rituals and Altered States of Consciousness*, Rotterdam, Balkema, 1977.

——*Cannabis in Africa*, Rotterdam, Balkema, 1980.

Efron, D. H., Holmstedt, B., and Kline, N. S. (eds), *Ethnopharmacological Search for Psychoactive Drugs*, New York, Raven Press, 1979.

Elferink, J. G., 'The narcotic and hallucinogenic use of tobacco in Pre-Columbian Central America', *Journal of Ethnopharmacology*, 1983, vol. 7, pp. 111–22.

Eliade, M., *Shamanism: Archaic Techniques of Ecstasy*, London, Routledge, 1972.

Elias, N., *The Civilising Process: The History of Manners*, Oxford, Basil Blackwell, 1978.

Emboden, W., *Narcotic Plants: Hallucinogens, Stimulants, Inebriants and Hypnotics, Their Origins and Uses*, London, Studio Vista, 1979.

Everett, M., Waddell, J. and Heath, D., (eds), *Cross-Cultural Aproaches to the Study of Alcohol*, The Hague, Mouton, 1976.

Flattery, D. S. and Schwartz, M., *Hoama and Harmaline: The Botanical Identity of the Indo-Iranian Sacred Hallucinogen 'Soma' and its Legacy in Religion, Language and Middle-Eastern Folklore*, Berkeley, University of California Press, 1989.

Flynn, J. C., *Cocaine: An In-Depth Look at the Facts, Science, History and Future of the World's Most Addictive Drug*, New York, Birch Lane Press, 1991.

Forrest, D., *Tea for the British: The Social and Economic History of a Famous Trade*, London, Chatto & Windus, 1973.

Furst, P. M., *Hallucinogens and Culture*, San Francisco, Chandler & Sharp, 1976.

Furst, P. M. (ed.), *Flesh of the Gods: The Ritual Use of Hallucinogens*, New York, Praeger, 1972.

Gernet, A. von, 'The transculturation of the Amerindian/pipe/tobacco/smoking complex and its impact on the intellectual boundaries between "savagery" and "civilization", 1535–1935', unpublished PhD thesis, Montreal, McGill University, 1988.

Goldstein, A., *Addiction: From Biology to Drug Policy*, New York, W. H. Freeman & Co., 1994.

Goodman, J., *Tobacco in History: The Cultures of Dependence*, London, Routledge, 1993.

Grinspoon, L. and Bakalar, J. B., *Cocaine: A Drug and Its Social Evolution*, New York, Basic Books, 1976.

Haberman, T. W., 'Evidence for aboriginal tobaccos in Eastern North America', *American Antiquity*, 1984, vol. 49, pp. 269–87.

Harner, M. (ed.), *Hallucinogens and Shamanism*, New York, Oxford University Press, 1973.

Hattox, R. S., *Coffee and Coffeehouses: The Origins of a Social Beverage in the Medieval Near East*, Seattle, University of Washington Press, 1985.

Heath, D. B., 'Cultural factors in the choice of drugs', in M. Galanter (ed.), *Recent Developments in Alcoholism*, vol. 8, New York, Plenum Press, 1990.

——'Prohibition or liberalization of alcohol and drugs? A sociocultural perspective', in M. Galanter (ed.), *Recent Developments in Alcoholism*, vol. 10, New York, Plenum Press, 1992.

Kennedy, J., *Coca Exotica: The Illustrated Story of Cocaine*, Rutherford, NJ, Farleigh Dickinson University Press, 1985.

La Barre, W., *The Peyote Cult*, New Haven, Yale University Press, 1938.

——'Twenty years of peyote studies', *Current Anthropology*, 1960, vol. 1, pp. 45–60.

——'Old and New World narcotics: a statistical question and an ethnological reply', *Economic Botany*, 1970, vol. 24, pp. 73–80.

——*Culture in Context*, Durham, NC, Duke University Press, 1980.

Lebot, V., Merlin, M. and Lindstrom, L., *Kava: The Pacific Drug*, New Haven, CT, Yale University Press, 1992.

Lee, M. A. and Shlain, B., *Acid Dreams: The Complete Social History of LSD: The CIA, the Sixties, and Beyond*, New York, Grove Weidenfeld, 1992.

Lewin, L., *Phantastica: Narcotic and Stimulating Drugs*, London, Kegan Paul, Trench, Trubner & Co., 1931.

Leyel, C. F., *Elixirs of Life* (Culpeper House Herbals), London, Faber & Faber, 1948.

Lindstrom, L. (ed.), *Drugs in Western Pacific Societies: Relations of Substance*, Lanham, Md., University Press of America, 1987.

Lovejoy, P., *Caravans of Kola: The Hausa Kola Trade 1700–1900*, Zaria, Ahmadu Bello University Press Ltd, 1980.

——'Kola in the history of West Africa', *Cahiers d'Etudes Africaines*, 1980, vol. 20, pp. 97–134.

McCullen, J. T., Jr., 'Indian myths concerning the origin of Tobacco', *New York Folklore Quarterly*, 1967, vol. 23, pp. 264–73.

McGovern, P. E., Fleming, S. J. and Katz, S. H., *The Origins and History of Wine*, New York, Gordon & Breach, in press 1995.

McKenna, T., *Food of the Gods: The Search for the Original Tree of Knowledge*, London, Rider, 1992.

Mann, J., *Murder, Magic and Medicine*, Oxford, Oxford University Press, 1994.

Marshall, M. (ed.), *Beliefs, Behaviors and Alcoholic Beverages*, Ann Arbor, Mich.,

University of Michigan Press, 1979.

Mennell, S., *All Manners of Food: Eating and Taste in England and France from the Middle Ages to the Present*, Oxford, Blackwell, 1985.

Mennell, S., Murcott, A., and van Otterloo, A. H., 'The sociology of food: eating, diet and culture', *Current Sociology*, 1992, vol. 40(2).

Merlin, M. D., *On the Trail of the Ancient Opium Poppy*, London and Toronto, Associated University Presses, 1984.

Merrillees, R. S., 'Opium trade in the Bronze Age Levant', *Antiquity*, 1962, vol. 36, pp. 287–92.

—'Highs and lows in the Holy Land, opium in biblical times', *Eretz-Israel* (Yadin Memorial Volume), 1989, vol. 20, pp. 148–53.

—'Opium again in antiquity', *Levant*, 1979, vol. 11, pp. 167–71.

Mintz, S., *Sweetness and Power: The Place of Sugar in Modern History*, Harmondsworth, Penguin, 1985.

Morgan, P. A., 'The making of a public problem: Mexican labor in California and the Marijuana Law of 1937', in R. Glick and J. Moore (eds), *Drugs in Hispanic Communities*, New Brunswick, NJ, Rutgers University Press, 1990.

Mueller, W., *Bibliographie des Kaffee, des Kakao, der Schokolade, des Tee und deren Surrogate bis zum Jahre 1900*, Bad Bocklet, Walter Krieg Verlag, 1960.

Musto, D. F., *The American Disease: Origins of Narcotic Control*, revised edn, New York, Oxford University Press, 1987.

——'America's first cocaine epidemic', *Wilson Quarterly*, 1989, vol. 13, pp. 59–64.

——'Opium, cocaine and marijuana in American history', *Scientific American*, 1991, vol. 265, pp. 20–7.

Nadelmann, E. A., 'Drug prohibition in the United States: costs, consequences, and alternatives', *Science*, 1989, vol. 245, pp. 939–47.

Paper, J., *Offering Smoke: The Sacred Pipe and Native American Religion*, Moscow, Idaho, University of Idaho Press, 1988.

Parssinen, T. M., *Secret Passions, Secret Remedies: Narcotic Drugs in British Society, 1820–1930*, Philadelphia, Institute for the Study of Human Values, 1983.

Price, J. M., *France and the Chesapeake: A History of the French Tobacco Monopoly, 1674–1791, and of Its Relationship to the British and American Tobacco Trades*, Ann Arbor, Mich., University of Michigan Press, 1973

Robicsek, F., *The Smoking Gods: Tobacco in Maya Art, History and Religion*, Norman, Okla., University of Oklahoma Press, 1978.

Rogoziński, J., *Smokeless Tobacco in the Western World 1550–1950*, New York, Praeger, 1990.

Rubin, V. (ed.), *Cannabis and Culture*, The Hague, Mouton, 1975.

Rubin, V. and Comitas, L., *Ganga in Jamaica: The Effects of Marijuana Use*, Garden City, New York, Anchor, 1976.

Rudgley, R., *The Alchemy of Culture: Intoxicants in Society*, London, British Museum Press, 1993.

Schivelbusch, W., *Tastes of Paradise: A Social History of Spices, Stimulants and Intoxicants*, New York, Pantheon, 1992.

Schultes, R. E., 'The botanical and chemical distribution of the hallucinogens', *Annual Review of Plant Physiology*, 1970, vol. 21, pp. 571–94.

Schultes, R. E. and Hofmann, A., *Plants of the Gods*, Rochester, Vt., Healing Arts Press, 1992.

Schultes, R. E. and Raffauf, R., *The Healing Forest*, Portland, Oreg., Dioscorides Press, 1990.

Scott, P. D., and Marshall, J., *Cocaine Politics: Drugs, Armies, and the CIA in Central America*, Berkeley, University of California Press, 1991.

Sherratt, A. G., 'Sacred and profane substances, the ritual use of narcotics in later

Neolithic Europe', in P. Garwood, D. Jennings, R. Skeates and J. Toms (eds), *Sacred and Profane: Proceedings of a Conference on Archaeology, Ritual and Religion*, Oxford University Committee for Archaeology Monographs 32, 1991.

Sherratt, A. G. and Sherratt, E. S., 'From luxuries to commodities, the nature of Mediterranean Bronze Age trading systems', in N. Gale (ed.), *Bronze Age Trade in the Mediterranean* (Studies in Mediterranean Archaeology 90), Jonsered, Paul Åströms Förlag, 1991.

Siegel, R. K., *Intoxication: Life in Pursuit of Artificial Paradise*, New York, E. P. Dutton, 1989.

Spence, J., 'Opium smoking in Ch'ing China', in F. Wakeman, Jr., and C. Grant (eds), *Conflict and Control in Late Imperial China*, Berkeley, University of California Press, 1975.

Springer, J. W., 'An ethnohistoric study of the smoking complex in eastern North America', *Ethnohistory*, 1981, vol. 28, pp. 217–35.

Taylor, A. H., *American Diplomacy and the Narcotics Traffic, 1900–1939*, Durham, NC, Duke University Press, 1969.

Tchernia, A., *Le Vin en Italie romaine: essai d'histoire économique d'après les amphores*, Paris, Bocard, 1986.

Ukers, W. H., *All About Coffee*, New York, The Tea and Coffee Trade Journal Company, 1922.

——*All About Tea*, New York, The Tea and Coffee Trade Journal Company, 1935.

Vigié, M. and Vigié, M., *L'Herbe à Nicot*, Paris, Fayard, 1989.

Völger, G. and von Welck, K. (eds), *Rausch und Realität*, Hamburg, Rowohlt, 1981.

——'Hallucinogens and the origins of the Iroquoian pipe/tobacco/smoking complex', in C. F. Hayes III (ed.), *Proceedings of the 1989 Smoking Pipe Conference*, Research Records No. 22, New York, Rochester Museum and Science Center, 1992.

Walker, W. O., *Opium and Foreign Policy*, Chapel Hill, NC, University of North Carolina Press, 1991.

——(ed.), *Drug Control Policy*, University Park, PA, The Pennsylvania State University Press, 1992.

Wasson, R. G., Kramrisch, S., Ott, J. and Ruck, C. A. P., *Persephone's Quest: Entheogens and the Origins of Religion*, New Haven, CT, Yale University Press, 1986.

Weil, A., *The Natural Mind: An Investigation of Drugs and the Higher Consciousness*, revised edn., Boston, Houghton Mifflin, 1986.

Weil, A. and Rosen, W., *Chocolate to Morphine*, Boston, Houghton Mifflin, 1983.

Weir, S., *Qat in Yemen: Consumption and Social Change*, London, British Museum Publications, 1985.

Wilbert, J., *Tobacco and Shamanism*, New Haven, CT, Yale University Press, 1987.

Zias, J., Stark, H., Seligman, J., Levy, R., Walker, E., Breuer, A. and Mechoulam, R., 'Early medical use of cannabis', *Nature*, 1993, vol. 363 (no. 6426), p. 215.

INDEX